M000011504

Object-Oriented Design Using Java

Dale Skrien

Boston Burr Ridge, IL Dubuque, IA New York San Francisco St. Louis
Bangkok Bogotá Caracas Kuala Lumpur Lisbon London Madrid Mexico City
Milan Montreal New Delhi Santiago Seoul Singapore Sydney Taipei Toronto

The McGraw·Hill Companies

OBJECT-ORIENTED DESIGN USING JAVA

Published by McGraw-Hill, a business unit of The McGraw-Hill Companies, Inc., 1221 Avenue of the Americas, New York, NY 10020.

This book is printed on acid-free paper.

1 2 3 4 5 6 7 8 9 0 DOC/DOC 0 9 8

ISBN 978–0–07–297416–4
MHID 0–07–297416–8

Global Publisher: *Raghothaman Srinivasan*
Executive Editor: *Michael Hackett*
Director of Development: *Kristine Tibbetts*
Developmental Editor: *Lora Kalb*
Executive Marketing Manager: *Michael Weitz*
Senior Project Manager: *Kay J. Brimeyer*
Senior Production Supervisor: *Laura Fuller*
Associate Design Coordinator: *Brenda A. Rolwes*
Cover Design: *Studio Montage, St. Louis, Missouri*
(USE) Cover Image: © *Comstock/PunchStock*
Compositor: *Newgen*
Typeface: *10/12 Times Roman*
Printer: *R. R. Donnelley Crawfordsville, IN*

Library of Congress Cataloging-in-Publication Data

Skrien, Dale John.
Object-oriented design using Java / Dale Skrien. — 1st ed.
p. cm.
Includes index.
ISBN 978–0–07–297416–4 — ISBN 0–07–297416–8 (hard copy : alk. paper) 1. Object-oriented programming (Computer science) 2. Java (Computer program language) I. Title.
QA76.64.S57123 2009
005.1’17–dc22

2007024087

www.mhhe.com

Dedication

To Pam, Julia, and Jason

Contents

This chapter expands on the material in the preceding chapter to discuss more thoroughly the role of inheritance in object-oriented software design, including its advantages and disadvantages, and to discuss alternatives to inheritance.

This chapter looks at issues concerning low-level code, such as readability, modifiability, and reusability. In this chapter, we assume that the classes and their desired behaviors have already been mapped out, and only the implementation of those behaviors remains to be done.

This chapter looks at object-oriented software development at a higher level. We discuss how to design classes to solve particular problems. That is, we discuss general principles to follow when deciding what classes to create, what their behavior will be, and with what other objects they will communicate.

This chapter is a small case study. It introduces several implementations of money, each a refinement of the preceding one.

This chapter introduces the reader to the topic of design patterns. We present four simple patterns as samples. The discussion of each pattern includes examples from earlier chapters of the book where the pattern was used but not explicitly stated. The succeeding chapters in the text introduce more design patterns in the contexts of their case studies.

This chapter gives a case study of a drawing application. We start with a very simple application, and in each section we add enhancements to it, which provides us with a context in which to introduce more design patterns and to use the design principles discussed earlier in the text. The sections include the discussion of several alternative designs and implementations of the application and their advantages and disadvantages.

This chapter gives a case study of code manipulators for a subset of the Java language, which provides us with a context in which to introduce more design patterns.

This appendix explains how to understand and use the four UML diagrams that appear in this text.

This appendix covers some of the material in Sun's coding conventions for Java. It covers Javadoc comments in quite a bit of detail.

Preface

BRIEF DESCRIPTION OF THE BOOK

This text is an introduction to object-oriented (OO) design for second-year or higher undergraduate computer science students. It discusses software design and implementation in terms of "elegance," which is defined in Chapter 1. It reviews the concepts of object-oriented programming and then covers fundamental software design techniques, coding style, refactoring, UML, and design patterns.

It uses many examples and one small and two moderate-size case studies to introduce design principles and patterns. The principles and patterns are introduced at the point where they are needed to solve a design problem. In this text, many examples and case studies start with an "obvious" solution to a problem, which evolves to a more elegant solution through a discussion of the advantages and disadvantages of that initial solution.

The book is not intended to be a complete, definitive "bible" regarding elegance in coding and design. Instead, it is an introduction to many of the topics that need to be addressed in order to achieve such elegance. References for further study are provided in the text for students who wish to pursue the topics further.

All the discussion and examples in the text use Java 1.5, but the concepts and principles presented are mostly of a general object-oriented nature and so apply to design and implementation using other object-oriented languages.

The book includes extensive exercises. There are an average of 18 exercises per chapter in each of Chapters 2 to 9. These exercises include simple tests of the students' understanding of the material in the chapters, but most of the exercises lead in directions that could not be covered in the current text without straying too far from the main subject and without making the text unwieldly large.

RATIONALE

The ACM/IEEE model curriculum (CC2001) states that "Introductory programming courses often oversimplify the programming process to make it accessible to beginning students, giving too little weight to design, analysis, and testing relative to the conceptually simpler process of coding. Thus, the superficial impression students take from their mastery of programming skills masks fundamental shortcomings that will limit their ability to adapt to different kinds of problems and problem-solving contexts in the future" [1].

This statement nicely summarizes the situation that I have encountered during the last 20 years of teaching computer science, especially when my department switched 10 years ago to using Java as the implementation language for the introductory course and many of the upper-level courses. After our students complete our CS1 and CS2 courses using Java, they know how to design and write code that works, but I have been frustrated that they don't know very much about designing and writing readable, maintainable code. I have also been frustrated that the students' understanding of the OO features of Java (inheritance, interfaces, static vs. instance variables and methods, dynamic method invocation) is very shallow. For example, they can use inheritance or an interface if it is given to them, but they cannot use inheritance or interfaces properly if they are asked to design their own software.

Part of this frustration is self-directed in that our CS1 and CS2 courses, including the times when I have taught those courses, have so much other materials to cover that there hasn't been time in the semester to address OO design and implementation principles in a meaningful way. One of the problems is that OO design principles really show off their advantages in large applications but seem, to the students, to be overkill in small applications, such as they see in our CS1 and CS2 courses. In upper-level courses involving large programming projects where OO design principles would be a big aid, students have not been able to appreciate good designs because they have had little prior experience with any large programs, good or bad.

As a professor I feel strongly that OO design, including the use of design patterns, is a very important skill that our students need to develop. Furthermore, I want to share with them my love of "elegant" designs. I want them to develop a sense of aesthetics when it comes to software development, so that they can tell when code "smells bad" (as Martin Fowler [2] puts it) and when it smells good. I want them to develop this sense to the degree that "shivers of joy run up and down their spine" (as I put it in class) when they see elegant code and also that they would feel "shudders of revulsion" when they see inelegant code. Donald Knuth [3] said that computer programming is an art as well as a science and involves creativity and beauty. I want my students to attempt to produce objects of beauty, like artists do. When successful, they should be sufficiently proud of their work that they want to sign it, as artists do.

This text was written to help teach the students to design and write beautiful object-oriented software.

INTENDED AUDIENCE

The text was designed for undergraduate computer science students who have taken an introductory programming course (CS1) and a data structures course (CS2), but whose courses did not include extensive coverage of object-oriented design principles and patterns. The text could be used as the main text in a sophomore-level course forming a third course in an introductory sequence, or it could be used as a supplementary text to the data structures course. Alternatively, it could be used as the main text or a supplementary text in an upper-level undergraduate course on object-oriented software design.

The text assumes the students have the following background:

- Programming experience as typically learned in a CS1 course
- Knowledge of elementary data structures as typically learned in a CS2 course

- Understanding of the fundamentals of Java, such as students would know if one of their previous courses were taught using Java
- A small amount of familiarity with the following Java features:
  - generics (from Java 1.5)
  - throwing and catching exceptions
  - inner classes
  - the AWT or Swing packages (for Chapter 8)

If the student is unfamiliar with these topics, they could easily be introduced to them at the appropriate time during the course. Java's reflection capabilities and Java threads are mentioned in the text and in some optional exercises, but no experience with these topics is required.

The text uses four UML diagrams (state, sequence, state machine, and use case), but no previous experience with the UML is required because the text introduces the appropriate parts of UML when it first uses them and covers the four diagrams in more depth in Appendix A.

PEDAGOGICAL APPROACH

The book attempts to teach students object-oriented design and implementation through the evolution of software solutions. As stated above, after having taken an introductory sequence of courses, students know how to find solutions, but they often don't appreciate the differences between competing solutions. Therefore the text attempts to build gradually on the students' understanding of the programming process by first presenting a problem and then discussing an "obvious," but usually inelegant, solution that students might initially create. The advantages and disadvantages of that solution are discussed and then a better design is presented. This new design, in turn, has advantages and disadvantages to be discussed, which often leads to even better designs. In this way, all the important software design principles and patterns are introduced in the context of solving a particular problem in an elegant manner.

THE CONTENT

The book can roughly be divided into four parts.

The first part (Chapter 1) is very short and is, in fact, very much like an introduction. It provides the motivation for the rest of the book and so is essential reading if students are to appreciate the material in the later chapters.

The second part (Chapters 2–3) consists of a review of the fundamental concepts of object-orientation, such as objects, classes, methods, inheritance, polymorphism, and dynamic method invocation. It continues with a detailed discussion of the use and misuse of inheritance.

The third part (Chapters 4–6) introduces design and implementation elegance. It begins with a discussion of low-level implementation issues, such as coding conventions and idioms. This in turn is followed by a discussion of general design principles. The book then works through one small-size case study (the design of a Money class).

The fourth part (Chapters 7–9) introduces design patterns. Chapter 7 introduces the concept of a design pattern and discusses several of the simplest patterns. This chapter is followed by two moderate-size case studies (a figure-drawing application and a language parser). These chapters introduce new patterns and principles gradually as new features are addressed in the case studies.

In addition, there are two appendices in the book. Appendix A discusses in some detail the four UML patterns used in this book (class, sequence, state machine, and use case). Appendix B covers many of the coding conventions for Java provided by Sun Microsystems[4], especially Javadoc notation. Most of the coding conventions, except possibly Javadoc, will probably be familiar to students but are included here for completeness.

Here are more details regarding the contents of each chapter:

1. Chapter 1 is a brief introduction to and overview of the text. In that chapter, "elegant" software is defined as software that is usable, complete, robust, efficient, scalable, readable, reusable, simple, maintainable, and extensible. I attempted to motivate the study of OOD so that students will appreciate the value of learning the material in the book.
2. Chapter 2 is a review of basic OO programming features. The purpose of the chapter is to cover again those OO topics that students have seen before but are possibly not completely comfortable using. Some motivation for those features is provided so that students can begin to develop an appreciation of what OO programming has to offer over non-OO programming.
3. Because implementation inheritance is quite complicated and can be easily misused, I felt that a significant amount of discussion of that topic was needed. Rather than try to cram it all into Chapter 2, I broke that material into a separate chapter. Therefore, Chapter 3 discusses when to use and when not to use implementation inheritance. It begins with a discussion of four possible justifications for inheritance and gives examples showing that most of those justifications by themselves are insufficient. It also discusses when to use delegation instead of inheritance.
4. Elegance is valuable not only at the design level, but also at the implementation level. Therefore, I added Chapter 4, which discusses principles to follow when implementing methods, including some coding conventions. It was added at this point in the text so that it could be referred to in later chapters of the book, as the need arose in the sample code and the case studies. I also wanted to start this section of the book with material that students are already likely familiar with. An extensive discussion of the `equals` and `clone` methods in Java is included to show students that you need to implement methods very carefully if your implementations are to obey the contracts expected of them.
5. In Chapter 5, I begin the main discussion of OO design. Many fundamental OO design principles are covered, including motivation for and examples of each.
6. Because such design principles can only be appreciated in the context of a large (or at least not small) example, I included such an example as a case study in Chapter 6. I wanted to include an example that was interesting to the students but also led to interesting design questions. I chose for the case study the design of a Money class.

7. Chapter 7 introduces the students to design patterns. It discusses several of the simplest patterns to show the students what patterns are and how they can be of help in developing elegant designs.
8. Chapter 8 includes the moderately large case study of a drawing program. This application is based on the HotDraw framework developed by Kent Beck and Ralph Johnson [5], and to some work of John Vlissides [6]. A simple drawing program is given initially, and then new features are gradually added. An elegant design of each of the features typically requires the introduction of a new design pattern.
9. In the final chapter, another case study is presented. This case study concerns a parser for a simple subset of Java. Several more design patterns are introduced, such as the Visitor pattern, as the chapter discusses uses of the abstract syntax tree generated by the parser.

CHAPTER DEPENDENCIES

Chapter 1 should be read before all other chapters because it provides the context for the material in the later chapters and defines design and code "elegance."

Chapters 2 and 3 concern fundamental OO concepts such as objects, classes, polymorphism, dynamic method invocation, and inheritance. All later chapters will use the material in these chapters. If the student is already very comfortable with those topics, these chapters can be skipped.

Chapters 4 and 5 are central to the textbook and should be read by all students, although they may be familiar with much of the material in Chapter 4.

Chapter 6 is optional. The case study in this chapter uses the design principles discussed in Chapters 4 and 5.

Chapter 7 introduces design patterns. If students are comfortable with the concept, they could skip this chapter. However, it would be good for them to learn the patterns introduced in this chapter. The motivation for design patterns comes from the material presented in Chapters 4 and 5.

Chapters 8 and 9 are optional. They introduce new design patterns in the context of two case studies. They depend on the material presented in Chapters 4, 5, and 7.

Appendices A and B are optional. When the book uses a UML diagram for the first time, it includes a very brief explanation of the diagram and its icons.

HOW THE TEXT FITS IN THE ACM MODEL CURRICULUM (CC2001)[1]

Two of the core knowledge units in the CC2001 curriculum are PL6 and SE1. These units include the following topics:

PL6 Object-oriented design
Encapsulation and information hiding
Separation of behavior and implementation
Classes and subclasses
Inheritance (overriding, dynamic dispatch)

Polymorphism (subtype polymorphism vs. inheritance)
Class hierarchies
Collection classes and iteration protocols
Internal representations of objects and method tables

SE1 Fundamental design concepts and principles
Design patterns
Software architecture
Structured design
Object-oriented analysis and design
Component-level design
Design for reuse

This book covers virtually all the material in these knowledge units. The case studies in the text also cover the material in PF5, most of the material in HC2, and some of the material in PL3 and PF3. It is also natural to include medium-size team-developed design projects, which the CC2001 Task Force believes are essential, in association with a course using this text.

SUMMARY OF THE DISTINGUISHING FEATURES

1. Discusses design and implementation in terms of code "elegance."
2. Uses several small and two moderate-size case studies to introduce many design principles and patterns. The principles and patterns are introduced in those case studies at the point where they are needed to solve a design problem.
3. Starts many examples and case studies with an "obvious" solution to a problem, which evolves to a more elegant solution through a discussion of the advantages and disadvantages of the initial solution.
4. Discusses the following topics:
   a. fundamental object-orientation concepts (class, object, inheritance, polymorphism, method)
   b. coding style and implementation issues, such as proper naming and documentation, including preconditions, postconditions, and invariants
   c. fundamental OO design principles, including virtually all the topics in the PL6 and SE1 knowledge units of the CC2001 model curriculum.
   d. design patterns, most of which are introduced in the context of solving a problem.
5. Includes a lot of exercises at the ends of the chapters (about 144 in total for an average of 18 per chapter) varying in difficulty from easy tests of the students' knowledge of the chapter material to exercises that ask them to significantly modify or enhance existing code.

SUPPLEMENTARY FEATURES

All the source code from the text will be readily available from a web site or from a CD-ROM accompanying the text.

An instructor's manual contains solutions for most of the exercises and descriptions of some moderate-size projects that could be assigned in conjunction with the text. The manual also includes pedagogical suggestions for presenting the material.

THANKS

The author wishes to thank and acknowledge the following students in the CSC (ECE) 517 course taught by Ed Gehringer at North Carolina State University in the Fall of 2005, who gave me permission to include in this text the examples, exercises, and explanations that they created for that class:

Chang Chih-Chieh Geoff
Rojas Cristian Gonzalo
Hodges Christopher John
Giang Donna Ngoc Dung
Mears Garrett Allan
Frink John Moore
Petty John T
Edwards Kevin James
Navoraphan Kanyamas
Kediyal Prashant Chakradhar
Hsiao Ping Lin
Kampanakis Panagiotis Theodorou
Kariath Riya Raju

The author also wishes to thank Ed Gehringer for his help, support, and encouragement and thank Colby College, for providing the financial support and computer equipment to enable me to write the book. I also wish to thank Alan Apt, Rebecca Olson, Kelly Lowery, and Emily Lupash at McGraw-Hill. Without their encouragement and support, this book would never have been created. I would like to thank all the reviewers who provided such excellent advice to improve the text. Last, but most important, I wish to thank my wife, Pam, and my children, Julia and Jason, for putting up with the long working hours I spent writing this text. Their patience and encouragement have been invaluable.

REFERENCES

1. *Computing Curricula 2001, Computer Science Volume*. 2001. [Cited March 28, 2007; available from *http://www.sigcse.org/cc2001/cs-introductory-courses.html*.]
2. Fowler, M., *Refactoring, Improving the Design of Existing Code*. Object Technology Series. 1999. Addison-Wesley. Reading, MA.
3. Knuth, D., *Literate Programming*. 1992. Chicago, IL: University of Chicago Press.
4. Sun Microsystems, I. *Code Conventions for the Java Programming Language*. 1999. [Cited March 28, 2007; available from *http://java.sun.com/docs/codeconv/html/CodeConvTOC.doc.html*.]
5. Beck, K. and R. Johnson, Patterns generate architectures. In *European Conference on Object-Oriented Programming (ECOOP'94)*. 1994. Bologna, Italy: Springer-Verlag.
6. Vlissides, J., Tooled composite. *C++ Report*. September 1999.

1

Elegance in Object-Oriented Design and Implementation

SECTION 1.0 INTRODUCTION

If you are a college student using this book in a course, you have probably already taken several computer science courses, including an introductory programming course. If you have been conscientious, you have learned the fundamental programming concepts in at least one programming language, you learned language constructs such as loops, assignments, and conditional statements, and you learned one or more ways to program each of those constructs. Hopefully, you also learned that computer science is not just programming and that, instead, programming is just a tool of a computer scientist.

Unfortunately, due to the lack of time in which to cover so many important topics in computer science, you might not have been taught the advantages and disadvantages of the different ways to write programs to solve the same problem. For example, at a low level, there are many ways to implement a structure such as a loop (e.g., you could use a `for` loop, a `while` loop, or recursion), some of which are better than others. At a higher level, there are many ways to perform a task (e.g., merge sort vs. selection sort), some considerably faster than others. At an even higher level, there are many ways to divide a program into modules such as classes and methods, some of which are better than others.

For an example of the last situation, consider the problem of writing a module that is supposed to maintain a collection of people and the dogs they own. Should the collection be a hash table or an array or some other kind of collection? Should the collection contain Person objects or maybe Person-Dog pairs of objects? Should a Dog object have an instance variable pointing to its owner? Should owners have an instance variable that refers to a collection of the dogs they own? If so, what kind of collection should it be? What other data should the Person object store? If the people are U.S. citizens, do you need to store their social security numbers? Should you keep the collection of people sorted for easier lookup? If a person's only dog dies, should that person be removed from the collection or left in as a person who owns no dogs?

You might reasonably ask whether the answers to these questions really matter. If two designs, one with few classes and methods and one with many, both solve a problem, does it matter which one you use? Similarly, if all versions of a loop correctly do a computation, does it matter which one you use? If two algorithms both work correctly, does it matter that one is faster, especially given the fantastic growth in hardware processing speeds each year?

The answer is, "Yes, it really does matter." In this chapter, we attempt to explain why. We will give you a set of criteria to apply to the designs and implementations of programs to help you learn to critique those programs. In later chapters of this text, we will show you principles that reflect the best practices of software engineers so that you can learn from the masters what works well and what works poorly.

Over the course of reading this text, we will show you not just what works, but also what makes some software "ugly" and other software "elegant" or "beautiful." That is, we want to help you develop a sense of aesthetics for designs and code. Mathematicians judge proofs of theorems based on their elegance—that is, two proofs may both be correct, but one may be more beautiful than the other—and computer scientists should similarly be able to judge software designs. It is possibly stretching the emotional aspects of these aesthetical judgments to say so, but it would be nice if you could develop an aesthetic sense to the degree that really good designs and code would send "shivers of joy up and down your spine" and bad designs would instead give you "shudders of revulsion."

SECTION 1.1 WHY WORRY?

A programmer who quickly throws together some code without considering design criteria might justify his actions by saying that he knows what is going on in the code and so there is no need to worry about a misinterpretation. Furthermore, he might say, the code is never going to be used again or viewed by anyone else so why devote time needlessly to design.

In the case of small "quick-and-dirty" programs written by one person and used only once, such as short shell scripts, the programmer is correct. It is usually not productive to spend a lot of time creating the most elegant possible version. All that is important is that the code work correctly. However, you also need to be aware that code that the programmer thought of as "throwaway" is often not thrown away. It ends up copied and pasted into another program, or it becomes the core of a more general, more complex program. In such cases, time devoted to make the design elegant would be time productively spent.

Designing software that is intended for long-term, heavy use requires a considerable investment of time and energy. For example, consider libraries of classes, such as Java's Swing package, which are used extensively by application developers. It is not sufficient that the library classes have no errors in them; it is also important that the classes have a good design. A poor design for any one of these classes can cause problems down the line for all of developers using the package. For example, if a valuable or important feature was omitted, developers will have to write their own code, possibly in a very awkward way, to accomplish what the library classes should have provided.

For large systems, in which many programmers are involved, it is even more important to spend a significant amount of time on the analysis of the problem and the design of the solution. In such cases, no one person can understand every part of the program, and instead each programmer works on one small part of it. If the solution has not been well designed, a change (a bug fix or an enhancement, for example) by one programmer in one line of code could easily introduce bugs in the code written by other programmers. The costs due to such bugs can range from very minor to disastrous.

Consider just a couple of the problems that have occurred over the years, some catastrophic, some financially devastating, and others merely annoying, as described in [1–3]:

1. In 1962, the Mariner I spacecraft lifted off for its voyage to Venus but was destroyed by the people running the mission because, due to a bug in the ground-based computer system, they incorrectly thought the booster rocket had malfunctioned.
2. Between 1985 and 1988, there were six cases of patients being given massive overdoses of radiation from a Therac25 radiation therapy system. Part of the blame is due to an error in the control software for the system.
3. In 1990, a bug in some new software that had been installed by AT&T in 114 electronic switching systems caused a 9-hour nationwide blockage, affecting an estimated 5 million calls. The bug was caused by the mistaken use of a break statement inside a switch statement in a C program.
4. In 1993, a bug in the SunSoft operating system I/O library held up a $20 million sale. The problem was traced to a statement that read `x == 2` instead of `x = 2` in a C program.
5. A mail program either read mail or sent mail, depending on the arguments passed to the mail function. It used a heuristic to parse the arguments to determine whether it was reading or sending. Unfortunately, the heuristic was not precise enough, and so the program failed to send mail to any addressee with the letter "f" as the second letter in their user name.
6. For a more recent example, it was reported in the online Guardian newspaper on January 16, 2003, that a software upgrade to improve security for cash machines had a flaw that allowed anyone to withdraw any amount of cash they liked using any password they wanted. About £850,000 were withdrawn before the problem was corrected.

These problems are just the tip of the iceberg. According to a National Institute of Standards report in 2002 [4], software bugs cost the U.S. economy $58 billion annually. The report further states that software developers spend 80% of their development time finding and fixing defects.

One might argue that all these problems merely indicate a failure on the part of the programmer to write error-free code. That is, one might argue that the problem is just incorrect software. In a sense, that argument is correct, but avoiding such failures is not that simple. When a program has thousands or millions of lines of code, it is inevitable that there will be bugs in it. The real issue is how to minimize the number of bugs that occur when the code is written in the first place, how to maximize the detection and removal of the bugs that do make it into the code, and how to minimize the number of new bugs that are accidentally introduced whenever the code is modified. Furthermore, this minimization and maximization process is not a one-time thing. Software continually changes due to patches introduced to fix bugs or due to enhancements added to the software. As shown in the cash machine example above, any such change can introduce more bugs.

In other words, thorough testing to remove bugs is important in software development, but it is just as important to design and write the software so that as few bugs as possible are introduced in the first place and so that it is easy to modify the code later without introducing new bugs.

So why don't software developers design and write software in a way that minimizes bugs? The answer is that, try as they might, there are forces working against them. Doing the job right takes time and money in the short term and the benefits do not appear until later. At the same time, software projects are under more and more pressure to be completed quickly and put into production before the window of opportunity for sales closes. As a result, the initial software design is often inadequately specified, and so a solid foundation has not been laid. In addition, after it has gone into production, the pressure to quickly fix the bugs and enhance the software works against major redesigns of the software. As a result, a software system tends to become a "big ball of mud," that is, a "haphazardly structured, sprawling, sloppy, duct-tape and bailing wire, spaghetti code jungle" [5]. The degradation over time of software into such mud balls makes finding and fixing bugs and adding enhancements harder and harder, costing more time and money and resulting in more pressure to put off large-scale redesign, and so the vicious cycle continues.

In addition, there are other forces pushing software toward the same balls of mud. Those forces are the lack of skill, knowledge, and experience of the software developers regarding how to write high quality software. If the developers have no experience with designing software systems of any size or complexity or if the developers are writing a business application but have no knowledge of that particular business domain and its needs and requirements, then it is easy for the software to become muddy. Even if developers understand a system completely, the mud in the system will not go away if the developers don't have the tools (skills or knowledge) to clean it up.

What can be done to fight the tendency of software systems to turn into mud balls? Addressing the pressures of cost and time are beyond the scope of this book. Our focus concerns the skills, knowledge, and experience that developers need in order to do high quality work. In this book, we will try to teach you some of the things a software developer should know in order to be able to design high quality software systems and to be able to redesign existing software systems in a way that fight the forces toward mud.

SECTION 1.2 SOFTWARE ENGINEERING

To create high quality software, you first need to know what it means for software to have high quality. Unfortunately, such quality is not easily measured. The field of software engineering was created with the purpose of understanding and devising ways of measuring the quality and reliability of software. One of its tools has been the application of engineering principles to software development [6].

Software engineering traditionally divides the software process into stages, including specification and analysis, design, implementation, and maintenance. These stages can be handled sequentially (finishing one stage before moving on to the next) or iteratively (returning to earlier stages when necessary to extend, complete, or correct the previous work at that stage).

In the specification and analysis stage, software engineers determine the precise behavior the final software system is to have. That is, they attempt to determine exhaustively what the system should do in all possible cases. This stage also includes determining what the user interface will be. It is performed in close cooperation with the clients of the system and some users of the system.

In the design stage, the engineers determine the parts of the software system, what each part is responsible for doing, and how the parts will interact. For example, this stage includes determining the data structures that will be used and the kind of data that will be stored in those structures.

In the implementation stage, programmers code the software system parts using an appropriate (or several appropriate) programming languages. In this stage, testing is an essential component.

In the maintenance stage, which occurs after the product has shipped, programmers repair defects and update or enhance the software to extend its usefulness. In this stage also, testing is of central importance.

In this text, we will focus mostly on the design and implementation phases. Therefore, our examples will typically already have a specification, and we will start working with the design phase. That is, we will usually assume that we know what the software is supposed to do and look like from the client's perspective, including the user interface. We will attempt to design the software to do what it is supposed to do and to do it in a way that results in high quality code. We will also discuss the implementation of the software once the design is complete.

SECTION 1.3 CRITERIA FOR ELEGANT SOFTWARE

What makes one software design better than another? One way to measure the quality of a design is to analyze the software with regard to the following properties:

1. Usability—is it easy for the client to use?
2. Completeness—does it satisfy all the client's needs?
3. Robustness—will it deal with unusual situations gracefully and avoid crashing?
4. Efficiency—will it perform the necessary computations in a reasonable amount of time and using a reasonable amount of memory and other resources?
5. Scalability—will it still perform correctly and efficiently when the problems grow in size by several orders of magnitude?
6. Readability—is it easy for another programmer to read and understand the design and code?
7. Reusability—can it be reused in another completely different setting?
8. Simplicity—is the design and/or the implementation unnecessarily complex?

9. Maintainability—can defects be found and fixed easily without adding new defects?
10. Extensibility—can it easily be enhaced or restricted by adding new features or removing old features without breaking code?

The first four properties mostly relate to the functional requirements of the software—that is, does it do what the requirements documents say it is supposed to do? Software does not perform correctly if, for example, it crashes in unusual situations.

The properties addressed by the last six properties are the ones with which we will mostly concern ourselves. They address the program style and how easily the software can be changed to eliminate defects or to add new features. For example, the software must be readable if the programmer is to easily find the bugs. The software must be maintainable if the fix is to involve as few changes as possible. Reusability implies that the software can easily be adapted with minimal or no change for use in another environment.

A few words should be said regarding the property of simplicity. The simplicity of the design affects almost all the other properties. For example, the simpler it is, the more easily the software can be read and understood by a developer. Simplicity also works against the software becoming a big ball of mud in that it is often easier to develop and modify simple software, thus saving on the cost and time of initial development as well as later modification. Furthermore, the need for simplicity works against any attempt by software developers to go overboard in their designs.

Other "ilities" could also be added to the list—such as testability, in that software that is hard to test is likely to have errors—but we will consider the ones mentioned above as the core set of properties required for high quality software. In this text, we will refer to software as *elegant* if it has these properties; that is, if it is usable, complete, robust, efficient, scalable, readable, reusable, simple, maintainable, and extensible. The definition of "elegant" given here is not traditional terminology in software engineering, but it is used in this text to remind the reader that software design is as much an art as a craft.

It is worth noting that we are not just referring to code when we talk about elegance. In Chapter 4, we will talk about well-written code, because that is important for readable software, but the rest of the book will be devoted to the discussion of high-quality software design.

How can software get these qualities that we lumped under the term "elegance"? One cannot get quality software just by writing code and then testing it for errors. It is almost impossible to add quality to sofware after it has been written; instead quality must be built in from the start.

How do you know when your design is elegant? In this text, we will discuss, from an object-oriented perspective, many design and implementation principles and patterns that can aid in the development and appreciation of elegant software. After enough practice using these principles and patterns, the reader can begin to develop a "feeling" for quality software. That is, even though it is hard to precisely define such software, the reader will know it when they see it.

To help the reader develop an appreciation for the elegant ways of solving a problem and the advantages they provide, we will often first present an "obvious" solution to the problem, that is, a straightforward way to solve the problem and then analyze what, if anything, is wrong with it. We will gradually modify it to remove ugly parts and make it more elegant.

In summary, this book is an introduction to many of the topics that you need to understand in order to start on the road to elegance in your own software development. References are included that provide more details on each of the topics we address to help you further develop your skills after you finish this text.

SECTION 1.4 ROAD MAP

In the remaining chapters of this text, we discuss code elegance from a variety of levels and from several case studies. Many of the chapters include one or more "rules" or "guidelines" that summarize the discussions of ways to make the design more elegant. You should strive to understand and appreciate these guidelines so that they become a standard part of your practice as you develop software.

In Chapter 2, we review the basics of object-oriented programming and the advantages that such programming can provide to the programmer and software designer for making the software more flexible, extendable, reusable, and scalable. Students with strong backgrounds in object-oriented programming may need only to skim this chapter.

In Chapter 3, we expand on the material in the preceding chapter to discuss more thoroughly the role of inheritance in object-oriented (OO) software design, including its advantages and disadvantages, and to discuss alternatives to inheritance.

In Chapter 4, we look at low-level code and ways to make it readable, maintainable, extensible, and reusable. In most of that chapter, we assume that the classes and their desired general behaviors have already been mapped out and only the implementation of those behaviors remains to be done.

In Chapter 5, we look at OO software development at a higher level. We discuss how to design classes to solve particular problems. That is, we discuss general principles to follow when deciding what classes to create, what their behavior will be, and with what other objects they will communicate.

In Chapter 6, we give a small case study involving monetary currency. We will start from an "obvious" solution and gradually enhance it to make it more elegant.

In Chapter 7, we introduce the reader to design patterns from [7]. These patterns are solutions to recurring problems in software design. We present a few simple patterns as examples.

In Chapter 8, we give a case study of a drawing application. In the context of developing this application, we introduce several more design patterns.

In Chapter 9, we give a case study of a pretty printer for a subset of Java, in which we introduce more design patterns.

Appendix A gives an overview of four UML diagrams: Class, State, Sequence, and Use Case. Those diagrams are explained in the text when they are first introduced, but Appendix A gives more details.

Appendix B discusses coding conventions, in particular, the Java coding conventions and Javadoc notation provided by Sun Microsystems.

EXERCISES

1. Read the article, "How to write unmaintainable code," by Roedy Green on the Web at *http://mindprod.com/jgloss/unmain.html.* It provides a nice introduction to some of the topics we will be discussing in this text.
2. For a list of disasters and other problems that can occur from improperly designed and coded software, read the Risks Digest on the Web at *http://catless.ncl.ac.uk/Risks.*
3. **a.** Look up the meaning of "elegance" in *The Hacker's Dictionary,* which is also available online as the Jargon Lexicon at URL *http://catb.org/~esr/jargon/.*

   b. Take some software you have written in the past and briefly explain why your software is or is not elegant according to that definition.
4. To learn more on the subject of whether software development is an art, craft, or science, read Donald Knuth's 1974 Turing Award lecture entitled, "Computer programming as an art" [8].
5. To see how much you already understand about software elegance, find two different implementations of the same sorting algorithm and compare and analyze them regarding the ten properties for high quality software listed in Section 1.3.

REFERENCES

1. Neumann, P., *Computer-Related Risks.* 1995. Addison-Wesley. Reading, MA.
2. Van der Linden, P., *Expert C Programming; Deep C Secrets.* 1994. Prentice Hall. Upper Saddle River, NJ.
3. Allison, R., *ATM Gives Out Free Cash and Lands Family in Court.* Web page, 2003. [Cited January 16, 2003; available from *http://www.guardian.co.uk/uk_news/story/0,3604,875749,00.htm.*]
4. NIST, *Software Errors Cost U.S. Economy $59.5 Billion Annually.* 2002. [Cited 2006, August; available from *http://www.nist.gov/public_affairs/releases/n02-10.htm.*]
5. Foote, B. and J. Yoder, *Big Ball of Mud.* Web article. [Cited March 28, 2007; available from *http://www.laputan.org/mud/.*]
6. IEEE, *IEEE Standard Glossary of Software Engineering Terminology.* 1990. IEEE. New York, NY .
7. Gamma, E., et al., *Design Patterns, Elements of Reusable Object-Oriented Software.* Professional Computing. 1995. Addison-Wesley. Reading, MA.
8. Knuth, D., Computer programming as an art. *Communications of the ACM,* 1974. 17(12): 667–673.

2

Fundamentals of Object Orientation

SECTION 2.0 INTRODUCTION

In this chapter, we review the fundamental concepts of object-oriented (OO) programming in order to understand how such programming is different from non-object-oriented programming and the advantages of OO programming as applied to elegant software design.

We assume the reader already has some familiarity with classes, objects, and variables, and so we will review those object-oriented concepts briefly and review how they are implemented in Java. We do not assume any familiarity with inheritance and polymorphism, and so those concepts are covered more completely, both in general terms and as specifically applied to Java. The discussion of inheritance will include implementation inheritance as well as specification inheritance, the second of which will lead to a discussion of "type." We will also introduce you to some of the uses of those concepts in producing high quality software.

Along the way, we will introduce you to the Unified Modeling Language (UML) class diagrams, and we will discuss the difference between overloading and overriding. In addition, we will mention accessibility options (e.g., public and private) of data, methods, and classes, as they apply to Java.

SECTION 2.1 OBJECT-ORIENTED PROGRAMMING VS. NON–OBJECT-ORIENTED PROGRAMMING

Overview of OO vs. Non-OO Programming

In non–object-oriented programming, a program is usually process-oriented or data-oriented. In such programs, there are typically data globally available and procedures globally available. The main program, or its subprograms, are in control and manipulate the data. That is, each part of the program goes to the global data, gets part of it, manipulates it, and then, if necessary, saves any changes to the data. One can think of the main program, through its subprograms, as having all the "intelligence" or behavior in the program and the data has no intelligence. In this case, the main program and its subprograms are responsible for everything.

In OO programming, a program is partitioned into a set of communicating objects. Each object encapsulates all the behavior and knowledge relating to one concept. In that way, one can think of an OO program as having distributed control in that the "intelligence," that is, the ability to do things, and the "knowledge" or data need to do those things, is distributed among the objects. When an object needs something from another object, it sends it a message to the other object, which then performs some action and possibly returns a value to the caller. The first object could even create the second object if no such object already exists. The second object, in turn, may need to communicate with other objects to help it accomplish its task. Therefore, to start up an OO program, you typically create a few objects and start them communicating with each other. In particular, this situation occurs when an object-oriented GUI (graphical user interface) is used as the human-computer interface in an application. The windows, menus, and buttons are objects that need to be created first, and then those objects just "sit there" waiting for the user to interact with them, in which case they send messages to each other (and to other invisible objects) to accomplish the desired task.

This view of OO programming, in which objects share the work and the responsibilities, should seem familiar in that it is the way humans typically interact with each other. One person, such as the owner of a business, doesn't do everything herself. Instead, she assigns tasks to her employees, each of whom is responsible not only for doing the assigned task, but for maintaining the data associated with that task. For example, a secretary might be responsible for not only typing papers, but also storing the papers in appropriate filing cabinets. Furthermore, if the data in the files is confidential, the secretary might also have the task of guarding the files and giving or denying access to the data. In the process of his work, a secretary may also need to call on the help of other people in or out of the office.

Object-Oriented Languages

Programming languages support the OO style of programming if they have certain features that make it easier for the programmers to create objects and have them send messages to each other. We call a programming language *object-oriented* if the language supports classes, objects, messages, inheritance, and (subtype) polymorphism. Java is an example of such a language. We will briefly review the subjects of classes, objects, and messages in this section and the next two sections and will discuss the last two features in the following sections of this chapter.

A *class* can be understood from a modeling perspective and a programming language perspective. When designing a software application, classes model abstract concepts that play an important role in the system with well-defined responsibilities and relations with other classes. In an OO programming language, classes can be viewed as templates for objects that describe a certain type of behavior or a certain set of responsibilities and any associated data, just as a job description for a secretary or police officer indicates the responsibilities of any person filling one of those roles. Individual secretaries have their own data (e.g., files, desks, bosses) to maintain, but they all have similar responsibilities for handling that data. In the same way, all police officers in a given precinct will have similar responsibilities but will have individual differences in the data involved in their work, for example, their name, which section of the precinct they are to patrol, who their partners are, and which patrol cars they will use.

In OO programming, an *object* is an instance of a class. An object is similar to an individual secretary or police officer. An object's associated class defines the type of data the object maintains and its behavior or responsibilities toward that data. But as with individual secretaries, individual objects have their own set of data (their own state) to maintain.

The way objects communicate and get each other to perform some action is by sending messages to each other. By sending a message to another object, the first object causes the second object to execute some code. That code is actually a procedure—which in object-oriented languages is called a *method*—associated with the second object. Therefore, message-sending is actually a request (or command) from one object to another object to execute one of its methods. Through this mechanism, objects can be thought of as servers that provide a service to any client who asks (by sending them messages).

For example, a Graphics object `g` (in the java.awt package) is an object designed to do you the service of drawing shapes, among other things, in visual components such as windows. For example, it can draw a rectangle for you in its associated component at whatever coordinates and of whatever size you want. To get it to do so, you just send it a message such as

```
g.drawRect(10, 10, 50, 100);
```

and `g`'s `drawRect` method will get executed, causing a rectangle with upper level corner at coordinates (10,10) and with width 50 and height 100 to be drawn in the component.

Advantages of OO Programming

One of the advantages of the OO approach over the non-OO approach defined above is that, because the intelligence is distributed among objects, each of which maintain the data necessary to perform their tasks, it is easier to keep things in small manageable units and to understand how the units affect each other. In contrast, if every procedure is interacting with an arbitrary part of a global set of data, the effect of one procedure on all the others and on the system as a whole is harder to understand. Thus, the distributed nature of OO programming can increase the readability of the code.

More importantly, a small change in the structure of the global data in a non-OO program may force a change to all procedures that access that data. In contrast, a well-designed OO program has little global data and instead stores the data in objects mostly for their local use. Hence, making a change to the way the data is stored in one class of objects often means that the only part of the program that needs to be changed is the code in that class. Similarly, if a programmer decides that a particular object is working too inefficiently, the programmer can redesign the object's behavior to be more efficient without affecting the rest of the system, thus supporting the maintainability of the software.

Similarly, since each object has typically one small well-defined role and carries the data it needs with it, it is usually easier to reuse these objects in other situations.

Thus, the use of OO programming techniques, if done well, increases the modifiability, readability, reusability, and maintainability of the software. We will be discussing these issues in more detail throughout the rest of this text.

SECTION 2.2 CLASSES, OBJECTS, VARIABLES, AND METHODS IN JAVA

In this section, we will briefly review how classes, objects, and methods are implemented in Java.

Ignoring for the moment the optional parts of a Java class definition, a class is defined using the keyword *class* followed by a class name and braces surrounding the declaration and implementation of the methods of the class and the declaration of the variables storing the data of objects of the class. For example, the following Java code defines a class Person that stores a name and birth date. It has two variables, a constructor, and two methods.

```
public class Person
{
  private String name;
  private Date birthdate;
  public Person(String name, Date birthdate)
  {
    this.name = name;
    this.birthdate = birthdate;
  }
  public String getName() {
    return name;
  }
  public Date getBirthdate()
  {
    return birthdate;
  }
}
```

The nonoptional parts of a method declaration include a return type, the method name, the list of parameters in parentheses, and then the body of the method enclosed in braces. A variable declaration includes the type of the variable, the name of the variable, and an optional initial value. Note how this class actually uses two other classes, namely String (in the java.lang package) and Date (in the java.util package), for storing the data of this class.

A user of the Person class would typically construct a Person object using the constructor, as in

```
Person firstPerson = new Person("Adam", new Date(0));
```

and then send the object a message, such as

```
String firstPersonName = firstPerson.getName();
```

As mentioned in the last section, the methods of a class correspond to messages that objects can send to an object of this class. These methods correspond to the behavior of objects of this class. They can also be thought of as the services that objects of this class can provide for other objects.

In order to execute their methods properly, most objects need to store data. This data is stored in *instance* variables (also called *fields*), which, in Java, are declared in the body of the class declaration but outside of the body of any method or constructor. Instance variables differ from *local* variables, which are variables declared in method or constructor bodies, in that local variables exist and store data only during the execution of the body within which they were declared whereas instance variables exist and store data during the whole life of the object. Therefore, instance variables provide state information for the objects. For example, a Person object has an instance variable called `name` that stores a reference to the String object containing the person's name. This String forms part of the state of the Person object.

It should also be noted here that in Java, only variables of a primitive type actually store their data in the variable. For all variables of an object type, the variables store a *reference* to the data. It is common to visualize the reference as a pointer from the variable to the data (see Figure 2.1), although the reference can actually be implemented through means other than direct pointers. Unless the difference between data and a reference to that data is relevant to the discussion, we will often use somewhat imprecise terminology and just say that the variable "stores" the object data.

The `public` and `private` accessibility keywords in front of the methods, variables, and class declaration restrict the objects that can access objects of the Person class and send them messages. In short, public classes are accessible by any other class, public methods can be invoked on an object by any other object, and public variables of an object can be accessed (read and written) by any other object. For example, if a class A has a public integer instance variable `x` and a public

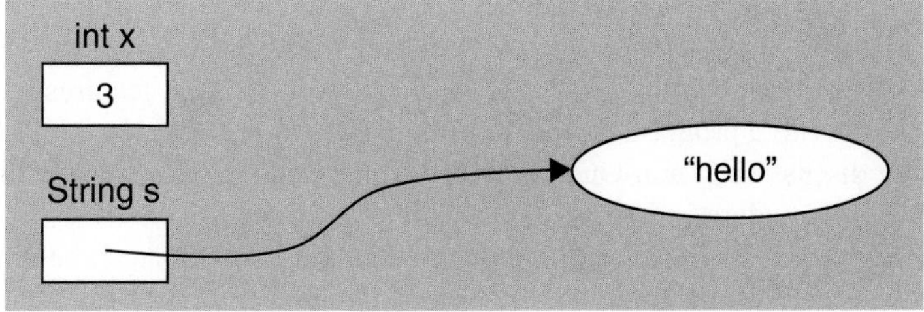

FIGURE 2.1 The variable `x` stores the primitive integer value 3 whereas the variable `s` stores a reference to the String object "hello."

method `proc` with no parameters and if another object's method has a reference to an object `a` of class A, then that method can contain the following code:

```
a.proc();
int y = a.x;
a.x = 4;
```

In contrast, if a method or an instance variable of a class is private, then it can be invoked or accessed only within the class body itself. A more detailed discussion of accessibility is given in the last section of this chapter.

Because two objects of the same class have the same set of methods and therefore can be sent the same set of messages, one might initially think that all objects of that class behave identically, in which case there would be little reason ever to create more than one object of a class. What distinguishes the behavior of two objects of the same class is their state. That is, the two objects may behave differently because the two objects' instance variables may have different values. For example, if the user creates two Person objects

```
Person firstMan = new Person("Adam", new Date(0));
Person firstWoman = new Person("Eve", new Date(1000000));
```

then both objects can respond to the `getName` message as in

```
String hisName = firstMan.getName();
String herName = firstWoman.getName();
```

but they will return different values. Because the result of a method call may vary depending on the state of the object, these methods are also called *instance* methods.

SECTION 2.3 ASIDE: CLASS METHODS AND VARIABLES IN JAVA

Introduction to Class Variables and Methods

As mentioned in the last section, methods contain the code that is executed when objects are sent messages, and instance variables contain any data that the object needs to maintain between method calls in order to execute the methods properly. In view of this use of variables as a way of maintaining objects' unique states and the use of methods as a way of communicating between objects, it may come as a surprise that Java also includes objectless variables and objectless methods, called *class* variables and methods. In fact, by using these objectless features of Java, it is possible to write a program that is almost completely non-OO. In the rest of this section, we discuss such non-OO variables and methods in Java so that the reader can more clearly understand when and when not to use them.

Footnote: Class methods can be thought of as messages that can be sent to the class itself instead of to an object of the class and class variables can be thought of as the "state" of the class itself.

Class Variables in Java and Their Uses

Both class variables and class methods are declared in Java using the key word "static." Class variables can be thought of as variables that are shared among all objects of a given class (and among objects outside of the class if the variable is made public) and so such variables cannot have unique values for each object of the class.

The typical use of class variables is for defining constants. Such constants are not only shared between all objects of the class, but are often made publicly available to be shared among all objects and classes in a program. In Java, a constant is indicated by the key word "final." For example, a programmer could define the physical constant *c* representing the speed of light in a vacuum in a class PhysicalConstants by including in the body of that class a line such as the following:

```
public final static int C = 299792458;
```

Since it is declared public and static, this constant can be accessed by any object at any time independently of any objects of class PhysicalConstants. A Java program could refer to this constant by using the notation "PhysicalConstants.C" as in

```
double distance = PhysicalConstants.C * 40;
```

which computes the distance in meters that light travels in 40 seconds.

In addition to its use in defining constants, class variables can be used to allow all instances (all objects) of a class to share a piece of data. For example, suppose all objects of a class need to know how many objects of that class have been created. One could give each object a copy of that data or to give each object a reference to that data. But in either case, not only is space wasted because of the duplication, but if the data is changed in one object, it becomes necessary to update in all objects of that class, which can waste time and easily lead to errors if one object is accidentally missed. A better solution is to make the count a static variable in the class shared by all objects.

Class Methods in Java and Their Uses

Class methods can be thought of as methods that are not a form of message passing to objects of that class and instead can be invoked independently of any objects of the class. In general, class methods are useful when objects of that class are stateless (i.e., have no instance variables) or when some of the methods do not use the state of the objects and instead merely manipulate the data passed in as parameters. For example, all the methods in the Math class are public class methods (they have the "public" and "static" modifier in their declarations) and so can be accessed and executed by any body of Java code without reference to Math objects. For example, the `sin` method in the Math class can be executed as in

```
double y = Math.sin(x);
```

It is appropriate that these methods are class methods because they perform mathematical operations on the arguments passed to those methods, and so a Math object would play no significant role. [1, p. 152]

When designing a class and figuring out what methods it should have, it is not always immediately obvious whether a method should be a class method or instance method. For example, suppose you were defining a Set class (different from the java.util.Set interface), objects of which behave like (finite, unordered) mathematical sets of integers. A natural operation to be performed on such a set is the intersection of it with another Set. There are (at least) two ways such an operation can be declared in your Set class:

- `public Set intersect(Set otherSet)`
- `public static Set intersect(Set firstSet, Set secondSet)`

In the first case, the user would get the intersection by sending a Set `s1` a message, asking it to return the intersection of itself and a second set `s2`, through a method call such as:

```
Set intersection = s1.intersect(s2);
```

In the second case, the user could find the intersection by calling the class method, passing both sets as parameters:

```
Set intersection = Set.intersect(s1, s2);
```

Which version is better? One advantage of the second version is that it displays the natural symmetry in the intersection operation, in which neither set plays a special role. Also, the second version will not necessarily fail with a NullPointerException if `s1` or `s2` happened to be null. That is, the `intersect(Set, Set)` class method in the second version could test the nullity of `s1` and `s2` and treat a null `s1` or `s2` as an empty set and so return an empty set. In contrast, the call in the first version will throw an exception before the `intersect(Set)` instance method even begins execution if `s1` is null.

However, an advantage of the first version is that it is a natural way to proceed from an OO perspective. That is, it is natural to think of asking a Set object to tell you what it has in common with another set. Also, unless the `intersect(Set)` instance method is declared "final," it can be overridden by subclasses of Set, which, although not obviously useful here, is a feature that future users may find very valuable. We'll discuss the topic of overriding later in this chapter.

Summary

Methods can be class (static) methods when objects of that class have no state or do not use their state in the body of that method. Variables can be class (static) variables when the piece of data they contain needs to be shared among objects of that class (and possibly other classes).

SECTION 2.4 BRIEF INTRODUCTION TO UML CLASS DIAGRAMS

It is not easy to keep in your mind all the important properties of classes and the relationships between classes as the number of classes and relationships grow. To aid in visualizing the design, a diagram can be very helpful. In this text, we will use many such diagrams to show the properties of classes and the relationships between classes and objects, and how messages are passed between them. There is a standard notation or language, called the *Unified Modeling Language* for such diagrams. There are 13 kinds of diagrams included in UML 2.0, among which are class diagrams, state diagrams, and sequence diagrams, the three kinds of diagrams that we will mainly use in this text. Wherever one of these diagrams is introduced for the first time, we will include a very short introduction to the diagram. All the diagrams that we use in this text can be studied in more detail in Appendix A, which also has references for even more details.

When you use UML, keep in mind that it is not a Java-only modeling language, and so its notations do not always directly correspond to Java notation or syntax. For example, a method named `foo` that takes an integer `x` as a parameter and returns a String is written

```
String foo(int x)
```

in Java, but in UML it would be written

```
foo(x: int): String
```

A UML *class diagram* shows classes and interfaces and the relationships between them. Such a diagram provides a static view of the classes and relationships rather than a dynamic view of the interactions among objects of those classes. A class is represented by a box divided into three sections. The top section gives the name of the class. The middle section gives the attributes or properties held by objects of the class. These properties are abstractions of the data or state of an object and so are usually implemented using instance variables. The bottom section gives the operations of a class, which correspond in Java to methods and constructors.

For example, see Figure 2.2 for the class diagram for the Person class discussed in Section 2.2. The diagram shows that this class has a "name" attribute that is a String and a "birthDate" attribute of type Date. In Java, such attributes are typically implemented by adding two instance variables to the Person class: a variable called `name` of type String and a variable called `birthDate` of type Date. The diagram also shows that this class has a constructor with two parameters, a method `getName` with no parameters that returns a String and a `getBirthDate` method with no parameters that returns a Date.

Notice several other things about this diagram:

1. The "−" symbol in front of the attributes indicate that the attributes are private. Similarly, the "+" symbol in front of the operations indicate that they are public operations.

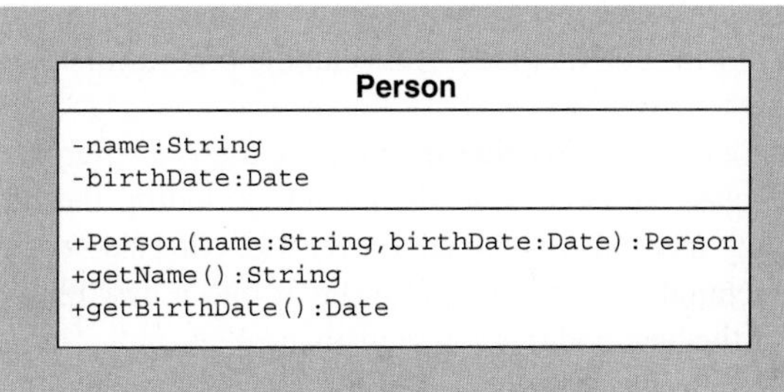

FIGURE 2.2 The class diagram for the Person class.

2. The types of the attributes, parameters, and return types of the operations are given after the names of the elements and are separated from them by colons.
3. The implementation of these attributes and operations are not included in the box, because a UML diagram is not usually concerned with such low-level details.

Any part of the details of a class except its name can be omitted from the diagram, including all attributes and/or operations, the public and private modifiers of those attributes and operations, and the parameters and/or return type of the operations. In fact, to avoid clutter and confusion, it is strongly recommended that the diagram leave out all details of the classes that are not relevant to the discussion. Therefore, it is important to remember that a class with no operations shown, for example, does not imply that the class has no operations. Rather, it implies that the operations were not relevant.

SECTION 2.5 IMPLEMENTATION INHERITANCE

One of the most significant features of OO programming is "implementation inheritance" or "subclassing," which greatly increases the reusability of classes and also minimizes the duplication of code. We will introduce implementation inheritance through several simple examples that show some of the standard uses to which inheritance is put and that will hopefully lead you to appreciate the benefits it can provide to a software designer. We will also devote all of the next chapter to the discussion of the proper use and the pitfalls of inheritance.

Specialization

Consider an example of a programmer who has been assigned to create a drawing program in which rectangles can grow, shrink, or move around on a panel under the control of the user. In order to deal with the rectangles, it is useful to have a Rectangle class that stores the relevant information about the rectangle, such as its size and position. Being appropriately lazy, the programmer doesn't automatically code a Rectangle class from scratch and instead spends a minute or two looking through existing libraries to see whether there is already a Rectangle class to be used. Sure enough, there are several Rectangle classes in the Java libraries, including java.awt.Rectangle, java.awt.geom.Rectangle2D.Double, and java.awt.geom.Rectangle2D.Float.

After studying these three classes, our programmer determines that java.awt.Rectangle is the closest one to satisfying his needs. However, he wants a class with a `getCenter()` method and a `setCenter(int x, int y)` method and the Rectangle class doesn't have such methods. How can the programmer get what he wants with minimal effort?

If the source code for the existing Rectangle class is available, the programmer could modify the class to suit his needs, including adding the new methods and possibly deleting any methods that he will never use. Alternatively, the programmer could copy the Rectangle class code and insert it into a new class EnhancedRectangle and then add the new code.

Code reuse is always a very appropriate action to take, but not in either of these ways. Both of these approaches have inelegant aspects. The first approach could cause problems with existing code that uses the original Rectangle class—there are now two versions of Rectangle floating around to confuse users and possibly the compiler. The second approach is better in that the new class will not affect existing code that uses the original Rectangle class, but there is major code duplication in this case, which introduces unnecessary complexity (remember that one of the properties of elegance is simplicity). For example, if the copied code is later found to have bugs, the programmer is going to have to remember to fix the bugs in the copy as well.

Furthermore, neither of these approaches works if only the compiled code, and not the source code, for the Rectangle class is available. One solution in this case is to have the programmer ignore the compiled code and define and implement his own EnhancedRectangle class. This action, however, does nothing in terms of reuse of existing code and so results in significant code duplication. In this case, we don't necessarily have exact duplication of method bodies, but we do have duplication of semantics, which can be just as bad. Furthermore, the Rectangle class was (presumably) thoroughly tested and the implementation of the new class could involve considerable effort just to bring it to the error-free level of the existing class.

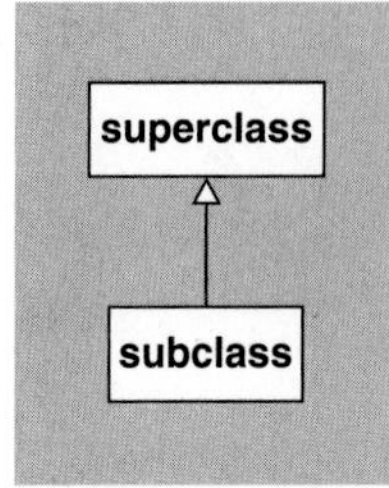

FIGURE 2.3
The UML notation for subclass and superclass.

To avoid all these problems, implementation inheritance can be used. Java (and other OO languages) allows the programmer to define one class as a *subclass* of another class (which makes the second class a *superclass* of the first class). A subclass *inherits* all the features (all the variables and methods, but not the constructors) of the superclass, which means all those features are automatically included in the subclass and, if not declared private, are accessible in the subclass. The UML notation for subclassing is shown in Figure 2.3. The arrow pointing from the subclass to the superclass is called a *generalization* relationship in UML.

In Java, subclassing is expressed using the keyword "extends." So our programmer could write

```
public class EnhancedRectangle extends Rectangle
{
  public EnhancedRectangle(int x, int y, int w, int h) //constructor
  {
    super(x, y, w, h);
  }
  public Point getCenter()
  {
    return new Point((int) getCenterX(), (int) getCenterY());
  }
  public void setCenter(int x, int y)
  {
    setLocation( x - (int) getWidth()/2, y - (int) getHeight()/2);
  }
}
```

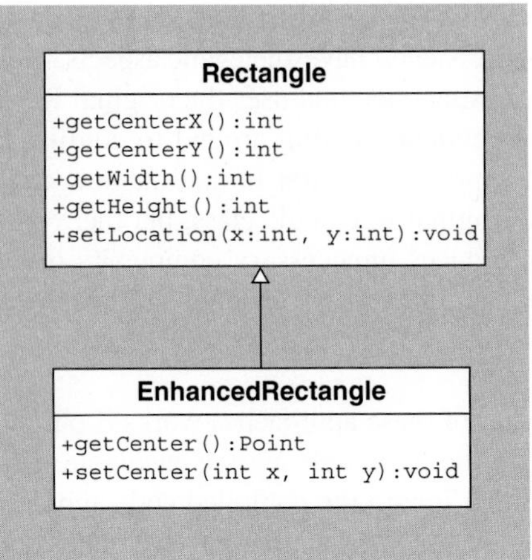

FIGURE 2.4 The relationship between Rectangle and EnhancedRectangle.

This declaration makes EnhancedRectangle a subclass of Rectangle and makes Rectangle a superclass of EnhancedRectangle. Because it is a subclass, the new EnhancedRectangle class inherits all the methods and all the data in the Rectangle class. Note that since constructors are not inherited, you need to create constructors for new subclasses (or let the Java compiler create a no-argument constructor for you, which it does if you don't implement any constructors in your class). The call to `super(x, y, w, h)` in the constructor above calls the superclass' constructor to initialize all the Rectangle data. The `getCenterX`, `getCenterY`, `setLocation`, `getWidth`, and `getHeight` methods that are used to implement the two new methods are all inherited from the Rectangle class. See Figure 2.4 for the UML diagram. (Note how, in this diagram, all instance variables and methods of the Rectangle class were omitted except for the ones relevant to the discussion.)

Now the clients of the EnhancedRectangle class can use it as follows:

```
EnhancedRectangle rectangle = new EnhancedRectangle(1, 2, 50, 60);
rectangle.setLocation(10, 10); //inherited method
rectangle.setCenter(50, 60); //subclass method
```

Note that EnhancedRectangle objects behave as if all methods inherited from the Rectangle class had been defined in their class.

In this way, subclassing provides a way to reuse the code and data of an existing class to create a new class that is identical except that it has more features (data and/or behavior). This process of extending an existing class by adding new features is called using inheritance for *specialization*.

The Object Superclass in Java

Before we continue, it is important to note that all Java classes that do not explicitly extend another class implicitly extend the Object class. Therefore, all Java classes extend the Object class either directly or indirectly via one or more intermediate classes in an inheritance chain. This means that your classes will automatically inherit the methods in the Object class: `clone`, `equals`, `finalize`, `getClass`, `hashcode`, `notify`, `notifyAll`, `toString`, and three versions of `wait`.

Another Use of Specialization

To see how implementation inheritance can be used to solve a slightly different problem involving specialization, consider another programmer working on a drawing program using the Java Swing package. Suppose that the program allows the user to draw ovals with white interiors and black borders and stores all drawn ovals in a collection of Oval objects. The Ovals know their locations and size and how to draw themselves:

```
public class Oval
{
    public int x, y, w, h;
    public Oval(int x, int y, int w, int h) { //constructor
        this.x = x; this.y = y; this.w = w; this.h = h;
    }
    public void draw(Graphics g) {
        g.drawOval(x, y, w, h);
    }
    public int getWidth() { return w; }
    public int getHeight() { return h; }
    public Point getTopLeftPoint() { return new Point(x,y); }
    //...other methods...
}
```

Suppose that the programmer has been asked to enhance the program to allow the user to draw filled ovals in addition to regular ovals. See Figure 2.5 for a picture of such ovals.

This programmer quickly realizes that she will need to create a FilledOval class that can be stored in a collection similar to the collection of Ovals. There are at least three ways she could proceed:

1. She could ignore the Oval class and design her own FilledOval class that she implements from scratch.
2. She could realize that the Oval is exactly what she needs except that Ovals do not have black interiors when drawn, and so she could copy and paste the Oval class source code into a new FilledOval class and then make small changes to it to change the way it draws itself.
3. She could use implementation inheritance and creates a new FilledOval class that is a subclass of Oval.

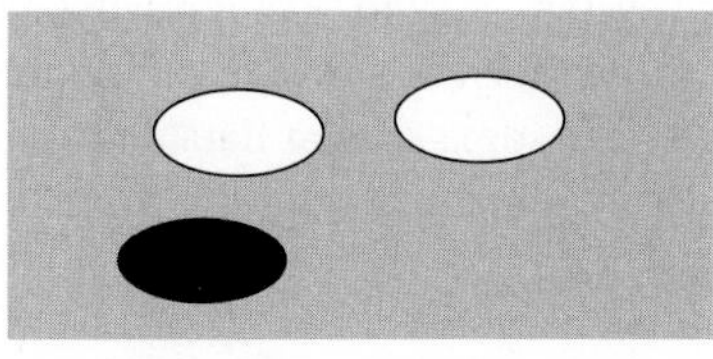

FIGURE 2.5 Two white ovals with black borders and a filled oval.

In the third case, the FilledOval inherits all the methods and data in the Oval class. Unfortunately, the programmer doesn't want the FilledOval to inherit *all* the behavior of Oval, since one of the methods of Oval, the `draw(Graphics)` method, displays the Oval with a black border and white interior. She wants her class to have a slightly different implementation of the same `draw` method. Luckily this change can easily be implemented in OO languages like Java through overriding. A method implemented in a subclass that has the same signature as a method implemented in the superclass is said to *override* the superclass' method. (The *signature* of a method consists of the method name and the list of types of the parameters.) We can override `draw` by including a new implementation of `draw` in the FilledOval class as follows:

```
public class FilledOval extends Oval
{
    public FilledOval(int x, int y, int w, int h)
    {
        super(x, y, w, h);
    }
    public void draw(Graphics g)
    {
        g.fillOval(x, y, w, h);
    }
}
```

Whenever the `draw` message is sent to a FilledOval object, the implementation of `draw` in the FilledOval class will be the one that is executed.

Do you notice also how much code reuse is going on in this example? The new class reuses all of the code in the superclass so that only a new constructor and a `draw` method need to be written.

Note also that, in this case, the programmer didn't want to enhance the Oval class by adding new attributes or behavior, but instead she wanted to modify it so that it behaved slightly differently (it should display itself differently in the window). In summary, subclassing can be used to create a new class identical to an existing class except with some modified behavior instead of (or as well as) some additional behavior. This is another way that inheritance can be used for the purpose of specialization.

Generalization

There are other common ways whereby subclassing can help clean up code. Let us assume a business has a billing system that keeps track of all its current customers. Because the business sells both to human customers and business customers, the designers of the billing system created two unrelated classes, BusinessCustomer and HumanCustomer. Unfortunately, this design might not be very elegant because both of these classes might have some similar data and some identical methods. For example, they both might store a name and have a `getName` method for retrieving that name.

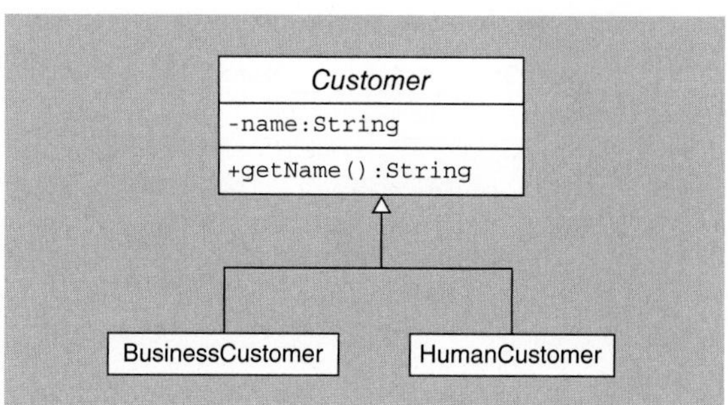

FIGURE 2.6 The Customer superclass with two subclasses.

One way to avoid code duplication is to introduce a new Customer class that is a superclass of both the BusinessCustomer and HumanCustomer classes and then move all common data and methods into the superclass. That is, we could remove the `name` instance variable and the `getName` method from the BusinessCustomer and HumanCustomer classes and add the variable and method to the Customer class. Since BusinessCustomer and HumanCustomer classes are both subclasses of Customer, they inherit the instance variable and method of the superclass. See Figure 2.6 for the UML diagram for this relationship.

In this example, that we would probably not want the user to create any Customer objects, since that class has been created merely as a place to put common features to avoid duplication. One way to prevent creation of Customer objects is to declare the class "abstract." To do so, you just need to include the keyword "abstract" in front of the word "class" in the declaration, for example,

```
public abstract class Customer
{ ... }
```

In UML class diagrams, abstract classes are indicated by putting the names of the classes in italics, as shown in Figure 2.6.

Now the user can proceed to create and use the two subclasses as if they both contained a `name` variable and `getName` method:

```
HumanCustomer human = new HumanCustomer(...);
BusinessCustomer business = new BusinessCustomer(...);
String humanName = human.getName();
String businessName = business.getName();
```

In summary, subclassing and superclassing can be used to avoid code and data duplication among several classes by creating a superclass to those classes and moving the duplicate code and data up into that superclass, which is commonly abstract. This process is called using inheritance for *generalization*.

Single Inheritance in Java

In Java, a class can have only one superclass and so you can't inherit some methods from one class and some other methods from another class by subclassing. This single inheritance feature of Java can interfere with your attempts at code reuse. For

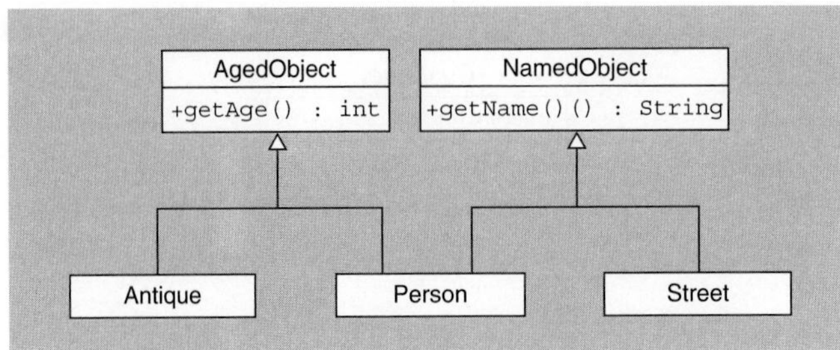

FIGURE 2.7 A Person class with two superclasses.

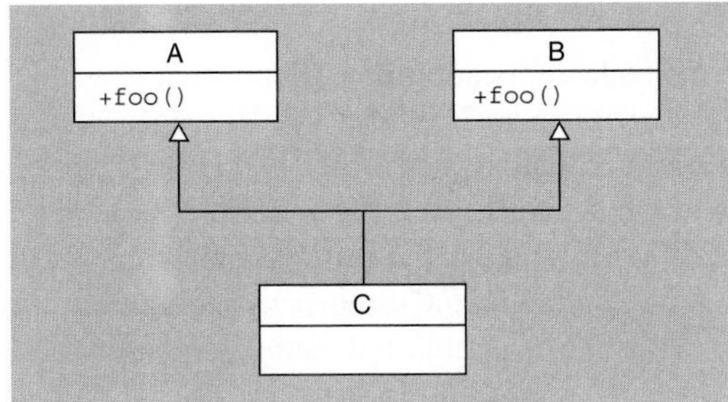

FIGURE 2.8 Class A inherits two `foo()` methods.

a very simplistic example, suppose you were given a project involving a Person class with name and age attributes, an Antique class with an age attribute, and a Street object with a name attribute. If you were told to maximize code reuse, you might be tempted to create a AgedObject superclass of Person and Antique to hold the age attribute, and you might wish to create a NamedObject superclass of Person and Street to hold the name attribute (see Figure 2.7). Unfortunately, you can't create two superclasses of Person.

This restriction to a single superclass is a shortcoming of Java, but it serves to keep the implementation of classes and inheritance simple and to simplify the understanding of such code. For an example of the issues that need to be addressed if multiple inheritance is allowed, consider a class C that inherits a `foo()` method from a superclass A and inherits another `foo()` method from a superclass B. See Figure 2.8.

Which of these methods will or should get executed when `c.foo()` is called for an object `c` of class C? There are a variety of ways of handling this ambiguity; the Java language designers handled it by eliminating multiple inheritance.

SECTION 2.6 TYPES, SUBTYPES, AND INTERFACE INHERITANCE

Another of the most powerful concepts of object-oriented programming is subtype polymorphism. In order to understand this concept, it is important to understand first what is meant by a "type."

Type

A *type* can be thought of as a set of data values and the operations that can be performed on them. For example, the "int" primitive type in Java can be thought of as the set of all 32-bit integers (with values ranging from −2,147,483,648 to 2,147,483,647) together with the set of operations that can be performed on integers, including, for example, addition, subtraction, multiplication, and division. For objects, types can be defined similarly, except the focus is more on the operations than on the values. For the purposes of this text, an object *type* will consist of a set of operations and a set of objects that can perform those operations.

There are two standard ways in Java to define new types. Any class C implicitly forms a type C. The set of public methods of the class form the set of operations for type C and the objects of class C or its subclasses form the set of objects of that type. For example, the class Person discussed in Section 2.2 defines a type "Person" with operations `getName()` and `getBirthDate()`. All objects of class Person or its subclasses can perform these two operations, and these objects form the set of objects of type Person.

The other way to define a type is to use Java interfaces. An interface can be thought of as a named set of operations. All objects whose classes explicitly "implement" the interface form the set of objects of that type. For example, the following interface defines a type Runnable:

```
public interface Runnable
{
    public void run();
}
```

The operations of type Runnable consist of just the `run()` method. The set of objects of type Runnable consists of all objects of all classes that implement Runnable. For example, consider the following class SimpleRunner:

```
public class SimpleRunner implements Runnable
{
    public void run() { System.out.println("I'm running." ); }
}
```

This class defines and implements a method `run()` of the form required by the Runnable interface and the class explicitly declares that it "implements Runnable." Therefore, all objects of class SimpleRunner can be considered as objects of type Runnable. In fact, since SimpleRunner is also a subclass of the Object class, objects of class SimpleRunner have three types: SimpleRunner, Runnable, and Object.

A UML diagram showing the relationship between SimpleRunner, Runnable, and Object is shown in Figure 2.9. Note that an interface is displayed in a UML class diagram similarly to a class, with the differences being that the top part of the box includes the designation «interface» and there are no attributes to an interface. The arrow with the dashed line pointing from the SimpleRunner class to the interface is called a *realization* relationship in UML and indicates that the class implements or "realizes" the interface.

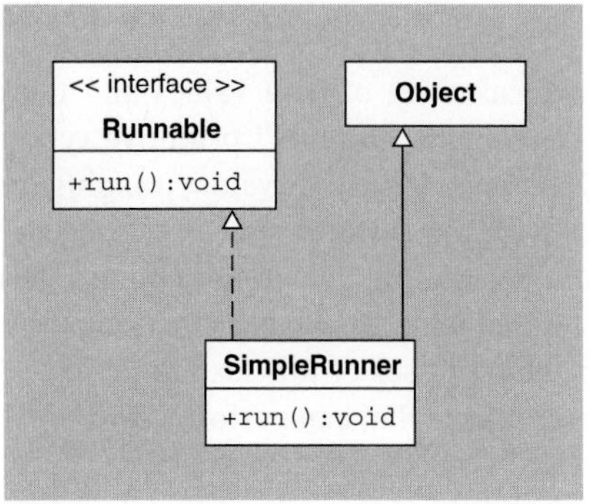

FIGURE 2.9 The Runnable interface and SimpleRunner class.

Note that objects of a subclass S of a class T are considered to be both of type S and of type T. There is a special relationship between the type of a subclass and the type of a superclass, in that a subclass of a class defines a subtype of the superclass' type. That is, one type S is a *subtype* of another type T (which, in turn, is called a *supertype* of S) if the set of objects of type S are a subset of the set of objects of type T and the set of operations of S are a superset of the operations of T. Note that, if type S is a subtype of type T, the set of operations of S must include all the operations of T and can possibly have more. For example, the type SimpleRunner is a subtype of Runnable since all objects of type SimpleRunner are also objects of type Runnable and since SimpleRunner includes all operations in the Runnable type. Similarly, SimpleRunner is a subtype of Object since it includes (inherits) all operations in Object and its objects are a subset of the set of all Objects.

It should be noted that interfaces can also have subinterfaces that inherit from them similar to the way inheritance works with classes. For example, consider the following interface:

```
public interface Movable extends Runnable
{
    public void walk();
}
```

The Movable interface defines a new interface with two operations: its `walk()` operation and the `run()` operation that it inherits.

As you might expect, a subinterface defines a subtype of the type defined by the superinterface. In summary, if a class B is a subclass of class A or if B implements an interface A or if B is a subinterface of interface A, then the type B is a subtype of the type A.

Polymorphism

Object-oriented programming languages support these notions of types and subtypes by allowing a variable of one type to store an object of a subtype. For example, in the Java statement

```
Runnable r = new SimpleRunner();
```

the variable `r` of type Runnable refers to an object of actual class SimpleRunner. The fact that an object of a subtype can be legally used wherever an object of a supertype is expected is called *subtype polymorphism.* As mentioned above, subtype polymorphism is one of the most important concepts in object orientation and is one of the main things that makes OO languages so useful. The Java libraries use polymorphism extensively. In fact, the Java 1.5 API includes over 1000 interfaces. Because you cannot create objects of an interface type and must instead create objects of a class that implements the interface, everywhere one of these Java interfaces is used, polymorphism is also being used.

The Value of Polymorphism

Why is subtype polymorphism so important in object-oriented languages? We will just give one example, but it will hopefully give you a feeling for the power and elegance that can be derived from the proper use of polymorphism.

When one discusses well-designed software, the concept of "plug-and-play" often arises. The idea of plug-and-play is that an item can be "plugged" into a system and immediately "played" without the need to do any extra work, such as reconfiguring the system. This terminology is normally used in discussions of computer hardware, such as plugging new cards into computer expansion slots and immediately being able to use them. However, the concept can also apply to software. In particular, if software is elegant, then one should be able to remove an object of one class and easily replace it with, or "plug in," an object of another "equivalent" class either on the fly or with only minimal code changes.

Consider the example of collection classes, which act as storage containers for other objects. For the purpose of discussion here, let us suppose you have used the java.util.LinkedList class extensively as the collection class in a large software system. Furthermore, suppose that after testing and using the system, it is found that, in some parts of the system, the LinkedList is too slow because the operation of retrieving the *n*th item requires traversing the first *n* elements of the list. At that point, it would be nice to replace some of the uses of the LinkedList class with a different collection class such as the ArrayList class, which stores its objects in an array and so has constant-time random access. The problem is that such a replacement might require significant changes to the system.

In particular, if the software was not designed with such a replacement in mind, then you would first need to find everywhere a variable of type LinkedList is declared and/or initialized in the system and then decide whether it needs to be replaced with the declaration and/or initialization of a variable of type ArrayList. However, such declarations and initializations can be scattered throughout the package. Errors can occur if all appropriate occurrences are not found and properly changed. (As you are surely aware, it is not sufficient to do a global search and replace—see the exercises for more on such an approach.)

Secondly, you might need to modify some of the method calls if you used methods unique to the LinkedList class, such as `addFirst` and `addLast`. You would need to replace those method calls with some equivalent code using ArrayLists.

Not only is making these changes a lot of work, but this whole process might need to be repeated again if it is later found that ArrayLists are also insufficient and a third different collection class is needed. Those changes would be time-consuming and, once again, they might accidentally introduce new errors. Ideally, we would be able to change the collection classes used by the system by making only one change to the system code.

To clean up the design once and for all so that future changes can be easily made, the first step is to realize that both these classes, LinkedList and ArrayList, implement the List interface. The next step is to see whether the methods in that interface are sufficient for all the collection class needs in your software system. If they are, then every place such a collection is used, one of those methods in the interface should be called rather than a method unique to LinkedList or ArrayList.

The third step is to deal with the declarations and initializations of variables of type LinkedList. To avoid having to change the declarations later, all collection variables should be declared to be of type "objects-that-implement-all-the-methods-in-our-List-interface" instead of declaring those variables to refer to objects of one specific class such as LinkedList. That is, declare your variables to be of some kind of the general type List that will allow such variables to refer to any object that implements the List interface. Then you will no longer need to change the variable declarations if you later change the design to use to a new collection class implementing the List interface.

See Figure 2.10 for a UML diagram relating these classes and interface.

Your software system can now have statements such as

```
List list = new LinkedList();
```

and

```
List list = new ArrayList();
```

Furthermore, regardless of whether the `list` variable refers to a LinkedList or an ArrayList, code such as

```
list.clear();
```

will execute the appropriate `clear` method, that is, the `clear` method of the object referred to by `list`.

Let us summarize how we are making our system plug-and-play regarding collection classes. By declaring our collection variables to be of type List then, if we need later to change our variables to refer to an ArrayList instead of a LinkedList, we do not need to change any method calls that use the variables nor do we need to change the declarations of any of those variables. These are the benefits of polymorphism.

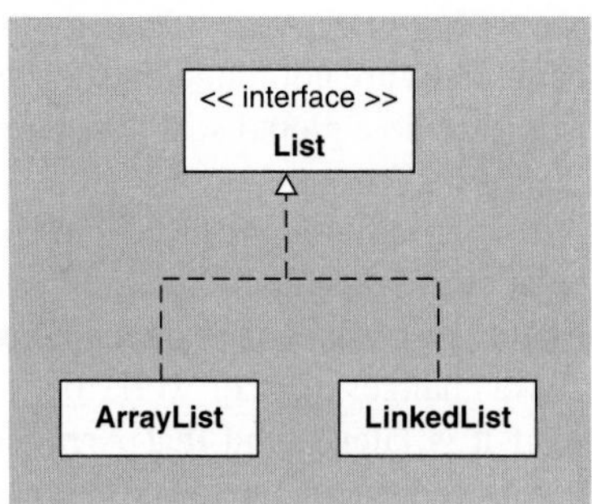

FIGURE 2.10 The List interface and two classes that implement it.

To complete this example, we should fix one more problem. That problem concerns not the declaration of our container variables, but their initialization. If we want to change our code to use some ArrayLists instead of LinkedLists, then everywhere our code has statements of the form

```
List list = new LinkedList();
```

we need to decide whether to change them to

```
List list = new ArrayList();
```

How can we minimize the amount of work and so minimize the chance of introducing errors for such changes in the variable initializations? Furthermore, can we make the code easier to modify in the future? The key to the solution is to localize the code that needs to be changed. Instead of using constructors to create new objects wherever our collection variables are initialized, as we do above, we could use a "factory" method, which is a method that (somehow) creates or finds and returns an object for you. This method may call a constructor to create a new object or it may recycle objects it already has available (stored in an object pool or "warehouse"). For example, your system might have a Manager class with a factory method `createNewList` that just creates and returns an object of the class LinkedList or ArrayList:

```
public List createNewList()
{
    return new LinkedList();
}
```

At first, it may seem like there is little to be gained by replacing a call to the LinkedList constructor with a call to the method `createNewList` that then turns around and calls the LinkedList constructor. The gain comes from the fact that the initialization statements for container variables can be replaced everywhere in your code with

```
List list = manager.createNewList();
```

where `manager` is an available object of class Manager. Then, if your system needs to be changed to use ArrayLists instead of LinkedLists, there is only one place in the whole system where code needs to be changed: the `createNewList` method of the Manager class. One way to proceed in that case would be to edit the method to read

```
public Collection createNewList()
{
    return new ArrayList();
}
```

An alternative, as discussed in Chapter 7, is to create and use a new subclass of Manager with a different implementation of `createNewList`.

In summary, interfaces and classes that implement those interfaces form a rich environment for exploiting polymorphism. The fact that a variable declared to be of an interface type can refer to objects of a variety of actual classes (that are subtypes of the interface type) enables you to write code that is much more flexible and reusable than would be the case if you had to fix the actual class of the values of the variable.

As a final point, note that, in contrast to inheritance where there can be only one superclass, classes can implement any number of Java interfaces. For example, a class D can implement interfaces A and B and extend a class C. There are no problems created by having a class implement multiple interfaces since the problems caused by multiple inheritance are due to inheriting one or more *implementations* of a method. There are no such implementations to be inherited with interfaces.

SECTION 2.7 INTERFACES VS. ABSTRACT CLASSES

What is the difference between interfaces and abstract classes? When should you use one and when the other? Before answering these questions, let us first review a property of abstract classes.

When declaring an abstract class, it is permissible to leave some of the methods in the class unimplemented. Such methods are indicated with the "abstract" keyword. For example, the following class is an abstract class that has one implemented method and one nonimplemented abstract method:

```
public abstract class AbstractClass
{
  public String toString() { return "An AbstractClass object"; }
  public abstract void visit(Object o);
}
```

Note that the declaration of the unimplemented method is similar to the declaration of methods in an interface except for the addition of the "abstract" keyword. In UML diagrams, abstract methods are indicated by putting the method name in italics.

Now suppose you have an abstract class with all abstract (unimplemented) methods and no instance variables. For example, consider the following abstract class:

```
public abstract class TotallyAbstractClass
{
  public abstract void clear();
  public abstract void visit(Object o);
}
```

Compare that class to the following interface:

```
public interface TotalInterface
{
  public void clear();
  public void visit(Object o);
}
```

How do they differ? If you needed to include one of them in your design, which should you choose?

Extending TotallyAbstractClass is virtually the same as implementing Total Interface, except that a given class can extend at most one superclass in Java. Therefore, one would rarely want to create an abstract class with all abstract methods and no instance variables instead of creating an interface with the same methods. Another way to think about this situation is that a programmer typically implements an interface to permit subtype polymorphism. In contrast, a programmer extends a class as a way both to permit subtype polymorphism and to inherit method implementations. If there are no implementations to inherit, then an interface is usually the preferable form.

SECTION 2.8 DYNAMIC METHOD INVOCATION

We have seen that inheritance provides at least two significant advantages for software designers. First of all, it provides a mechanism for code reuse. Secondly, if a class B is a subclass of a class A, then B can also be considered a subtype of A, and so subtype polymorphism can be used. In this section, we will discuss how such subtype polymorphism together with a concept called *dynamic method invocation*, gives designers and programmers even greater power and flexibility.

Consider the following code that uses the Customer example discussed earlier in this chapter:

```
Customer customer = new HumanCustomer(...);
String name = customer.getName();
```

Because the HumanCustomer type is a subtype of the Customer type, the assignment statement in the first line is legal. Furthermore, the HumanCustomer class inherits the `getName` method from the Customer class and that method will be executed correctly in the second line to return the name of the customer.

Things are a little more complicated if the subclass overrides one or more of the methods of the superclass. Consider the example of the FilledOval class discussed earlier and look at the following code:

```
Oval oval = new FilledOval(1,2,10,20);
oval.draw(g); //for some Graphics object g
```

Recall that FilledOval inherits a `draw` method from Oval and also implements its own version of `draw`. Which of those two implementations of `draw` will be executed in the second line of this example? Due to the fact that `oval` is declared to be of type Oval, you might be tempted to think that the Oval implementation of `draw` is executed. However, Java, like other object-oriented languages, uses dynamic method invocation. *Dynamic method invocation* means that the Java runtime environment, when asked to invoke a method on an object, looks at the actual class of the object to find the method implementation to execute. For example, when asked to execute `oval.draw(g)`, the Java environment does not look in the declared class of `oval` (namely, Oval) but instead looks in the actual class of the object referred to by `oval` (namely, FilledOval) for the `draw` method to execute. More generally, when a subclass overrides an inherited method then the overriding method implementation in the subclass is always invoked when the method is called on an object of the subclass.

In fact, dynamic method invocation is used when classes implement interfaces as well. For example, consider our List interface mentioned earlier and look at the following code:

```
List list = new ArrayList();
list.clear();
```

The `clear` method that is invoked in the second line is determined dynamically (at runtime) by the Java environment by looking at the actual class of the object referred to by `list`. In this case, that object is of class ArrayList and so the implementation of `clear` in the ArrayList class is the one that is executed.

To better understand subtype polymorphism and dynamic method invocation, let us look at another, more complicated, example. Consider an Automobile class and the Sedan, Minivan, and SportsCar subclasses shown in Figure 2.11. You can see from the figure that the Automobile class is abstract, as indicated by the use of italics for its name. (It would be better for the Automobile class to be an interface, as discussed in the preceding section, but for the sake of discussion regarding dynamic method invocation, we will use an abstract class here.)

Because Sedan is a subtype of Automobile, it is perfectly legal in Java to have a statement such as

```
Automobile auto = new Sedan(Color.black);
```

Although `auto` is expected to have a value of class Automobile, it can be assigned a value of class Sedan because of subtype polymorphism.

Assuming the Minivan and SportsCar classes, like the Sedan class, have constructors that take a Color as an argument, the following code is legal:

```
Automobile[] fleet = new Automobile[3];
fleet[0] = new Sedan(Color.black);
fleet[1] = new Minivan(Color.blue);
fleet[2] = new SportsCar(Color.red);
```

FIGURE 2.11 The Automobile class and its subclasses.

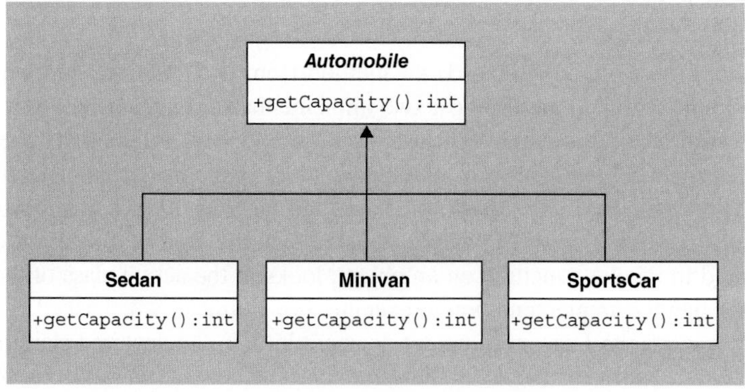

Aside: In this example, any features (methods or data) that an Sedan has but an Automobile doesn't have are still part of the object referred to by `auto`, but those features are hidden in that they are not accessible directly through the variable `auto`. For example, suppose that the Sedan class has a `getStyle` method that is not in the Automobile class. In that case, the compiler will complain if you attempt the following statement,

```
System.out.println(auto.getStyle()); //compiler error
```

even though `auto` refers to an Sedan object with a `getStyle()` method. To access the hidden features of `auto`, you need to downcast the value of `auto` to the subtype Sedan. *Downcasting* a value means indicating to the compiler that the value is actually of a subtype of the declared or implied type. Downcasting is done by including the name of the subtype in parentheses in front of the value. For example, you can write:

```
Sedan sedan = (Sedan) auto;
System.out.println(sedan.getStyle());
```

The first line tells the compiler that the object referred to by `auto` is actually a Sedan rather than an Automobile and so can be assigned to the variable `sedan` of type Sedan. More simply, but possibly less readably, you can combine these two lines and write:

```
System.out.println(((Sedan) auto).getStyle());
```

It is important to realize that downcasting does not dynamically change an object from one class to another. It merely indicates to the compiler that the variable `auto` actually refers to an object of the subtype even though the variable was declared to be of a supertype. If the variable did not refer to an object of the subtype and an attempt was made to downcast, it would result in a ClassCastException.

Note that the array is being assigned values from three separate classes, but, since they are all subclasses of Automobile, the assignments are legal.

To see the advantages that dynamic method invocation provides, let us suppose that our Automobile class' `getCapacity` method (indicating the number of passengers it can hold) has a default behavior of returning 0. Note that each subclass' `getCapacity` method overrides the inherited method to return the appropriate capacity, say 7 for Minivans, 5 for Sedans, and 2 for SportsCars.

Now suppose that we want to determine the total capacity of all the automobiles in the array `fleet`. Here's a naive way of doing so:

Version 1

```
int totalCapacity = 0;
for( int i = 0; i < fleet.length; i++ ) {
   if( fleet[i] instanceof Sedan )
      totalCapacity += ((Sedan) fleet[i]).getCapacity();
   else if( fleet[i] instanceof Minivan )
      totalCapacity += ((Minivan) fleet[i]).getCapacity();
   else if( fleet[i] instanceof SportsCar )
      totalCapacity += ((SportsCar) fleet[i]).getCapacity();
   else
      totalCapacity += fleet[i].getCapacity();
```

Recall that `c instanceof C` is a boolean expression that is true if and only if `c` refers to an object of class C or one of its subclasses. The naive approach in Version 1 works, but it is ugly and, due to dynamic method invocation, totally unnecessary. In fact, all we need in order to compute the total capacity is the following code:

Version 2

```
int totalCapacity = 0;
for( int i = 0; i < fleet.length; i++ )
   totalCapacity += fleet[i].getCapacity();
```

The runtime system dynamically (that is, during execution) looks at the *actual* class of the object referred to by `fleet[i]` rather than the *declared* type of `fleet[i]` and executes the `getCapacity` method in the actual class. As a result, `totalCapacity` will end up with the value 14 (i.e., 5 + 7 + 2).

It is important to realize that if the three subclasses implement `getCapacity` methods but the superclass does *not* mention such a method (e.g., if the Automobile class had no `getCapacity` method or if there were no Automobile class and so the three subclasses had Object as their immediate superclass), then overriding would not be occurring. Instead, the compiler will complain about Version 2, saying that `fleet[i]` is of class Automobile but the Automobile class has no `getCapacity` method. That is, there are two parts to the invocation of `fleet[i].getCapacity()`. The first part occurs at compile time when the compiler sees that `fleet[i]` is declared to have type Automobile, at which point the compiler determines which method is to be called by looking for a `getCapacity` method in the Automobile class. The second part occurs at runtime, in that the *implementation* or body of the `getCapacity` method that is actually executed is selected dynamically by looking at the actual class of the object referred to by `fleet[i]`. Hence, if there were no Automobile superclass or if the Automobile class did not mention a `getCapacity` method, then the naive code in Version 1—after removing the last else clause—would be the only way to get the capacities of the automobiles in the array.

Do you see the beauty of Version 2? Not only is the code shorter and simpler, but also if a new subclass of Automobile is later introduced, for example, an SUV, and objects of that class were added to the array `fleet`, then the Version 1 programmer would have to modify the conditional statement to test one more case. However, Version 2 can handle the objects of the new subclass without any changes. There is a natural elegance to code like this that uses polymorphism to avoid conditional statements that test whether a value is of a particular type. Using polymorphism to avoid such conditionals is considered to be one of the "OO" ways of doing things.

SECTION 2.9 OVERLOADING VS. OVERRIDING

The difference between *overloading* method names and *overriding* methods is an important one. In this section, we will attempt to clarify that difference and further explore how dynamic method invocation works.

Two methods in the same class with the same name but different parameter lists (more precisely, different lists of parameter types—the parameter names are irrelevant) cause the method name to be *overloaded*. This means that the method name is being used for two completely different methods in the same class. Note that overloading occurs within one class and refers to two or more methods with the same name but different signatures. Contrast this with overriding, which requires a superclass and subclass and refers to two methods, one in each class, with exactly the same signatures.

The three versions of `wait` in the Object class form one example of overloading. The String class' two `substring` methods provide another example. One of the `substring` methods has one integer parameter and the other has two integer parameters:

```
public String substring(int beginIndex)
public String substring(int beginIndex, int endIndex)
```

The first method returns the substring starting at the given index and continuing to the end of the string. The second method returns the substring between the given indices.

You should notice how the two `substring` methods perform almost identical actions. It should go without saying that you should only overload a method name if the methods with the same name do essentially the same thing, just as these `substring` methods do.

It is a bit harder to understand which method actually gets called when the two methods with the same name have parameters that involve subtypes.

Let us consider our Automobile class again. As discussed in Section 2.5, all classes in Java are subclasses of the Object class and so inherit a method from the Object class with the following header:

```
public boolean equals(Object obj)                          (1)
```

Suppose that you now add to the Automobile class a method with the following header:

```
public boolean equals(Automobile auto)                     (2)
```

FIGURE 2.12 The Automobile and Object classes.

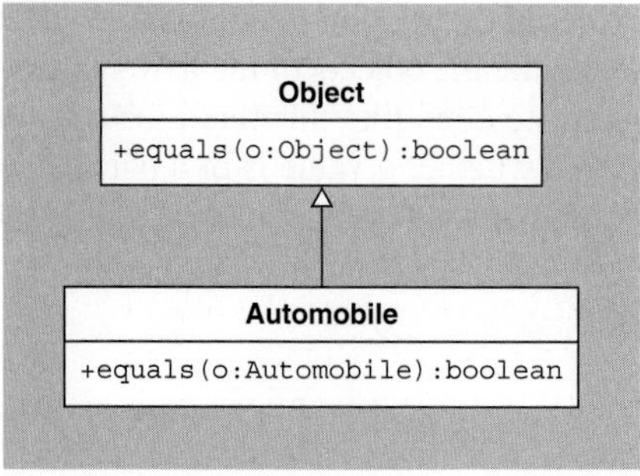

See Figure 2.12 for a UML diagram of the Automobile and Object classes.

Note that the parameter of the second `equals` method is of a different type than the parameter of the first (inherited) `equals` method. Because of the difference, the second method does not override the inherited `equals` method, and instead the `equals` method name is now overloaded in the Automobile class. That is, there are now two completely different methods in the Automobile class (one inherited and one local) that happen to share a name and one of whose parameter types is a subtype of the other's parameter type. As a result, it can be confusing as to which of these overloaded methods will be called when an object sends the `equals` message to an Automobile object `auto`.

For example, consider the following code:

```
Object o = new Object();
Automobile auto = new Automobile();
Object autoObject = new Automobile();
auto.equals(o);
auto.equals(auto);
auto.equals(autoObject);
```

For each of the three calls to `equals`, can you tell which of the two `equals` methods in the Automobile class is invoked? Is it the first method (1) that was inherited from the Object class and contains an Object as a parameter or the second method (2) that contains an Automobile as a parameter?

In general, the method that is executed depends on the declared type of the object being sent the message and the declared or inferred type of the arguments (not the actual value of the arguments) passed to the method. As a first step, the compiler determines the signature of the method that is to be called. For example, when the compiler sees a method call such as `auto.equals(o)`, it looks at the declared type of `auto` (in this case, Automobile) and looks in that class or interface and its superclasses or superinterfaces for all methods named `equals`. It then looks at the parameter lists of those methods and finds the list whose types most closely match the declared or inferred types of the arguments. The chosen signature is the one with this parameter list. In our example, the argument `o` has declared type Object. Therefore, the `equals` method with an Automobile as the parameter has too narrow a parameter type, and so the `equals` method with a parameter of type Object is chosen. That is, the compiler chooses the signature "equals(Object o)."

The second step occurs at runtime when the actual class of the object being sent the message is searched for a method with the chosen signature. If that class doesn't contain such a method, the chain of superclasses is climbed until a method with the desired signature is found. In our example, the method with the chosen signature is found in the superclass Object and so that method is the one that is executed.

For another example, consider the call `auto.equals(auto)`. The compiler again looks in the Automobile class (since `auto` is declared to be of type Automobile) and finds two `equals` methods in that class (one declared in Automobile and one inherited from Object). In this case, the one with the parameter type that most closely matches the type of the argument `auto` is the `equals` method (2), and so the compiler chooses the signature `equals(Automobile auto)`. At runtime, the actual class of `auto` is searched for a method with the chosen signature, which is method (2), and that method is executed.

When the compiler sees `auto.equals(autoObject)`, it notes that `autoObject` is declared to be of type Object, and so it chooses the signature "equals(Object o)." At runtime therefore, method (1) is executed.

Note that the actual class of the argument plays no role in determining which method is executed. The declared or inferred types of the arguments are the only part of them that plays a role.

To solidify these concepts, let us consider six other calls to `equals` using the same variables `o`, `auto`, and `autoObject`:

```
o.equals(o);
o.equals(auto);
o.equals(autoObject);
autoObject.equals(o);
autoObject.equals(auto);
autoObject.equals(autoObject);
```

In all six cases, the compiler notes that `o` and `autoObject` are declared to be of type Object, and so it looks in the Object class for all methods named `equals`. It finds only one such method and so in every case, the signature "equals(Object o)" is chosen. Therefore, method (1) is the one always executed.

In this example, there were no overriding methods. The situation is somewhat different if we include a method in the Automobile class, with header

```
public boolean equals(Object o)                               (3)
```

that overrides the `equals` method inherited from the Object class. See Figure 2.13 for the UML diagram.

Note that the Automobile class still has exactly two `equals` methods, but both of these methods are now implemented in the Automobile class rather than any being inherited.

Let us now reconsider the nine method calls discussed above:

```
Object o = new Object();
Automobile auto = new Automobile();
Object autoObject = new Automobile();
```

```
auto.equals(o);
auto.equals(auto);
auto.equals(autoObject);
o.equals(o);
o.equals(auto);
o.equals(autoObject);
autoObject.equals(o);
autoObject.equals(auto);
autoObject.equals(autoObject);
```

In this case, the compiler is going to behave exactly as it did in the earlier case. That is, in all nine cases the compiler will determine the signature of the `equals` method to be called just as before. However, the method that actually gets executed now changes because of dynamic method invocation. Recall that dynamic method invocation causes the Java environment to look at the actual class of the object being sent the message to determine which of several overridden versions of a method to call.

In the case of `auto.equals(o)`, the compiler determined that the signature of method to be called is `equals(Object o)`. At runtime, the actual class of `auto` (namely Automobile) is searched for a method with the chosen signature. Therefore, method (3) is executed. Similarly, method (3) will be executed in the calls `auto.equals(autoObject)`, `autoObject.equals(o)`, `autoObject.equals(auto)`, and `autoObject.equals(autoObject)`. Method (1) is executed in the calls `o.equals(o)`, `o.equals(auto)`, and `o.equals(autoObject)`, and method (2) is executed only in the call `auto.equals(auto)`.

In summary, the compiler looks at the various overloaded versions of the method to find an appropriate signature by looking at the declared type of the object being sent the message and the declared types of the arguments to the method call. The actual implementation of the method with that signature is chosen at runtime by dynamic method invocation using the actual value of the object being sent the message. The actual classes of the arguments to the method call do not play a role.

Other languages differ from Java in this respect. Some languages, like CLOS, an object-oriented extension to the Common Lisp language, are multimethod languages in which methods are not treated like messages sent to one particular object.

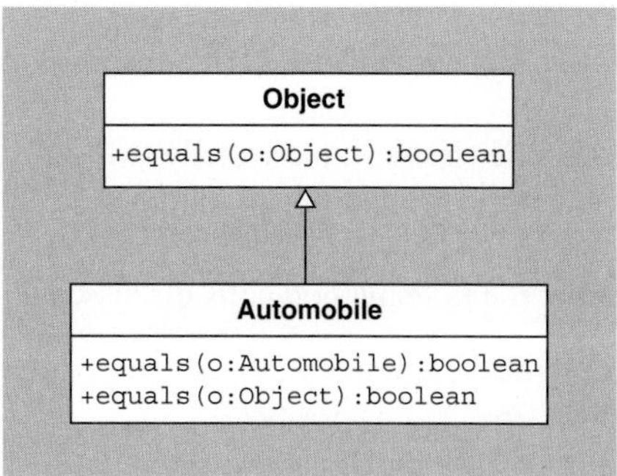

FIGURE 2.13 The new relationship between Automobile and Object.

Instead, all objects involved in the method call are passed to the method as arguments, and at runtime the method body to be executed is determined by considering the actual values of all of the arguments.[2, p. 98]

What is a programmer to do to create elegant code when overloaded method names threaten to confuse everyone? One approach would be to avoid overloading method names altogether, but that choice is too extreme. Overloading a method name can result in much more readable code if the methods with the overloaded names are performing similar actions. A better approach is to use overloading only in ways that clearly indicate which method with the overloaded name is being referred to.

For examples of the kinds of overloading to avoid, consider the following four code blocks.

1. `{ foo("hi", "there"); }`
2. `{ Object o1 = "hi"; foo(o1, "there"); }`
3. `{ Object o2 = "there"; foo("hi", o2); }`
4. `{ Object o1 = "hi"; Object o2 = "there"; foo(o1, o2); }`

At first glance, it appears that they all do the same thing. However, in certain situations, they will in fact do different things. Try to figure out how such a situation could occur before reading further. Hint: It depends on overloading `foo`.

In fact, if the class containing the four code blocks has three `foo` methods with signatures

1. `foo(Object, String)`
2. `foo(String, Object)`
3. `foo(Object, Object)`

that do different things, then the four code blocks will also do different things. More precisely, the last three code segments will call the three versions of `foo` in the given order. The first code segment will cause a compiler error since the Java compiler cannot determine which of the three versions of `foo` most closely matches the types of the arguments in the call to `foo`. To understand better what causes this compiler error, see [3].

In summary, to avoid confusion due to overloading, avoid overloading a method name with two versions that have the same number of parameters in the same order but with the types of parameters in one version being subtypes of the corresponding parameters in the second version. In particular, it is a good idea to try to ensure that your methods with overloaded names have different numbers of parameters, which makes it very easy to see which version will be executed.

SECTION 2.10 CONTROLLING ACCESS TO METHODS AND DATA (PUBLIC, PRIVATE, PROTECTED, PACKAGE)

When it is said that a subclass inherits all data and methods of its superclass, that doesn't mean that the subclass can directly access all that data or those methods. Instance variables and methods can be labeled "private," in which case the data or methods can only be accessed within that class itself. In particular, subclasses cannot use a superclass' private data or methods except indirectly by calling other methods in the superclass that in turn call the private methods or use the private data. Instance variables and methods can also be labeled "public," which means that any other object can access those variables and methods, not just objects of that class and its subclasses.

There are two other categories of access that provide more restrictive access than public but less restrictive access than private, which we will only briefly discuss here. If instance variables or methods of a class C are labeled "protected", then they can be accessed by any subclass or by any class in the same package as C. If no access label ("public," "private," or "protected") is used for an instance variable or method, then it is said to have "package" access, which means that other classes in C's package can access it. In [4], the analogy is made that subclasses are like family members and package members are like close friends. Hence, data and methods that have package access are those data and methods that you would be willing to share with your close friends, but not necessarily your family. Data and methods with protected access are those that you would be willing to share with your family and close friends. Of course, data and methods that have public access are shared with the whole world.

When should you use protected or package access for data? A good rule of thumb is "never," basically because it exposes too much of the internal implementation of a class. For example, if nonconstant data is made nonprivate, then other classes are aware of and can manipulate that data, which makes it much harder to later modify the implementation of the class. Furthermore, if other classes can arbitrarily modify that data, then it is hard to ensure that the objects' data will always have legal, well-formed values.

Just as importantly, the fact that other classes can access nonprivate fields and methods means that those fields and methods must be treated as part of the permanent external interface of the class, and so they cannot later be changed easily, since changes to them potentially force changes to other classes that use this class. For these reasons, it is a good rule of thumb to think of "protected" and "package" as a form of "public."

However, there are a few situations where it does make sense to allow protected or package access to instance or class variables. If you think of a package as an integrated component of classes that provide a specific functionality to users, then, for efficiency reasons, it might make sense to allow the classes in the package to have direct access to the data in other classes in the package. A drawback to such use of package access is that a change in the implementation of one of the classes in the package may require changes to other classes in the package, but at least the changes are restricted to the package.

Similarly, although methods should usually be labeled public or private, there are a few situations in which it makes sense to give methods protected or package access. For example, suppose you have a class with private data and public "getter" methods for access to some of that data. If you do not want to let users change the value of that data, then you should omit any modifier methods from that class. However, if you wish to make your class as generally reusable as possible, then you need to anticipate the fact that subclasses of your class may want to modify that data. But subclasses cannot change inherited data if the data are private and if there are only public getter methods in the superclass. The solution is to add *protected* modifier methods in your class. Then subclasses can call these protected methods and so modify the data. Here is how it would work in the trivial case of a class used to "wrap" an object around a social security number:

```
public class SSNWrapper
{
   private int socialSecurityNumber;
   public SSNWrapper(int ssn) { socialSecurityNumber = ssn; }
   public int getSSN (){ return socialSecurityNumber; }
   protected void setSSN(int ssn) { socialSecurityNumber = ssn; }
}
public class SettableSSNWrapper extends SSNWrapper
{
   public SettableSSNWrapper(int ssn) { super(ssn); }
   public void setSSN(int ssn) { super.setSSN(ssn); }
}
```

Any users of SSNWrapper objects cannot modify the value of the `socialSecurityNumber` variable unless those users are objects of subclasses of SSNWrapper or in the same package as SSNWrapper. However, all users of SettableSSNWrapper can modify the value stored in the object.

For our purposes in this text, the public and private access categories will suffice.

SECTION 2.11 SUMMARY

Here is a summary of the ideas introduced in this chapter.

- An object-oriented program is one that is partitioned into a set of communicating objects, each of which encapsulates all the behavior and knowledge relating to one concept. The proper use of OO programming techniques can increase the modifiability, readability, reusability, and maintainability of a program.
- An object-oriented programming language supports the OO style of programming by providing classes, objects, messages, inheritance, and polymorphism.
- In Java, methods can be class or static methods when objects of that class have no state or do not use their state in the body of that method. Variables can be class or static variables when the piece of data they contain needs to be shared among objects of that class (and possibly other classes).
- Implementation inheritance or subclassing is a way for one class (the subclass) to use all the methods and variables implemented in another class (the superclass) as if the methods and variables had been implemented directly in the subclass. Inheritance is typically used either to specialize the behavior of the superclass in the subclass by adding new features or overriding existing features or to generalize the behavior of classes by moving common behavior to a common superclass.

- Some languages, such as C++, allow multiple implementation inheritance, which means that a class can have more than one superclass. Java, in constract, is a single implementation inheritance language in that it allows only one superclass for each class.
- A type is a set of data values and the operations that can be performed on them. Any class defines a type, the objects of which are the data values associated with the type and the operations of which are the public methods of the class. Java interfaces also define types. All objects of classes that implement the interface are data values of that type.
- Types can have subtypes. A subclass is a subtype of its superclass and a class is a subtype of any interface that it implements. In this way, an object of a class can actually be a data value of many different types.
- Subtype polymorphism refers to the ability of a variable of a given type to actually refer to an object of any of its subtypes. If a method is invoked on such an object, the implementation of that method specific to the subtype will be executed. This process is called dynamic method invocation.
- In contrast to an overriding method, which is a method in a subclass with the same signature as a method in its superclass, an overloaded method name refers to two or more methods in the same class with the same name but different signatures.
- Public methods and data can be accessed by objects of other classes, private methods and classes can be accessed only by objects of the same class, protected methods and data can only be accessed by objects of the same class or any subclass or objects whose class is in the same package, and package methods and data can only be accessed by objects whose class is in the same package.

EXERCISES

1. Briefly describe how OO programming, as compared to non-OO programming, makes it easier to write elegant software, as discussed in Section 1.3 of Chapter 1.
2. In Section 2.2, a Person class is defined and then a Person object is created by the following line of code:

   ```
   Person firstPerson = new Person
   ("Adam",  new Date(0));
   ```

   In what month and year and on what day is Adam's birth date? Hint: Look at the documentation of the Date class in the java.util package.
3. Give a specific example, other than the example of constants, where it would make sense to have a class variable (that is, a variable declared "static"). That is, give an example where it would make sense for all objects of a class to share a variable.
4. In Section 2.3, we mentioned that the Set class' static method `intersect(Set s1, Set s2)` can treat a null `s1` or `s2` as an empty set and so return an empty set. Assuming we really want a static method for determining set intersections (rather than an instance method), is this particular behavior with null parameters a good design? Why or why not?
5. Look in the Java APIs for the javax.swing .JOptionPane class. It contains many class methods. Why would the Java class designers choose to make them class methods instead of instance methods?
6. In the Rectangle example in Section 2.5, the programmer desired a class like Rectangle except with `getCenter` and `setCenter` methods, and so the programmer subclassed Rectangle. An alternative solution to the programmer's problem is to use the Rectangle class and wherever a call to `setCenter` or `getCenter` is desired, instead "inline" the call. That is, instead of calls to `getCenter` and `setCenter`, there could be code to get and set the center manually. For example, instead of

   ```
   Point center = r.getCenter();
   ```

   the programmer could write

   ```
   Point center;
   center.x = r.getCenterX();
   center.y = r.getCenterY();
   ```

which accomplishes the same objective. Then the programmer wouldn't have to subclass Rectangle. Discuss whether this solution is preferable to the solution involving subclassing.

7. In Section 2.5 we mentioned that you can use implementation inheritance to create a subclass that specializes a superclass either by adding some new behavior or by changing existing behavior. We can also use implementation inheritance to *remove* some existing behavior. Explain how it would be done and discuss the elegance or inelegance of this use of inheritance.
8. In Section 2.5, we introduced HumanCustomer, BusinessCustomer, and Customer classes, but no complete implementations of such classes were given. Implement all three classes. Assume that, in addition to a name, the HumanCustomer class has a spouse and a list of children as attributes with `getSpouse` and `getChildren` methods and that a BusinessCustomer has a size attribute giving the number of employees and a `getSize` method. Don't forget to create appropriate constructors for all three classes.
9. In the Customer example of Section 2.5, the Customer class was created to avoid code duplication in the BusinessCustomer and HumanCustomer classes. An alternative approach that also avoids such duplication is to combine the two classes into one Customer class that includes all the instance variables and methods of both classes. There would also be an extra boolean variable `isHuman` that is true if the Customer corresponds to a human and is false if the customer is a business. Using the value of this extra variable, you could decide how to respond to any request (i.e., any method call) regarding the customer. What do you think of this implementation? Explain.
10. In Section 2.5, we talked about using inheritance to create a common superclass to two subclasses and then move duplicated code into the superclass. Following this reasoning, one might be tempted to create a common superclass of classes Pet, Person, Street, City, and Country objects, if they all have a `getName` method, to avoid duplication of code. If there were such classes, would a superclass be appropriate here? Briefly explain. If it is appropriate to have such a superclass, what would you call the superclass and should it be abstract? More generally, when is it inappropriate to create a common superclass of classes with common behavior or attributes?
11. In Section 2.5, we introduced a FilledOval class whose `draw` method overrode the parent's `draw` method. However, the Oval's instance variables are public, which, as we later discussed, is not optimal. Change those instance variables to private and reimplement any code that depended on the public accessibility of those instance variables.
12. In Section 2.6, we mentioned that, to replace a LinkedList object in the package with an ArrayList object, it is not sufficient to do a global search and replace. Give one reason why this approach is insufficient.
13. In Section 2.6, we said that "if software is elegant, then one should be able to remove an object of one class and easily replace it with, or 'plug in,' an object of another 'equivalent' class either on the fly or with only minimal code changes." Explain what "equivalent" and "minimal" mean based on the discussion in Section 2.6.
14. In Section 2.6, we talked about the problems of changing the type of list in our application. In our discussion, we assumed that once the type of list was chosen, it remained fix for the duration of the execution of the application. However, what if we wanted our application to be able to change the type of list on the fly? That is, during execution, the user or the program itself might decide that we need to start using ArrayLists instead of LinkedLists for all lists that will be created in the future (we will allow existing lists to remain as is). Tell how this would be implemented (a) using a factory method and (b) without using a factory method. Is the factory method version more elegant? Explain.
15. In Section 2.8, we gave the Automobile class' `getCapacity` method a default behavior of returning 0 to help us explain how dynamic method invocation and overriding works. However, this design is not very elegant, and, in fact, the Automobile should be an interface. Briefly explain why.
16. Consider an Automobile class with the following implementations of `equals` methods:

```
public boolean equals(Object o) {...}
  //version A, inherited from Object
public boolean equals (Automobile o)
  {...} //version B
```

and a class Sedan that is a subclass of Automobile with the following methods:

```
public boolean equals(Automobile o)
  {...} //version C
public boolean equals(Sedan o)
  {...} //version D
```

and a class Minivan that is a subclass of Automobile with the following methods:

```
public boolean equals(Automobile o)
   {...} //version E
public boolean equals(Minivan o)
   {...} //version F
```

Now suppose you have the following six variables:

```
Object o = new Automobile();
Automobile auto = new Automobile();
Automobile sedanAuto = new Sedan
   (Color.black);
Automobile minivanAuto = new Minivan
   (Color.blue);
Sedan sedan = new Sedan(Color.grey);
Minivan minivan = new Minivan
   (Color.pink);
```

There are 36 ways each of these variables can be paired off in a call to `equals`, where one of the 6 variables is being sent the `equals` message and one of the 6 is the argument to `equals`. For each such pair, indicate which of the `equals` methods will be executed. For example, if there is a call

```
auto.equals(auto)
```

then version B of `equals` will be called. Figure out which `equals` method will be executed for the other 35 combinations.

17. In Section 2.9, we mentioned two `substring` methods in the String class. Suppose it was your job to implement these two methods. Describe how you would go about avoiding code duplication in the bodies of these two methods.
18. In Section 2.10, we gave the example of a SSNWrapper class that allowed subclasses to modify the `socialSecurityNumber` instance variable through a protected modifier method. Wouldn't it be a whole lot easier to just make `socialSecurityNumber` itself protected and so avoid the need for the protected `setSSN` method in the SSNWrapper class? In that case, the code would look like this:

```
public class SSNWrapper
{
   protected int socialSecurityNumber;
   public SSNWrapper(int ssn)
      { socialSecurityNumber = ssn; }
   public int getSSN() { return
      socialSecurityNumber; }
}
public class SettableSSNWrapper
   extends SSNWrapper
{
   public SettableSSNWrapper(int ssn)
      { super(ssn); }
   public void setSSN(int ssn)
      { socialSecurityNumber = ssn; }
}
```

By making this change, we've eliminated the need for the protected method in the SSNWrapper class. Is this version better or worse than the version in the text? Explain.

19. In the java.awt.event package, there is an ActionListener interface that many classes implement when they want to be made aware of events that occur, such as mouse clicks in buttons. Why is ActionListener an interface instead of an abstract class? How would making ActionListener an abstract class decrease the usability of the class?
20. For each of the following pairs of classes, tell which class of the pair should be a subclass of which, if either. Briefly explain why or why not.
    a. Car and Tire
    b. Car and Truck
    c. Card (with suit and value instance variables) and Deck (of 52 cards)

REFERENCES

1. Riel, A.J., *Object-Oriented Design Heuristics.* 1996. Reading, MA: Addison-Wesley.
2. Bruce, K., *Foundations of Object-Oriented Languages.* 2002 Cambridge, MA: MIT Press.
3. Gosling, J., B. Joy, G. Steele, and G. Bracha. *Java Language Specification.* 3rd ed. The Java Series. 2005. Upper Saddle River, NJ: Prentice Hall.
4. Campione, M., K. Walrath, and A. Huml, *The Java Tutorial: A Short Course on the Basics,* 3rd ed. The Java Series. 2000. Reading, MA: Addison-Wesley.

3

Elegance and Implementation Inheritance

SECTION 3.0 INTRODUCTION

In the last chapter, we discussed all the features that make a language object-oriented, but we discussed very few of the advantages and disadvantages of the various possible competing OO designs of a solution to a problem. In particular, we didn't discuss all the trade-offs involved in designs using implementation inheritance. For example, the Java compiler will let you declare your classes to be subclasses of virtually any other class (as long as the inheritance hierarchical structure is a tree), but that fact does not mean it is a good idea to do so. Because there are so many issues to be addressed in this topic, we are devoting a full chapter to it. We will see that the use of inheritance can greatly increase the elegance of the design or greatly decrease it.

We will first analyze four different justifications for using inheritance to see whether they are valid individually or in combinations. From the discussion and the examples presented there, we will also develop guidelines for using inheritance and for deciding on other relationships or associations among classes, such as aggregation and message forwarding. We will also show some of the downsides or costs of using inheritance.

We will then give three examples, one involving men and women, one involving a drawing program, and the third concerning sorting, that show how inheritance can clean up the design and code. Because the sorting example uses inheritance of array types, we include a short discussion of the special issues related to such inheritance.

We end by revisiting of the issue of inheritance versus message forwarding.

In this chapter, whenever we mention "inheritance," we mean implementation inheritance (subclasses in Java) rather than interface inheritance (interfaces in Java).

SECTION 3.1 FOUR PERSPECTIVES ON INHERITANCE

Suppose you are a team leader designing a software system and one member of your team comes to you with a sample design that, among other things, has two classes A and B associated with each other through inheritance. If you question your worker about this design decision, she could come up with at least four reasons for including this inheritance relationship between A and B.

Code Reuse Perspective

Your team member might say that class B has some code (data or methods) that is identical to code in A and so, through inheritance, this duplicate code can be eliminated and instead B can inherit the code from A.

Is-A Perspective

The team member might argue that every B object "is an" A object. That is, the set of all objects of class B is a subset of the set of all objects of class A. Because the sets of objects have a subset relationship, it is natural to make B a subclass of A.

Public Interface Perspective

The team member might point out that the public interface of B includes the public interface of A. Therefore, it is appropriate that B should be a subclass of A.

Polymorphism Perspective

The team member might show you how it would be beneficial to be able to use polymorphism to assign an object of class B to a variable declared to be of type A. This benefit justifies the use of inheritance.

Let us look at all four perspectives in more detail.

SECTION 3.2 SUFFICIENCY OF CODE REUSE

One of the real benefits of inheritance, as we mentioned in the last chapter, is code reuse. But is code reuse alone a sufficient reason for using inheritance?

Let us look at an example. Suppose your design includes a Dog class and a Person class, both of which have a `name` field and a `getName` method. To avoid duplicating that field and method, you could remove the `name` field and `getName` method from the Person class and make the Person class a subclass of the Dog class. See Figure 3.1 for a UML diagram showing this relationship.

Unfortunately, in Java, subclasses inherit everything in their superclasses. Therefore, the Person class would also inherit the `bark` and `getLastRabiesShotDate` methods, which are rather inappropriate for Person objects.

Alternatively, you could put the `name` field and `getName` method in the

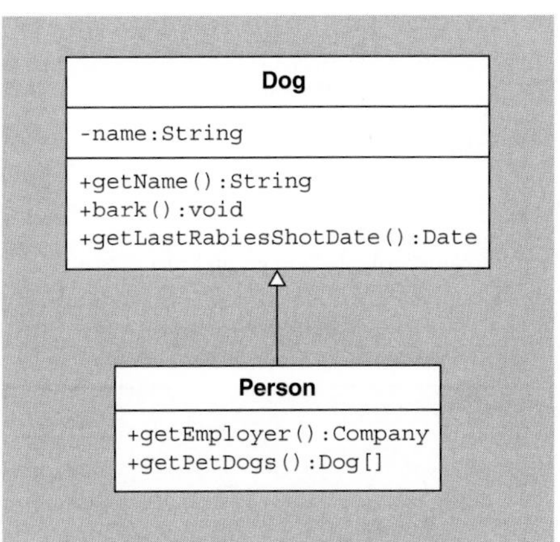

FIGURE 3.1 A misuse of inheritance.

Person class and then make the Dog class a subclass of Person. Clearly this solution is just as inappropriate; it makes little sense for the Dog class to inherit the `getEmployer` and `getPetDogs` methods.

In situations such as these, you really want to reuse only some of the code. If a subclass could selectively choose which code to inherit and which not to inherit, an argument favoring the use of inheritance here would have more merit.

What is a better way to avoid the code duplication in the Dog and Person classes? One way would be to create a NamedObject class with the `name` field and `getName` method and make Dog and Person both subclasses of NamedObject. This approach is particularly feasible in programming languages with multiple inheritance, where such a superclass would be called a "mixin." However, the fact that there is no multiple inheritance in Java limits the use of mixins because you might not want to "use up" the single inheritance on a mixin class.

What if *all* the methods in one class are duplicated exactly in another class? Would it then be appropriate to use inheritance to make one a subclass of the other? It would certainly be more appropriate, but even in this case, as we will see in Section 3.4, there may be alternatives that are preferable.

In summary, being able to inherit code that would otherwise have to be duplicated is a useful feature of object-oriented languages, and therefore one should always consider this feature when deciding whether to use inheritance. But code reuse by itself rarely justifies inheritance.

SECTION 3.3 SUFFICIENCY OF CODE REUSE AND THE IS-A RELATIONSHIP

The problem with using inheritance for the Dog and Person class in the preceding section is that dogs are not people and people are not dogs. That is, there is no "is-a" relationship between the concepts that the classes model. Is the combination of code reuse and the "is-a" relationship among the classes a sufficient reason for using subclassing?

FIGURE 3.2 The Square class is a subclass of Rectangle.

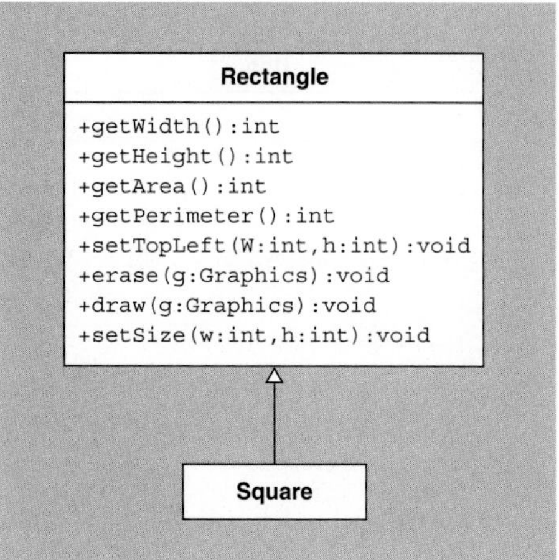

Let us consider another example. Suppose a software designer needs to model geometric shapes, and so he creates a Square class and a Rectangle class. Should inheritance be used between these two classes? It is clearly the case that, from a geometrical perspective, every square "is a" rectangle. Furthermore, there are certainly good opportunities for code reuse between them. For example, the implementations of methods involving moving or finding the area or perimeter of the rectangles and squares are probably identical in both classes. Therefore, it seems natural to make the Square class a subclass of the Rectangle class. But is this a good decision?

Consider the following Java implementation of the Square and Rectangle classes using inheritance. See Figure 3.2 for a UML diagram of these classes. Notice how much code reuse we have here in that the Square class doesn't need to implement anything but a constructor.

```
public class Rectangle
{
  private int x, y, width, height;
  public Rectangle(int x, int y, int w, int h) {
      this.x = x; this.y = y; width = w; height = h;
  }
  public int getWidth() { return width; }
  public int getHeight() { return height; }
  public int getArea() { return width * height; }
  public int getPerimeter() { return 2 * (width + height); }
  public setTopLeft(int newx, int newy) { x = newx; y = newy; }
  public erase(Graphics g) { ... }
  public draw(Graphics g) { ... }
  public void setSize(int w, int h) { width = w; height = h; }
}
```

```
public class Square extends Rectangle
{
  public Square(int x, int y, int side) {
    super(x, y, side, side);
  }
}
```

However, as you may have noticed, there is a serious problem with this design. Because of the fact that subclasses inherit all methods of their superclasses, the Square class now inherits a `setSize` method that has two parameters. A call to this method can make the width and height of the Square unequal, a rather undesirable outcome. A `setSize` method for Squares should just take one parameter.

What can we do about this situation? Before throwing away inheritance, let's try to patch the problem up by other means. One way to do so is to nullify the negative effects of the inherited `setSize` method by overriding it in the subclass. For example, we might add the following method to the Square class:

```
public void setSize(int w, int h) { width = h; height = h; }
```

thereby allowing users to modify the size of the square but doing it in a way that preserves its "squareness."

Unfortunately, this solution is not a very good one either. To see why, suppose that the user adds the following method to his drawing program:

```
public void stretch(Rectangle r, int dx, Graphics g)
{
  r.erase(g);
  r.setSize(r.getWidth() + dx, r.getHeight());
  r.draw(g);
}
```

When this method is executed, the user expects to see a rectangle being stretched horizontally by the amount `dx`. But if, unbeknownst to the user, a Square object is passed as the first argument, then the user will be surprised or confused to see no stretching. Code is not considered elegant if the user of that code is surprised or confused by the behavior of that code.

Our problem here is that the subclass does not have behavior consistent with the behavior of its superclass. Such consistent behavior is necessary for elegant code.

Guideline

A similar interface (that is, similar method signatures) is not sufficient for an elegant subclass/superclass or class/interface relationship; consistent behavior is also required. In particular, a class B should not inherit class A's methods and then nullify them or change their behavior to do something completely different.

One consequence of this guideline is that the designer of an interface or a class needs to specify clearly in any documentation the semantics of each method. If, instead, an interface is defined containing a method `foo`, for example, but no documentation for `foo` is provided, then any class implementing this interface can legitimately give `foo` any semantics it wants, which can result in horribly confusing code.

This guideline can also be phrased in terms of astonishment.

Guideline (The Principle of Least Astonishment)

If a client thinks he has a reference to an object of type A but actually has a reference to an object of subtype B, there should be no surprises when he sends messages to the object.

For example, a client using a Square object as the value of `r` in the `stretch` method above will almost surely be surprised by its behavior, indicating a problem with the inheritance hierarchy.

What are the implications of following this guideline? The answer depends on what we mean by a "surprise." There are two definitions of that word that we could provide. In the more restrictive case, a surprise is any difference in the behaviors of objects of the two classes. If we use this definition, then, by the principle of least astonishment, we are not allowed to change any of the inherited behavior in the subclass, which means overriding superclass methods is pretty much prohibited. Therefore, subclasses can only add new behavior rather than modify existing behavior. The new behavior is invisible when the subclass objects are being treated as if they were of the type of the superclass. This restrictive version of the principle could better be called the *Principle of No Astonishment*.

A less restrictive definition of surprise would be to say that a surprise is any difference in the *documented* behavior of objects of the two classes. Consider the FilledOval subclass of Oval defined in the previous chapter. If the client thinks he has a reference to an Oval and instead has a reference to a FilledOval, is the client going to be surprised when the FilledOval is drawn on the screen? The answer depends on the documentation for the Oval class. If the documentation mentions nothing about the color of the inside area of a drawn oval, then subclasses are free to draw that interior any way they desire. Therefore, under this less restrictive definition of surprise, it is perfectly acceptable to have the FilledOval class be a subclass of Oval and the principle of least astonishment will be satisfied.

This discussion is all very well and good, but it is still rather vague. How, more precisely, can you tell if your subclass is behaving properly in relation to its superclass' behavior? That is, how can you more precisely determine whether your class design satisfies the principle of least astonishment? The Liskov Substitution principle[1; 2, pp. 148 and 174–181; 3] gives a good answer.

Liskov Substitution Principle (LSP)

It is acceptable to make a class B a subclass of class A or to make B an implementer of interface A only if, for every method in both A's and B's interfaces, B's method accepts as input all the values that A's method accepts (and possibly more) and does everything with those values that A's method does (and possibly more).

Let us look back at our Square and Rectangle example with regard to the LSP. The `setSize` method of the Rectangle class has the behavior of modifying the width independently of the height. A `setSize` method of the Square class cannot have that behavior and still preserve squareness, and therefore the Square class' `setSize` method does not do everything that the Rectangle class' `setSize` method does. The conclusion is that Square should not be a subclass of Rectangle.

There is another aspect of the Square/Rectangle example that you may have noticed. The original is-a relationship between geometric squares and rectangles as viewed by mathematicians holds only because, in mathematics, all geometric shapes are fixed, or immutable. If a mathematician talks about stretching a rectangle, he is really talking about creating a new rectangle rather than modifying the old one. Therefore, if the Rectangle class and Square class were made immutable (a class is *immutable* if objects of the class cannot have their state changed in a way that is noticeable to outside objects), they would better model the mathematician's idea of rectangles and squares. In fact, if the classes were made immutable by removing the `setTopLeft` and `setSize` methods, it would be perfectly acceptable to make the Square class a subclass of the Rectangle class.

Guideline

A class A that is identical to another class B except that it has extra restrictions on its state should not be a subclass of B unless both classes are immutable.

So what is the proper relationship between mutable rectangles and mutable squares? Should Rectangle be a subclass of Square instead of the other way around? A Rectangle, by definition, can have unequal width and height unlike a Square and so it should not be a subclass of Square. Therefore, either these two classes should be completely unrelated or they should be related in some way other than as subclass and superclass, such as having a third class as their common superclass. For example, you could define an abstract Rectangle class with three subclasses—MutableRectangle, MutableSquare, and ImmutableRectangle—and have ImmutableSquare be a subclass of ImmutableRectangle. See Figure 3.3 for a UML diagram of this relationship. Although it lacks symmetry in the way it handles the mutable

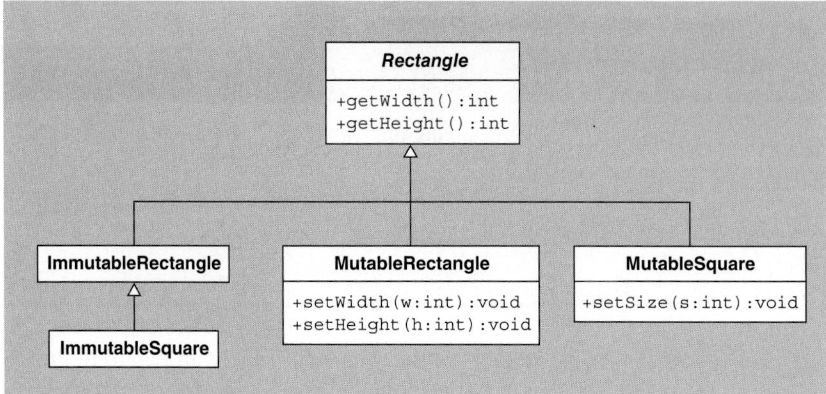

FIGURE 3.3 A possible Rectangle and Square class relationship.

and immutable version of rectangles and squares, it uses inheritance in a way that avoids inelegant surprises.

An alternative would be to make an immutable Rectangle class with an immutable Square subclass, and let each of them have a mutable subclass, such as shown in Figure 3.4.

There is another important point to consider in this discussion. Before adopting any of the Rectangle/Square class structures, designers should ask themselves whether they really need a Square class. What does it provide that the Rectangle class doesn't provide? They cannot claim that any memory is saved with the implementation of the ImmutableSquare class given above, since the ImmutableSquare class inherits all four instance variables of the ImmutableRectangle class even though it doesn't need all of them. Furthermore, if the user needs to distinguish square from nonsquare rectangles, a boolean `isSquare()` method could easily be added to the Rectangle class that merely checks whether the width and height are equal. Also, in the case of mutable squares and rectangles, a square can be thought of as just a temporary state of a rectangle, and so it is not clear that a Square class is really that valuable.

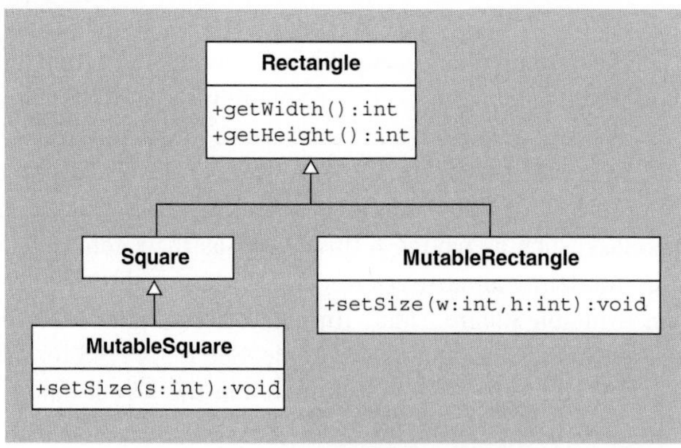

FIGURE 3.4 Another possible Rectangle and Square class relationship.

Guideline

Consider removing from your design any classes that provide little or no unique behavior.

SECTION 3.4 SUFFICIENCY OF CODE REUSE, THE IS-A RELATIONSHIP, AND PUBLIC INTERFACES

As mentioned in the preceding section, the problem with the is-a relationship between the original Square and Rectangle classes was the fact that the Square and Rectangle's *behaviors* didn't match. That is, a Square is not a Rectangle if a Rectangle has the ability to modify its width separately from its height. Another way of saying it is that the public methods of the Rectangle class were not all appropriate for the Square class. But what happens if we do have similar public interfaces with similar behaviors between two of our classes in addition to code reuse and an is-a relationship. Do we now have a sufficient reason for using subclassing?

Consider a classical example often used to introduce people to the concept of inheritance, namely the classes of Student and Person. Clearly a Student "is a" Person (as long as the student is attending an elementary school, high school, or college, for example, and not dog obedience school). A Student, has all the properties and behavior of a Person, such as name, address, date of birth, and, in addition, has other attributes like the school in which he or she is currently enrolled, the number of credits earned, the grade point average(GPA), the class schedule, etc. The methods they have in common clearly have common behavior and so there is a great opportunity for code reuse here.

Therefore, you could argue that the Student class should be a subclass of Person. But should it? Let us suppose we include this inheritance in our design and consider a large university that uses our design to store its records on each student. Furthermore, suppose the university stores its records on employees in Employee objects (where Employee is, by following the same line of reasoning, another subclass of Person). See Figure 3.5.

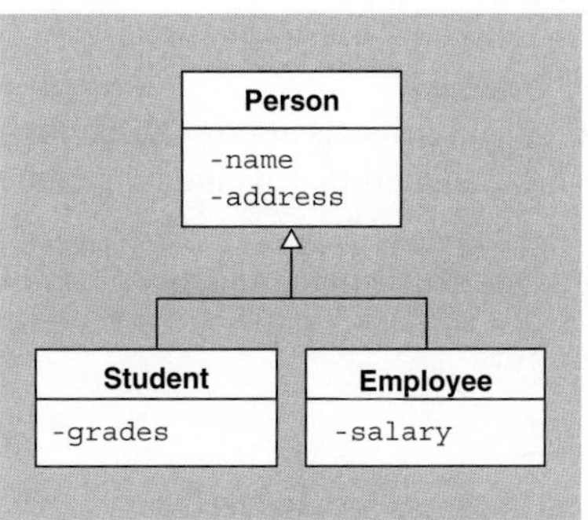

FIGURE 3.5 An inheritance hierarchy among Person, Student, and Employee.

Now, suppose one of the students graduates and starts to work for the university, and so becomes an employee. Or suppose the student becomes an employee of the university while still a student there. What must the university do to update its records in these cases?

In the case of a student graduating and becoming an employee, the university could just replace the Student object with an Employee object. However, this approach has two potential problems. If there are many references to the Student object in the university's records, those references need to be updated to refer to the new Employee object. Also, there might be data that needs to be preserved in the Student object, for example, the student's transcript, that is not included in the Employee object.

Alternatively, the university could create two distinct objects to represent the person: an active Employee object and an inactive Student object that might be archived. However, this approach is inelegant because it duplicates all the common Person data in both objects, which can easily become unsynchronized, for example, if the person's state changes (e.g., if the person moves to a new address) and the university accidentally updates the state of only one of the two objects.

The problems could be resolved easily if it were possible to change an object dynamically to belong to a different class (and so change the Student object into an Employee object). However, such a change is not possible in Java or many other OO languages.

A better approach avoids inheritance altogether and looks at the student and the employee as *roles* being played by the person. Such roles are typically temporary aspects of the person, in that the person is not always a student or employee. Because of the temporary nature of the roles but the more permanent nature of the person, inheritance is not an appropriate way to associate students, employees, and people.

A better design uses referencing, in which a Student object has an underlying Person to whom it refers. In this case, we could have exactly one Person object for each real person, which would be independent of all the roles currently played by that person.

For example, the Person class might be defined as follows:

```
public class Person
{
  private String name;
  private String address;
  public String getAddress() { return address; }
  ...other methods and data...
}
```

Then, as new roles are played, objects representing those roles, such as Student or Employee objects, can be created that include a reference to the Person playing those roles.

For example, the Student class might be defined as follows:

```
public class Student
{
  private Person me;
  private AcademicRecord myRecord;
```

```
    public String getAddress() { return me.getAddress(); }
    public float getGPA() {
      ...compute it from the academic record...
   }
    ...other methods and data...
  }
```

Notice how any Person-specific behavior required of a Student is performed by forwarding the request to the Person object. For example, if Student objects are asked for their addresses, the Student objects, in turn, ask their underlying Person objects for them. The Student object would handle student-specific tasks, such as computing GPAs and managing course schedules, and the underlying Person object would handle all personal tasks.

Similarly, the Employee class might have a reference to the Person being employed. See Figure 3.6 for a diagram of these alternatives using the Student, Employee, and Person classes. (The arrows in the UML diagram on the right side of Figure 3.6 are explained in the next section.)

By using such forwarding of responsibilities, it now becomes easy to keep track of the changing role of a person. When a person initially becomes a student, both a Student object and Person object are created and the Student object is given a reference to the Person object. When the student becomes an employee, a new Employee object is created that refers to the same Person object. Note that it is perfectly acceptable to have both Student and Employee objects referring to the same Person object. When the person no longer plays one of the roles (e.g., if the student graduates or quits her job at the university), that role object can be deleted or archived and the other roles can remain active. In this way, the Person object can be considered to exist permanently, but the person's roles can come and go. Furthermore, there is no duplication of data.

Guideline

If class B models a role played by class A, especially a temporary role, then B should not be a subclass of A. Instead objects of class B should have references to objects of class A.

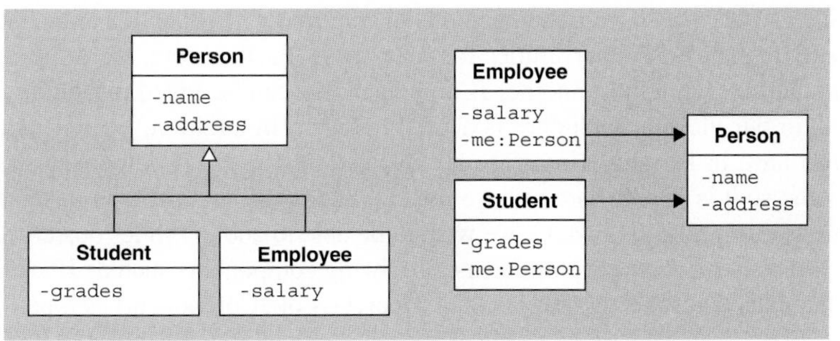

FIGURE 3.6
Inheritance (left) vs. referencing (right).

SECTION 3.5 HAS-A RELATIONSHIPS AND UML ASSOCIATIONS

In the person/student/employee example in the preceding section, we decided that a design using referencing was better than a design using inheritance.

To draw the "has-a" or reference relationship in a UML class diagram, as we did in Figure 3.6 on the right, we need some additional features of UML. An *association* is a structural relationship between classes. For example, if objects of one class maintain a reference to objects of another class or if you need to navigate from objects of one class to objects of another, you would represent the connection between the classes by an association, which is drawn in UML class diagrams as a line between the class boxes.

Association lines can have many optional adornments, such as numbers at one or both ends, indicating multiplicity (the number of objects on that end of the association). They also might have an arrow at one end to indicate one-way navigability or one-way awareness. From objects of the class at the tail of the arrow, you can easily "get to" objects of the class at the arrow head. Another way of describing one-way navigability is that objects of the class on the tail of the arrow are aware of objects of the class at the head of the arrow. A plain line with no arrows could indicate two-way navigability, or it could indicate that the direction of navigability, is not important and so was left out.

SECTION 3.6 SUFFICIENCY OF CODE REUSE, THE IS-A RELATIONSHIP, PUBLIC INTERFACES, AND POLYMORPHISM

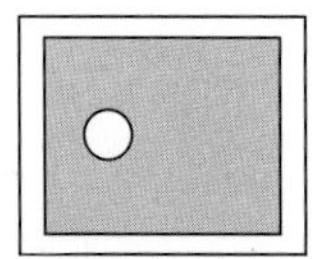

FIGURE 3.7
A 2DSlider with a knob that can be dragged anywhere within the box.

What if we have a situation in which we have code reuse, an is-a relationship, similar public interfaces with similar behaviors between two of our classes, and we have the need for polymorphism? Do we now have a sufficient reason for using subclassing? Probably so.

For example, suppose we wish to enhance the available graphical user interface (GUI) components in the javax.swing package. In particular, suppose we wish to add a 2-D slider with a knob that can be moved not just along a horizontal or vertical axis like a JSlider, but anywhere in a box. For this purpose, we plan to create a new 2DSlider class. See Figure 3.7 for an example.

Such a class will have many methods in common with other JComponents, and so there are plenty of opportunities for code reuse. Furthermore, we want our new slider to be considered just another JComponent that can be added to a GUI window and so, in our view, a 2DSlider "is a" JComponent. In addition, we will want our slider to have in its public interface all the methods in the JComponent class and more, and so it is appropriate to have the 2DSlider type be a subtype of the JComponent type. Finally, as we said, we wish to be able to add 2DSlider objects to windows just as we add other components, but Swing components such as JPanels have `add` methods that take a Component (a superclass of JComponent) as a parameter.

Therefore, we need to use polymorphism to pass a 2DSlider object as the value of a parameter of type Component. In this situation, it makes very good sense to use inheritance and make the 2DSlider class a subclass of JComponent.

SECTION 3.7 COSTS OF USING IMPLEMENTATION INHERITANCE

By now, you are hopefully realizing that (implementation) inheritance, as wonderful as it possibly first sounded, is actually quite limited in its usefulness. There are even more costs to be considered when using inheritance, in addition to those we've already addressed.

One problem with inheritance, especially a deep inheritance tree with many generations, is that the code for the methods of a class low in the tree is spread out among all its ancestors higher in the tree, which makes it harder for the reader of the code to follow the flow of execution. That is, suppose someone is reading code and sees that a method `foo` is invoked on an object. If the object's class does not implement `foo`, then the reader needs to look to the object's immediate superclass. If that class does not implement `foo`, then a further search up the inheritance hierarchy needs to be made. To complicate matters, `foo` may invoke another method `bar` on the same object. There need be little relationship between the locations of `foo` and `bar` in the inheritance tree, and so the reader again needs to start at the object's class and search up the inheritance tree, to find the implementation of `bar`. Matters are even worse if the reader is not sure of the object's class and knows, for example, only that the object could belong to any of the subclasses of a given class. In such cases, it is impossible to figure out exactly which method body of which class gets executed at any given time.

Another problem with inheritance is that all subclasses are very tightly tied with their superclasses. This coupling comes from the fact that, to guarantee certain behavior in a subclass, that subclass needs to know significant parts of the implementation of the methods of the superclasses.

For a simple example, consider the Rectangle class mentioned earlier and suppose that you want to create a type of Rectangle, called a ChangeMeasuredRectangle, that keeps track of the number of times the width of the Rectangle is changed. In this case, inheritance seems very appropriate, and so the ChangeMeasuredRectangle class can be made a subclass of Rectangle. See Figure 3.8 for the UML class diagram of these classes. Note that the subclass needs to override the `setWidth` and `setSize` methods in the Rectangle class in order to keep track of the number of changes made to the width, but all other inherited behavior can be left as is.

So what is the problem? Well, consider how we might implement the ChangeMeasuredRectangle class. Here is one such implementation:

```
public class ChangeMeasuredRectangle extends Rectangle
{
  private int widthChangeCounter = 0;
  public ChangeMeasuredRectangle(int w, int h) { super(w,h); }
  public int getNumWidthChanges() { return widthChangeCounter; }
```

FIGURE 3.8 The Rectangle and ChangeMeasuredRectangle classes.

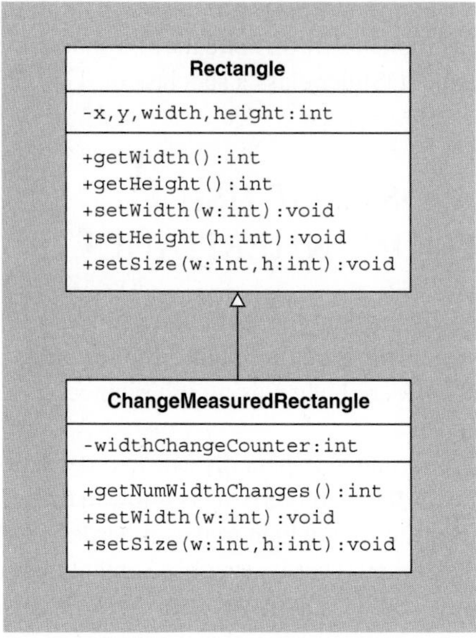


```
  public void setWidth(int newWidth) {
    if( newWidth != getWidth() ) {
      widthChangeCounter++;
    }
    super.setWidth(newWidth);
  }
  public void setSize(int newWidth, int newHeight) {
    if( newWidth != getWidth() ) {
      widthChangeCounter++;
    }
    super.setSize(newWidth, newHeight);
  }
}
```

Note how the `setWidth` and `setSize` methods first check to see whether the width will change and, if so, increment the counter. Then they call the superclass' `setWidth` and `setSize` methods, an elegant reuse of code.

Everything looks great, right? Well, unfortunately, this code may incorrectly count the number of width changes! The correctness of it depends on the implementation of the Rectangle class. See if you can figure out what might be wrong before reading ahead.

Suppose the Rectangle class is implemented as follows:

```
public class Rectangle
{
  private int width, height;
```

```
    public Rectangle(int w, int h) { width = w; height = h; }
    public int getWidth() { return width; }
    public int getHeight() { return height; }
    public void setWidth(int newWidth) { width = newWidth; }
    public void setHeight(int newHeight) { height = newHeight; }
    public void setSize(int w, int h) { setWidth(w); setHeight(h); }
}
```

This implementation also seems very elegant, including the use of `setWidth` and `setHeight` to help implement `setSize`. However, because `setWidth` is called within `setSize` in the Rectangle class, any change to the width of a ChangeMeasuredRectangle through a call to `setSize` will result in the counter being incremented twice.

Here is what happens when `setSize` is invoked on a ChangeMeasuredRectangle. If the new width is different than the old width, then the counter is incremented. Then the superclass' `setSize` method is called. This method in turn calls `setWidth`. But the ChangeMeasuredRectangles implementation of `setWidth` is the one that is executed since our object is actually a ChangeMeasured Rectangle. Therefore, the counter will be incremented again. To correct this problem, the overriding implementation of `setSize` should be removed from the subclass.

In summary, the designer of the ChangeMeasuredRectangle class needed to know the implementation of the `setSize` method in the Rectangle class in order to implement properly the ChangeMeasuredRectangle class. In particular, he needed to know whether the `setSize` method in the Rectangle class called the `setWidth` method.

In conclusion, the implementation of a class must be exposed to designers of subclasses if those subclasses are to be implemented correctly. This need for exposure is unfortunate, especially because it is often the case that designers do not have access to the implementation of all classes they would like to subclass nor, even if they did have them, do they want to spend the time studying those implementations.

To make matters even worse, suppose that, after the ChangeMeasuredRectangle class has been implemented to work correctly with the Rectangle class, the author of the Rectangle class decides to make it more efficient by replacing the original implementation of `setSize` with the following version:

```
    public void setSize(int w, int h) { width = w; height = h; }
```

When this seemingly innocuous change is made, the ChangeMeasuredRectangle no longer correctly counts the number of times the width of the Rectangle changes, and so it must be changed as well!

In other words, the implementation of a class has to be made far more visible to its subclasses than is usually desirable, and any change to a superclass, even an innocuous implementation change in a method to make it more efficient, may cause unforeseen changes in any of its subclasses.

SECTION 3.8 EXAMPLE: PERSON, WOMAN, AND MAN

Up to now, we have discussed where inheritance can be used and the drawbacks to using inheritance, but we have not given many examples that show how inheritance can clean up designs and the implementation of those designs. In the next three sections, we will give such examples. In the first example, we will clean up the code for a class whose objects satisfy mixed constraints on the values of their instance variables. [6, pp. 64–65]

Let us consider a Person class that was created as part of a program to study the transmission of diseases. To understand how diseases are transmitted, it is important to know the amount and kind of direct physical contact a person has had with other people. This contact can come about in a variety of ways, including handshaking and kissing. However, women also have forms of physical contact that men do not, such as breast feeding and giving birth, both of which could cause the transmission of diseases from the mother to the child. That is, women have different behaviors that are relevant to the subject under study.

These differences between men and women could be dealt with in the Person class by assuming men are exactly like women except that they never breast feed their babies and that they never give birth to children, but this method of handling the differences is awkward because the option of breastfeeding and giving birth simply should not be available for males. Another approach is to use code that tests for the sex of the person under study and only if she is female do you deal with issues of breast feeding and childbirth. This approach, because of the need for such conditional tests, makes the code more complex than it needs to be.

A cleaner solution is to have an abstract class Person with two subclasses: Man and Woman (see Figure 3.9). The common behavior of the Man and Woman classes would be inherited from the Person class, and the behavior unique to each subclass would reside in that subclass. This use of inheritance cleans up the code so that objects have only appropriate behavior and fewer complicated conditionals.

Guideline

If you have a class with behavior that applies to only some of the objects of the class, then consider splitting the class into two classes associated by inheritance either directly or through a common abstract class or interface.

FIGURE 3.9 Two subclasses of Person.

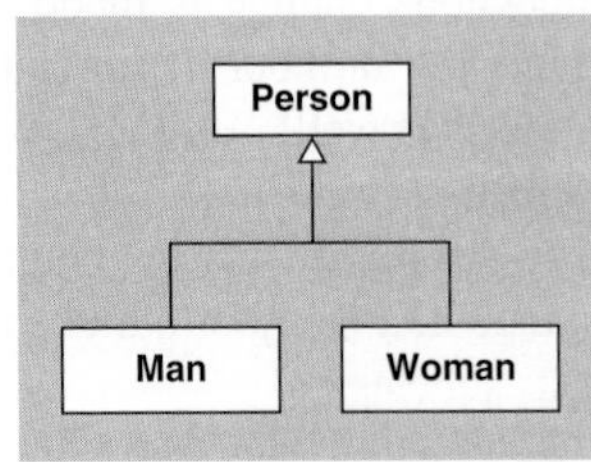

SECTION 3.9 EXAMPLE: DRAWING POLYGONS

Consider a drawing program in which the user is able to draw polygons, possibly including quadrilaterals (four-cornered figures), rectangles, squares, triangles, lines (two-cornered figures), points (one-cornered figures), etc. Suppose that the drawing program displays a window with two parts: a large drawing canvas and a toolbar across the top of the window with tool buttons, one for each polygon. The user is supposed to click on a toolbar tool button to select a polygon and then click in the drawing canvas, at which time a copy of the selected polygon appears in the canvas centered at the point of the click. See Figure 3.10 for a picture of such an application that draws only triangles, squares, and rectangles of fixed sizes.

We will discuss other aspects of this example in other sections and, in fact, will devote all of Chapter 8 to it. But for right now, we will focus on the design of one small part of this program, namely, the part that redraws all the polygons whenever the canvas needs refreshing (e.g., if it was partially covered up and then uncovered again). We will show how inheritance can help us create an elegant design.

In order for the application to be able to draw and redraw polygons, those polygons and their positions must be stored in some collection or collections. Therefore, let us assume that the canvas maintains a collection of polygons so that it can readily redraw them when necessary.

Let us focus on the collection of polygons that the canvas has. Of what form should the collection be and of what form should the polygons be? That is, what classes and what relationships should we use to store polygons?

Design 1 (a poor design): A simple design is to have the drawing canvas store two ordered collections, one containing Strings indicating the types of the polygons that have been drawn, and the other containing Points indicating the centers of the corresponding (fixed-size) polygons. Let us use an ArrayList <String> called `polygonNames` for the types of the drawn polygons and an ArrayList <Point> called `centerPoints` for the locations of the corresponding polygon. Whenever

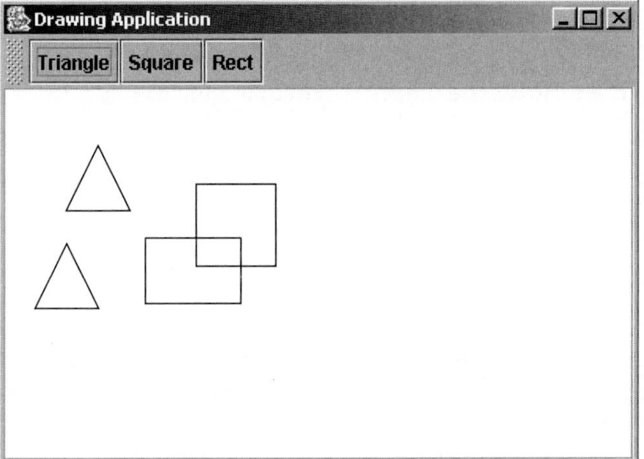

FIGURE 3.10 A simple polygon-drawing application.

the polygons need to be redrawn, a `paint` method in the canvas is called. That method can be implemented as follows:

```
public void paint(Graphics g)
{
  for( int i = 0; i < polygonNames.size(); i++ ) {
    String currentPolygon = polygonNames.get(i);
    Point currentCenter = centerPoints.get(i);
    if( currentPolygon.equals("triangle") )
      ...draw a triangle centered at currentCenter...
    else if( currentPolygon.equals("square") )
      ...draw a square centered at currentCenter...
    else if ...
}
```

If you've had a bit of experience with such tasks, or even if you haven't, you probably notice the inelegance of this code. Using two separate collections, one for the kind of the polygon and one for the location of the polygon is inelegant because it can lead to errors if the two collections become unsynchronized (e.g., if you delete an item from one collection and forget to delete the corresponding item from the second collection). Also, the `paint` method is inelegant in that it includes all the instructions for drawing each of the shapes. A third drawback of this version is that if the drawing program is later enhanced to draw pentagons and hexagons, for example, the implementation of this `paint` method will need to be enlarged to include even more conditionals.

Design 2 (not much better): Combine the two ArrayLists into one "polygons" list, each of whose items stores the necessary data for drawing one polygon. For example, the items in the list could be PolygonData objects such as the following:

```
public class PolygonData
{
  private String name;
  private Point center;
  public PolygonData(String n, Point c)
  { name = n; center = c; }
  public String getName() { return name; }
  public Point getCenter() { return center; }
}
```

The `paint` method can now get all the data it needs to draw one polygon from one PolygonData object:

```
public void paint(Graphics g)
{
  for( int i = 0; i < polygon.size(); i++) {
    String currentPolygon = polygons.get(i).getName();
    Point currentCenter = centerPoints.get(i).getCenter();
    if( currentPolygon.equals("triangle") )
      ...draw a triangle centered at currentCenter...
```

```
        else if( currentPolygon.equals("square") )
            ...draw a square centered at currentCenter...
        else if ...
    }
```

Although the data structure is now a little better in that the data for each polygon is stored together in one object, the actual code in the `paint` method is in some ways worse. Also, this change doesn't deal with the other drawbacks to the first design.

Design 3 (a better design): Instead of storing the type of polygon in a String in a PolygonData object, let us store that information in the class type itself. That is, let us create a separate class for each kind of polygon, all with a common superclass. For example, we could define an abstract Polygon class with "concrete" subclasses of Square, Rectangle, and Triangle ("concrete" is not a Java key word; it is just a useful adjective here to indicate a nonabstract class). See Figure 3.11.

In this design, the drawing canvas saves Square, Rectangle, and Triangle objects in a list. Furthermore, let us give these shapes a little intelligence and make them responsible for knowing their locations and for drawing themselves. That is, let us suppose that the Polygon class includes an abstract `draw` method that takes a Graphics object as parameter and suppose that each concrete subclass implements that `draw` method appropriately to draw its shape. It is certainly the case that this inheritance hierarchy is appropriate from the "is-a" perspective, the subtyping perspective, and the polymorphism perspective. If there are data and methods shared by all the concrete classes, then, by moving the common elements to the superclass, our design is also appropriate from the perspective of code reuse and avoiding duplication.

Once these classes have been created, the `paint` method for the canvas can be nicely simplified to the following form (here we assume the polygons are stored in an ArrayList<Polygon> named `polygons`):

```
public void paint(Graphics g)
{
    for(Polygon poly : polygons) {
        poly.draw(g);
    }
}
```

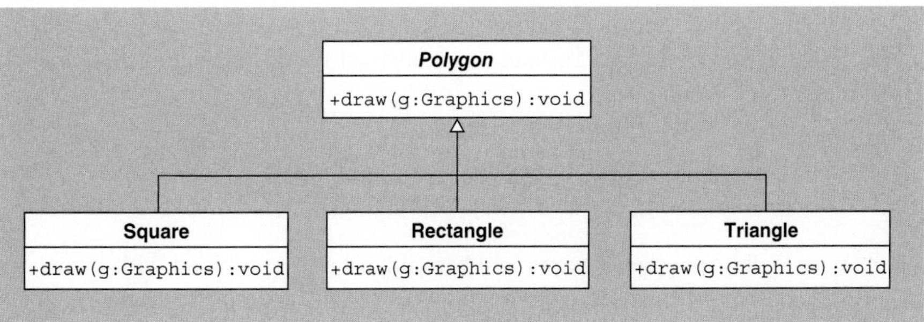

FIGURE 3.11 The Polygon class and its subclasses.

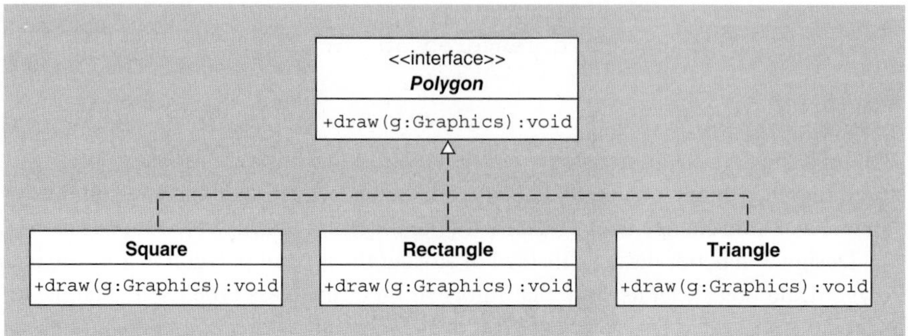

FIGURE 3.12 Design 4.

Note that polymorphism and dynamic method lookup allow the desired implementation of the `draw` method to be executed each time.

There is a natural elegance to a code like this that uses polymorphism to avoid conditional statements, especially conditionals that test whether a value is an instance of a particular class. As mentioned in Chapter 2 when introducing dynamic method invocation, this approach is considered to be one part of the "OO way" of doing things.

Guideline

Use inheritance, polymorphism, and dynamic method invocation to avoid ugly conditionals.

Design 4 (a better design in a special case): Should anything be done differently if there is no common code shared among the concrete subclasses of Polygon? That is, suppose the Polygon class has only abstract methods and no instance variables. In that case, the design allows no code reuse, and so it is no longer appropriate to use inheritance from the code reuse perspective. As discussed at the end of Chapter 2, an abstract class with only abstract methods should be replaced with an interface. Therefore, the best design in the case where there is no code reuse is the one in which Polygon is an interface instead of an abstract class. See Figure 3.12 for the UML diagram for Design 4.

SECTION 3.10 EXAMPLE: SORTING

Let us now look at one more example where inheritance combined with interfaces makes the code more generally useful and elegant. This example is one with which you should already be familiar. It concerns the java.util.Arrays class and its various sorting methods. Note that we are including this discussion of sorting not to intro-

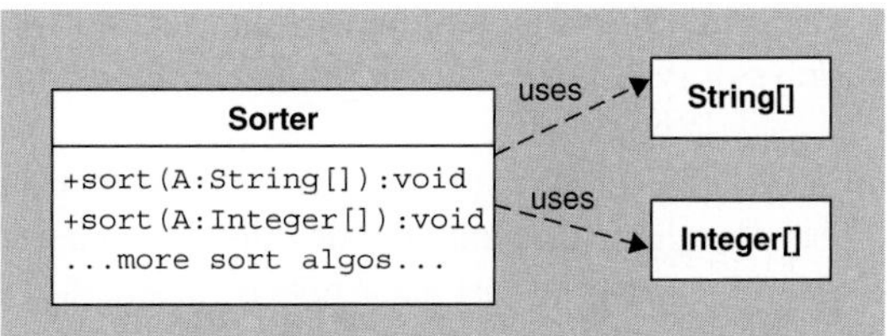

FIGURE 3.13 Our initial Sorter class.

duce you to a topic that you haven't seen before, but rather to show you an example of how to incrementally improve an existing design, a valuable skill to have in software design, and how inheritance can help during that process.

We will start with the problem of creating methods for sorting arrays of various kinds of objects, and we will present an initial inelegant solution. We will then gradually modify it to introduce elegance in the design and will see how it naturally leads to the methods in the Arrays class. Our improvements will mostly be the result of following the guidelines of avoiding code duplication and using polymorphism to avoid conditionals.

Note that we will ignore the generic types in the Java 1.5 Arrays methods to simplify the discussion. An exercise will ask you to compare these solutions with the solutions you get when you add generics.

Suppose you are asked to implement a class whose sole purpose is to sort arrays of data in place (i.e., using modifier methods that rearrange the data in the array). For example, the class might look like this:

```
public class Sorter
{
  public static void sort(String[] A)
  { ...code for sorting String arrays... }
  public static void sort(Integer[] A)
  { ...code for sorting Integer arrays... }
  ...methods for sorting other kinds of arrays...
}
```

See Figure 3.13. We will assume that the arrays to be sorted contain objects, and so arrays of primitive types of data, such as int or char, will not be considered. (You are asked in an exercise to consider the case of arrays of primitive data.)

Note that there is a new feature in the UML diagram, consisting of a dashed arrow labeled "uses." This indicates a dependency of the Sorter class on the String[] class and Integer[] class, in that the Sorter class' `sort` methods use those types of data.

This class seems quite useful and it seems like it might be easy to implement in an elegant way, except for (at least) three things:

1. How many `sort` methods should Sorter implement? If you don't include a `sort` method for a particular array type, then what will happen if someone needs to sort an array of objects of that type? Or, suppose that after the implementation of Sorter, you define a new class C and want to sort an array of

C objects? Our Sorter class cannot handle this case unless it includes a `sort` method for arrays of type Object[], and, in that case, we have to ask what sorting means for generic objects.

2. The code in the bodies of each of the `sort` methods are almost identical to each other. There is a large amount of code duplication here.
3. What if we sometimes want to sort the arrays from smallest to largest and other times from largest down to smallest? Also, what if we want to sort the array of Strings ignoring the case (upper or lower) of the letters? What if we want to sort using some other attribute of the Strings in the array, such as the length of the Strings? To be most useful, our Sorter class should be able to handle a variety of sorting options for each array type.

Suddenly the design of the Sorter class doesn't seem quite so elegant. Let us incrementally improve it.

Let's first consider how we can avoid duplicate code in each `sort` method. For the purpose of discussion and for code simplicity, we will look at implementations of the `sort` methods for Integers and Strings using the selection sort algorithm, even though that algorithm is not usually the sorting algorithm of choice. Here are two such implementations:

```
public static void sort(Integer[] data)
{
  for (int i = data.length-1; i >=1; i–) {
    // in each iteration through the loop
    // swap the largest value in data[0]..data[i] into position i
     int indexOfMax = 0;
     for (int j = 1; j <= i; j++) {
       if (data[j] > data[indexOfMax])
         indexOfMax = j;
}
//     swap the largest value into position i
Integer temp = data[i];
data[i] = data[indexOfMax];
data[indexOfMax] = temp;
}
}
public static void sort(String[] data)
{
  for (int i = data.length-1; i >=1; i--) {
     // in each iteration through the loop
     // swap the largest value in data[0]..data[i] into position i
     int indexOfMax = 0;
     for (int j = 1; j <= i; j++) {
       if (data[j].compareTo(data[indexOfMax]) > 0)
         indexOfMax = j;
       }
// swap the largest value into position i
```

```
String temp = data[i];
data[i] = data[indexOfMax];
data[indexOfMax] = temp;
}
}
```

Notice that the two methods are identical except in three places (shown in bold in the code above):

1. The two methods take a different type of array as their parameter.
2. The first method extracts the integer values from the objects and uses ">" to compare the values, and the second method uses the String's `compareTo` method to compare the values.
3. When swapping the data, the two methods use temporary variables of different types (Integer in the first method and String in the second method).

All the other `sort` methods in the Sorter class will be similar. How can we avoid the duplication in the bodies of all these methods?

One way to avoid duplication is to create one generic selection sort method that could sort all these kinds of arrays. In order to create such a method, it is important to realize that the most significant difference in the `sort` methods above is how the objects in the arrays are compared to each other. Therefore, our first step toward removing the duplication will be to factor out that difference. To factor out the different ways of comparing items, let us try creating a new object, a `Comparator` object, to do the comparing of objects for us. Our first attempt at creating a Comparator class will have many methods for comparing the data, one for each type of data:

```
public class Comparator

{
  public int compare(String o1, String o2)
  {
    return s1.compareTo(s2);
  }
  public int compare(Integer o1, Integer o2)
  {
    int i1 = o1.intValue();
    int i2 = o2.intValue();
    return i1 - i2;
  }
  ...compare methods for the other types of data we wish to sort...
}
```

These methods all return a negative integer if `o1` is "less than" `o2`, zero if `o1` "equals" `o2`, and a positive integer if `o1` is "greater than" `o2`. Notice all the method name overloading that is going on in this class.

If we add a "comp" parameter of type Comparator to the sort method, then we can modify the sort method for arrays of Strings as follows (the changes are highlighted in bold):

```
public static void sort(String[] data, Comparator comp)
{
  for (int i = data.length-1; i >=1; i--) {
    // in each iteration through the loop
    // swap the largest value in data[0]..data[i] into position i
  int indexOfMax = 0;
  for (int j = 1; j <= i; j++) {
    if (comp.compare(data[j], data[indexOfMax]) > 0)
      indexOfMax = j;
  }
    // swap the largest value into position i
    String temp = data[i];
    data[i] = data[indexOfMax];
    data[indexOfMax] = temp;
  }
}
```

We can use the same Comparator to modify the `sort` methods for the other types of arrays. At the cost of complicating our design by the addition of another class, we have made the String array, Integer, and other array `sort` methods look a little more alike.

The remaining differences in the Integer array and String array `sort` methods consist of the different types of the first parameter and the different types of the `temp` local variable used for swapping. To eliminate these differences, we will try replacing those types with the Object type, which is a superclass of String and Integer and all other classes in Java. Notice how subtype polymorphism is enabling us to make this change. That is, since an array of Strings is also an array of Objects, we can use an array of Strings where an array of Objects was expected. The resulting version of our sort routine looks like this:

```
public static void sort(Object[] data, Comparator comp)
{
  for (int i = data.length-1; i >=1; i--) {
    // each iteration through the loop
    // swaps the largest value in data[0]..data[i] into position i
  int indexOfMax = 0;
  for (int j = 1; j <= i; j++) {
    if (comp.compare(data[j], data[indexOfMax]) > 0)
      indexOfMax = j;
  }
    // swap the largest value into position i
    Object temp = data[i];
    data[i] = data[indexOfMax];
```

```
      data[indexOfMax] = temp;
    }
}
```

We have now removed all duplication in the `sort` methods in the Sorter class. In fact, using this method, we can completely eliminate all the original `sort` methods, since this new `sort` method handles all kinds of data. See Figure 3.14 for our new design.

However, there is a problem. Try to spot it before reading ahead. (Hint: The compiler will not accept the code above.)

The problem is that, in this new version of `sort`, the compiler can't determine which `compare` method of the Comparator class to call. The compiler sees only that the two arguments to `compare` are of declared type Object, and so it looks for a `compare` method that takes two Objects as parameters. However, our Comparator class has no such `compare` method, and so the compiler will generate an error message. (Note that if Java used multimethods, this problem would be easily solvable.)

To solve this problem, let us modify the Comparator so that it has a `compare` method that takes two objects of class Object as parameters. Then this method is the one that will *always* be called by the generic `sort` routine above, so we can eliminate the other `compare` methods in the Comparator class and replace them with one that is general enough to deal with all the cases:

```
public class Comparator
{
  public int compare(Object o1, Object o2)
  {
    if( o1 instanceof String && o2 instanceof String )
      return ((String) o1).compareTo((String) o2);
    else if( o1 instanceof Integer && o2 instanceof Integer )
      return (Integer) i1 - (Integer) i2;
    else
```

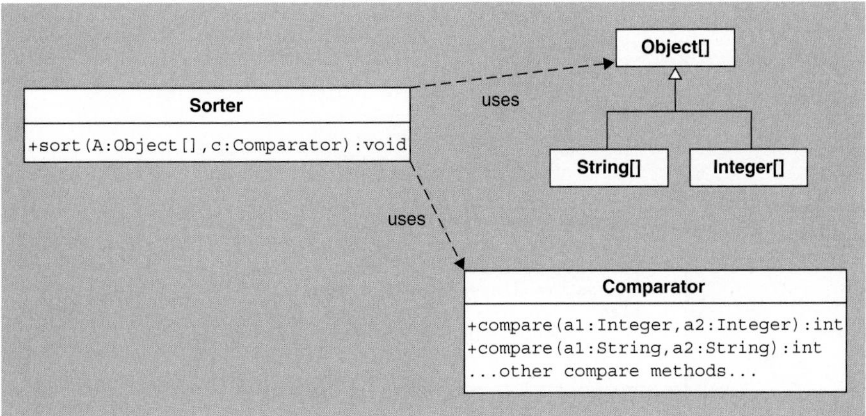

FIGURE 3.14 Our new Sorter class using our Comparator class.

```
            ...deal with all the other types of data...
        }
    }
```

See Figure 3.15 for our new design.

Now we've done it! Or have we? The latest version of our generic `sort` routine will correctly take any array of Strings or Integers and sort it based on the comparisons done by the generic Comparator, but is it really a significant improvement?

A very inelegant aspect of our latest implementation is that we've cleaned up the generic sort routine but at the expense of the Comparator. The Comparator's `compare` method is inelegant in that it has many conditionals based on the type of an object. As we discussed earlier, the OO way of doing things is to use polymorphism instead of such conditionals. Furthermore, the Comparator still won't handle all desirable cases. For example, what if you wish to sort an array of C objects where C is a new class created after the Comparator was written? The C type won't be in the Comparator's list of types that are compared. Or, as we mentioned earlier, what if you want to sort an array of Strings sometimes alphabetically using case, sometimes ignoring case, and sometimes based on the length of the Strings? How can the Comparator distinguish these cases?

The problem here is that one Comparator is trying to do too many things in its generic `compare` method. Note that when we're sorting Strings, we only need to consider the comparison of Strings. Similarly, when we're sorting Integers, we only need to consider the comparison of Integers. So our final modification of the code is to make Comparator an interface and create several classes that implement

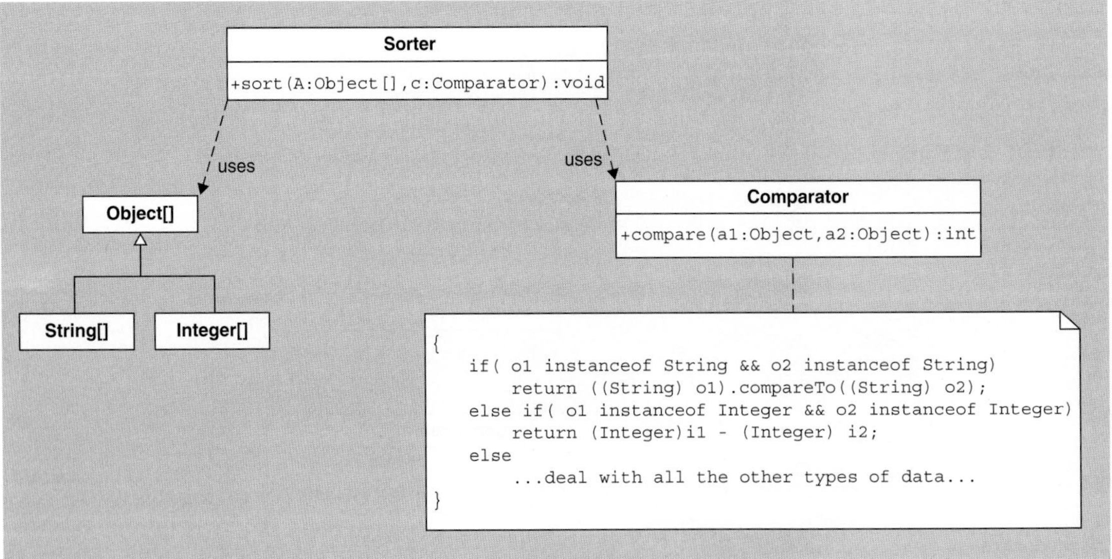

FIGURE 3.15 Our Sorter class and new Comparator class.

Comparator, one for each type of data. In fact, the Java library includes just such an interface in the java.util package:

```
public interface Comparator
{
  public int compare(Object o1, Object o2);
  public boolean equals(Object o);
}
```

We can create concrete classes implementing the Comparator interface that compare two objects of one particular type and throw an exception in all other cases. For example, we could create the following classes:

```
public class StringComparator implements Comparator
{
  public int compare(Object o1, Object o2)
  {
    String s1 = (String) o1;
    String s2 = (String) o2;
    return s1.compareTo(s2);
  }
}
public class IntegerComparator implements Comparator
{
  public int compare(Object o1, Object o2)
  {
    return (Integer) o1 - (Integer) o2;
  }
}
```

Each of these two classes just compares one type of object and the `compare` methods throw an exception if the arguments are not of the right type. (Note also that these classes do, in fact, implement the Comparator interface even though they do not directly implement `equals`, because they inherit an implementation of `equals` from the Object class.)

A client who wants to sort an array of Strings alphabetically might use our Sorter's `sort` method by passing the array and a StringComparator as parameters to the `sort` method:

```
String[] data = ...initialize the data array...
Comparator comp = new StringComparator();
Sorter.sort(data, comp);
```

To sort an array of Strings ignoring the upper or lower case of the letters, the user can do exactly the same thing except define a different class implementing Comparator as follows:

```
public class StringIgnoreCaseComparator
{
```

```
    public int compare(Object o1, Object o2)
    {
      String s1 = (String) o1;
      String s2 = (String) o2;
      return s1.compareToIgnoreCase(s2);
    }
  }
```

and then use it in exactly the same way:

```
String[] data = ...initialize the data array...
Comparator comp = new StringIgnoreCaseComparator();
Sorter.sort(data, comp);
```

Do you see how subtype polymorphism helps here? Since the Comparator parameter in the generic `sort` method can take as its value any object of any subtype of Comparator, we can pass any kind of Comparator we want as the second argument to the `sort` method. If we pass in an array of Strings for the data, we can pass in a StringComparator as the comparator. If we pass in an array of Integers for the data, we can pass in an IntegerComparator as the comparator. Similarly for the other types of data. If such arguments are passed to the `sort` routine, then the polymorphic method-calling mechanism will ensure that the `compare` method of the Comparator subtypes will be called by the `sort` routine and that the `sort` method will correctly compare and sort the data.

Note: Here is a situation where documentation is important—the `sort` routine documentation must clearly state that the Comparator passed as the second argument must be of the proper type to compare the objects in the array passed as the first argument or else an exception will be thrown.

Notice how nice and general this sort routine is (assuming, of course, that you want to use selection sort to sort your array). To sort the same array in different orders, just create different Comparators. This generic routine can sort any kind of array of objects, even objects of a class that hasn't yet been defined, as long as the user defines an appropriate Comparator to go with the new class. See Figure 3.16 for a UML class diagram showing the relationships among these classes. It should be noted that the java.util.Arrays class implements a similar `sort` method.

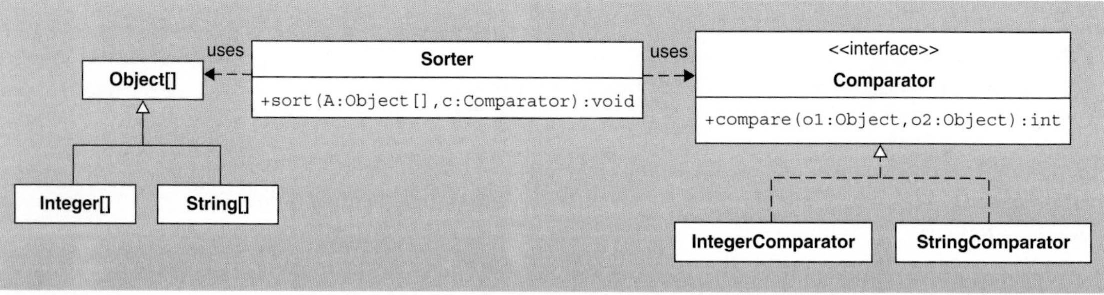

FIGURE 3.16 The Sorter and Comparator relationships.

Here is the final code for our Sorter example, including the StringComparator and IntegerComparator classes that implement the Comparator interface, and a Main class with a main method that demonstrates how to use the Sorter and Comparator objects.

```
public interface Comparator
{
  public int compare(Object o1, Object o2);
  public boolean equals(Object o);
}
public class StringComparator implements Comparator
{
  public int compare(Object o1, Object o2)
  {
    String s1 = (String) o1;
    String s2 = (String) o2;
    return s1.compareTo(s2);
  }
}
public class IntegerComparator implements Comparator
{
  public int compare(Object o1, Object o2)
  {
    return (Integer) o1 - (Integer) o2;
  }
}
public class Sorter
{
  public static void sort(Object[] data, Comparator comp)
  {
    for (int i = data.length-1; i >=1; i--) {
      // in each iteration through the loop
      //   swap the largest value in data[0]..data[i] into position i
      int indexOfMax = 0;
      for (int j = 1; j <=i; j++) {
        if (comp.compare(data[j], data[indexOfMax]) > 0)
           indexOfMax = j;
      }
      // swap the largest value into position i
      Object temp = data[i];
      data[i] = data[indexOfMax];
      data[indexOfMax] = temp;
    }
  }
}
public class Main
```

```
{
  public static void main(String[] args)
  {
    String[] B = {"John", "Adams", "Skrien", "Smith", "Jones"};
    Comparator stringComp = new StringComparator();
    Sorter.sort(B, stringComp);
    Integer[] C = {new Integer(3), new Integer(1),
      new Integer(4), new Integer(2)};
    Comparator integerComp = new IntegerComparator();
    Sorter.sort(C, integerComp);
  }
}
```

To reinforce the lessons learned here, let us review how we used polymorphism, as well as other design techniques, to create a Sorter class that is much more elegant than the original version.

- By factoring out the comparison operation to a separate Comparator object, we were able to make the implementations of the various sorting methods in the original Sorter class very similar to each other.
- By using polymorphism on the arrays and the objects within the arrays, we were able to complete the generalization of the sorting algorithm, and, as a result, the Sorter class needed only one `sort` method.
- To clean up the Comparator class, we turned it into an interface that we implemented with the various kinds of comparators.

Although we ended up with many more classes and interfaces than we had originally (namely, the Comparator interface and its implementations), the resulting design displays all the features of elegance discussed in Chapter 1.

SECTION 3.11 SUBCLASSING ARRAYS IN JAVA

In the preceding section, we stated that a generic sort routine should have a parameter of type Object[] because then we could pass in any kind of array of objects that we want. Let's look at this argument a little more closely because there are subtle issues regarding inheritance of array types in Java that everyone should be familiar with.

One of the java.util.Arrays `sort` method has header

```
public void sort(Object[] data, Comparator comp)
```

Consider the kind of arrays we can pass in as the first argument. We could, for example, pass in an array of type Object[] containing strings:

```
Object[] data = new Object[3]{"Larry", "Curly", "Moe"};
Sorter.sort(data, new StringComparator());
```

In this case, the data array is of type Object[], but the data in it are of type String, a subtype of Object. This subtyping will not be a problem, and the `sort` routine will work correctly.

We could also pass in an array of type String[] containing strings:

```
String[] data = new String[3] {"Larry", "Curly", "Moe"};
Sorter.sort(data, new StringComparator());
```

This time, the data array is of type String[]. The compiler will accept this array as a legal argument to the `sort` routine because, in Java, if A is a subclass of B, then A[] is a subclass of B[]. Therefore, an array of type String[] is acceptable wherever an array of type Object[] is expected.

But "Is it accepted by the compiler in Java?" and "Should it be accepted by the compiler in Java?" are two different questions. Did the Java language designers make a good language design decision here?

It is clearly advantageous to be able to pass an array of type String[] or Integer[] wherever an array of type Object[] is expected, or else our generic sort routine would not be nearly as useful. However, there is also a design flaw in allowing subclassing of arrays in this way. Consider the following code segment:

```
String[] stringData = new String[3] {"Larry", "Curly", "Moe"};
Object[] objectData = stringData;
objectData[0] = new Integer(3);
```

Before reading any further, try to guess what the compiler will say when it checks the last statement of the code segment.

This code will be accepted by the compiler. The second line is legal according to the compiler because `stringData` is of type String[], which is a subtype of Object[]. The last line is legal according to the compiler because `objectData` is of type Object[], and the compiler thinks it is perfectly acceptable to assign any object to any slot of an array of type Object[]. But when we try to execute these lines of code, the program crashes (more precisely, an ArrayStoreException is thrown), since you cannot assign an Integer to a slot of an array of type String[], which is what `objectData` refers to. Since it is always better to have errors reported at compile time than run time, the Java subclass/superclass relationship between array types is not ideal. Unfortunately, there is no easy solution to this problem.

In summary, if A is a subclass of B, then there are both advantages and disadvantages to having a collection of objects of A considered as a collection of objects of type B. For more discussion of this issue, see [4, pp. 80–83] or, for a discussion using C++, see [5].

SECTION 3.12. INHERITANCE VS. REFERENCING REVISITED

In preceding sections, you saw how referencing is preferable to inheritance in some situations that at first seemed like ideal ones for inheritance. We showed that sometimes it is better to have objects of class B contain references to objects of class A and forward requests to those objects instead of making B a subclass of A. We will see many more similar situations in later chapters of this text as we discuss competing designs. In those discussions, we will ask ourselves whether it is better to inherit the responsibilities of another class or to retain a reference to an object of that other class and forward appropriate messages to that object.

For example, if a clickable button in a dialog box needs to notify several other objects when it is clicked, should the button do the notifying or should it maintain a reference to some kind of "NotificationManager" object and assign notification responsibilities to that manager? That is, instead of keeping a list of all objects to notify and notifying them itself, the button might assign the responsibility of maintaining the list of objects that request notification to the notification manager, then the button just needs to signal the notification manager, that the button has been clicked, and the manager handles all the notifications.

Let's consider one more example. Suppose you want to have a Stack class with only pure stack operations (`push`, `pop`, `peek`, `isEmpty`). There is the java.util .Stack class that you can use, but it has many more operations than the pure stack operations you desire. For example, in that Stack class you can insert or extract an object at an arbitrary location in the Stack. One way to design your pure stack is to subclass java.util.Stack and "void out" the other operations—that is, override them with empty methods that do nothing or just return null. However, as discussed in Section 3.3, it is not very elegant to do such restrictive subclassing.

A better solution might be to create from scratch your own Stack class with just the given operations. However, this is somewhat akin to reinventing the wheel—there are already nice storage classes, such as java.util.Stack, that handle all the details for you; why not use them?

Therefore, an even better solution would be to create your own MyStack class with just the desired operations but have it contain a java.util.Stack object and then forward all requests to that object. See Figure 3.17.

Here is what MyStack might look like:

```
public class MyStack
{
  private java.util.Stack stack;
  public MyStack() { stack = new java.util.Stack(); }
  public void push(Object o) { stack.push(o); }
  public Object pop() { return stack.pop(); }
  public object peek() { return stack.peek(); }
  public boolean isEmpty() { return stack.empty(); }
}
```

Notice how the java.util.Stack object does all the work. The MyStack class can be thought of as a class that merely cleans up the Stack's interface to remove all the non-

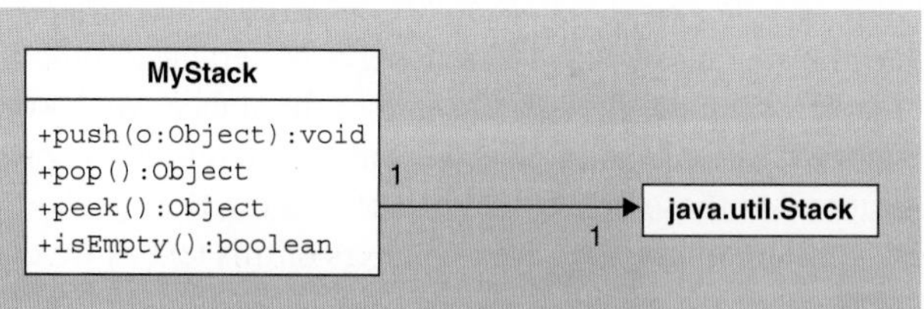

FIGURE 3.17 Forwarding requests to the java.util.Stack class.

stack operations that the java.util.Stack class contains. Such thinking should lead you to realize that one can also generalize things a little further and create a PureStack interface:

```
public interface PureStack
{
   public void push(Object o);
   public Object pop();
   public Object peek();
   public boolean isEmpty();
}
```

and then implement it with MyStack. The only change necessary to the MyStack class is the addition of the phrase "implements PureStack" in the definition header for the class. This approach allows users to concern themselves only with the PureStack type and ignore whether or not there is a MyStack object involved.

Now that we have looked at several examples where inheritance works well and several examples where referencing works well, let's summarize the advantages and disadvantages of each. That is, suppose we wish to design and implement a class B that is very similar to an existing class A. Two of our choices are to (a) make B a subclass of A or (b) pair B with an object of class A to which it assigns some responsibilities. See Figure 3.18 for the differences between these two choices.

For each of the following categories, let us compare the two choices in terms of flexibility and features:

- Polymorphism: If B is a subclass of A, then subtype polymorphism is possible and so an object of class B can be used anywhere an object of class A was expected, a definite advantage. In contrast, if B is composed with A, then this subtype polymorphism does not apply to B. Therefore, inheritance wins in this category.
- Interface: If B is a subclass of A, then B inherits *all* methods of A, and so the interface of B must include all the methods in the interface of A, whether B wants them all or not. Furthermore, it is usually not appropriate to "void out" or nullify the methods of A that B doesn't want. In contrast, if B is composed with A, then the public interface of B need not be related at all to the public interface of A, and so you have the flexibility to design B exactly the way you want. Referencing wins here.
- Efficiency: If B is a subclass, there is direct execution of any inherited methods. In contrast, if B forwards requests to A, then the methods of B must call methods of A, which results in slightly higher overhead costs. Inheritance wins

Property	Relationship	Structural form	UML
inheritance	"is-a"	generalization/ specialization	A ◁— B
reference	"has-a" or "refers to"	association	B → A

FIGURE 3.18
Two possible relationships between classes A and B.

here, but the efficiency gain is almost surely negligible and so it is not much of a win.

- Amount of Code: If B is a subclass of A, you need to implement in B only the methods of B that aren't already inherited from A. In contrast, if B forwards requests to A, then you must implement all of B's methods yourself. Although many of these methods might merely call a corresponding method in A, there is still more code to write and therefore more chance of errors. Inheritance wins here.
- Dynamic changeability: If B is a subclass of A, then at runtime, there is no way to change the behavior of the inherited methods. However, if B forwards requests to A, then at runtime, B can change the object of class A or a subclass of A to which it forwards requests and in this way reconfigure itself.

So who is the overall winner? Of course, neither one is. There are times when you want to use each one. Use referencing when you want the functionality but not the interface. Use inheritance when you want the functionality and interface. In the situations where it is not immediately obvious which approach is better, a natural tendency for new programmers is to want to demonstrate their knowledge of inheritance and so they consider it first. However, inheritance is overrated for many of the reasons given in this chapter, and so you should always consider referencing first.

SECTION 3.13 SUMMARY

Here is a summary of the ideas and guidelines introduced in this chapter.

- A similar interface (that is, similar method signatures) is not sufficient for an elegant subclass/superclass or class/interface relationship; consistent behavior is also required. In particular, a class B should not inherit class A's methods and then nullify them or change their behavior to do something completely different.
- The Principle of Least Astonishment: If a client thinks he has a reference to an object of type A but actually has a reference to an object of subtype B, there should be no surprises when he sends messages to the object.
- Liskov Substitution Principle: It is acceptable to make a class B a subclass of class A or to make B an implementer of interface A only if, for every method in both A's and B's interfaces, B's method accepts as input all the values that A's method accepts (and possibly more) and does everything with those values that A's method does (and possibly more).
- A class B that is identical to another class A except that it has extra restrictions on its state should not be a subclass of A unless both classes are immutable.
- Consider removing from your design any classes that provide little or no unique behavior.
- If class B models a role played by class A, especially a temporary role, then B should not be a subclass of A. Instead referencing should be used.
- Inheritance between a superclass A and a subclass B is appropriate if it promotes code reuse, each object of class B "is an" object of class A, the public interface of class B includes the interface of class A and the behavior of the methods in this interface in both classes is similar in both classes, and there is a need for polymorphism to allow a variable of type A to refer to an object of type B. Otherwise, inheritance is probably inappropriate.
- Inheritance makes it hard to follow the flow of execution through the code of a program, and it makes it hard for the programmer to change one

of the classes in the hierarchy without affecting the others.

- If you have a class with behavior that applies to only some of the objects of the class, then consider splitting the class into two classes associated by inheritance either directly or through a common abstract class or interface.
- Use inheritance, polymorphism, and dynamic method invocation to avoid ugly conditionals.
- When designing a class B that will be very similar to an existing class A, use referencing if you want the functionality of A but not the interface, and use inheritance only when you want the functionality and interface of A.

EXERCISES

1. Determine the proper relationship between the following classes. That is, which ones should be subclasses of others and which should be composed of others? You may add extra classes or interfaces (for example, a common superclass or interface of two of the classes) if you feel they will help clarify the relationship. Explain your reasoning.
   a. Boat, BoatHouse, House, HouseBoat, Garage, Car
   b. USMoney (with dollars and cents attributes) and Money (with an attribute indicating the kind of currency as well as the amount)
   c. Class1 and Class2, where both classes have methods with headers "public Object get()" and "public void put(Object o)." In Class1, the get and put methods behave like a stack's pop and push methods with LIFO behavior, and in Class2, the get and put methods behave like a queue's dequeue and enqueue methods with FIFO behavior.
2. A person might say that "Fluffy is a cat" and "A cat is a mammal," and therefore Fluffy should be a subclass of Cat and Cat should be a subclass of Mammal, because we have two "is-a" relationships. What is wrong with this reasoning?
3. In determining whether a class B should be a subclass of A, we said that there should be no surprises to the client who thinks she has an object of class A when she really has an object of class B. However, suppose B is any subclass of any class A and consider the following code:

```
public String getClassNameOf(A a)
{
   return a.getClass().getName();
}
```

   The client will always be expecting to see "A" returned regardless of the argument, but if an object of class B is the value of the parameter a, then "B" will be returned. Won't that surprise the client? Does this mean that no class should ever be a subclass of another class because there will always be this surprise?
4. Consider the following almost-identical classes A and B:

```
public class A
{
   public int foo(int x)
   {
      if( x >= 0)
         return x*x;
      else
         throw new RuntimeException();
   }
}
public class B
{
   public int foo(int x) throws Exception
   {
      if( x >= 0)
         return x*x;
      else
         throw new Exception();
   }
}
```

   If we make B a subclass of A, then the compiler generates an error when we compile these two classes, whereas if we make A a subclass of B, then the compiler compiles the classes without complaint. Explain this compiler behavior in terms of the Liskov Substitution Principle we stated in Section 3.3.
5. In Section 3.3, we discussed the Rectangle and Square classes in the case where they were both immutable or both mutable. Discuss the elegance of the following designs:
   a. Make a mutable Square class a subclass of an immutable Rectangle class,
   b. Make an immutable Square class a subclass of a mutable Rectangle class,

c. Make a mutable Rectangle a subclass of a mutable Square class.

6. In Section 3.3, we discussed an inheritance hierarchy including an abstract Rectangle class with three direct subclasses—MutableRectangle, ImmutableRectangle, and MutableSquare—and an ImmutableSquare class that is a subclass of Immutable Rectangle. However, it seems like mutable squares should somehow be more closely related to mutable rectangles than the hierarchy shows. Can you redesign the inheritance hierarchy in an elegant way so that the mutable squares and mutable rectangles are more closely related?
7. In Section 3.3, we discussed an inheritance hierarchy including an abstract Rectangle class that had MutableRectangle and ImmutableRectangle as two of its subclasses. Assume that the MutableRectangle class has a `move(dx, dy)` method that shifts its position horizontally by `dx` and vertically by `dy`. Suppose you are told by your boss to add a FirstQuadrantRectangle class that is the same as MutableRectangle except that the *x* and *y* coordinates of the top-left corner must always be positive. Redesign the inheritance hierarchy in an elegant way so that the FirstQuadrantRectangle class is included. Also, discuss whether the new class is a useful addition to the class hierarchy.
8. Consider the last approach discussed in Section 3.4 for the Student and Person problem. In that approach, a Student was not a subclass of Person, but instead held a reference to a Person object. One disadvantage of this solution is that there is now no type relationship between Person and Student. For example, suppose that you want to have a collection of Students and non-Student Persons mixed together in an array. More precisely, suppose you are working for a newspaper and are storing in an array all the information regarding subscribers to the paper and suppose that you want to distinguish between student subscribers and nonstudent subscribers because students get a reduced rate. What should the type of the array be? It can't be an array of Persons since Students aren't Persons. It can't be an array of Students since Persons aren't Students. One option would be to make it an array of Objects, but then you lose all the compile-time type information of the objects in the array and so have to do downcasting and type checking at runtime. Come up with a better option.
9. In Section 3.7, we implement a ChangeMeasured Rectangle class that assumed that the Rectangle class' `setSize` method called the `setWidth` method. As noted in that section, if the `setSize` method is modified so that it doesn't call `setWidth`, then the ChangeMeasuredRectangle class is broken. Is it possible to implement the ChangeMeasuredRectangle class so that it will correctly work regardless of the implementation of the `setSize` method in the Rectangle class? If so, give such an implementation.
10. In Section 3.9, the Polygon class and its subclasses were given `draw` methods, which seemed to make sense from an OO perspective. However, now consider a geometer who wants to study and analyze polygons from a mathematical point of view (e.g., to prove theorems about polygons), and she doesn't care at all about drawing them. Ideally, from the perspective of code reuse, it would be nice if she could use the Polygon class we created. Unfortunately, our Polygon class is tied to the Graphics class and a `draw(Graphics)` method, and so carries this extra baggage around that is irrelevant from the geometer's perspective. Suggest some solutions to this dilemma.
11. In the Sorter class defined in Section 3.10, the sort methods are declared "static," and so they are class methods. Is this a good design decision? Why or why not?
12. In the Sorter class defined in Section 3.10, the sort methods took a Comparator as a parameter. Why not make the Comparator an instance or class variable of the Sorter class instead of passing one in as a parameter? Why not use a public variable from another class that is of type Comparator?
13. An alternative to using Comparators to determine which elements of the array come before other elements is to use the `compareTo` method of the elements, as was done in the original version of the `sort` method for arrays of Strings. This approach, in fact, is taken in one of the `sort` methods in the java.util.Arrays class. What are some of the advantages and disadvantages of this approach?
14. The StringComparator discussed in Section 3.10 throws an exception—more precisely a ClassCastException—if either of the two objects passed into its `compare` method is not a String. Is there any reasonable way for the StringComparator to avoid throwing an Exception and instead always return an integer? If so, what should the Comparator do with a non-String argument?
15. In the Sorter class defined in Section 3.10, it was mentioned that the generic sort method won't work for arrays of primitive types. Come up with an elegant way of handling such arrays.

16. Does the use of generics—specifically, Comparator<T>—simplify the final sorting method that we created in Section 3.10? If so, how?
17. Write a StringLengthComparator that implements the Comparator interface and allows users to sort arrays of String by the length of the Strings (from smallest to largest). Two Strings of the same length should be neighbors in the sorted array but can be in any order.
18. Redo the previous exercise so that all Strings of the same length are in alphabetical order. That is, the primary sorting mechanism is by String length but the secondary sorting mechanism is by alphabetical order.
19. One problem with the Sorter class in Section 3.10 is that it uses selection sort, a rather inefficient sorting algorithm. One should really rename the class as SelectionSorter. Similarly, one could use a different sorting algorithm, such as quick sort, and create a QuickSorter class. Is there a way to avoid code duplication between these two sorter classes? Read and write a short report on how such duplication is handled in [7]
20. In Section 3.12, we raised the question as to whether a button should handle all the notifications that it was clicked or whether the button should have a notification manager object and forward the notifications to it to handle properly. Which approach is taken by the javax.swing.JButton class?
21. Consider the inheritance hierarchy in which a Person class has a ParttimeEmployee subclass, which in turn has a NewFulltimeEmployee subclass, which has a TenuredFulltimeEmployee subclass. When asked to justify this hierarchy the designer of it gave the following two reasons:
    - Every employee is a person.
    - The three categories of employees are identical except each subclass has more benefits than its superclass. For example, parttime employees have a few benefits, for example, salary, but new fulltime employees get more, for example, health insurance, and tenured fulltime employees get even more, for example, stock options and dental insurance.

    What do you think of this hierarchy? Evaluate it based on the discussion in this chapter. Come up with a better design for these categories of employees.
22. Suppose a person needs to model the concept of balloons and so, wishing to use inheritance to make an elegant design, the person creates three classes, a RubberObject class, an InflatableBag class, and a Balloon class that is a subclass of those two classes. (For the purpose of this exercise, assume that Java, like C++, allows multiple inheritance.) Can you see any problems with this design?
23. The java.util.Collection class has a method with the following header:

```
public static List unmodifiableList(List
  list)
```

that returns an immutable copy of the list passed in as a parameter. The immutable copy throws an UnsupportedOperationException if you call any of the modifier methods in the List class. Discuss the elegance of this design.

REFERENCES

1. Martin, R.C., The Liskov substitution principle. *C++ Report*, March, 1996.
2. Liskov, B., *Program Development in Java: Abstraction, Specification, and Object-Oriented Design*. 2001. Reading, MA: Addison-Wesley.
3. Wiki. *Liskov Substitution Principle*. Web page, 2003. [Cited March 28, 2007; available from *http://c2.com/cgi/wiki?LiskovSubstitutionPrinciple*.]
4. Bruce, K., *Foundations of Object-Oriented Languages*. 2002. Cambridge, MA: MIT Press.
5. Cline, M., *C++ FAQ Lite*. Web page, 2003. [Cited March 28, 2007; available from *http://www.parashift.com/c++-faq-lite/proper-inheritance.html#faq-21.3*.]
6. Riel, A.J., *Object-Oriented Design Heuristics*. 1996. Reading, MA: Addison-Wesley.
7. Nguyen, D. and S. Wong, "Design patterns for sorting" is a paper in the *SIGCSE BULLETIN* 33:1, March, 2001. Pages 263–267 Published by ACM Press, New York, NY.

4

Elegance and Methods

SECTION 4.0 INTRODUCTION

It is useful to distinguish between the different perspectives or levels of software design. Based on the ideas in [1], we will consider OO design on three levels:

1. Conceptual
2. Specification
3. Implementation

At the highest level, the conceptual level, software components, such as objects and their associated classes, have responsibilities, for example, geometric shapes might have the responsibility to draw themselves and to compute their area, or students might have responsibilities to get to class on time rather than expecting a parent to prod them. At this level, the components are language-independent.

At the specification level, we are concerned with the precise interfaces and associations between components. For example, a geometric Shape interface may specify methods with headers `public void draw(Graphics g)` and `public double area()`.

At the implementation level, concrete classes that implement these interfaces are of concern to us. Such classes have instance variables and code for their methods, for example, a Circle object might have `x` and `y` integer variables corresponding to the coordinates of the center and a float variable `r` corresponding to the radius, and the `area` method might have `return 3.14*r*r;` in its body.

Introductory programming classes are mostly taught at the implementation level. In a data structures course, instructors usually talk about both the implementation and specification levels. In a software engineering class or a software design class, the conceptual level is the usual focus of discussion. In the next three chapters, we will talk about how to design elegant OO programs from all three perspectives.

This chapter focuses mostly on implementation and specification issues. More precisely, this chapter discusses standard forms for methods and elegant implementations of methods, including standard coding conventions. As discussed in Chapter 1, one important factor in determining the elegance of code is its readability. In fact, Abelson and Sussman [3] said, "Programs must be written for people to read, and only incidentally for machines to execute." Source code should flow like a good novel, with no unnecessary words, with delightful names, and with a message to communicate to the reader, so that the reader can put it down later with satisfaction and a "well done."

We will say little in this chapter about the interactions and relationships between classes (e.g., through association or inheritance). Those issues will be presented in Chapter 5, which focuses on specification and conceptual issues, and Chapter 6, which provides a case study of a money class, in which we will have a chance to apply many of the ideas discussed up to that point.

SECTION 4.1 CODING STYLES AND NAMING CONVENTIONS

There are many coding styles for writing the bodies of classes and their methods using Java. Everyone has their own preferences, and those preferences can be based on a logical analysis of the options or just an aesthetic sense of layout. However, there are valid reasons for following certain agreed-upon stylistic conventions as much as possible. For example, if programmers in a team each follow different conventions, team members will have a harder time understanding each others' code than if they agreed to use a particular coding convention.

Sun Microsystems suggests certain conventions when writing Java programs. For example, Sun suggests that you use at most 80 characters per line, because longer lines do not print properly on some printers nor are easily viewed in some environments. You can find all the conventions at `http://java.sun.com/docs/codeconv/`. If you have no prior preferences and if you have not been given other conventions to use, it is suggested that you follow these guidelines.

A review of many of Sun's conventions, including a discussion of Javadoc conventions, is included in Appendix B.

Guideline

Choose a standard coding style and follow that style throughout all your code.

One of the most important coding conventions affecting readability and elegance of code is the proper naming of your variables, classes, and methods. Unfortunately, good names for variables, classes, and methods are not things that a development environment can provide for you in the same way that it can reformat your code. Instead good names are things that you much choose very carefully. Therefore, we include a discussion of that naming here rather than in Appendix B.

Classes and interfaces should have names that reflect the role or intention of the objects of those types. The name of a class is the reader's first clue as to the actual role the class plays in a design, and so it is worth spending time finding an appropriate name for the class. Class names typically are nouns, such as Date or ComputerCard. Interfaces often have names ending in "able" or "ible," such as "Cloneable" or "Iterable."

Method names also need to be chosen carefully. The method name should indicate the intent of the method, that is, what the method is supposed to accomplish. The name should not indicate *how* the method accomplishes its goal but rather *what* that goal is. A method that does not return a value (a method with return type "void") should have a name consisting of a verb or verb phrase, such as "print" or "setName." Clearly, vague names like "doIt" are inadequate. A method that returns a value should have a name reflecting the value being returned, for example, "isVisible" or "size." Such a method could also have a verb phrase for a name, the convention being the word "get" followed by the value being returned. For example, the `size` method could be renamed `getSize`. See also [4–6] and the Intention Revealing Selector pattern.

Finally, variables need to be named appropriately to promote readability. Consider a program that has a variable in it called "nT." An argument in favor of such a name is that it is short and so saves typing time and therefore helps shorten your lines of code. However, the name is completely meaningless in terms of indicating the role of the variable, and so the reader is forced to memorize that role. In contrast, calling the variable "numberOfThreads" instead of "nT" increases dramatically the ease with which your code can be understood.

It is also possible to go overboard in giving variables descriptive names, such as "theNumberOfThreadsInTheCurrentApplicationRunningRightNow." Keep in mind that "clarity is often achieved through brevity." [7, p. 3]

A boolean variable should have an appropriate name representing the event to which it refers. It usually should not represent the negation of an event, for example, don't call your variable "notYetDone," which could possibly result in the need for expressions such as the double negative "! notYetDone." Instead, it would be better to call it "done" and use the expression "! done" wherever "notYetDone" would have been used. Of course, you shouldn't be using "done" either, since the word does not contain enough information to aid the reader in understanding the role of the variable. That is, it is not clear to the reader *what* activity is done or not done. For example, if this variable is being used to indicate that a graphic image is done loading and is now visible, a better name would be something as simple as "doneLoading."

Using good names is even more important for constants, because they are often used in a context far from where they are defined, and so the reader needs to spend more time searching for the declaration of such a constant than they would with a local variable.

Finally, not only is choosing the right names important, but also following convention in the capitalization of the names is important. For example, readers used to seeing class names begin with capital letters will be misled when they see a class name starting with a lower case letter. Follow a consistent capitalization scheme, such as starting your class and interface names with capital letters and starting your variable and method names with small letters, as is used in this text.

Guideline

Use intention-revealing names for all variables, methods, and classes so that they accurately describe the role or intentions of the things they are naming.

SECTION 4.2 METHODS AND DECOMPOSITION

The public methods of a class provide the public behavior of the class that other classes can call upon. But those methods and especially private auxiliary methods can also be used to raise the level of abstraction at which code can be viewed. That is, the separation of large segments of code into methods and the replacement of those sections of code with method calls allows the programmer to think about the computational process on a higher level. Programmers can treat methods as if they were built-in higher-level features in the programming language, and so they can conceptualize larger sections of code than they would otherwise be able to do. In this way, methods improve the readability of the code. This process of breaking code into methods is called *functional decomposition,* a process you should already be familiar with, but which is worth reviewing.

The decomposition of code into well-designed methods not only improves the readability of the code, it also promotes reusability. A well-designed method becomes another tool for the programmer to use whenever he or she needs code to accomplish a particular objective.

When should a method be decomposed into other methods? One overly simplistic rule of thumb suggests that if the method body can't all fit on a computer screen at the same time, it is probably too long and should forward some of the work to other methods. (Although, interestingly enough, some studies have shown that method bodies of up to 200 lines can have advantages over shorter bodies [8, p. 93].)

Decomposition should also be considered when there is duplicate code. That is, if a program has two places where the same sequence of instructions is being executed, it is almost always beneficial to move the duplicated code into a separate method and then replace the code in each place with a method call.

For example, suppose you are developing a class of objects one of whose responsibilities is to parse an input string, such as a complicated mathematical expression. Part of the process of parsing involves checking that the input is valid. So the class might have a method like this:

```
public void parse(String expression)
{
   ...do some parsing...
   if( ! nextToken.equals("+") ) {
      //error
      System.out.println("Expected +, but found " + nextToken);
      System.exit(1);
   }
   ...do some more parsing...
   if( ! nextToken.equals("*") ) {
      //error
      System.out.println("Expected *, but found " + nextToken);
      System.exit(1);
   }
   ...
}
```

It should be clear that it would be appropriate here to replace the body of the two conditional statements with a method call. Here is one way of cleaning up that code:

```
public void parse(String expression)
{
    ...do some parsing...
    if( ! nextToken.equals("+") )
        handleError("Expected '+', but found" + nextToken);
    ...do some more parsing...
    if( ! nextToken.equals('*') )
        handleError("Expected '+', but found" + nextToken);
    ...
}
private void handleError(String message)
{
    System.out.println(message);
    System.exit(1);
}
```

Not only is the code in the new version of the `parse` method much cleaner and more readable, but it is also much easier to change the error handling. For example, if you decide later that your parser needs to throw an exception instead of printing a message and quitting, you only need to change the code in one place, namely inside the body of the `handleError` method. The exercises at the end of the chapter ask you to clean up the code to reduce the duplication even further.

Note that there is a special mechanism for removing duplicated code in constructors in Java called *constructor chaining*. This mechanism involves one constructor calling another one using the "this" construct. For example, consider the following class with two constructors. It assumes a family always has a father and mother and zero or more children.

```
public class Family
{
    public Family(Person father, Person mother, Person[] children)
    {
        ...code...
    }
    public Family(Person father, Person mother)
    {
        this(father, mother, new Person[0]);
    }
    ...other methods...
}
```

The second constructor calls the first constructor and so is merely a convenience constructor that allows the user to specify a family that does not (yet) have any children without requiring the user to create an empty array.

Guideline

Use methods, especially private auxiliary methods, for decomposition to reduce duplication of code and to raise the level of abstraction of the code.

We have already mentioned other forms of code duplication, such as duplicate methods in two classes and how to avoid such duplication through inheritance. In the next chapter, we will again visit duplication, especially as it relates to duplication of responsibility.

SECTION 4.3 COHESIVE METHODS

In the preceding section, we gave some reasons *why* methods should be created, especially private auxiliary methods, but they don't explain *how* to create useful methods. That is, they don't explain what should and should not be included in a method. In this section, we will discuss some guidelines regarding the design and role of all methods, whether public or private.

One important property of methods is that they should be as self-contained as possible. For example, if a method uses instance variables or calls private methods of its class, then the method is only useful in the context of that class. In contrast, if the method can take all of its data through its parameters and invokes methods only on those parameters, then the method could be moved into any class you wish, which gives you much more flexibility in organizing your code.

Another important property of methods is that they do only one thing. When you create or intend to create a method, ask yourself whether you can describe completely, in one sentence, what a method does without using the word "and." If not, you probably have a method that should be divided into two or more methods.

Guideline

A method should do one thing only and do it well.

In [4, pp. 21–22; 5, pp. 3–7; 9, pp. 271–275], this guideline is called *Composed Method*. A method following this guideline is also said to have strong "functional cohesion" [8, Sec. 5.3].

For example, the `substring` method in the String class is cohesive in that it does one very simple, but very useful, task. It just returns a new string consisting of the specified sequence of characters from the original string. If it also performed another unrelated task such as printing that substring to the console, it would be far less useful (and the name would be far less intention-revealing).

Here's an example of a noncohesive method:

```
void doThisOrThat(boolean flag) {
  if( flag ) {
    ...twenty lines of code to do this...
  }
  else {
    ...twenty lines of code to do that...
  }
}
```

This method is clearly trying to do two things and using the flag to determine which of them to do. It would be better to have two separate auxiliary methods, such as `doThis` and `doThat`, neither of which needs a flag. Once we have these methods, then we can rewrite our method above to read:

```
void doThisOrThat(boolean flag) {
  if( flag )
    doThis();
  else
    doThat();
}
```

This code is now acceptable (except for the non-intention—revealing names "flag," "this," and "that") since the method is just acting as a dispatch center and so is doing one thing only and doing it well.

There is one other point we can make about this `doThisOrThat` method. Suppose we had rewritten our method halfway so that it called an auxiliary method to hand the "do this" case but it handled the "do that" case itself. As a result, the code would look like:

```
void doThisOrThat(boolean flag) {
  if( flag ) {
    doThis();
  }
  else {
    ...twenty lines of code to do that...
  }
}
```

Is some ways, this code is even worse than the original code in which the method handled both the "do this" and "do that" cases itself. The reason the new code is worse is that, not only doesn't it do one thing only, but it is now uncomfortably unbalanced in that the `doThis` auxiliary method does not have a matching `doThat` method. We can think of the `doThisOrThat` method as now working on two different levels. It is acting as a high-level dispatch method calling other auxiliary methods to do the work, but it is also acting at a lower-level in that it itself is doing some of the work.

Guideline

All code in a method should execute at the same level.

There is another implication to the statement that a method should do one thing only. The implication is that a method should not both return a value and modify the state of some object. Therefore, it follows that all modifier methods (that change the state of one or more objects—such methods are also called *commands* or *mutators*) should have "void" return type and that all functions (that return a value—such methods are also called *queries*) should not change any existing object's state. That is, in an ideal world, functions should have no side effects and modifier methods' behaviors should just cause side effects. Meyer [10] calls this guideline the *Command-Query Separation Principle.*

Note, however, that there are standard methods in the Java library classes that do not follow this guideline. For example, the `pop` method in the Stack class both modifies the Stack and returns a value. Similarly, the `next` method in the java.util.Iterator interface modifies the state of the Iterator and returns a value. Also, modifier methods are sometimes designed to attempt a modification and then to return a value indicating whether the attempted modification was successful. This is a common programming form in many languages, including Java, such as in several methods in the java.util.Collection interface. However, a Java programmer should also consider an alternative course of action such as throwing an Exception if the modifier method does not succeed. [11, p. 279; 12]

Guideline

Functions (which return a value) should not modify any existing object's state in a way visible to other objects and modifier methods (which modify one or more objects' state) should have "void" as the return type.

You may ask why you should be expected to follow this guideline when the designers of the standard libraries, such as the Java libraries, didn't do so. The reason is that some methods, like `pop`, are now so standard that changing them to fit the guideline or removing them because they don't follow the guideline would actually reduce the readability of code (programmers would ask why `pop` wasn't used). Some other cases, such as the case where a modifier method returns a boolean value indicating success or failure, are also somewhat of a standard, especially in languages that don't have exception-throwing mechanisms. In any case, whether you or others attain it or not, the guideline is worth striving for. Consider it a challenge to see whether you can design your methods better than previous designers have done with their methods.

SECTION 4.4 WELL-FORMED OBJECTS AND CLASS INVARIANTS

If the designers of classes and methods follow the guidelines in preceding sections, then their functions will never affect or modify the state of any existing objects. However, modifier methods will do so. There is an important guideline for such methods to observe if they are to do their jobs well.

> **Guideline**
>
> Public methods should always keep objects in a well-formed state.

To understand what we mean by this guideline, consider a MyLinkedList class that has an instance variable `head` of type Node that refers to the first node of a noncircularly linked list of nodes and another instance variable `length` of type int that indicates the number of nodes. Consider what would happen if the value of `length` was different than the actual number of nodes. Then the user would get two different values for the length, depending on whether she checked the `length` instance variable or iterated over the nodes and counted them. Clearly, we need the two values to be the same if the class is to be usable. It is this kind of internal consistency that we mean when we say a class is "well-formed."

How do we state the requirements of consistency for a class? That is, how do we know whether an object of that class is well-formed? A good way is to specify what makes objects of a class well-formed is to list the class invariants. A *class invariant* is a statement about the state of objects of the class between public method calls. The statement of equality of the value of `length` and the number of Nodes in an object of the MyLinkedList class is an example of a class invariant.

Note that there is another class invariant for our MyLinkedList class, assuming the links are maintained by `next` pointers in each Node, namely the `next` instance variable of the last node on the list must have null or some other special placeholder object as its value. That is, it is required that the `next` variable not point back to an earlier node in the list.

It is valuable to test a class' invariants often, especially when debugging your code. For example, it is useful to create a boolean method `satisfiesInvariants` that tests some or all class invariants, returns true if the invariants are satisfied, and then calls this method at the end of every modifier method. Java 1.4's `assert` construct comes in handy here. For example, at the end of every modifier method, you could just add the statement

```
assert satisfiesInvariants() : <error message>
```

This statement invokes `satisfiesInvariants`. If it returns true, then nothing happens and execution moves on to the next statement in the program. If it returns false, then an AssertionException is thrown with the error message passed as an argument to the AssertionException's constructor. One feature of assert statements is that they can all be disabled at once by a command line switch when they are no longer needed.

Notice that class invariants refer to the state of an object when it is not executing one of its public methods. That is, in the body of a public method, it is okay for the object to temporarily break one or more of its invariants, but before the method returns, the object should be back in a well-formed state. This means, in particular, that all constructors for the class need to return a well-formed object.

One more point should be made regarding the MyLinkedList example. Is it a good idea to have such a `length` instance variable, as we described above? After all, you can compute the length of the list whenever you want by traversing it and counting the number of nodes. What's wrong with just computing the length in this way every time it is needed? The advantage to computing it each time is that it reduces the complexity of your class in that you have one fewer instance variables and one less invariant to satisfy. The main disadvantage of computing the length each time is the computation will take more time than just reading the value from a variable.

Guideline

Be aware that, although it can increase the efficiency of your code, caching values instead of computing them when they are needed can also increase the complexity and number of invariants of your class.

SECTION 4.5 INTERNAL DOCUMENTATION

A software package, no matter how well designed otherwise, is almost worthless if documentation is not included. Consider the frustration of a software designer knowing that a library almost surely has the tools she needs but she can't tell for sure because the documentation of the library's components is inadequate. Or consider the frustration of the person faced with the task of fixing a bug in a large section of code that contains little or no comments explaining why it does things the way it does. Elegant software avoids both of these situations by including appropriate documentation.

In this section and the following one, we will explain what we mean by "appropriate documentation." In this section, we will consider internal documentation, and in the next section, we will consider external documentation.

Internal documentation is the documentation for someone who is looking at the source code. Such documentation should provide information not readily available from the code itself. It should summarize what is being done, why it is being done, and why it is being done this particular way. For example, the documentation might explain that a method has been implemented a particular way to allow easy modification later, or because the method is most efficient this way, or because this way is the simplest way. It should explain the trade-offs that were involved among the various possible implementations.

Internal documentation should also clearly state any class or method invariants that exist. A person modifying an existing method without being aware of those invariants is almost surely going to write code that breaks them.

Internal documentation should not repeat what the code says. Instead, it should summarize the *intent* or purpose of the code or gives a higher-level explanation. One reason to include the intent in the documentation is so that future maintainers of the code, when fixing errors in it, can understand what the method/variable/class *should* have been doing.

Helpful internal documentation might also give an overview of the implementation. An internal method comment might explain the algorithm used by the method if the algorithm was not already mentioned in the external documentation. For example, a `sort` method's internal documentation might say that the quicksort algorithm was used:

```
public class sort(int[] A)
{
  /* sorts the array A using recursive quicksort */
  ...
}
```

Internal documentation mostly consists of comments in the source code, but the code itself can be a useful part of the documentation if the code is well written. If the programmer uses intention-revealing names of methods and variables and appropriately combines them, there is often little need for further documentation.

Guideline

Always strive for "self-documenting code" that is so clear that no comments are necessary.

Unfortunately, self-documenting code is an ideal that is rarely met, and so additional comments are necessary. Such comments can be helpful in understanding code, or they can hinder the understanding, especially if the comments are not also updated when the code is updated.

Code needing a large number of comments usually indicates poor code. That is, if you find yourself needing comments to explain the code, then the code should probably be rewritten. In particular, if you write a lot of comments that summarize sections of code in a method, the method may be doing too many things.

Guideline

If your code is so complicated that it needs explaining with lots of internal or external documentation, then the code should probably be rewritten.

When should comments be added to the code? It is easy for a new programmer to say that he doesn't "do" comments until after he has written and debugged the code, because otherwise he ends up wasting too much time writing comments for code that is later deleted. Such a thought process, however, is counterproductive.

Thinking about and documenting what a method is going to do and how it is going to do it before implementing it leads to simpler and clearer software. In particular, thinking about and documenting the method and class invariants before implementing the class forces the programmer to consider all the implications of those invariants and use them to maximum benefit.

Guideline

Write comments before or while writing the code, not after. "Build it in, don't add it on."

What should you do if you are given code that someone else wrote that needs fixing but that you cannot fix right away? In such a case, it is tempting to add internal documentation indicating what is wrong and what needs to be done. You clearly want to record this information somewhere and putting it near the code that needs to be changed seems an appropriate place. However, such comments can easily be overlooked and/or forgotten, except by code readers who wonder when, if ever, the changes are going to be made. It is more appropriate in many respects to keep a separate document with proposed changes in the design or the implementation.

Kernigan and Plauger [13] summarize nicely the role of documentation:

1. If a program is incorrect, it matters little what the documentation says.
2. If documentation does not agree with the code, it is not worth much.
3. Consequently, code must largely document itself. If it cannot, rewrite the code rather than increase the supplementary documentation. Good code needs fewer comments than bad code does.
4. Comments should provide additional information that is not readily obtainable from the code itself. They should never parrot the code.
5. Mnemonic variable names and labels, and a layout that emphasizes logical structure, help make a program self-documenting.

In this text, we have striven to write self-documenting code, and so little internal documentation has been included. The user is encouraged to study how well this code succeeds at being self-documenting and to learn from it, whether as an example of good documentation or bad.

SECTION 4.6 EXTERNAL DOCUMENTATION

External documentation is for the users of the code who can't look at or don't care about the source code itself. It describes the public classes, interfaces, methods, fields, and packages and how to use them. External documentation might also include design documents such as UML diagrams indicating the relationships between and the roles played by the classes. Such documentation, if done correctly, describes all aspects of the behavior of each method on which the caller must rely.

It is important to understand that the only behavior of a method on which the user should rely is the documented behavior. Reliance should be limited in this way because, during maintenance of the system, a programmer might need to modify the method. That programmer may feel free to change any undocumented behavior, which then can cause serious problems with anyone relying on that behavior.

What should be included in the external documentation of a method? This documentation must include the full method signature and return type so that the user knows the syntax to use in a method call, but much more is needed as well. For example, consider the method in the java.lang.Math class with the following header:

```
public static double rint(double a)
```

Some reference books give you no more details than this header regarding how to use this method or what this method does. For an experienced programmer who already knows about `rint`, this information is sufficient to remind him or her of the type of the argument and the return type. But for everyone else, the signature is quite useless without further documentation. A more descriptive name would go a long way toward clearing up any confusion, but, even with such a change, a textual description of what the method returns and how it uses the parameter is essential for proper usage.

To understand more specifically what should be included in external documentation, let us step back and consider the creation of a new method. It comes about when the designer of a system has a need for certain behavior in one of the classes in the system and so decides that a method with that behavior must be included in the design of the class. One of the important steps in such a design process is the development of a precise specification of the behavior of the method before the method is implemented. This specification is useful to the designer so that he or she can document exactly the role the method will play in the system, but it is also useful later to the person implementing the method in that it tells precisely what behavior needs to be coded into it and to any users of the method so that they can determine whether the method actually does what they want and, if so, how to call it.

If the designer's specification is too vague and general, problems can occur during the implementation phase. For example, consider the following documentation for an `nthRoot` function:

```
public double nthRoot(double value, int n)
  returns the n-th root of the double value.
```

This documentation is clearly inadequate. It does not specify what happens in special cases, such as when `value` is −1 and `n` is 2. If the designer wants the method to behave in a certain way in those special cases, then she must include that behavior in the documentation to guide the implementer. Here is an example of more complete documentation for the `nthRoot` method:

```
public double nthRoot(double value, int n)
  returns the n-th root of the double value.
  If n is even, the positive n-th root is returned.
  If n is odd, the n-th root will have the same sign as the
    value.
  If n < 0 or if n is odd and value < 0 then an
    IllegalArgumentException is thrown
```

Another problem with external documentation can occur if the designer, instead of being overly general and vague, is overly restrictive, specifying too many details. In that case, he or she is forcing the implementer to code the method in a way that may not be optimal. That is, if the designer specifies *how* a method computes a value instead of just *what* value is computed, then the implementer has no choice regarding how to implement the method, even if there is another more efficient way to do so.

For example, let us revisit the Set class discussed in Section 2.3 and in Exercise 4 in Chapter 2. In particular, consider the following documentatiton for the `intersect` method discussed in that exercise.

```
public static Set intersect(Set s1, Set s2)
  returns a Set with the common elements of s1 and s2 by first creating an
  empty Set to be filled with the common elements and then stepping through
  the elements of s1 using an iterator and testing whether those elements are
  also in s2 by calling s2.contains(e), where e is the next element of s1 to be
  tested. If s2 contains e, then e is added to the Set that is returned.
```

This documentation is inappropriate for several reasons. It is inadequate in that it does not specify what happens if `s1` and/or `s2` is null. As mentioned earlier, if the designer expects certain behavior in special cases such as these, then she needs to include that behavior in the documentation. Similarly, the documentation does not clearly specify the side effects, if any, on `s1` and `s2`. Presumably they are to be unmodified, but this presumption should be made explicit somewhere in the documentation.

But just as importantly, this documentation is inappropriate in that it is overly detailed regarding the implementation, unless that particular implementation is an essential part of the method. The implementer may have an alternate way of determining the intersection—such as cloning `s1` and then removing the elements that are not also in `s2`—but he is not allowed to implement it that way because of the documentation.

Guideline

The external documentation for a method should be sufficiently specific to exclude implementations that are unacceptable but sufficiently general to allow all implementations that are acceptable.

How do you determine when the external documentation for a method is just right? To answer this question, it is valuable to think of it as a service an object of that class will perform for others who request/demand it. In order for users of your class to know what that service entails and therefore whether they want to use that service, you need to specify clearly what the users need to do (e.g., the arguments they need to provide) and what your object will do in return when it executes the method. That is, think of the method in terms of a contract. If a user provides appropriate arguments, then your method promises to perform a specific service. One way to specify the contract and what "appropriate parameters" and "specific service" mean is with preconditions and postconditions.

A *precondition* is a condition that must be true in order for a method to work. A *postcondition* tells what the method guarantees will happen when it is executed. If the caller (client) can guarantee that all preconditions are satisfied, the callee (server) guarantees that the postconditions will be satisfied after the call. That is, the method promises that it will do what the postconditions say if the client is careful to ensure that the preconditions are satisfied.

Note that it is up to the client to make sure the preconditions are satisfied before attempting the method call. If the client attempts to use the method without satisfying the preconditions, then all bets are off and the method can have unspecified behavior, including crashing the program, running forever, or seemingly running correctly but actually generating garbage.

Guideline

Specify precisely all preconditions and postconditions for each of your methods in the external documentation. These conditions form the contract for your method.

For example, consider again the `intersect` function mentioned above. The documentation gave the postcondition but did not specify any preconditions. As a result, the user is led to believe that the method will produce a useful result for all values of the two parameters, even null. Better external documentation would warn the user that the two parameters must not be null:

```
public static Set intersect(Set s1, Set s2)
  Precondition: s1 and s2 are not null.
  Postcondition: returns a Set with the common elements of s1 and s2.
```

With this documentation, the user has been warned that the behavior of the method is unspecified if `s1` or `s2` is null.

Although unspecified behavior is acceptable in the case where a precondition fails, it is usually better for the clients of the method to know what will happen in all cases. A well-designed method will usually do some well-defined, appropriate action such as throw an exception if the preconditions are not satisfied and that behavior will be stated as part of the contract. This information will help clients prepare for situations where things go wrong.

Therefore, an example of even better documentation of the `intersect` method is the following:

```
public static Set intersect(Set s1, Set s2)
  Precondition: none
  Postcondition: returns a Set with the common elements of s1 and s2
    if s1 and s2 are not null.
    If s1 or s2 is null, an IllegalArgumentException is thrown.
```

By adding the exception-throwing behavior to the method, we have removed the precondition, in that the method now promises to work for all possible inputs. In this case, the postcondition describes two very different behaviors that can happen (a value can be returned or an exception thrown), depending on the input values.

Let us reiterate the advantages of complete documentation. If a method specifies a precondition and the user accidentally calls that method with illegal arguments, the result may be that an incorrect value is returned. The user's program may then continue to execute with incorrect values, which makes it hard later to detect where the error occurred or even that an error occurred.

The last version of the `intersect` method does not allow this to happen, in that it throws an exception if illegal arguments are used, which notifies the user immediately of the error. Furthermore, the exception mechanism allows the user to catch the error and handle it robustly in a way appropriate to the user's needs.

Guideline

Try to make your methods do something appropriate in all cases so that there are no preconditions.

This guideline is one example of a practice called *defensive programming.* You know errors are almost certainly going to occur and illegal input is going to be given to methods, so make sure that your methods can defend against such input by doing something explicit in a way that is helpful to the user of those methods.

There are situations where this guideline needs to be ignored. In particular, the extra code needed to test for legal input and, if the test fails, throw an exception may be quite expensive in terms of resources. For example, consider a method that performs binary search on an integer array. A precondition to using binary search is that the array is sorted. To eliminate that precondition, the binary search method could first check the array to see if it is sorted and, if not, throw an exception. However, in that case the method's efficiency is reduced from $O(\log n)$ to $O(n)$, where n is the array size.

We note here that, with the notion of precondition and postcondition, we can now state a more precise version of the Liskov Substitution Principle discussed in the preceding chapter concerning when it is acceptable for a class B to be a subclass of a class A:

> It is acceptable to make B a subclass of A only if for every public method with identical signatures in both A and B, the preconditions for B's method are no stronger than the preconditions for A's method and the postconditions for B's method are no weaker than the postconditions for A's method.

As with internal documentation, one problem with writing external documentation concerns keeping it synchronized with the code as the design evolves. As the code is modified (e.g., errors are fixed, features are added), it is tempting, especially under time pressure, to postpone updating the documentation, resulting in documentation that no longer matches the code. One way to solve the problem of keeping documentation in synchronization with source code is to generate external documentation from the source code or vice versa so that they are always synchronized.

Javadoc [14] is a tool and documentation technique designed for such document generation. It specifies a syntax to be used for comments in the source code that are then gathered by the Javadoc application and converted into external documentation. Javadoc was used to generate the Java API documentation [15]. Using Javadoc will not, unfortunately guarantee that the external documentation will always be synchronized with the source code. It only guarantees that the external documentation is synchronized with the Javadoc-formatted comments in the code, not the actual Java code.

For an example of Javadoc notation, the method header for the `nthRoot` method discussed earlier is presented here using that notation:

```
/**
  * returns the n-th root of the double value.
  * If either n < 0 or n is even and value < 0,
  * then an IllegalArgumentException is thrown.
  *
  * @param value the double whose root is desired
  * @param n the integer indicating the root to be computed
  *
  * @return the n-th root of the value
  *   If n is even, the positive n-th root is returned.
  *   If n is odd, the negative n-th root is returned.
  *
  * @throws IllegalArgumentException
  *   if either n < 0 or n is even and value < 0.
  */
```

For a more detailed discussion of Javadoc syntax, especially the meaning of the special fields such as `@param`, `@return`, and `@throws`, see Appendix B.

SECTION 4.7 CASE STUDY: OVERRIDING THE EQUALS METHOD IN JAVA

In this section, we will discuss the issue of implementing an `equals` method for a class both because it is an issue you should address whenever you create or change a class and because it will give us a chance to demonstrate the use of some of the guidelines mentioned earlier in this chapter and in preceding chapters. We will concern ourselves initially with the question as to whether `equals` can be implemented elegantly. We will then consider the implications of overriding the `equals` method. More discussion concerning whether you should override `equals` is included in the next chapter.

Suppose you have created a new class and have decided to override the `equals(Object)` method inherited from the Object class or another superclass.

You can't, of course, change the method arbitrarily and still expect to have an elegant design. In particular, the Liskov Substitution Principle says that if a method behaves in a certain way in a class, then users will expect an overriding method in a subclass to behave similarly. Therefore, you need to understand the behavior of the inherited method before you can properly implement the overriding method.

The Java API specifies the following equivalence relational properties for the Object class' `equals` method [2]:

- It is *reflexive*: for any nonnull reference value `x`, `x.equals(x)` should return `true`.
- It is *symmetric*: for any nonnull reference values `x` and `y`, `x.equals(y)` should return `true` if and only if `y.equals(x)` returns `true`.
- It is *transitive*: for any nonnull reference values `x`, `y`, and `z`, if `x.equals(y)` returns `true` and `y.equals(z)` returns `true`, then `x.equals(z)` should return `true`.
- It is *consistent*: for any nonnull reference values `x` and `y`, multiple invocations of `x.equals(y)` consistently return `true` or consistently return `false`, provided no information used in `equals` comparisons on the object is modified.
- For any nonnull reference value `x`, `x.equals(null)` should return `false`.

Notice that these properties specify postconditions and that there are no preconditions. The `equals` method must return true or false for all possible arguments, even null.

Because the `equals` method of the Object class implements an equivalence relation, all overriding `equals` methods in subclasses are also expected to do so (due to the Liskov Substitution Principle). Even if they weren't required, these equivalence relation properties are clearly desirable. For example, you obviously want an object to be equal to itself. You also clearly want `x.equals(y)` to return the same value as `y.equals(x)`—consider how horrible it would be if, whenever you wanted to test two objects `a` and `b` for equality, you had to worry about whether to call `a.equals(b)` or `b.equals(a)`. In particular, in situations where you don't know the precise class of `a` or `b` (which is possible if they refer to objects that are of unknown subtypes of the declared type of `a` and `b`), it would be impossible for you to distinguish between the two calls to `equals`, and so you would be effectively flipping a coin when choosing which call to make.

How is `equals` implemented in the Java library classes, especially the Object class? The implementation of the `equals` method in the Object class tests object identity. That is, `a.equals(b)` returns true if and only if `a == b`, which means that `a` and `b` both refer to exactly the same object (another way to think of it is that `a` and `b` contain references pointing to the same location in memory). Some standard Java classes, such as String and Point, override this method to test equality in a different way. The String class overrides `equals` so that for Strings `s` and `t`, `s.equals(t)` returns true if and only if `s` and `t` have the same sequence of characters, regardless of whether `s` and `t` refer to exactly the same object. Similarly, in the java.awt.Point class, two Points are considered equal if and only if they have the same *x* and *y* coordinates. After a little reflection, you can convince yourself that all these implementations satisfy the equivalence relation properties.

With this information in mind, let us now determine how to implement `equals` in a class of our own so that it implements an equivalence relation. At first glance, it may seem fairly straightforward, but in actuality it must be done quite carefully, not just for the sake of elegance, but for the sake of correctness. To show you the subtleties involved, we will override the inherited `equals(Object)` method for a Triangle class and a ColoredTriangle subclass.

Here is the basic code for the Triangle and Colored Triangle classes:

```
public class Triangle {
  private Point p1, p2, p3; //the three corners
  public Triangle(Point p1, Point p2, Point p3) {
    if( p1 == null ) p1 = new Point(0,0);
    if( p2 == null ) p2 = new Point(0,0);
    if( p3 == null ) p3 = new Point(0,0);
    this.p1 = p1; this.p2 = p2; this.p3 = p3;
  }
  ... other methods...
}
public class ColoredTriangle extends Triangle {
  private Color color;
  public ColoredTriangle (Color c, Point p1, Point p2, Point p3) {
    super(p1, p2, p3);
    if( c == null ) c = Color.red;
    color = c;
  }
  ... other methods...
}
```

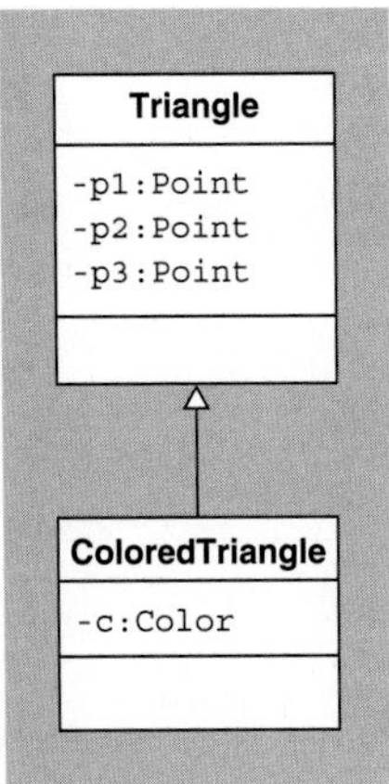

FIGURE 4.1
The Triangle and ColoredTriangle classes.

See Figure 4.1 for a UML diagram of these classes.

Note that the constructors ensure that the fields `p1`, `p2`, `p3`, and `color` are all nonnull. In particular, we will assume that the Triangle and ColoredTriangle classes have the class invariant that the fields are always nonnull (and hence any modifier methods must also ensure that those fields are never null). The case where the fields are allowed to be null is assigned as an exercise.

We want to consider two Triangles `t1` and `t2` to be equal if they have the same *x* and *y* coordinates at each corner. For simplicity, we will consider them to be equal only if the first point `t1.p1` matches `t2.p1`, the second points `t1.p2` and `t2.p2` match, and the third points match. We leave the case where the order of the corners can be different as an exercise.

Note that the `equals` method we wish to override takes an Object as a parameter, not just a Triangle, and so a user of the `equals` method might legitimately pass in a Rectangle, for example, as the argument to `equals` to test whether that Rectangle is equal to a Triangle. Therefore, the first step for the Triangle's `equals` method is to test the class of the argument and return false if it is not a Triangle. So here's a simple implementation of Triangle's `equals` method that includes this step:

```
//version 1 – in Triangle class
public boolean equals(Object obj)
{
  if( ! (obj instanceof Triangle) ) return false;
  Triangle otherTriangle = (Triangle) obj;
  return (p1.equals(otherTriangle.p1) &&
          p2.equals(otherTriangle.p2) &&
          p3.equals(otherTriangle.p3));
}
```

Note how this method elegantly uses the `equals` method of its components.

Does this `equals` method implement an equivalence relation? It correctly handles the case where `obj` is null, in that null is not an "instanceof" Triangle, and so false is returned. Also, it is easy to see that our method has the property of reflexivity.

Let us see next whether symmetry holds. It is easy to see that it holds if the argument is another Triangle, but what happens if the argument is a subclass of Triangle, such as ColoredTriangle? The answer depends on the implementation of the `equals` method in the ColoredTriangle class. Let us first assume that the ColoredTriangle does not override the `equals` method inherited from Triangle.

Consider the following test code:

```
Triangle t = new Triangle(new Point(0,0), new Point(1,1), new Point(2,2));
ColoredTriangle ct = new ColoredTriangle(Color.red, new Point(0,0),
                     new Point(1,1), new Point(2,2));
System.out.println(t.equals(ct));
System.out.println(ct.equals(t));
```

Before you read any further, try to figure out what will be printed by the last two lines of code.

This code will print "true" twice, and so the symmetry property holds in this case. The reason symmetry works here is that, in the `equals` method, the ColoredTriangle object is never treated as anything but a Triangle object, and so the fact that they both have the same corner points means they will be equal. More precisely, a ColoredTriangle object is an instance of Triangle, and so the `instanceof` test in the Triangle's `equals` method succeeds when `obj` is a ColoredTriangle. Also, the ColoredTriangle class inherits the `equals(Object)` method from the Triangle class and so `ct.equals(t)` similarly works properly.

Let us consider one more example of test code:

```
ColoredTriangle redTriangle = new ColoredTriangle(Color.red, new Point(0,0),
                              new Point(1,1), new Point(2,2));
ColoredTriangle blueTriangle = new ColoredTriangle(Color.blue, new Point(0,0),
                               new Point(1,1), new Point(2,2));
System.out.println(redTriangle.equals(blueTriangle));
System.out.println(blueTriangle.equals(redTriangle));
```

Symmetry again is preserved in this example in that the last two statements will both print "true."

Furthermore, the properties of transitivity and consistency are also preserved by this implementation of `equals`, regardless of whether the parameters are Triangles, ColoredTriangles, or other objects. Therefore, version 1 of the `equals` method above correctly implements an equivalence relation and so can legitimately be used in the Triangle class without violating the Liskov Substitution Principle.

However, there is one problematic aspect of this implementation of `equals`. According to this method, red ColoredTriangles are equal to blue ColoredTriangles if they have the same corners. Do we really want them to be equal? If we want to insist that equal ColoredTriangles must have the same color, then we need to create a new `equals` method for ColoredTriangle to override the one it inherits from Triangle. Let us see what happens when we attempt to do so.

It seems reasonable to implement the ColoredTriangle's `equals` method in a way similar to the Triangle's `equals` method:

```
//version 1 – in ColoredTriangle class
public boolean equals(Object obj)
{
  if( ! (obj instanceof ColoredTriangle) ) return false;
  ColoredTriangle otherColoredTriangle = (ColoredTriangle) obj;
  return super.equals(otherColoredTriangle) &&
    this.color.equals(otherColoredTriangle.color);
}
```

This code looks elegant, including such niceties as the reuse of the superclass' `equals` method. Furthermore, if you now test red ColoredTriangles against blue ColoredTriangles, you will find that they are not equal, as desired, and that symmetry is again preserved in that case.

So are we done? Not quite. Try retesting the Triangle object against the ColoredTriangle object that we considered in our first example:

```
Triangle t = new Triangle(new Point(0,0), new Point(1,1), new Point(2,2));
ColoredTriangle rct = new ColoredTriangle(Color.red, new Point(0,0),
                          new Point(1,1), new Point(2,2));
System.out.println(t.equals(rct));
System.out.println(rct.equals(t));
```

This code, when executed, will now print "true" and then "false." In other words, symmetry is no longer satisfied! Before we can fix it, we need to decide which is the "right" answer. That is, should `t` and `rct` be equal or not? Before reading any further, see whether you can figure out what went wrong and what you might do about it.

To fix the symmetry, we could change the ColoredTriangle's `equals` method so that, if the argument is a Triangle rather than a ColoredTriangle, then the method just calls and returns the result of the superclass' (Triangle's) `equals` method, which checks only the equality of the corners and ignores the color. Here is some such code:

```
//version 2 — in ColoredTriangle class
public boolean equals(Object obj) {
  if( obj instanceof ColoredTriangle ) {
    ColoredTriangle otherColoredTriangle = (ColoredTriangle) obj;
    return super.equals(otherColoredTriangle) &&
      this.color.equals(otherColoredTriangle.color);
  }
  else if( obj instanceof Triangle ) {
    return super.equals(obj);
  }
  else
    return false;
}
```

Using this version of the method, `rct.equals(t)` will return true, and so, since `t.equals(rct)` also returns true, we have preserved symmetry. However, transitivity is now violated. For example, let `bct` denote a blue ColoredTriangle with the same corner points as the red ColoredTriangle and the Triangle. Then calls to `rct.equals(t)` and `t.equals(bct)` will return both true. Therefore, by transitivity, `rct.equals(bct)` must also return true, but it does not.

One way to get both symmetry and transitivity to hold is to have `rct.equals(t)` and `t.equals(rct)` both return false. In order to get the Triangle's `equals` method to return false, it needs to distinguish between the Triangle class and subclasses of Triangle, which its `equals` method does not currently do. The easiest fix to this method is to test the class of the parameter `obj` using the `getClass` method instead of using the `instanceof` operator. Here is the new `equals` method for the Triangle class:

```
//version 2 — in the Triangle class
public boolean equals(Object obj)
{
    if( obj == null ) return false;
    if( obj.getClass() != this.getClass() ) return false;

    Triangle otherTriangle = (Triangle) obj;
    return (p1.equals(otherTriangle.p1) &&
            p2.equals(otherTriangle.p2) &&
            p3.equals(otherTriangle.p3));
}
```

In this implementation, if the argument `obj` is null or is not of the Triangle class, the method immediately returns false. This method now correctly deals with all the issues we discussed and is quite elegant. In particular, the method now implements an equivalence relation.

We can also change the ColoredTriangle class' `equals` method similarly into the following form:

```
//version 3 - in ColoredTriangle class
public boolean equals(Object obj)
{
  if( obj == null ) return false;
  if( obj.getClass() != this.getClass() ) return false;
  if( ! super.equals(obj) ) return false;
  ColoredTriangle otherColoredTriangle = (ColoredTriangle) obj;
  return this.color.equals(otherColoredTriangle.color);
}
```

Once again, if the argument `obj` is null or is not a ColoredTriangle, the method returns false. If the `equals` method has not returned false after the first two lines, then we know that `obj` is a ColoredTriangle. Therefore, to finish the test of equality, we need to test that `this` and `obj` are equal as Triangles and that they have the same color. The best way to test equality as Triangles is to call the superclass' `equals` method, which tests the equality of any inherited properties of a class. If the superclass' equality test succeeds, then the remaining test, namely the equality of the color of the two ColoredTriangles, is applied to determine the final result.

These latest versions (version 2 of `equals` in the Triangle class and version 3 of `equals` in the ColoredTriangle class) both implement equivalence relations. So, are we done? Unfortunately, in the process of getting the equivalence relation properties to work, we introduced a new problem.

To see what this new problem is, suppose a user has three variables t1, t2, and t3 of type Triangle and the user knows that the objects referred to by all three variables have the same corner points. However, suppose that the user does not know that t2 is actually a ColoredTriangle. Consider now the following two function calls:

```
t1.equals(t3)
t2.equals(t3)
```

According to the Liskov Substitution Principle, the user should never be surprised by the output of a method if a subclass object is substituted for a superclass object as the object being sent the message. However, the two function calls above return different values (true in the first call and false in the second call). Therefore, our latest `equals` methods still fail the Liskov Substitution Principle!

What is going on here? In the process of getting reflexivity, symmetry, and transitivity to work, we ended up giving the ColoredTriangle class' `equals` method significantly different behavior than its superclass' `equals` method. But a subclass' method should never different significantly from the overridden method in its superclass or else that subclass should not legitimately be considered a subclass of its superclass, as discussed in the last chapter.

This problem is not unique to the Triangle and ColoredTriangle classes. If you have any two classes A and B where A has an `equals` method overriding the Object class' `equals` method and B is a subclass of A with an `equals` method overriding A's `equals` method, then you will have the same problem of a violation of the Liskov Substitution Principle. Therefore, we have two choices:

1. Allow two classes in an inheritance chain to override the Object class' `equals` method, but accept the fact that the Liskov Substitution Principle will be violated.
2. In any inheritance chain, have at most one class that overrides the Object class' `equals` method.

To see the implications of these choices, let us apply them to our Triangle and ColoredTriangle classes. There are several things we can do, none of which is totally satisfactory. The first approach is to eliminate one of the two overriding `equals` methods. For example, we can eliminate the ColoredTriangle class' `equals` method, but then any tests for equality of ColoredTriangles will ignore the color and will consider only the corners. Alternatively, we can eliminate the Triangle class' `equals` method, but then two Triangle objects will be considered equal only if they are the same object. Another approach is to remove the subclass/superclass relationship between the ColoredTriangle and Triangle classes. To minimize code duplication, we could use composition, as discussed in the preceding chapter. That is, the ColoredTriangle class could have a Triangle field, which maintains the corners of a ColoredTriangle object. But by using this approach, we lose the ability to use subtype polymorphism with the two classes. Finally, we could accept the fact that the Liskov Substitution Principle is violated. The particular solution that should be adopted depends on the context and how the classes will be used.

It is worth mentioning that, if we eliminate the ColoredTriangle's `equals` method or if we choose composition over inheritance, then we can actually use the original (version 1) implementation of `equals` for the Triangle class.

It is also worth mentioning that whenever you implement the `equals` method in a class, then you might also want to include an additional version of `equals` for convenience that takes an object of that class as its parameter. For example, in the Triangle class, we might want add the following method that takes a Triangle as its parameter:

```
public boolean equals(Triangle otherTriangle) //in Triangle class
{
   return (p1.equals(otherTriangle.p1) &&
           p2.equals(otherTriangle.p2) &&
           p3.equals(otherTriangle.p3));
}
```

Note that this `equals(Triangle)` method does not override the inherited `equals(Object)` method and instead it overloads `equals`. It is merely a convenience method that is helpful if you know that you are comparing two nonnull objects from the same class, which is often the case. Furthermore, this method can be used to simplify slightly the implementation of the `equals(Object)` method in the Triangle class as follows:

```
public boolean equals(Object obj) //in Triangle class
{
  if( ! (obj instanceof Triangle) ) return false;
  return this.equals((Triangle) obj);
}
```

You might wonder how the Java library developers handled the implementation of `equals` for the library classes. At least some of them, such as the `equals` methods for some Collection classes, were implemented so that objects of two different classes can be equal. For example, the expression

```
new HashSet().equals(new TreeSet())
```

returns true. Therefore, this version of `equals` does not require class identity. Instead, the Java developers specified in the Set interface the required semantics of the `equals` method for any class implementing this interface. In particular, they said that two Sets are equal if they have the same size and if every member of one Set is also a member of the other Set. This requirement prohibits any class implementing the Set interface from implementing the `equals` method in any other way, and so the Liskov Substitution Principle is satisfied.

As a final note, if you do decide to override the inherited `equals(Object)` method from the Object class, you should also override the Object class' `hashCode` method so that whenever two objects are equal, they also have the same hash code value. This property is needed to ensure that objects of your class can properly be used as keys in a hash table. See the references for more details.

SECTION 4.8 CASE STUDY: OVERRIDING THE CLONE METHOD IN JAVA

Let us do one more cases study. In this case, we will consider the `clone` method inherited from the Object class. This method's intention is to create and return an object that is a clone of the object on which the method is invoked. We will discuss how you properly go about overriding it in your class. It has even more subtle issues than `equals`.

Despite the fact that all classes inherit a `clone` method from the Object class, objects are not actually clonable unless their class implements the Cloneable interface. This interface is just an empty "flag" interface indicating that objects of your class are allowed to be cloned. That is, if someone calls the `clone` method on an object of a class that does not implement that interface, a CloneNotSupportedException will be thrown. Furthermore, the `clone` method inherited from the Object class is protected rather than public, which means not all objects have permission to invoke that method.

If you want to allow everyone to clone objects of your class, you need to state that your class implements the Cloneable interface and you need to implement a public `clone` method in your class with the following header:

```
public Object clone()
```

You also need to determine how deep a clone you want to create. That is, if the object to be cloned includes references to other objects in its instance variables (the way the Triangle class refers to Point objects in its instance variables), you need to decide whether those objects should be cloned as well. A *shallow* clone is one for which only the object itself is copied and, as a result, the data referred to by the object's instance variables are shared among all copies. This is the default behavior of the Object class' `clone` method, which just makes a bit copy of the object being cloned, and so all references in the object to other objects are copied but the other objects themselves are not copied. A *deep* clone is one in which all objects referred to by instance variables are also (deeply) cloned.

For example, in the case of the Triangle class discussed above, a deep clone is a completely independent object. However, a shallow clone is tied to the original object in that they share Point objects in their instance variables. In the latter case, any change to the *x* or *y* value of a Point forming a corner of the clone or the original will also cause a corresponding change in the other object.

To help you understand these issues better, let us write both deep and shallow `clone` methods for the Triangle and ColoredTriangle classes discussed above.

Let us first write a shallow `clone` method for these classes to see how it needs to be implemented. An obvious approach to implementing Triangle's `clone` method is to create a new Triangle and assign to its instance variables the same values as the original:

```
//in the Triangle class—inelegant shallow clone implementation
public Object clone() {
  return new Triangle(p1, p2, p3);
}
```

This method works fine, unless a subclass of Triangle, such as ColoredTriangle, doesn't have its own `clone` method and instead inherits its superclass' `clone` method. In that case, if `ct.clone()` is invoked on a ColoredTriangle `ct`, the result will not be an object of class ColoredTriangle, but instead will be an object of class Triangle, which is not what was desired. As a result, if this implementation of `clone` is used for the Triangle class, then all subclasses of Triangle, such as ColoredTriangle, will need to include their own implementations of `clone` to override the Triangle's `clone` method. Furthermore, the Triangle's `clone` method cannot be reused to help implement the subclass' `clone` method since a call to `super.clone()` will return a Triangle object instead of the desired subclass object. Therefore, this implementation of `clone` for the Triangle class is less than elegant.

The Object class' implementation of `clone`, as mentioned above, creates a bit copy of the object being cloned and so always produces an object of the correct class. Therefore, the proper way to implement `clone`, whether for a shallow or deep clone, is to start by calling `super.clone()`. Hopefully the ancestors of your class have also followed the rule of either not implementing `clone` at all or implementing it in a way that starts with a call to `super.clone()`. If so, the object returned by `super.clone()` will be a new object of the correct class, all of whose inherited attributes have already been set to the proper values. All that remains to be done is to adjust, if necessary, the values of the attributes of the subclass that are not inherited from its superclass. If we just want a shallow clone of the Triangle class, the values assigned to the attributes of a Triangle object by the Object class' `clone` method do not need to be changed. In that case, the proper implementation of Triangle's `clone` is just:

```
//in the Triangle class—correct shallow clone implementation
public Object clone() {
  try {
    return super.clone();
  } catch (CloneNotSupportedException e) {
    e.printStackTrace();
    return null;
  }
}
```

Note that the Object class' `clone` method may throw a CloneNotSupported Exception, which should be caught by the public `clone` method in your class unless one of your class' ancestors already caught this exception in its `clone` method. The exception will never be thrown if your class implements the Cloneable interface, and so, in that case, the body of the `catch` block can be rather arbitrary.

Now ColoredTriangle's shallow `clone` method can be implemented a little more simply:

```
//in the ColoredTriangle class—correct shallow clone implementation
public Object clone() {
  return super.clone();
}
```

or ColoredTriangle can just inherit the Triangle class' `clone` method. The result is the same in either case.

Let us now create deep `clone` methods for our Triangle and ColoredTriangle classes. A logical and correct approach to implementing `clone` for the Triangle class is as follows:

```
//in the Triangle class—correct deep clone implementation
public Object clone() {
  try {
    Triangle clone = (Triangle) super.clone();
    clone.p1 = (Point) p1.clone();
    clone.p2 = (Point) p2.clone();
    clone.p3 = (Point) p3.clone();
    return clone;
  } catch (CloneNotSupportedException e) {
    e.printStackTrace();
```

```
      return null;
    }
  }
```

Notice how we elegantly use the `clone` method of the Point class (which implements Cloneable) to copy the endpoints.

For the ColoredTriangle class, we can attempt to implement the deep clone similarly:

```
  //in the ColoredTriangle class—incorrect implementation
  public Object clone() {
    try {
      ColoredTriangle clone = (ColoredTriangle) super.clone();
      clone.color = (Color) color.clone();
      return clone;
    } catch (CloneNotSupportedException e) {
      e.printStackTrace();
      return null;
    }
  }
```

Notice how the superclass' `clone` method handles deep cloning of the inherited attributes, and so the color attribute, is the only thing left to be deep cloned in this method. Unfortunately, this code doesn't quite work. The Java compiler will complain because the Color class does not implement Cloneable. What do we do now? (It turns out that actually we do not need to clone Color objects because they are immutable—for more details see the discussion of immutability in the next chapter—but for the sake of discussion, let us pretend we want to clone the color field of the ColoredTriangle.) We have run into a general problem: How do you create a deep clone of an object if the attributes of the object do not implement Cloneable? Let us attempt to solve this problem in the case of the ColoredTriangle class by using the Color class' constructor:

```
  //in the ColoredTriangle class—incorrect implementation
  public Object clone() {
    try {
      ColoredTriangle clone = (ColoredTriangle) super.clone();
      clone.color = new Color(color.getColorSpace(),
                    color.getColorComponents(color.getColorSpace(),
                    null), color.getAlpha());
      return clone;
    } catch (CloneNotSupportedException e) {
      e.printStackTrace();
      return null;
    }
  }
```

This code is inelegant but is actually quite typical of what you need to do when you want to make a deep clone of a class whose attributes do not also implement Cloneable.

However, the inelegance is the least of this method's problems. More importantly, this method is not always going to produce an exact deep clone. Suppose you created a subclass of Color:

```
public class NamedColor extends Color
{
  private String name;
  public NamedColor(String s, int rgb) {
    super(rgb);
    name = s;
  }
  public String getName() { return name; }
}
```

and now consider the following user code:

```
NamedColor mauve = new NamedColor("Mauve", 3456);
ColoredTriangle ct = new ColoredTriangle(mauve, new Point(0,0),
                         new Point(1,1), new Point(2,2));
ColoredTriangle clone = (ColoredTriangle) ct.clone();
```

The clone will be a legitimate ColoredTriangle object, but it will not be a deep clone of the original object `ct` since the clone's color is of class Color whereas `ct`'s color is of class NamedColor. The lesson here is that it is hard to create a deep clone of an object if the object's attributes are not Cloneable. Furthermore, even if all instance variables refer to Cloneable objects, those objects' `clone` methods may produce shallow clones of themselves, in which case, your `clone` method will not create a true deep clone.

Because of these problems, there are alternatives to using the `clone` method for copying objects. One alternative is to use reflection to find the exact class of an object and call one of its constructors.

What have we learned in these two case studies? In the preceding section of this chapter, we learned that an elegant `equals` method can be implemented in your classes as long as you are aware of all the pitfalls. In contrast, creating an elegant `clone` method depends not just on your understanding of the pitfalls, but also on the proper behavior of the superclasses of your class and, in the case of a deep clone, the behavior of the attributes of your class. That is, those classes must also properly implement their `clone` methods or your `clone` method may fail to produce the clone you want.

SECTION 4.9 REFACTORING

The preceding case studies were examples of attempts to make the code not just correct but also of high quality. But what if your code ends up being correct and of poor quality? For example, you might have variables or methods with poor names or your code might be brittle (*brittle* code is code that is hard to modify without breaking it). Code with those properties is said to "smell bad" [11]. Despite the bad smells, you may, justifiably, be hesitant to change the code to get rid of the smells for fear of introducing bugs.

The situation of needing to change existing, working code arises far more often than you might think. Even if you have working high quality (good smelling) code, you may need to change it. For example, after you have written such code, there is nothing to prevent your boss from coming to you and informing you that changes need to be made right away because of new requirements desired by customers. As they say, "Change happens. Deal with it."

When you have to make changes to working code, your goal should be to end up with code that is at least as well-designed, readable, and correct as the original code. Unfortunately, whenever you introduce changes, you can easily introduce bugs or new bad smells. For example, even if your code is well-designed so that changes are easy to make without breaking it, you may find that, after making the modifications, methods might no longer do what their names originally suggested or might do two or more completely different things. You might also find that the inheritance hierarchy for a class no longer is appropriate. When you notice such situations appearing in your code or design, then you should modify your code further to make it elegant again. But how do you do so without introducing new bugs?

Luckily, there are techniques that have been developed for modifying working code in a systematic way that get rid of existing bad smells and minimize the chance of introducing new bugs. These techniques are called *refactoring*. Martin Fowler, in his classic book on refactoring, says that "refactoring is the process of changing a software system in such a way that it does not alter the external behavior of the code yet improves its internal structure. It is a disciplined way to clean up code that minimizes the chances of introducing bugs"[11, pp. xvi and 53–54].

Refactoring makes the most sense within a testing framework. The idea behind it is to subdivide the process of changing the code into a sequence of small steps, each of which does not break the code. That is, after each step in the process of refactoring, the code should still be correct. As a result, you can (and should) be able to run your test suite and get exactly the same results as you did before the step, thus ensuring that you didn't break your code when you made changes.

To give you an idea of how refactoring works, let us look at a code sample. Suppose the following method is part of a hotel management package you wrote for determining the bills for customers. Such a method might need to use in its calculations the room rate, the number of days the customer stayed, the tax, and any discount coupons.

```
public double getRoomCharge()
{
  return ...an expression that computes room charge...
}
```

Now let us suppose that the management decides that the whole bill, which includes meal and movie charges, should be computed instead of just the room charge.

As a result, you insert additional code to compute those new charges and get the following:

```
public double getRoomCharge()
{
  //compute room charge, meal charge, and movie charge and return the sum
  return ...an expression that computes the sum of the room charge
          and meal charges and movie charges...;
}
```

Although this method may compute the correct result, it is also inelegant for two reasons. First of all, the name of the method is no longer totally appropriate in that the method now computes more than the room charge. Secondly, the method is much too complicated and doing too much work, resulting in a long and hard-to-read body. A clue that the body is too complicated is the need for a comment explaining what it is computing. Therefore, we will refactor the method to give it a new name and refactor it to clean up the body. After we have finished, we will review the code to see whether any more refactorings need to be done.

How do we give a method a new name and clean up the body of a method in a systematic way so that we don't break working code? There are two refactoring patterns, the "Rename Method" and "Introduce Explaining Variable" patterns [11, pp. 124–127 and 273–274] that have been designed to handle exactly this situation.

The Rename Method refactoring explains how to systematically change the name of the method in both the declaration of that method and in every applied occurrence of the method. In the following box, we explain how the Rename Method refactoring works.

The Rename Method Refactoring

The Rename Method refactoring is used to change the name of the method to something intention-revealing. The process of renaming a method might appear trivial at first glance in that all it involves is changing the method name and using the new name wherever the method is called. To find all the places that the method is called, you could just change the name of the method and then look for all the errors when you try to compile it. However, this approach is not the way refactoring is done. When refactoring, each step should leave the coding working correctly so that you can run your test suite to ensure no bugs were introduced during that step.

To change the name of a method, the Rename Method refactoring suggests the following steps:

1. Create a new method with the new name.
2. Copy the body of the old method into the new method.
3. Change the body of the old method to call the new method.

4. For each reference to the old method, change it to refer to the new method.
5. Eliminate the old method.

Note that none of these steps individually should break the code.

There are also other issues that need to be addressed when renaming methods. For example, if the original method overrides a superclass' method, then the programmer needs to decide whether the superclass' method name should also be changed so that the renamed method continues to override the inherited method. Also, if the original method name was part of an interface, the interface may need to be changed, which can lead to changes to other classes implementing the interface. If the interface cannot or should not be changed, then the original method needs to remain along with the new method, although, to avoid code duplication, the original method can just call the new method.

For example, consider a class that implements the ActionListener interface:

```
public class ButtonListener implements ActionListener {
    public void actionPerformed(ActionEvent e) {
        ...get the point where event occurred...
        ...create a Rectangle object centered at the point...
        ...draw the Rectangle in a window...
    }
}
```

You may not like the name of the `actionPerformed` method, and you might want to change it to something more intention-revealing like `drawRectangle-AtEvent`. But if you blindly use the Rename Method refactoring to do so, the compiler will complain that your class no longer implements the ActionListener interface. A better way to refactor the code is use the Extract Method refactoring to extract the body of the `actionPerformed` method and then have the `actionPerformed` method call the extracted method. Here is what the code looks like after such changes:

```
public class ButtonListener implements ActionListener
  {
  public void actionPerformed(ActionEvent e) {
    drawRectangleAtEvent(e);
  }
  private void drawRectangleAtEvent(ActionEvent e) {
    ...get the point where event occurred...
    ...create a Rectangle object centered at the point...
    ...draw the Rectangle in a window...
  }
}
```

Let us apply the Rename Method refactoring to our example to rename the method from `getRoomCharge` to `getTotalBill`. We first add a new method with the new name:

```
public double getTotalBill() { return 0; /* default value */ }
public double getRoomCharge()
{
  return ...an expression that computes the sum of the room
            charge and meal charges and movie charges...;
}
```

After testing that this change didn't break the code, we copy the body of `getRoomCharge` into `getTotalBill`:

```
public double getTotalBill()
{
  return ...an expression that computes the sum of the room
            charge and meal charges and movie charges...;
}
public double getRoomCharge()
{
  return ...an expression that computes the sum of the room
            charge and meal charges and movie charges...;
}
```

After testing again, we change the old method to call the new method:

```
public double getTotalBill()
{
  return ...an expression that computes the sum of the room
            charge and meal charges and movie charges...;
}
public double getRoomCharge()
{
  return getTotalBill();
}
```

After further testing, we change all the references in the code base to call the new method (not shown here) and test. We then eliminate the old method and end up with just our new method:

```
public double getTotalBill()
{
  return ...an expression that computes the sum of the room
            charge and meal charges and movie charges...;
}
```

Next we can apply the Introduce Explaining Variable refactoring to further clean up the code. This refactoring takes an expression or part of an expression and replaces it with a variable with an appropriate name. The details of it are in the following box.

The Introduce Explaining Variable Refactoring

The Introduce Explaining Variable refactoring involves replacing parts of an expression with new variables with intention-revealing names. Its intent is to break down a complicated expression into something more understandable. The steps are quite simple:

1. Declare a new local variable initialized to one part of the expression you want replaced.
2. In the complicated expression, replace that part with the new local variable.
3. Repeat this process for the other parts of the expression.

In our example, we will introduce three explaining variables, one for each of the three parts of the expression. We will call the three variables `roomCharge`, `mealCharge`, and `movieCharge`.

We first declare and initialize the local variable `roomCharge`:

We end up with the following code:

```
public double getTotalBill()
{
   double roomCharge = ...part of expression that computes room charge...;
   return ...an expression that computes the sum of the room charge and meal
            charges and movie charges...;
}
```

After testing, we replace the part of the expression corresponding to room charge with the `roomCharge` variable:

```
public double getTotalBill()
{
   double roomCharge = ...part of expression that computes room charge...;
   return roomCharge + ...an expression that computes the sum of the meal
                         charges and movie charges...;
}
```

Then we test again before we do the same for the other two new variables, to get the final form:

```
public double getTotalBill()
{
  double roomCharge = ...part of expression that computes room charge...;
  double mealCharge = ...part of expression that computes meal charge...;
  double movieCharge = ...part of expression that computes the movie charge...;
  return roomCharge + mealCharge + movieCharge;
}
```

Our code looks much better. Each expression is much more understandable, as is the final sum that is returned.

If each expression is still somewhat long and complicated and especially if that expression needs to be used again elsewhere, then it would make sense to continue refactoring. For example, we could use the Replace Temp with Query refactoring[11, pp. 120–123] . This refactoring extracts the expression assigned to a local variable and puts it into a new method. It then replaces every occurrence of the variable with a call to that method. The details of this refactoring are in the following box.

Let us use this refactoring for each of our three local variables. Initially, we will consider `roomCharge`. After declaring it final and compiling to ensure it is only assigned to once, we copy the right-hand side of the assignment and put it into a new method:

```
public double getTotalBill()
{
  final double roomCharge = ...expression that computes room charge...;
  double mealCharge = ...expression that computes meal charge...;
  double movieCharge = ...expression that computes movie charge...;
  return roomCharge + mealCharge + movieCharge;
}
public double getRoomCharge()
{
  return ...expression that computes room charge...;
}
```

After testing, we replace the right-hand side of the assignment with a call to the new method:

```
public double getTotalBill()
{
  final double roomCharge = getRoomCharge();
  double mealCharge = ...expression that computes meal charge...;
```

The Replace Temp with Query Refactoring

The Replace Temp with Query refactoring involves extracting an expression that was assigned to a local variable and putting that expression into a method. It then replaces every use of the local variable with a method call. Its intent is to simplify the method body by eliminating a local variable and to make the expression available outside the method body. Here are the steps:

1. Find a local variable that is assigned to only once.
2. Declare the local variable as final and recompile (to ensure it really is assigned to only once).
3. Copy the expression on the right-hand side of the assignment and put it into the body of a new method.
4. Replace the right-hand side of the assignment with a call to the new method.
5. Replace every use of the local variable with a call to the new method.
6. Remove the assignment statement and the declaration of the local variable.

There are some special situations that will need to be dealt with before this refactoring can be done. For example, the local variable that you want to replace may be assigned to more than once. In that case, try converting it "into" several local variables, each assigned to only once, using the Split Temporary Variable refactoring[11, pp. 128–130].

Also, if the expression has side effects, use Separate Query from Modifier refactoring to remove the side effects. (This refactoring should be done even if you do not intend to use the Replace Temp with Query refactoring, since an expression with side effects has a very bad smell.)

Another problem might be that there are other local variables that are used in the expression. In that case, the new method won't compile because those local variables are not declared in the new method. One solution is to pass these variables into the new method as parameters.

You may wonder about the performance hit of this refactoring, because, instead of computing the expression once and storing it in a local variable, you are recomputing it every time it is needed. If performance is a problem, the local variable can be put back, but most likely your performance problem is due to some other part of your code.

```
    double movieCharge = ...expression that computes movie charge...;
    return roomCharge + mealCharge + movieCharge;
}
public double getRoomCharge()
{
    return ...expression that computes room charge...;
}
```

We then test again and next replace every use of `roomCharge` with a call to the new method:

```
public double getTotalBill()
{
  final double roomCharge = getRoomCharge();
  double mealCharge = ...expression that computes meal charge...;
  double movieCharge = ...expression that computes movie charge...;
  return getRoomCharge() + mealCharge + movieCharge;
}
public double getRoomCharge()
{
  return ...expression that computes room charge...;
}
```

After testing, we eliminate the declaration of and assignment to `roomCharge`.

```
public double getTotalBill()
{
  double mealCharge = ...expression that computes meal charge...;
  double movieCharge = ...expression that computes movie charge...;
  return getRoomCharge() + mealCharge + movieCharge;
}
public double getRoomCharge()
{
  return ...expression that computes room charge...;
}
```

After more testing, we do the same refactoring for the `mealCharge` and `movieCharge` local variables. We end up with the following code:

```
public double getTotalBill()
{
  return getRoomCharge() + getMealCharge() + getMovieCharge();
}
public double getRoomCharge()
{
  return ...expression that computes room charge...;
}
public double getMealCharge()
{
  return ...expression that computes meal charge...;
}
```

```
public double getMovieCharge()
{
    return ...expression that computes movie charge...;
}
```

Look at how much more elegant our code is. Each of our methods is shorter and much clearer, because they are each doing one thing only and doing it well. Note also that, by using intention-revealing names for the methods and variables, the comments that were necessary in the original code sample are no longer necessary.

It is a good idea to get used to doing refactoring and testing continuously during code writing, whether that coding consists of adding functionality or just fixing errors. In particular, when you are adding new features to existing code, you should alternate between refactoring code (and testing) and adding new code (and testing).

As you may have noticed, refactoring can be a time-consuming process, especially when you are new at it, because of the need to break the refactoring into steps and test after each change. For this reason, software developers are sometimes reluctant to do refactoring when writing code. It is tempting to either leave the code with the bad smells or else attempt refactoring using short cuts that might result in new defects. Therefore, we are happy that some major advances in automating refactoring have occurred in recent years that simplify the process of refactoring. In particular, virtually all modern development environments (such as Eclipse and NetBeans) now include tools to do some of the most-used refactorings for you. You only need to specify the section of code to be refactored and the particular refactoring technique to apply to it, and the tool does the actual refactoring for you. In other words, the tool allows you to do a refactoring in just one step instead of many. For example, you can select a variable declaration in your code, choose the Rename Variable refactoring tool, specify a new name, and then the tool will change the declaration and all occurrences of the variable to the new name. However, not all refactoring patterns have been automated. Also, this automation does not eliminate the need for testing. The difference is that, with automated refactoring, you only need to test after each refactoring instead of after each step within each refactoring process.

Many of the guidelines we've introduced in this chapter or earlier chapters directly relate to the refactorings listed in [11]. Here are examples:

- If you find yourself needing comments to summarize sections of code in a method, the method may be too long and doing too many things. You should consider making each section a separate method using the "Extract Method" refactoring [11, p. 110].
- If you find a method that has been poorly named or whose role has changed so that its name is no longer intention-revealing, it is important at that point to change the name using the "Rename Method" refactoring [11, p. 273].
- If a section of code is repeated more than once, you should make the duplicated section into its own method using the "Extract Method" refactoring [11, p. 110].
- If a method is both a modifier with observable modifications and a function, use the "Separate Query from Modifier" refactoring [11, p. 279; 12].

- If you find a class that has a public instance variable, use the "Encapsulate Field" refactoring [11, p. 206].
- If you have magic numbers in your code, use the "Replace Magic Number with Symbolic Constant" refactoring [11, p. 204].
- If a method does one of two very different things based on a parameter, create separate methods for each parameter value using the "Replace Parameter with Explicit Methods" refactoring [11, p. 285].
- If you find that one of your public methods is really just a utility or auxiliary method that is used only by other methods in the class, make it private using the "Hide Method" refactoring [11, p. 303].
- If you find that two classes have common methods, use the "Pull Up Method" refactoring [11, p. 322] to move the method to a common superclass.

In later chapters of this text, you will find references to more refactorings, especially when we consider case studies in which we will iteratively enhance the code.

SECTION 4.10 CODE OPTIMIZATION

One final aspect of elegant code that needs to be mentioned in this chapter is efficiency. Well-written code performs its tasks using a reasonable amount of resources such as time and memory. Unfortunately, making complex changes to the code to optimize it is very hard on the readability of the code. How can you maximize the readability of the code and at the same time get the performance that you need?

A good programmer will write code that is readable and only later worry about optimization. Donald Knuth [16] found that "less than 4 percent of a program generally accounts for more than half of its running time." Therefore, you should first find out which code consists of that 4 percent, for example, by using code profiling, and then optimize only it.

Programmers make a common mistake when they try to optimize their code too early, for example, before the code has been written and thoroughly tested. Hand optimization may not be necessary because good compilers will do many optimizations for you. In fact, your hand optimizations may not only make the code less readable, but they may also make it harder for the compiler to do its optimizations.

That said, you should not leave *all* aspects of efficiency until after the code is written. The best optimizer is between your ears. Only you, and not the compiler, can choose the appropriate data structures and algorithms so that your code will execute efficiently. For example, you should always do simple time and/or space complexity analyses of your algorithms. If you need to write a sorting routine, implement an $O(n \log n)$ algorithm instead of an $O(n^2)$ one, unless you know it will never be used on large collections.

Guideline

Balance optimization needs with readability needs.

SECTION 4.11 SUMMARY AND FURTHER READING

Here is a summary of the ideas and guidelines introduced in this chapter.

- Choose a standard coding style and follow that style throughout all your code.
- Use intention-revealing names for all variables, methods, and classes so that they accurately describe the role or intentions of the things they are naming.
- Use methods, especially private auxiliary methods, for decomposition to reduce duplication of code and to raise the level of abstraction of the code.
- A method should do one thing only and do it well.
- All code in a method should execute at the same level.
- Functions (which return a value) should not modify any existing object's state in a way visible to other objects, and modifier methods (which modify one or more objects' state) should have "void" as the return type.
- Public methods should always keep objects in a well-formed state.
- Be aware that, although it can increase the efficiency of your code, caching values instead of computing them when they are needed can also increase the complexity and number of invariants of your classes.
- Always strive for "self-documenting code" that is so clear that no comments are necessary.
- If your code is so complicated that it needs explaining with lots of internal or external documentation, then the code should probably be rewritten.
- Write comments before or during writing the code, not after. "Build it in, don't add it on."
- The external documentation for a method should be sufficiently specific to exclude implementations that are unacceptable but sufficiently general to allow all implementations that are acceptable.
- Specify precisely all preconditions and postconditions for each of your methods in the external documentation. These conditions form the contract for your method.
- Try to make your methods do something appropriate in all cases so that there are no preconditions.
- Balance optimization needs with readability needs.

More detailed discussions of many of the topics in this chapter can be found in [4–6; 17, Appendix C; 18, Chapter 6].

Further references to documentation can be found in [6; 8, Chapter 19; 18, pp. 248–254; 19, item 28].

A more detailed discussion of testing and optimization techniques can be found in [9, Chapters 1–3 and 13].

EXERCISES

1. Back in Section 2.5, we created a class EnhancedRectangle that extends Rectangle. Give a better name for the EnhancedRectangle class and explain why it is better.
2. In Section 4.2, we used a parser as an example of how to extract code and put it into a new auxiliary method to remove code duplication. Study that example and suggest a way to remove even more code duplication than was done there.
3. Suggest new methods to replace `pop()` in the `Stack` class and `next()` in the `Iterator` interface so that the new methods follow the functions and modifiers rule given in Section 4.3, which states that every method should either be a void modifier method or a function method that does not modify the state of any objects.
4. Consider an object that maintains an array of integers whose values change over time. Suppose the object keeps track of the number of times it is asked to search the array for specific values. If the number of searches exceeds a threshold, then the object sorts the array to speed up future searches. In such an object, a call to

a search method, which should be a function that just returns a value, causes side effects in that the number of searches is incremented and the array is possibly sorted. Therefore, this object's search method appears to be breaking the guideline in Section 4.3 that says that functions should not have side effects. Does this fact mean that the object should cease and desist in counting the searches and in sorting? Briefly explain.

5. Tell what is inelegant about the following implementation of a class. Hint: It relates to class invariants.

```
/* Objects of this class are labels
   with red backgrounds.*/
public class RedLabel extends JLabel
{
    public RedLabel() { }
    public void initialize()
    {
        setBackground(Color.red);
    }
}
```

6. Consider the following method and its Javadoc-formatted header:

```
/**
 * Copies the values of array A into
 * array B in the same order.
 * The old values in B are lost.
 * The array B must have the same
 * length as array A.
 *
 * @param A the integer array to be
 * copied
 * @param B the integer array into
 * which the values will be copied
 */
public void copyArray(int[] A, int[] B)
  { ... }
```

   a. What are the preconditions for this method?
   b. Is there any ambiguity in its behavior?
   c. What are the postconditions?

7. Suppose a class has an invariant condition that must be true for any objects of that class to be well-formed. You have at least two options regarding checking the invariant:
   a. You could check the invariant in each modifier method just before it returns and throw an exception if the invariant fails.
   b. You could document the invariant but not include any code that checks the invariant.

   Each option is better in certain situations. Give at least one such situation where the first option is better and one where the second option is better.

8. Suppose you create a doubly linked list DLL that has three instance variables: head, tail, length. The data is stored in Node objects with next and prev pointers. For each implementation below, give all the class invariants that must be satisfied for a DLL to be well-formed.
   a. Implementation 1: The head and tail pointers point to null if the list is empty.
   b. Implementation 2: The head and tail pointers always point to special dummy Nodes that are just placeholders.

9. Suppose you are implementing a method to compute a formula that involves dividing a quantity by a variable x. You realize that if x is 0, then an ArithmeticException will be thrown. How should you handle this exceptional situation? Here are some alternatives:
   a. Ignore the problem and let your method throw an ArithmeticException.
   b. Test for x == 0 before doing the computation and, if found, print an error message and return 0.
   c. Surround the computation with a try/catch block and print an error message in the catch block before returning 0.

   Compare these alternatives. Is there a fourth alternative that is better than these three?

10. In Section 4.7, our final version of the `equals(Object)` method for the Triangle class included the line

```
if( obj == null ) return false;
```

   Why was that line included in the method? What is wrong with letting the `equals` method throw a NullPointerException instead?

11. In Section 4.7, we settled on the following implementation of the `equals(Object)` method for the Triangle class:

```
public boolean equals(Object obj)
{
    if( obj == null ) return false;
    if( obj.getClass() != this.getClass() )
        return false;
    Triangle otherTriangle = (Triangle)
        obj;
    return (p1.equals(otherTriangle.p1) &&
            p2.equals(otherTriangle.p2) &&
            p3.equals(otherTriangle.p3));
}
```

Some experts suggest that we add one more test at the beginning of this method:

```
if( this == obj ) return true;
```

Why would they suggest this additional test? Comment on the advantages and disadvantages of adding it.

12. In Section 4.7, we settled on the following implementation of the `equals(Object)` method for the Triangle class:

```
public boolean equals(Object obj)
{
   if( obj == null ) return false;
   if( obj.getClass() != this.getClass() )
       return false;
   Triangle otherTriangle = (Triangle)
       obj;
   return (p1.equals(otherTriangle.p1) &&
           p2.equals(otherTriangle.p2) &&
           p3.equals(otherTriangle.p3));
}
```

What, if anything is wrong with replacing the line

```
if( obj.getClass() != this.getClass() )
  return false;
```

with the line

```
if( obj.getClass() != Triangle.class )
  return false;
```

Explain your answer. Hint: Look at the implementation of the ColoredTriangle class' `equals (Object)`method.

13. The final version (version 3) of the `equals` method for the ColoredTriangle class in Section 4.7 can actually be simplified a little, because of the final form of the `equals` method in its Triangle superclass. Do the simplification.
14. Consider the following situation:
   a. A class A has Object as its superclass and a class B has class A as its superclass.
   b. Class A has a no argument constructor.
   c. Class B has an integer field `x` and a constructor with an integer argument for initializing `x`.
   d. A does not override the `equals` method inherited from Object.
   e. Class B overrides `equals` so that two objects of class B are considered equal if their field `x` has the same value in both objects:

```
public boolean equals(Object obj) //in
class B
{
  if( obj == null ) return false;
  if( obj.getClass() != this.getClass() )
      return false;
  if( ! super.equals(obj) ) return false;
  B b = (B) obj;
  return this.x == b.x;
}
```

   f. We test these classes with the following code:

```
B b1 = new B(1);
B b2 = new B(1);
System.out.println(b1.equals(b2));
```

   and "false" gets printed.

   The reason for overriding `equals` in class B was to allow two objects of class B to be equal if their fields x had the same value, but the test code shows that something is wrong. What is wrong? What is the fix?
15. In the Triangle and ColoredTriangle code in Section 4.7, we assumed that the fields always had non-null values. If we eliminate that assumption—that is, if we allow the fields to have the value null—then we need to modify the code in both class' `equals` methods, or else they might throw NullPointerExceptions. Fix both `equals` methods so that they never throw an exception, even if one or more fields are null.
16. In the Triangle (and ColoredTriangle) code in Section 4.7, we say two Triangles t1 and t2 are equal only if they have equal values in their corresponding instance variables. But shouldn't two Triangles be considered equal as long as they have the same three corner point values regardless of which instance variable stores which value? For example, what if, for Triangles t1 and t2, it were the case that `t1.p1 == t2.p1`, `t1.p2 == t2.p3`, and `t1.p3 == t2.p2`? Shouldn't the Triangles be considered equal in that case as well?
   a. Explain why or why not. Does it make a difference if our objects are four-sided figures instead of three-sided?
   b. Fix the Triangle class' `equals` method so that two Triangles are equal if they have the same three corner point values regardless of which instance variable stores which value.
17. Read the literature to determine a good way to override the Object class' `hashCode` method for any class and create a good implementation of that method for the Triangle class discussed in

Section 4.5. Assume that the Triangle class overrides the inherited `equals` method, as discussed in that section.

18. An alternative to cloning using constructors or calls to `super.clone()` is to serialize and then deserialize the object you wish to clone. The deserialization process will create a new copy of the object. Investigate Java's serialization features and implement a `clone()` method for the Triangle class that uses serialization to create the new copy.

19. An alternative to cloning is a "copy constructor." This constructor takes an object of the same class as an argument and creates and returns a new copy of that object. For example, consider the following shallow copy constructor for the Triangle class from Section 4.7:

```
public Triangle(Triangle t) {
   this.p1 = t.p1;
   this.p2 = t.p2;
   this.p3 = t.p3;
}
```

Create a similar copy constructor for the ColoredTriangle class. What happens if you call the Triangle class' copy constructor with a ColoredTriangle object as the parameter? What should happen?

20. Create a class A that has an ArrayList of java.awt.Rectangle objects as an instance variable. Make the class implement Cloneable by adding a `clone()` method that produces a deep copy.

21. Consider the following code:

```
String[] s = {"a", "b", "c"};
String[] sClone = s.clone();
s[0] = "d";
System.out.println(sClone[0]);
```

What is printed? Why?

22. Give an example of a situation where
    a. A shallow clone is preferable to a deep clone.
    b. A deep clone is preferable to a shallow clone.
    c. You do not want an object to be cloned.

23. In Section 3.10 of the preceding chapter, we used some refactorings to clean up the sorting code, but we never mentioned those refactorings by name. Which refactorings did we use?

24. In Section 4.9, we refactored the `getTotalBill` method by moving the calculations of the room charge, meal charge, and movie charge into three separate methods. An alternative that reduces the number of auxiliary methods and possible code duplication within those methods would be to rewrite the `getTotalBill` method as follows:

```
public double getTotalBill() {
  return chargeFor(ROOM) +
  chargeFor(MEALS) + chargeFor(MOVIES);
}
private double chargeFor(int type) {
  if( type == ROOM ) ... compute room
    charges ...
  else if( type == MEALS ) ... compute
    meal charges ...
  else if( type == MOVIES) ... compute
    movie charges ...
}
```

Is this refactoring better or worse than the one presented in Section 4.9? Explain.

25. Suppose you need functions to convert temperatures between the Fahrenheit and Celsius scales. Here are three ways to do it.
    a. Create two functions: `f2c` and `c2f` that each take a temperature as a double and return a double indicating the converted temperature.
    b. Do as in part (a) except name the functions `FahrenheitToCelsius` and `CelsiusToFahrenheit`.
    c. Create just one `convertTemperature(double temperature, int fromScale, int toScale)` function that takes three parameters: the temperature to be converted, the scale used by that temperature, and the scale to be used for the converted temperature .

    Which of those three approaches is most elegant? Explain.

    Suppose you are asked to include the Kelvin temperature scale as a third alternative, and so you need to write code that converts from any one of the three scales to any other of the three scales. Find the most elegant approach.

26. (For students familiar with the Swing and AWT packages) Use a series of refactoring techniques to make the following code more elegant. Do it step-by-step giving the new code after each refactoring. You are welcome to use the refactoring tools in your development environment if you wish.

```
import javax.swing.*;
import java.awt.*;
public class ExerciseRefactoring
{
  public static void main(String[] args)
  {
    MessageBox box = new MessageBox();
```

```
      box.createBox();
   }
}
class MessageBox
{
   public void createBox()
   {
      //create dialog box
      JFrame frame = new JFrame("A
          message for you");
      Container contentPane = frame.
          getContentPane();
      //add a row, include message in
      //this panel with a JLabel
      JPanel row2Panel = new JPanel();
      row2Panel.setLayout(new
          FlowLayout());
      JLabel message = new JLabel("Hi
          there");
      row2Panel.add(message);
      contentPane.add(row2Panel);
      frame.pack();
      frame.setVisible(true);
   }
}
```

27. Suppose a class has an instance variable whose name, due to refactorings, is no longer intention-revealing. In that case, the name should be changed. Give several reasons why it is not sufficient to search the class globally for occurrences of the name and change those occurrences to the new name. Does it make a difference whether the variable is public, private, protected, or package? What's wrong with just changing the name of the variable where it is declared and then letting the compiler find the other changes that need to be made?

28. Suppose a `Person` object knows the birthday of the person it represents and can tell you that birthday. Consider the method

    ```
    int processPerson(Person p)
    ```

    that computes and returns the age of the Person `p` by finding the difference between the current date and that person's birthday. If that action is all that the `processPerson` method does, then find a better signature for the method and explain why the new signature is better.

29. Suppose a `Person` object knows the height of the person it represents and can tell you the height through a `getHeight` method that returns the height in inches as an integer. Consider the method

    ```
    int getAverageHeight(Person p1,
        Person p2, Person p3)
    {
      int result = 0;
      int p1Height = p1.getHeight();
      int p2Height = p2.getHeight();
      int p3Height = p3.getHeight();
      result = (p1Height + p2Height
              + p3Height) / 3;
      return result;
    }
    ```

    that computes and returns the average height of the three Persons. Why isn't this method very elegant? Suggest changes to the design and implementation of this method to make it much more elegant. Give the Javadoc header and the declaration (but not implementation) of your new method.

30. Suppose you need to determine whether two Array Lists are equal except you don't care whether the orders of the elements in the two lists are the same. Here is one method that purportedly solves this problem:

```
public boolean specialArrayListEquals
    (ArrayList a1, ArrayList a2){
  boolean result = true;
  a1 = new ArrayList(a1); //clone a1
  a2 = new ArrayList(a2); //clone a2
  if(a1.size() == a2.size()){
    for(int i = 0; ((i < a1.size()) &&
    (result == true)); i++){
      Object o = a1.get(i);
      result = a2.contains(o);
      if(result){
        a1.remove(o);
        a2.remove(o);
      }
    }
  }
  return result;
}
```

    Debug this code, list everything you can think of that makes this code inelegant, and then come up with an elegant solution to the problem. Can you come up with an even more elegant solution if you know that there are no duplicate elements (i.e., no two equal elements) in each ArrayList?

31. Rewrite the following class using all the issues discussed in this chapter to make it as elegant as possible.

```
public class smelly {
  public static void main(String[]
    args){
    int[] x = new int[5];
    int kkk;
    for( kkk = 5; kkk > 0; kkk– )
      x[kkk-1] = kkk;
    stinky(x, 0);
  }
  public static void stinky(int[] y,
    int c){
    int[] z = new int[5];
    int ww;
    if( c == 4 ) {
      ww = 0;
      while( ww < 5 ) {
        System.out.print(y[ww] + " ");
        ww++;
      }
    }
    if( c == 4)
      System.out.println();
    if( c != 4 ) {
      for( ww = 1; ww <= 5; ww = ww+(z.
        length-4) ) {
        z[ww-1] = y[ww-1];
      }
      for( ww = c; ww < 5; ww++ ) {
        int f = z[ww];
        z[ww] = z[c];
        z[c] = f;
        stinky(z,c+1);
}}}}
```

32. (For students familiar with XML) Suppose a class A's purpose in life is to convert an object of another class B into textual form for storage to a file. Suppose there are three parts to objects of class B that we will call `var`, `const`, and `virtual`. Class A will convert these parts into Strings and enclose them in tags of the form `<tag kind="var">` and `</tag>` where the `kind` indicates the type of part, which for our purposes we will suppose are var, const, and virtual. These parts might also be nested. A well-designed class A will have a method to convert each kind of part of B into a String, and then it will append those strings to finish the conversion. Each method might look like the following:

```
public String convertVar() {
  String result = "<tag kind=\"var\">";
  //...convert rest of var part of B...
  result += "</tag>";
  return result;
}
public String convertConst() {
  String result = "<tag kind=\"const\">";
  //...convert rest of const part of B...
  result += "</tag>";
  return result;
}
public String convertVirtual() {
  String result = "<tag
  kind=\"virtual\">";
  //...convert rest of virtual part of
  B...
  result += "</tag>";
  return result;
}
```

a. What is a better name for class A?

b. There is duplicated code in these three methods in the way they add the starting and ending tags. Refactor these methods to eliminate the duplication and clean up the code.

REFERENCES

1. Fowler, M. and K. Scott, *UML Distilled,* 1st ed. Object Technology Series. 1997. Reading, MA: Addison-Wesley.
2. Sun Microsystems, I. *Java 2 Platform, Standard Edition, v 1.4.2, API Specification*. 2003. [Cited April 8, 2007; available from *http://java.sun .com/j2se/ 1.4.2/docs/api/.*]
3. Abelson, H. and G. Sussman, *Structure and Interpretation of Computer Programs*, 2nd ed. 1996. Cambridge, MA: MIT Press.
4. Beck, K., *Smalltalk Best Practice Patterns*. 1997. Upper Saddle River, NJ: Prentice Hall.
5. Langr, J., *Essential Java Style: Patterns for Implementation*. 2000. Prentice Hall.

6. Langr, J. *Enlightened Java Style*. Web page 2002. [Cited April 18, 2007; available from *http://www.sdmagazine.com/documents/s=4077/sdm0203c/0203c.htm.*]
7. Kernigan, B.W. and R. Pike, *The Practice of Programming*. Professional Computing Series. 1999. Reading, MA: Addison-Wesley.
8. McConnell, S., *Code Complete, A Practical Handbook of Software Construction*. 1993. Redmond, WA: Microsoft Press.
9. Larman, C. and R. Guthrie, *Java 2 Performance and Idiom Guide*. 2000. Upper Saddle River, NJ: Prentice Hall.
10. Meyer, B., *Object-Oriented Software Construction*. 2nd ed. 1997. Upper Saddle River, NJ: Prentice-Hall.
11. Fowler, M., *Refactoring, Improving the Design of Existing Code*. Object Technology Series. 1999. Reading, MA: Addison-Wesley.
12. Henney, K., A tale of two patterns. *Java Report*, 2000. 5(12) 84–88.
13. Kernigan, B.W. and P.J. Plauger, *The Elements of Programming Style*. 1978. New York: McGraw-Hill.
14. Sun Microsystems, I. *Javadoc*. 2006. [Cited April 8, 2007; available from *http://java.sun.com/j2se/javadoc/.*]
15. Sun Microsystems, I. *Java 2 Platform, Standard Edition, v 1.5.0, API Specification*. 2004. [Cited April 8, 2007; available from *http://java.sun.com/j2se/1.5.0/docs/api/.*]
16. Knuth, D., *An empirical study* of FORTRAN programs. *Software Practice and Experience*, 1971. 1(2): p. 105–133.
17. Eckel, B., *Thinking in Java*. 1998. Upper Saddle River, NJ: Prentice Hall.
18. Hunt, A. and D. Thomas, *The Pragmatic Programmer, from Journeyman to Master*. 2000. Reading, MA: Addison-Wesley.
19. Bloch, J., *Effective Java Programming Language Guide*. The Java Series. 2001. Reading, MA: Addison-Wesley.

5

Elegance and Classes

SECTION 5.0 INTRODUCTION

In previous chapters, we have discussed some foundational topics necessary for developing a good object-oriented design of a software system. In particular, we discussed the features of object-oriented languages and some of the advantages over other types of languages that they provide to a designer and programmer. We also discussed low-level implementation issues regarding these features.

In this chapter, we will discuss how and when to use these features and we will introduce other guidelines to help design and build elegant systems "from scratch." We will compare various possible competing designs of systems in terms of the classes involved, their responsibilities, their relationships with their collaborators, and their implementations.

SECTION 5.1 STARTING OUT FINDING CLASSES AND THEIR RELATIONSHIPS

In [1], the authors state, "The hard part about object-oriented design is decomposing a system into objects." In this section, we will discuss some techniques to help you get started with such a decomposition.

Let us suppose that we are asked by a customer to create a new application. As we briefly discussed in Chapter 1, we should not start by writing code. Instead, we need start at a higher level. Here is a simplified outline of the steps that should be taken:

1. We need to develop a precise specification of the software system.
2. We need to determine what classes to create and what will be the responsibilities or behaviors of objects of those classes and of the other objects with which they collaborate.
3. We need to specify these behaviors more precisely by designing the *protocol,* or public interfaces, of the classes in the design.
4. Finally, we can code the classes and the methods that implement their protocols.

We will discuss these concepts and some of the issues they raise by considering a very simple project. Let us suppose that our goal is to develop a program for a customer that allows us to gather statistics on the frequency of occurrence of words in text files. More precisely, let us suppose that the project was initially presented to us by the customer in the form of the following statements:

```
When the Java program starts, it analyzes the specified
text file. It constructs a summary report regarding each
word that occurs in the file and the number of times that
word occurs, sorted from most frequently occurring word to
least frequently occurring.
```

Students with one or two semesters of Java programmming should quite easily be able develop a Java program with the specified behavior, but there is a good possibility that the program could be rejected by the customer as inadequate. Do you see the problem? The description of the desired program is far too vague. Before moving to steps 2–4 of the outline above, the customer needs to be queried for further clarification to avoid wasting time writing code that is not what the customer really wants. In other words, before the design can begin, a precise specification needs to be created.

Let us see what is wrong with the specification for our word frequency program. You should be able to easily come up with a half dozen unanswered questions about the program. Here are some such questions:

1. What is the user interface for this program? In particular, how does the program know what text file to analyze? For example, does the program display a dialog box, does it ask the user to type a file name on a command line, or does it expect the user to supply the name as a command-line argument when starting up the program?
2. What should happen if the user specifies the name of a file that is nonexistent?
3. What should the format of the summary be? Can it be specified by the user?
4. When counting occurrences of words, does capitalization matter? Can the user specify how to treat capitalization?
5. Can the same execution run of the program be used to analyze several text files, or do you need to rerun the program whenever you want to analyze another file?
6. What is meant by a "word"? What distinguishes a word from an arbitrary sequence of characters? Are we counting only words that appear in a dictionary? If so, which dictionary?
7. When counting occurrences of words, do we distinguish between singular and plural forms of the same word, such as "shell" versus "shells"? How about "mouse" versus "mice"?
8. When reporting the results, what order should be used for two words that have the same frequency of occurrence?
9. Is the efficiency of the program regarding space or time an important concern?
10. Is the program going to be enhanced later to deal with input other than text files and with other forms of summary reports?

One of the techniques that are useful for clarifying the vague parts of a specification is to create, with the help of the customer, "use cases" or "user stories." A *use case* is a sequence of steps indicating how the program is to behave in a certain situation to achieve a particular goal. To develop a complete specification, there should be a use case for each of the various ways the system is expected to behave for each goal. Because our project is so simple, there won't be many use cases. In fact, for our project, only one use case is needed.

Let us suppose that the customer decided that the use case should have the following steps:

1. The user starts up the program by typing the following command on the command line of a console window: "java," followed by the name of the program, followed by the full path name of the text file. For example, the command might be

```
java WordCounter /users/smith/Hamlet.txt
```

2. The program checks that the file exists. If not, it reports an error message and exits.
3. The program traverses the file, treating each byte as a character and treating each sequence of characters not containing any delimiters as a word. The delimiter characters are Java's default whitespace characters.
4. The program keeps track of the number of occurrences of each word. Two words are considered equal if and only if they contain exactly the same sequence of characters.
5. The program prints to the console window a list of all the words and their frequencies, with words with the highest frequency first and with one word and frequency (separated by a tab) per line.
6. The program quits.

Notice that the use case actually has two variations, one of them successful and one unsuccessful. These variations define different *scenarios* of the use case. The successful scenario is the one where the word frequencies get computed and displayed. The unsuccessful scenario is where the program detects that there is no file with the given name and reports an error message.

The different use cases for a software system can be displayed in a UML use case diagram. Our application is so simple that such a diagram is not all that helpful, but for more complex software systems, it can provide a very helpful overview of the goals and uses of the system. See Figure 5.1 for a use case diagram for our word frequency counter application. In such a diagram, each circle corresponds to another use case. The stick figure corresponds to an *actor*, which is a role that a user

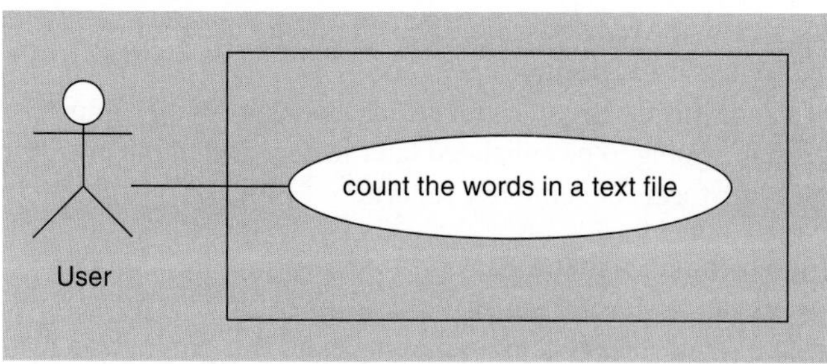

FIGURE 5.1 A use case diagram for our word frequency counter application.

of the system can play. In our case, there is only one such role, namely the role of the user typing in the command on the command line to run the program. See Appendix A for more information regarding UML use case diagrams.

Note that the steps in the use case provide answers to the first seven of the unanswered questions above, but it doesn't give us all the information we need. To finish our specification so that we can proceed to the next steps in the software design process, let us answer the remaining questions somewhat arbitrarily:

- If two words have the same frequency, they should be reported in alphabetical order using the ASCII ordering.
- The efficiency of the program is important enough that only one read-through of the text file is permitted by the program. Furthermore, the program is not allowed to copy the whole text file into memory, since it might use up too much memory.
- The program is going to be enhanced later to deal with other inputs and outputs of an as-yet-unknown form.

Now that we have a more precise specification of the project, we can begin to think about the design. In particular, we need to determine what objects and classes will be used in our design.

There are many possible candidates for classes, there are many ways to divide the work among them, and there are many ways to have the classes interact. For example, the number of classes in a design could be one or it could be in the hundreds. The responsibilities could all be in one class with the other classes being just behaviorless data holders, or a design could divide the responsibilities evenly among the participating classes of objects. The collaborations between the objects could be extensive, with every object communicating directly with every other object, or the collaborations could be minimal, with each object communicating with as few other objects as possible. With virtually unlimited choices, how should you proceed?

Before reading any further, it is valuable to attempt to come up with your own design to compare to the forthcoming design. You may even come up with a better design than we do.

Extract Nouns and Verbs

An initial but overly simplistic way to obtain candidate classes for a design is to study the project specification and extract all the nouns. Each noun can correspond to a potential object or class. Similarly, by extracting the verbs, we can get potential actions or behaviors of the objects.

Here are some of the nouns used in our specification:

program, user, file, word, number, times, report, pathname, capitalization, characters, line, window, name, character

Some of those nouns seem to correspond to useful classes, such as a Program class that could be in charge of the whole process (although a better name could also be chosen for such a class) and File and Report classes. But it is not clear whether the rest of the nouns would correspond to meaningful classes in our design. For example, do we need a User class? Do we need a Word class, or will the String class suffice for representing words?

Let's also look at some of the verbs in the specification:

starts, analyzes, constructs, returns, occurred

Again, it is clear that some of those words do correspond to useful actions that we will want our objects to perform, such as "construct" and "analyze," but most of the verbs are not at all helpful in determining what behaviors our objects should have.

Use Concepts from the Application Domain

One problem with the noun and verb technique is that it relies too much on the particular words used in the specification. In addition to the candidates that that technique provides, it is valuable to look at the problem domain for additional candidates. For example, if you are designing a Monopoly game, the problem domain is board games. Natural candidates for classes in this domain include Player, Piece, and Board, and candidates for actions include moving a piece. If you are designing an application for drawing pictures, natural candidates for classes include Picture, Tool, Paint, and Color, and candidates for actions include drawing and erasing.

Use CRC Cards

One excellent approach for deciding on the classes, their behaviors, and their responsibilities is to use CRC cards. A *CRC card* is just a note card (4″ × 6″ or maybe 5″ × 7″) that corresponds to one class in the design. CRC stands for "class, responsibilities, and collaborators" in that the card is divided into three sections, one for the class name, one for the class' responsibilities, and one for the class' collaborators. One of the advantages of using actual paper cards is that their small size forces you to summarize the responsibilities of each class in a few words and so helps the design team avoid getting bogged down in low-level details too soon. Another advantage of using paper cards (in contrast to cards on a computer screen) is that they can be easily moved around, regrouped, and carried by members of the design team during role playing or during design activities.

A good way to use such cards is through role playing. When doing role playing, blank cards are handed out to members of the design team, one card per person. Then the people act out a use case for the project. As the team members play their roles, they may realize that a new class may need to be created, in which case one of the members with a blank card writes the name of that new class on his/her card. From that point on, that person plays the role of an object of that class. Each time some new action needs to be performed, the team decides which class has the responsibility for performing that task, and the team member holding the card for that class writes the responsibility down on the card. The team member also writes down the other classes that the class needs to collaborate with in order to accomplish the job. Such role playing should be performed for the main use cases of the application.

Role playing can also be augmented in many ways. For example, it is sometimes helpful to use an actual physical object to pass around to indicate whose method is currently being executed in the thread under discussion.

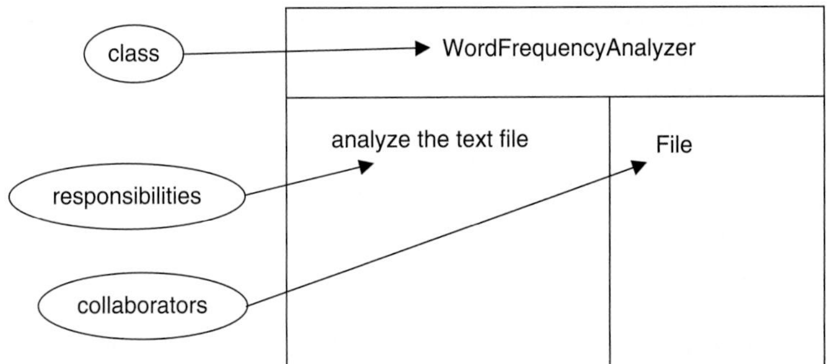

FIGURE 5.2
A CRC card for the WordFrequencyAnalyzer class.

Let's use CRC cards to help us with the design of the word frequency counter project. Along the way, you'll notice that we go back and forth between the cards as we refine our design.

The core of the program is the analysis of the text file. A class has to be responsible for that analysis, and so let us start by creating a "WordFrequencyAnalyzer" class and give it that responsibility. See Figure 5.2 for our first CRC card. Let us suppose that a WordFrequencyAnalyzer object will be given a File from which it will get the words to analyze, and so the WordFrequencyAnalyzer object will collaborate with a File object. We have added its basic responsibility and its collaborator to the card in Figure 5.2.

Do we now need to create a CRC card for the File class? Technically, we should do so and we should list the responsibilities and collaborators of that class. However, to simplify our presentation and because the standard File class in the java.io library meets our needs, we won't create a CRC card for it at this time.

Once the WordFrequencyAnalyzer has finished its analysis, the results need to be printed. The WordFrequencyAnalyzer could be responsible for this action, but it seems more elegant to give a different object that responsibility. This decision then leads to the question as to how the WordFrequencyAnalyzer is going to store and make available the results of its analysis. Because storing or maintaining information is a responsibility that seems just as important as manipulating information, let us create a new WordFrequencyCollection class that stores the results of the analysis. We now have a second CRC card to create. See Figure 5.3. Once we add

WordFrequencyCollection	
store and edit data regarding words and their frequencies make data available	

FIGURE 5.3 The WordFrequencyCollection CRC card.

this new class, we need to go back to the CRC card for WordFrequencyAnalyzer and add new responsibilities and a new collaborator. The new collaborator is the WordFrequencyCollection class, and the new responsibilities include creating, adding data to, and then making available the WordFrequencyCollection that contains the results of the analysis of the text file.

We will make the WordFrequencyCollection class responsible for making all its data available for clients, but we will leave formatting and print that data to other classes.

We now have a rough, very high-level design of our system. The program will create a WordFrequencyAnalyzer object, pass it the file to analyze, tell it to analyze the file, and finally tell it to return the resulting WordFrequencyCollection object. Then the program will get the data from this object and print it to the console.

Let us now refine our design a little. First of all, where does the WordFrequencyAnalyzer get the File to analyze? Our top level design says it comes from the program. Therefore, let us add a new CRC card for a class containing the main program. Let us call that class the WordCounter class. See Figure 5.4 for its CRC card. It has responsibilities for checking for a nonexistent file, creating the File and WordFrequencyAnalyzer, and asking the analyzer to analyze the file. It is also responsible for getting and printing the result. That result is stored in a WordFrequencyCollection object.

Next, let us refine the method by which the WordFrequencyAnalyzer analyzes the text file. This object needs first to create an empty WordFrequencyCollection object. It then needs to repeatedly get the next word from the file and process it. But how can it do that job? The File object corresponding to the text file has no methods for extracting words from the file. A FileReader object from the java.io library might be useful here, except that it reads only a character at a time and we want it to read a word at a time. It turns out that the java.util.Scanner class has just the abilities we need. Therefore, we will add it as a collaborator in the WordFrequencyAnalyzer's CRC card. The final copies of our three CRC cards are as they appear in Figures 5.2–5.4 except that the WordFrequencyAnalyzer's card has two more collaborators: WordFrequencyCollection and Scanner.

We now have a sufficiently refined design to be able to proceed to the next step. However, we would first like to point out that there are many possible variations on

FIGURE 5.4 The WordCounter CRC card.

WordCounter	
report an error if there is no file with a given name create a File and a WordFrequencyAnalyzer initiate the analysis get and print the result	File WordFrequency-Analyzer WordFrequency-Collection

this design. For example, the WordCounter could create the Scanner and pass that object to the WordFrequencyAnalyzer instead of a File object. Which is better? This question is an exercise at the end of the chapter.

We would also like to point out that in a larger project, further low-level details of the design and issues related to the other use cases of the system would need to be considered in order to develop a more complete design before moving on to the next step of the process. Since our design is so simple and since we are just introducing these topics rather than attempting to cover them exhaustively, we will move on now.

Class Protocols

Now that we have potential classes and their responsibilities and collaborators, we will proceed to construct the protocols, or public interfaces, of all the classes in our design. As a first step, we will convert each CRC card to a class and each responsibility to a method. However, keep in mind that, in general, not all responsibilities of a class will ultimately correspond to methods of that class. Similarly, not every CRC card will ultimately end up being implemented as a class nor will all classes in the final implementation necessarily come from the initial set of CRC cards. For example, we never created a card for the String class, although we will certainly use that class. Also, a card could correspond to a Java interface, and we might need to create one or more concrete classes that implement that interface.

Here is our first attempt at the classes and protocols, obtained by turning each responsibility into a method and adding constructors:

```
public class WordCounter
{
  public WordCounter(); //constructor
  public void checkFileExistence(String filename);
  public File createFile();
  public WordFrequencyAnalyzer createAnalyzer();
  public void initiateAnalysis();
  public getAndPrintResult();
}
public class WordFrequencyAnalyzer
{
  public WordFrequencyAnalyzer(); //constructor
  public void analyzeText(File file);
  public WordFrequencyCollection getResults();
}
public class WordFrequencyCollection
{
  public WordFrequencyCollection(); //constructor
  public void editCollection();
  public String toString();
}
```

Note that, in the process of constructing these protocols for the classes on our CRC cards, we kept in mind the issues discussed in the last chapter regarding methods and method signatures. That is, we attempted to use intention-revealing method names, and we used verb phrases for names of modifier methods.

At this point, it is valuable to step back and decide whether these protocols are appropriate. The methods in the second class seems appropriate, but not the methods in the WordCounter class or the WordFrequencyCollection class. Let us inspect these classes in more detail.

Almost all the responsibilities of the WordCounter class are just steps of the main method that the user would call to do the analysis. They could be implemented as private methods in the WordCounter class, but they do not belong in the public interface. Therefore, a more appropriate protocol for the WordCounter class is the following:

```
public class WordCounter
{
  public static void main(String[] args);
}
```

Regarding the WordFrequencyCollection class, what does the `editCollection` method do? It is quite meaningless. The responsibility of "managing the collection" is too vague and should be refined down to several methods. The only one we really need for our application is a method for adding new words to the collection. So we will add that method to our protocol:

```
public class WordFrequencyCollection
{
  public WordFrequencyCollection(); //constructor
  public void add(String word);
  public String toString();
}
```

The WordFrequencyCollection class is also responsible for making the results available. The protocol above does so through the `toString` method. However, such an approach is not very helpful to clients. According to Java conventions, the `toString` method is supposed to create a humanly readable form of the state of the object, not to make available data from the class to users of the class. Consider, for example, a user who only wants to know how many different words appear in the file, regardless of their frequency. Under the current design, that user would need to search and parse the output of the `toString` method to find that information. How can we better make the data in the collection available?

There are a variety of approaches that could be taken. For example, the collection could have an `iterator` method that returns an Iterator over the words in the collection. Also, there could be a method that, for each word, returns the frequency of occurrence of that word. Following this approach, we get a much better protocol for the WordFrequencyCollection class:

```
public class WordFrequencyCollection implements Iterable<String>
{
  public WordFrequencyCollection(); //constructor
  public void add(String word);
```

```
    public Iterator<String> iterator();
    public int getFrequency(String word);
}
```

With these protocols in place, we have reached the point where we can begin implementing these classes. For example, here is one possible implementation of the `main` method of the WordCounter class:

```
public class WordCounter
{
  public static void main(String[] args)
  {
    //create the file
    File file = new File(args[0]);
    //test to see whether the file exists and can be read
    try {
      new FileReader(file);
    } catch (FileNotFoundException e) {
      System.out.println("error: file cannot be read");
      System.exit(0);
    }
    //analyze the file
    WordFrequencyAnalyzer analyzer =
                                    new WordFrequencyAnalyzer();
    analyzer.analyzeText(file);
    //get and display the results
    WordFrequencyCollection collection = analyzer.getResults();
    for(String word : collection) {
      System.out.println(word + ":" + collection.getFrequency(word) );
    }
  }
}
```

There is still some low-level design left to work out before implementing the remaining classes, such as determining how the WordFrequencyCollection stores its data. We leave the remaining design and implementation as an exercise.

The class diagram containing these three classes is shown in Figure 5.5.

The Big Picture

Let us review the process we followed with our program. The first step was to get a precise specification of the problem. Use cases were helpful in this step. The next step was to determine what classes and their responsibilities and collaborators are needed to accomplish our task. CRC cards were helpful in this step. The third step consisted of determining the precise protocol or public interface of the classes in our design. The final step was implementing the classes.

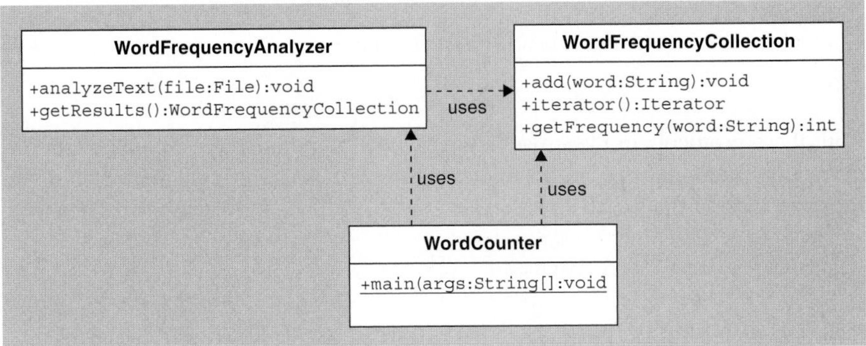

FIGURE 5.5 The word frequency analyzer classes.

The word frequency counter example should give you the basic idea of how to execute each of these steps of the design process and the tools that you might want to use along the way. You may choose to use a different approach for designing and implementing a program, but the general lessons learned here and the tools introduced, such as CRC cards and use cases, should be valuable regardless of your approach.

One of the lessons to be learned from this discussion can be summarized very generally:

Guideline

When working in the early high-level design phase, keep the discussion at a high level. In particular, avoid wasting time on implementation details and low-level data representations at the initial stages.

How well have we stayed at a high level in the initial stages of the design of the word frequency counter program? We could have done better at avoiding references to low-level value classes. For example, we could have referred to the words of the text file as objects of a "Word" class instead of as Strings. One advantage of storing our words in such an object instead of in a String is that other behavior can be added to it and other information than the sequence of characters can be stored in it, such as the line and column number of the start of the word in the original text file. This extra behavior and information might make the Word class more generally useful. For example, knowing the line and column number of a word would be useful in an enhanced version of our program that highlights the occurrence of words in a window displaying the contents of the text file.

Similarly, we could have represented the text file by a TextFile object instead of automatically using the java.io.File class, and we could have created a FileScanner class for extracting the words from the file instead of automatically using the java .util.Scanner class.

Another way of stating the guideline is, in the initial design phase, you should avoid trying to map your classes to existing Java library classes and instead design the "ideal" classes for your program. Then, as you refine the design, you can use the Java library classes as necessary to implement your ideal classes.

SECTION 5.2 MAXIMIZING COHESION

As you have hopefully seen in the preceding discussion, an extremely important part of the design process is determining which class should be responsible for which behavior. When making such determinations, it is useful to recall one of the guidelines from Chapter 4. In that chapter, we said that methods should do one thing only and do it well. As you shall see, one of the fundamental design principles presented in this chapter is that *classes* should behave the same way.

Guideline

Every class should be responsible for doing one thing only and doing it well.

This rule does not mean that each class should have exactly one method. Instead, it says that a class should model one concept, and all the methods in the class should be related to and appropriate for that concept. That is, all the responsibilities of the class should focus on the concept being modeled by the class. One advantage of following this guideline is that a class' behavior and its role in a software system is much clearer to everyone. Furthermore, the class is more reusable if it isn't encumbered with responsibilities and data irrelevant to its main purpose for being.

For example, a class that does one thing quite well is the String class. All the methods and data of that class refer to one and only one concept, namely a sequence of characters. The methods of that class provide useful tools for manipulating that sequence.

A simple example of an ill-formed class would be one that is responsible for storing all the information relating to a person (e.g., name, address, age) and all the information relating to that person's current car (e.g., the brand, model, color, age). Instead, the person data and car data should be stored in separate objects, which, if necessary, have references to each other. These two classes are much more reusable than the original class.

Another ill-formed class is a "god" class that controls all other objects in a large program (see Figure 5.6). Such a class acts like a master class with all the responsibilities in the program, and all other classes are treated like slave classes or just data holders. As discussed in Chapter 2, this approach is counter to the OO paradigm. In OO programming, there should be decentralized control, with the responsibilities for various actions spread out among the cooperating classes.

Another term that can be used for describing the focused nature of a class is "cohesion." When we say we want each class to "do one thing only," we mean that

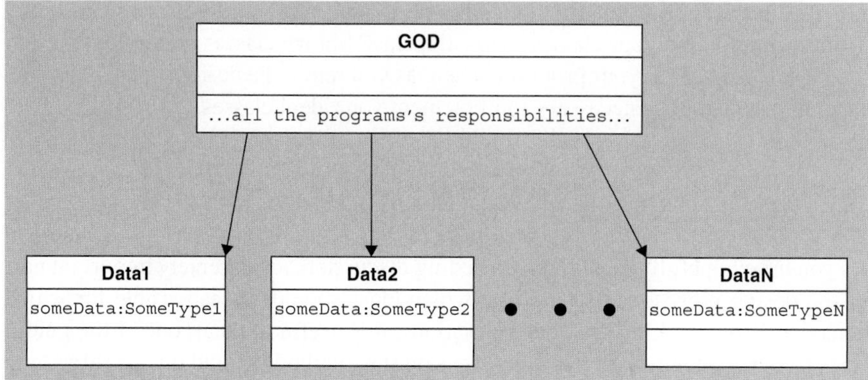

FIGURE 5.6 A god class and its data classes.

we want each class to have high cohesion in that all the class' behaviors and responsibilities are tightly related. The design principle of maximizing cohesion is one of the patterns of GRASP (general responsibility assignment software patterns) documented in [2].

One simple measure of the cohesiveness of a class is how easy it is to describe the purpose of the class in a simple sentence without using the word "and." If you cannot do so, then the class is probably less cohesive than it should be.

SECTION 5.3 SEPARATION OF RESPONSIBILITY

Another way of saying that a class should do one thing only is that different kinds of responsibilities should be delegated to different classes. Unfortunately, it is not always easy to decide how the responsibilities should be spread out among classes that do one thing only and do it well. Consider the following examples.

1. When an array of objects needs to be sorted, the objects need to be compared to each other. Should the objects know how to compare themselves to other objects with a method similar to the `compareTo` method in the Comparable interface, or should a separate object, such as the Comparator discussed in Section 3.10, be responsible for doing the comparing? There is no one right answer to this question, which is why the Java API includes both options. For example, the Arrays class in the java.util package includes two methods that sort arrays of objects. One method uses the `compareTo` method of each object, and the other uses a Comparator to do the comparing.
2. A *graph* is a set of nodes each of which is connected by edges to an arbitrary number of other nodes. See Figure 5.7 for a picture of a graph. A graph could be modeled by a Graph class that has a collection of Node objects and each Node object has a collection of references to the other Nodes to which it is connected. Users of graphs often visit the nodes by traversing the edges—for example, to

find a path from one node to another. In such cases, the users need to keep track of which nodes in the graph have already been visited so that they don't visit them again. To keep track of the already-visited nodes, there are several approaches that could be taken:

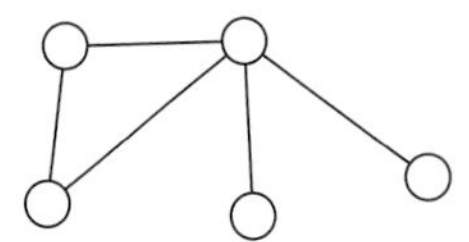

FIGURE 5.7
A graph with five nodes and five edges.

a. There could be a public `setVisited` method in each Node that the user can call to set the Node as visited and a `getVisited` method that the user can call to see whether the Node has been visited.

b. The Graph object could have a public `setVisited(Node n)` method that sets the Node as visited and a `getVisited(Node n)` method that returns true or false indicating whether the Node has been visited.

c. An object other than the Nodes and Graph objects could keep track of the visited Nodes.

One major problem with the first two approaches is that they do not allow two concurrent traversals of a graph. That is, if one traverser visits certain nodes first, then the other traverser may likely miss those nodes since they have already been marked as visited. Even if traversals are done sequentially, things can go awry if the first traverser, when finished, forgets to reset all the Nodes to unvisited before the second traverser begins. The third option is best. The object keeping track of the visited nodes could be the traverser or some other object employed by the traverser.

3. Consider the drawing program mentioned in Section 3.9. Suppose that the user of the program can select (i.e., highlight) any number of the shapes by clicking on them. Who should be responsible for keeping track of which shapes are currently selected? Again, there are several options, including:

a. The shapes themselves keep track of whether they are selected.

b. The view displaying the shapes keep track of the selected shapes.

c. Some other object keep track of the selected shapes.

The first approach seems most appropriate from an OO perspective; after all, shouldn't the shapes be responsible for their own behavior and state? However, consider what happens when the program needs to delete the currently selected shapes. In that case, the only way to find the selected ones is for some object (e.g., the view) to traverse the collection of all the shapes and ask them individually whether they are selected, and, if so, delete them. This can be inefficient if there are a large number of shapes and only a few of them have been selected. In the case of the second and third options, should the shapes themselves also know whether they are selected? This problem has no obvious best solution—the programmer should choose the solution that is most appropriate based on the context.

From these examples, you may have realized the point we are driving at:

Guideline

Different kinds of responsibilities should be separated among different objects.

How can you tell whether you have given a class too many responsibilities? There is no easy answer, although it is helpful to think of the three categories of responsibilities [3] that a class can have: knowing, doing, and controlling or deciding. A class that is only a data holder can be thought of as having "knowing" responsibilities; it is a class that knows some information and provides some kind of access to it. A class that manipulates data that it knows or that is passed to it or gathered from other objects has "doing" responsibilities. A class that controls the action of various other objects, deciding which object is to do what and when, has "controlling" responsibilities. Very broadly, one should consider separating knowing, doing, and controlling behaviors into different classes.

There is another general rule that can help you decide which class gets which responsibilities. In the third example at the beginning of this section, we suggested that, if only the shapes know they are selected and if we want to delete the selected shapes, then some object needs to find the selected shapes and delete them. What object should do that job of finding and deleting? The natural choice is the object that maintains the collection of shapes. That object has the necessary data to perform the desired tasks, and so it should be the one to do so. This principle is called the *Expert* pattern, another instance of the use of GRASP [2].

Guideline (Expert pattern)

The object that contains the necessary data to perform a task should be the object that performs the task.

The String class follows this pattern. A String object contains a fixed finite sequence of characters and can do most of the tasks you might want done with that sequence. For example, it can give you the substring starting at a given index, and it can tell you where a given character occurs in the sequence and whether its sequence comes before or after another String's sequence alphabetically.

For another example, consider a CarDealer object that stores, among other things, a collection of Car objects corresponding to the cars currently in stock. Suppose you want to know if there are any blue minivans in stock. You (the user) can do the work yourself by asking the CarDealer for a list of all cars and then traversing the list looking for a blue minivan. Or you can ask the CarDealer object if it has any blue minivans in stock. The latter option is clearly preferable. The CarDealer is the object with the necessary data to perform the task, and so it should be the one that does so.

In summary, the Expert pattern is being violated whenever a class A has a method that gets several pieces of data from an object of class B, manipulates those pieces, and then possibly returns a result. The object of class B has all the necessary data, and so that object should be performing the manipulation rather than the A object. That is, the method in class A should probably be a method in class B. The Move Method refactoring [4] would be very useful here.

Others have rephrased the Expert pattern in alternate forms. For example, Owen Astrachan presents it as a fundamental law of OO design [5]: "Ask not what you can do to an object, ask what an object can do to itself." The Expert pattern can also be rephrased in the form of a question, "What is it I'm doing with this data, and why doesn't the class do it for me?"[6].

One hint that your objects may not be doing their jobs properly is the existence of a lot of calls to accessor methods (`getX` methods). If there are many such calls, then you should ask yourself what the other objects are doing with the data they get when they call one of those methods? Shouldn't your object with the `getX` methods be doing that job for them?

Notice how this issue relates to our earlier concept of a well-designed class doing one thing only and doing it well. An object that does its job well not only retrieves data for you, but also it manipulates that data for you, if appropriate, instead of expecting you to do all the manipulations yourself.

The word "appropriate" was used in the preceding paragraph because there is usually a tension between the principle of doing one thing only and doing it well and the Expert pattern. For example, consider an application that is the front end of a database. The application gets some data from the database and then displays it in a window. The Expert pattern suggests that the database be responsible for displaying its own data. However, a database object should also have high cohesion, which suggests it should not be responsible for two completely different activities, namely, managing the data stored in it and displaying that data in a GUI.

Now that we have some design guidelines under our belts, let us go back to the design of our word frequency counter application in Section 5.1 and consider how well that design follows these guidelines. Do the classes in that design do one thing only and do it well? Do they follow the Expert pattern? Do they separate responsibilities appropriately? We cannot answer these questions fully without looking at the complete implementation of the classes, but we can make some remarks based on the class' protocols.

The WordFrequencyCollection class is very cohesive. It is responsible for maintaining a collection of data, and it does nothing else. The `iterator` and `getFrequency` methods are appropriate ways for it to return the information it has gathered. If it were to print the data, as well, then it would be doing something it shouldn't. Instead it appropriately lets others deal with the printing. Furthermore, it protects the data from damage by only exposing it via the `iterator` and `getFrequency` methods.

The WordFrequencyAnalyzer is also cohesive. It is responsible only for analyzing a file and returning the results. If its `getResults` method returns the original copy of the collection, then one could argue that it doesn't protect its data as strongly as possible, in that another object could manipulate that collection unbeknownst to the analyzer, but that flaw is implementation dependent. One could also argue that the class doesn't do its thing very well because of the division of its work into the two `analyzeText` and `getResults` methods. These two methods are inevitably called one right after the other, so one could argue that they should be combined into one method that analyzes the text and returns the result. There is some merit to that argument.

The WordCounter program is cohesive in that it has one method and so does only one thing. Namely, it provides a simple interface to the user who wants to just pass in a filename and get the results back. The use of a simple interface for a common task is an example of the *Facade* pattern, which we will study in more detail in Chapter 9.

Finally, one could argue that all of these classes lack some desirable methods, but that argument is not related to the cohesiveness of the class or whether it properly separates responsibilities. We will address that argument in a later section of this chapter.

SECTION 5.4 DUPLICATION AVOIDANCE

In the preceding section, we talked about separating the responsibilities among classes and, in particular, making sure that no class has too many different kinds of responsibilities. But there is another question about responsibilities that we haven't yet addressed: Is there anything wrong with two different classes having the same responsibility? Must there be one and only one class given each responsibility? The answer is easy to guess.

Guideline

Avoid duplication.

This guideline is also known as the *DRY* principle: "Don't repeat yourself." It actually says much more than "don't duplicate the responsibilities among classes." Duplication can occur in many forms, some of which have been addressed in earlier chapters. For example, there might be duplicate copies of the same information, there might be duplicated code within a method or between two methods, there might be duplicate methods in two different classes. In addition, there might be duplication of processes, that is, unnecessary duplicate execution of a piece of code. All of these forms of duplication result in designs and code with bad smells.

What's actually wrong with duplication? In summary, code with duplication is less readable and less maintainable than code with no duplication.

To give you a better feeling for the problems that can occur from duplication, let us consider data duplication. Why should duplicate copies of the same data be avoided? If several classes need to know the same information—for example, if there are several school administration objects that need to access the same student records—doesn't it make sense to give them all copies of that information? In some cases it does make sense if the information never changes (i.e., it is immutable). In that case, duplicate copies are okay, although they can waste space, especially if they are large. However, if the information that is duplicated is modifiable, then it is very easy for the copies to become unsynchronized; that is, one copy might be updated while, for some reason, maybe accidentally, one or more of the other copies are not.

Instead of duplicating the data, how about keeping only one copy of the data but allowing duplicate points of access to that data? Is that also bad? For example, suppose you have an object of class Company that is responsible for maintaining a collection of Employee objects. Suppose the Company class implements its collection with an ArrayList<Employee>. Other objects may need to use the Employee objects and so the Company might have a `getEmployees` method that returns the ArrayList of Employee objects. As a result, two objects may have access to the same ArrayList. Is that bad?

The problem is that the other objects may maliciously or unintentionally render the collection invalid by removing Employees who should be there or by adding new Employee objects to the ArrayList or even adding null. In this case, the Company is not properly maintaining the data against intentional or unintentional corruption by others.

What should the Company do instead of handing over its collection to anyone who asks? There are several options:

1. Replace the `getEmployees` method with an `iterator` method that returns an Iterator over the ArrayList. Iterators are discussed in more detail in Chapter 7.
2. Have the `getEmployees` method return an ArrayList of the Employees, but make it a new ArrayList that is a shallow clone of the Company's ArrayList.
3. Assuming that other objects rarely need to see all the Employee objects, have a getter method that finds and returns an employee specified by particular criteria.
4. Have the Company class follow the Expert pattern and do all the manipulation of Employee objects for the other objects so that the Employees are always hidden. That is, do not give other objects direct access to Employee objects, and instead force those other objects to ask the Company to access the Employee objects for them.

The issue here relates to how much you trust your collaborators. A class' default behavior should trust no one. In particular, if the Company doesn't trust other objects, then it should never let them see the actual ArrayList itself, but only the data in the ArrayList.

Guideline

Only one class should be responsible for knowing and maintaining a set of data, even if that data is used by many other classes.

A corollary to this guideline is that you should always keep data in only one place.

In a good design, one class is chosen as being the "gatekeeper" for the data, that is, the one responsible for maintaining the primary source of data. Other objects must ask the gatekeeper for a reference to that data when they need access to it. The other objects can then temporarily use or even modify the data passed to them, if appropriate. But they should not, in general, have a permanent reference to the primary source of the data nor should they create or maintain their own copy of it except on a temporary basis.

Also, just as methods should always keep objects in a well-formed state, so must the gatekeeper always keep its data is in a well-formed state, which requires it be the sole object with access to the information.

That said, consider the situation in which you have a gatekeeper of a massive collection of objects. If the collection changes infrequently but there are frequent requests for the size of the collection, then it makes little sense to traverse the collection counting the number of objects every time its size needs to be known. Instead, for efficiency, it makes sense to have a separate variable holding the size of the collection that is updated when the collection changes and can then be returned when a request is made for the collection's size. But doesn't this situation violate the guideline against duplication? That is, the collection itself contains the information concerning its size (although you have to traverse the collection to get that information), and the extra variable also contains information about the collection's size, thus duplicating that information. In fact, this is not a serious violation of the guideline against duplication. The key idea of the guideline is that there should be one *primary* source of the information. Other secondary sources, such as the size variable, can exist, as long as it is acknowledged that the primary source is where the actual data resides.

What about the other forms of duplication we mentioned above, such as code duplication within a method or method duplication? Like data duplication, the problem with code duplication is the copies can become "out of sync" when one copy is updated but not the others. Many of these forms of duplication of code can be handled by refactoring. For example, if you have a method with duplicate sections of code, refactor it by extracting the duplicated section into a new auxiliary method. If you have two classes with duplicate methods, then move the duplicated method up into the superclass. Removing code duplication more generally, however, is not so easy because sometimes it can be subtly hidden.

In addition, as mentioned in Section 4.6, there is another form of duplication that can cause problems, namely, the duplication between the actual software itself and the documentation (internal or external) of that software. External and internal documentation must precisely reflect the design and the implementation of the software because, if they become out of sync, then the documentation becomes misleading, which can be worse than no documentation at all. If you could generate the documentation from the source code or generate the source code from the documentation automatically, then duplication problems are avoided, but such generation is not easy to do. Javadoc tools will convert one form of documentation to another, but they do not help keep the code and documentation in sync.

Duplication of processes should be also avoided for efficiency reasons. An example of where such duplication might occur is the checking of preconditions, as discussed in Section 4.5. If a method has preconditions that must hold for it to work properly, who should check those preconditions? Should the caller of the method check, or should the method itself do the checking when it first starts executing? It would be wasteful of resources if they both checked. That is, the duplication of the process of checking the preconditions should be avoided. It is interesting, however, to note that the practice of defensive programming can lead to such duplication. A good defensive programmer, like a defensive driver, always assumes that others will do something wrong and so is prepared. Such preparation naturally includes checking preconditions. But if the calling program and the callee are both coded defensively, this precondition check may in fact be duplicated.

Finally, in addition to everything we have said so far about duplication of data, code, documentation, and processes, you should keep in mind that the appearance of any form of duplication in your software might be a symptom of a bigger problem in your design or implementation. If you see a lot of duplication, you should probably rethink the roles, responsibilities, and relationships among the classes and components involved to see whether a better design can be found that eliminates the duplication.

Is there any duplication in our word frequency counter classes? The WordFrequencyCollection class is the gatekeeper for the word frequency data. It only returns the data via `iterator` and `getFrequency` methods and so trusts no one, as is appropriate. The WordFrequencyAnalyzer class creates the WordFrequencyCollection, fills it with words, and then returns the collection to anyone who asks for it. As a result, others could modify the collection. Does that mean that the analyzer is failing in its task of gatekeeping the collection? In fact, the analyzer's responsibility is to create and fill the collection using words from a file, not to manage the collection after that point. So, in that sense, it is not failing at its task. There is, in fact, little duplication between the three classes, although, depending on the implementation, there may be some duplication within any one of the classes.

SECTION 5.5 COMPLETE AND CONSISTENT PROTOCOLS

Up to this point in this chapter, our discussions have centered on determining the purpose of each class. That is, what concept should each class represent or what role should a class play? The preceding sections argued that each class should play one and only one role in order to maximize cohesion and separate responsibilities. Furthermore, they argued that each responsibility should be assigned to exactly one class.

But once we have decided on the role of a class, then we still need to decide what behaviors and attributes the class should have with regard to that role. Do we include just the minimal necessary behavior? Or, while we are at it, should we add more behavior to the class in the hope of making it more reusable? What methods should we include to implement this behavior?

The answers to these questions vary from class to class. Some classes are very application specific. In particular, a class with just the main method that executes when an application starts running is not a class that will be reusable for other applications, and so it makes little sense to spend a lot of energy designing that class for reusability. However, considerable attention and energy should be devoted to the design of other classes, especially classes that will become part of a library on which many other applications will depend. For the rest of this section, we will assume we are talking about such classes, and so we will consider their design very carefully.

Guideline

Give classes a complete interface.

By "complete," we mean that the class should have the full set of appropriate behavior so that it can perform any reasonable action related to the role that it plays. If, for example, we have a GUI component and it has a `setSelected` method that highlights the component, then it should have a `setUnselected` method to remove the highlighting. Even better would be to have one method `setSelected(boolean b)` that highlights the component if `b` is true and unhighlights it if `b` is false. For completeness, such a component should also have an `isSelected` boolean function that tells you whether the component is currently highlighted.

How full should the set of behaviors be? That is, how many public methods should be included? One extreme is to create the minimum number of essential methods. By "essential" methods, we mean methods that any class that does one thing well must have. Such methods' implementations typically are intimately tied to the representation of the data stored in the class. Informally, we can think of an essential method as one that cannot be implemented by calling other methods of the class. All nonessential methods we call *convenience* methods. At the other extreme from a class with only essential methods is a class that has a large number of convenience methods in addition to the essential methods.

For example, consider a rotatable Rectangle class with a `rotate(double degrees)` method. Suppose that a significant number of the rotations that are expected to be performed are actually 90-degree counterclockwise rotations. Then a `rotateLeft` method could be included in the Rectangle class for convenience. The `rotateLeft` method is not essential, in that it can be implemented by a call to `rotate(90)`. An alternative is to leave the `rotateLeft` method out of the Rectangle class, and let subclasses define that method if necessary. As a third alternative, you could create a RectangleUtilities class that is not a subclass of Rectangle and that has a number of static utility methods that take a Rectangle as one parameter and do things to it, such as rotate it by 90 degrees.

A designer needs to be careful not to overwhelm the users by adding too many methods to a class in an attempt to ensure completeness. In other words, don't try to anticipate all possible uses to which your class will be put. It is better to include a core set of essential methods, and a few convenience methods, and let the users construct their own convenience methods or extend the class through subclassing if they need a larger range of methods. The key is to make sure that the core set is sufficiently large so that users can create any convenience methods they deem worthwhile.

If you do add convenience methods to your class, should you implement them by calls to other methods or by directly accessing the data stored in the class? The advantage of the direct access is that you might be able to make the convenience methods more efficient. However, there are also advantages to implementing convenience methods through calls to the essential methods. For example, consider the java.util.AbstractCollection class, which was created to make it easy for programmers to implement the Collection interface. The AbstractCollection class implements all the methods in that interface except the `iterator` and `size` methods. The implemented methods in AbstractCollection get information about the data in the collection through calls to `size` and `iterator`. Therefore, a programmer who wishes to create a class that implements the Collection interface need only create a concrete subclass of AbstractCollection and, in that subclass, implement the `iterator` and `size` methods. To create a modifiable Collection, the programmer will also need to override the `add` method and implement the `remove` method in the Iterator returned by the `iterator` method. In summary, by implementing all the convenience methods in terms of the essential methods (`iterator`, `size`, `add`, and the Iterator's `remove`), the AbstractCollection class saves programmers a significant amount of work.

There is one more issue that needs to be addressed regarding a well-formed, reusable class.

Guideline

A well-formed class has a consistent interface.

By "consistent," we mean that the methods that do similar things should be laid out similarly. For example, suppose a class maintains and manipulates an indexed collection of people, and the class has a method that allow the user to set the *i*th person's name and another that allows the user to set the *i*th person's age. In that case, the two methods should have similar names and they should have similar arguments in the same order. That is, the method signatures should be something like `setAge(int age, int index)` and `setName(String name, int index)`. It would be very confusing to the user and hard to remember if, for example, the first method used the index as the first parameter and the second used the index as the second parameter.

Overriding toString, hashCode, clone, and equals

When designing a complete set of methods for a new class, one decision the designer must make is whether to override the toString, hashCode, clone, and equals method implementations inherited from the Object class. In Sections 4.7 and 4.8, we addressed *how* to implement the equals and clone methods if you decide to override the inherited versions, but we had little discussion regarding *when* to override them. Here are some guidelines.

Consider a class that is mutable. In choosing the implementation of equals, you need to ask yourself whether you want to require that two objects that are equal remain equal for the duration of the program, even if the state of one of the objects changes. If so, then object identity (the inherited version of equals) is probably the one that makes the most sense. Or do you want them to be considered equal only when their transient states happen to match? In that case, you need to override the inherited equals method.

In contrast, consider a class in which its objects are immutable. In that case, you typically want to consider two objects to be equal if their (fixed) states are the same, in which case you would want to override equals to test equality of state rather than object identity.

However, when you are deciding whether to override equals, you need to consider the guideline discussed in the preceding chapter that states that, if you don't want to violate the Liskov Substitution Principle, then, in any inheritance chain, there should be at most one class that overrides the Object class' equals method. Therefore, if one of your class' superclasses already overrides equals, then your class should not do so.

The hashCode method should be overridden whenever the equals method is overridden, to avoid problems when the objects are used as the keys in hash tables. In particular, it is important that for all objects a and b, if a.equals(b) is true then a.hashCode() == b.hashCode(). A good discussion of this issue can be found in [7].

An overriding toString method of your class should almost always be added. The purpose of the toString method is to display the state of the object as text in a humanly readable form. The default implementation of toString in the Object class displays the name of the class of the object followed by "@" and the object's hash code value, which is not the kind of information you normally want.

When should you override the inherited clone method? If your class is immutable, then it makes no sense to use clone at all. (Why would you ever need a copy?) In contrast, if your class is mutable, it might make sense to override clone if you want to let others create copies of your object. Keep in mind, as discussed in Section 4.8, cloning has to be done very carefully (for example, do you want a deep or shallow clone?). Also there are other alternatives that you should seriously consider instead of cloning that provide the same service. For example, you could provide a copy constructor for your class. That is, for a Triangle class, provide a constructor of the form

```
public Triangle(Triangle t)
```

that constructs a new Triangle that is in the same state as the Triangle passed as a parameter. This constructor has effectively created a clone for you. Another alternative is to provide a factory method similar to the factory method discussed at the end of Section 2.6. Such a method for the Triangle class might look like

```
public static Triangle
   createInstance(Triangle t)
```

This method could even be in a separate factory class that also creates instances of other classes. But keep in mind that, regardless of whether you override clone, use a copy constructor or use a factory method , the issues discussed in Section 4.8 must be addressed, especially if you want a deep clone.

An example of inconsistent behavior-in this case not within a class but among several classes—is the way the size of a Java Collection is determined. To find the size of an array `A`, you use the public instance variable `A.length`. To find the size of an ArrayList `v`, you use `v.size()`. To find the size (number of characters) of a String `s`, you use `s.length()`. Avoid this kind of inconsistency as much as possible.

To finish this section, let us see how well our three word frequency counter classes conform to the guidelines in this section. The WordCounter class is an example of a class that is application-specific, and so giving it a complete and consistent interface is not very appropriate. The WordFrequencyAnalyzer makes one computation and returns the result, and so there is little else that is needed. We could extend its behavior to make it a little more complete by having it reuse the same WordFrequencyCollection in every analysis and adding a `clear` or `reset` method that clears the WordFrequencyCollection. Separating the resetting from the analyzing puts an extra burden on the users in that they need to remember to call `clear` if they want to start over with new text. But it also gives them the flexibility of being able to accumulate the word frequencies from more than one file. The WordFrequencyCollection is the worst offender of this section's guidelines. For example, it has an `add` method but not a `remove` method. To be reusable, it should, in fact, implement most or all of the methods in the java.util.Collection interface.

SECTION 5.6 MUTABILITY VS. IMMUTABILITY REVISITED

In the preceding section, we talked about the need for symmetry in our class' public interface. In particular, if there is a `get`*X* method, you should consider adding a matching `set`*X* method. This makes sense for mutable classes, but not for immutable ones. Therefore, as the design of a project is being refined, one of the issues that needs to be addressed is whether various classes should be made mutable or immutable. The Java libraries include both kinds of classes. For example, the java.util.Date and java.awt.Point classes are mutable, but the String is class immutable. How do you decide which path to take for each of your classes? In this section, we will address that question.

One of the reasons the Java API designers made the String class immutable is to allow the sharing of Strings. Every place the String `"hello"`, for example, is needed in a program, exactly the same String object can be used, which can save a considerable amount of memory. (To handle the case where the user wants to modify a string, the Java designers created the StringBuffer class, whose objects are mutable.)

One can think of immutable objects as ones with guaranteed behavior. You never need to worry about whether they follow particular invariants, nor do you ever need to recheck their state once they have been created. In particular, an immutable object will always give the same result from repeated calls to one of its functions, if those functions don't access external data.

One of the disadvantages of immutability is that there can be no modifier methods, which means that if you want change the state of an object, you need to create a whole new object, even if you will never use the original object again. For example, if you have a very long string `s` and you want an extra letter `"a"` at the front, you have to create a StringBuffer object to use or else write code such as

```
s = "a" + s;
```

which will create a new string from `"a"` and `s` instead of modifying or reusing the old string referred to by `s`.

What classes in your design should be immutable? The general answer is "as many classes as possible" because the advantages to immutability far outweigh the disadvantages. In particular, objects at the lowest level, that is, representing data, that are just "value objects" should be immutable. The class wrappers for the primitives types (Integer, Float, etc.) are examples of such immutable classes.

Once you've decided that one of your classes A should be immutable, how do you go about making sure it is so? The three most important things to do are to:

1. Make all instance variables of A private (which should be done in virtually all classes anyway for reasons mentioned earlier).
2. Exclude any modifier methods from A.
3. Prevent the overriding of methods by subclasses of A by making A final or by making all of A's methods final.

To guarantee immutability, there are some more subtle problems to consider as well, some of which are discussed in the exercises, the rest of which are beyond the scope of this book. A more detailed analysis of the issues surrounding immutability can be found in [7].

What if you need the use of a class that is identical to a mutable class except you need your class to be immutable? For example, suppose you need an immutable version of the java.awt.Point class. One approach would be to ignore that Point class and write your own independent FixedPoint class from scratch, since such a class is so simple.

A second approach would be to make FixedPoint a subclass of Point that overrides the modifier methods (`move`, `translate`, and `setLocation`) so that they either do nothing or throw an exception. See Figure 5.8. Note that the Collections

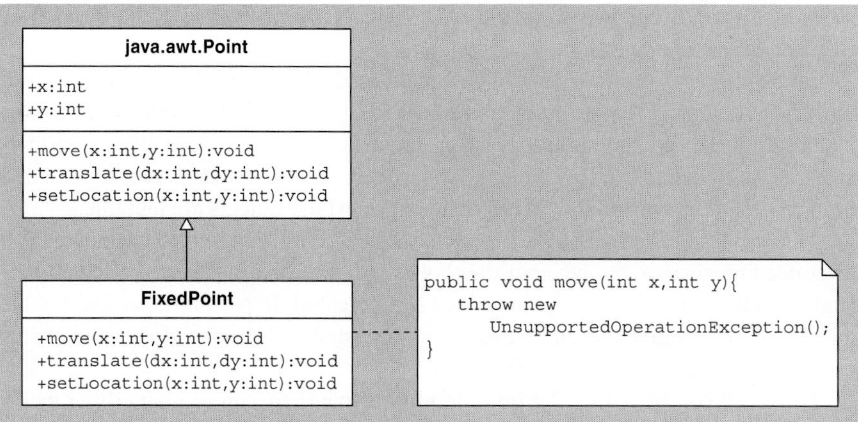

FIGURE 5.8 FixedPoint class implemented as a subclass of java.awt.Point.

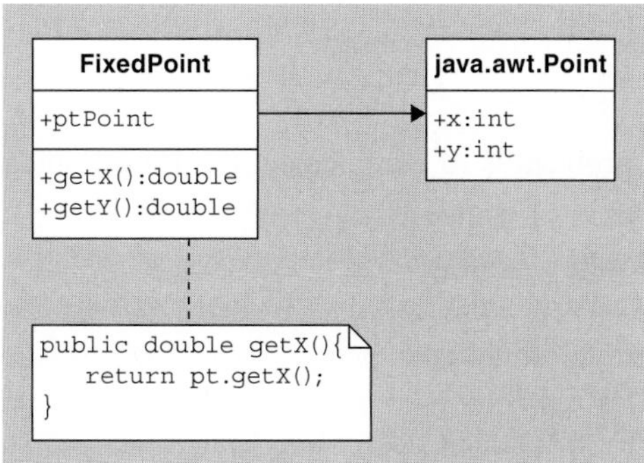

FIGURE 5.9 FixedPoint implemented using delegation to java.awt.Point.

class in the java.util package takes this approach in that it has six methods named `unmodifiableX`, where *X* is Collection, List, Map, Set, SortedMap, or SortedSet. These methods take an object of class *X* that is modifiable and return a new read-only (immutable) view of *X*. In the new collection, any call to a modifier method results in an `UnsupportedOperationException` being thrown. This approach unfortunately will not work for us. Our FixedPoint class will not be immutable even if `move`, `setLocation`, and `translate` are overridden because the Point class has public instance variables `x` and `y`, which are accessible and modifiable from anywhere. Subclasses of Point cannot hide these inherited public instance variables.

A third approach is to use delegation instead of inheritance. See Figure 5.9. That is, create a new "wrapper" class with a read-only interface that contains a Point object in which it stores its data. Consider the following example:

```
public class FixedPoint //attempting immutability using delegation
{
  private Point pt;
  public FixedPoint(Point p) //constructor
  { this.pt = p; }
  public FixedPoint(int x, int y) //constructor
  { this.pt = new Point(x, y); }
  public double getX() { return pt.getX(); }
  public double getY() { return pt.getY(); }
  public Point getLocation() { return pt; }
}
```

Notice that there are no modifier methods, and so the interface is much cleaner than if you were to subclass Point. Unfortunately, we are not out of the woods yet. This FixedPoint class, at first glance, might look like an immutable class, but there are two problems. The first one is that the `getLocation` method returns the Point being wrapped, which leaves it exposed to modification by the user. That is, the user could write code like the following, which modifies the FixedPoint:

```
FixedPoint fp = new FixedPoint(3, 4);
System.out.println(fp.getX()); //prints 3
```

```
Point loc = fp.getLocation();
loc.x = 5;
System.out.println(fp.getX()); //prints 5
```

One way to fix that problem is to reimplement the FixedPoint's `getLocation()` method as follows:

```
public Point getLocation()
{
  return pt.getLocation();
}
```

(Why does this version fix the problem? Hint: read the documentation for the `getLocation` method in the java.awt.Point class.)

But even with that fix, there is another subtler problem with our class that makes it mutable. Here is some user code that shows this problem:

```
Point p = new Point(3, 4);
FixedPoint fp = new FixedPoint(p);
System.out.println(fp.getX()); //prints 3
p.x = 5;
System.out.println(fp.getX()); //prints 5
```

The problem is that the internal point has external references to it and so can be modified. To avoid this problem, the FixedPoint class needs either to get rid of the constructor that takes a Point as an argument or to make a "defensive copy" of the Point passed in as the argument and then use this hidden copy. Here is code that will work:

```
public final class FixedPoint //corrected version
{
  private Point pt;
  public FixedPoint(Point p)
  { this.pt = new Point(p); } //copy constructor
  public FixedPoint(int x, int y)
  { this.pt = new Point(x, y); }
  public double getX() { return pt.getX(); }
  public double getY() { return pt.getY(); }
  public Point getLocation() { return pt.getLocation(); }
}
```

With this implementation, the `pt` instance variable refers to a Point object to which there is no outside reference and to which there is no way to get an outside reference, even with subclassing. So the FixedPoint class really is immutable.

SECTION 5.7 DESIGNING FOR CHANGE

Much of our discussion in this chapter and earlier chapters has had to do with reusability and readability of software. For example, we want intention-revealing names so that our code will be readable. We want our classes to have cohesion and a complete and consistent interface so that they can be easily reused. However, there are other, just as important issues to consider when designing classes. These are the issues of maintainability, modifiability, and extendibility.

There are many reasons why modifications to existing classes may be necessary, including fixing bugs, making optimizations, and adding new behavior. The hard part of making such modifications is doing it in a way that does not introduce new bugs or make the code "brittle". In fact, the technique of refactoring, discussed in the preceding chapter, was developed for just the purpose of changing code without adding bugs.

Well-written code is designed with the possibility of future change in mind. This statement has also been phrased as [8]: "Change happens. Deal with it." Another way to say it is [9]: "To prosper, an interface must be well suited for its task—simple, general, regular, predictable, robust—and it must adapt gracefully as its user and its implementation change." In other words, to have a maintainable, modifiable, and extendible system, you need to accept the fact that changes will need to be made to it and prepare for them.

Guideline

Design your classes and interfaces so that they can handle change.

The rule above is easier stated than followed. How can you design for change when change can come in so many forms? In fact, you can't anticipate all the forms of change, but there are general guidelines that you can follow as you design your code that will greatly improve the ability of your classes to handle change when it does happen. One such guideline is known as the Open-Closed Principle [10].

One way to state the Open-Closed Principle is: "Software entities (classes, modules, functions, etc.) should be open for extension, but closed for modification"[11]. That is, you should design your classes and modules so that they are easy to extend if new behavior is needed, but design them in a way so that existing classes never need to be modified. That is, design them so that they are easy to extend by adding new classes, extending existing classes, and reusing existing classes, but without modifying existing classes. Note that "extension" here does not just mean Java inheritance. Rather we are referring more generally to extending a system by adding new features or new behavior.

The benefit of following this principle should be clear. When software needs to be changed, as it always does, one approach is to change the existing classes. For example, you can change your software by adding new methods or changing existing methods of your classes. Unfortunately, this approach will likely require you to change other classes as well that depend on the changed classes, which in turn may require you to change classes that depend on these classes, and so on. Not only are all these cascading changes time consuming, but they are likely to introduce new errors in the code. Clearly it is advantageous to minimize the modification of existing, working code and instead to extend that code by adding new classes that incorporate the changes, leaving the old classes alone.

Guideline

Follow the Open-Closed Principle when designing software. That is, design software to be open for extension but closed for modification.

One situation for which it is particularly important that you follow the Open-Closed Principle is when you are writing code for libraries. The users of such libraries often do not have access to the source code for the classes in the libraries, and so they cannot modify the code even if they want to. But even if they have access to the source code, changes to that code are likely to introduce new bugs and break other code. Think about the mess they would be in if, for example, programmers rewrote the Swing classes every time they needed new behavior from them instead of subclassing them or combining them in new ways! In contrast to libraries, code that is specific to one application is more likely not to be reused or extended, and so you have to decide whether it is worth the time and energy to follow the Open-Closed Principle.

How do you design classes so that the Open-Closed Principle holds? Let us start with some examples.

Suppose you were told to write a program to manage the purchase/maintenance/disposal of a company's fleet of vehicles, which happen to all be Ford minivans. Can you assume that in the future the vehicles will always be Ford minivans? Not if you want the software to be closed to future modification. Can you assume that the vehicles will always be purchased from Ford? Not if you want your software to be closed. In particular, if you have a Vehicle class with an instance variable `dealer`, the type of dealer should not be FordDealer that stores information about the Ford dealer from whom the company purchased the vehicle. Instead, the instance variable should be of type Dealer, which could represent all kinds of dealers.

For another example, consider an electrical outlet in your home that currently (pun intended) provides power to an electric clock you purchased from Acme 10 years ago. There are at least three ways to view the outlet, with analogies in OO design:

1. If we think of the outlet only as a Acme clock outlet (that is, if we reserve that outlet only for clocks of the brand of the current clock), then, if Acme stops making clocks, the outlet becomes useless when your clock breaks. In this view, the outlet is analogous to a AcmeClock variable that can refer to (plug in) only clocks of type AcmeClock.
2. If we think of the outlet as a "electric clock" outlet, then, when our current clock breaks or becomes obsolete, we can buy a new electric clock of any brand or style and plug it into the outlet. In this view, the outlet is analogous to a variable of the type of an abstract ElectricClock class that can refer to objects of any subclass (brand) of ElectricClock. This view of the outlet is much more useful that the first view, but it is still restrictive in that only electric clocks are allowed to use the outlet.
3. However, if we think of the outlet as an "electric appliance" outlet, then, we can plug any appliance, not just a clock, into the outlet. The appliances need have

no relationship with each other other than the fact that they have a plug that fits the outlet (the electrical interface). This view corresponds to having an ElectricAppliance interface and a variable of type ElectricAppliance that can contain any object of any class that implements the ElectricAppliance interface.

It is clear that the third view provides much more flexibility to the users of your classes by making it easier to change the value of the variable when necessary. The idea is to define your variables and values to have the widest possible type rather than the narrowest type. The widest possible type in Java is an interface that can be implemented by any number of classes.

For another simple Java example, consider a library with the following method that returns true if the given object is in the given linked list:

```
public static boolean contains(Object o, LinkedList L)
{
  for( Object l : L )
    if( l.equals(o) )
      return true;
  return false;
}
```

This method might be useful for someone with a LinkedList to search, but it is not useful if that person stores her data in some other structure. Can we improve this method to make it more generally useful? If you look carefully at the implementation, you will see that the only behavior of the LinkedList class that is being used is its `iterator` method. Therefore, the `contains` method will still work correctly and be much more generally useful if we replace "LinkedList" with "Collection" as the type of parameter L. Then any class that implements the Collection interface can be searched by this method. But we shouldn't stop there. We can make it even more generally useful by widening the parameter type further. A wider type than Collection is Iterable, the interface implemented by all classes with an `iterator` method. In summary, by converting the signature of the method to

```
contains(Object o, Iterable L)
```

we still have a correct method, but we have made it as generally useful as possible.

Guideline

Code to interfaces, not classes. That is, wherever possible write your code so that objects are referred to by the interfaces they implement instead of by the concrete class to which they belong.

One way to view coding to interfaces or, more generally, designing your classes to handle change is to think of it as a way of making it easy to back out of any design or implementation decisions that you previously made. For example, if you hard wire your code to refer to a TreeSet, then it is hard to back out of that design and instead use another container such as a HashSet. In contrast, if you had written your code so that the TreeSet was stored in a variable of type Set (an interface) and only the interface's methods were used, then it would be easy to replace the TreeSet with a HashSet and little or no other code would need to be modified.

Note that much of our discussion in this section can be thought of in terms of minimizing the interconnections between parts of the program. For example, by coding to interfaces instead of to a concrete class, you reduce the interdependence among the concrete classes. The concept of reducing such connections goes by the name of "minimizing coupling." Other equivalent terminology for this concept is "keeping classes orthogonal" and "minimizing the interdependence among classes." The principle of minimizing coupling is another example of using GRASP [2].

We can also consider interdependence on a larger scale, such as among groups of classes, than just between two classes. For example, suppose we decide that we need to replace a group of classes that work together to accomplish a task with another group of classes that accomplish the same task. More specifically, let's assume our application uses 20 classes, and a group of 5 of them need to be replaced with a group of 4 new classes. Suppose further that each of the 20 classes uses every other class. In this case, the UML class diagram for those 20 classes will contain 380 associations and will look like a complete graph with 20 vertices. In this case, every class will have to be modified to accommodate the replacement of the five classes. However, if the classes had been designed so that each class is minimally coupled with the other classes, then the group of 5 cooperating classes may have lots of associations among themselves, but the 15 classes outside the group of 5 would most likely have only a few connections to the group of 5, making it much easier to replace those 5 classes. In other words, to accommodate change, it is advantageous for a UML class diagram to look more like a tree than a complete graph.

What else can you do to your software design so that the Open-Closed Principle holds? Two techniques that can help, if used properly, are encapsulation and information hiding.

Encapsulation [1] means grouping together related items and putting a wall around them or protecting them from access by others. Although encapsulation can be done in most any programming language, object-oriented languages like Java provide a natural mechanism, called a *class*, for encapsulating data and the methods that operate on that data. Java also provides a package mechanism for encapsulating groups of classes.

How can the encapsulated items be protected? One technique that is helpful is *information hiding*, which means keeping information hidden from others. In particular, it is helpful to keep the implementation of a class or group of classes hidden as much as possible from the users of the class or classes. If information in a class is exposed, then clients are likely to use it, resulting in tighter coupling between that class and the clients' classes. One way to hide information has been mentioned before: keep all its instance variables private. This privacy is necessary if in the future we want to be able to change the implementation of a class without requiring other classes to also change. But there is another reason to keep instance variables private even if the implementation of the class will never change. We will explore that reason through an example.

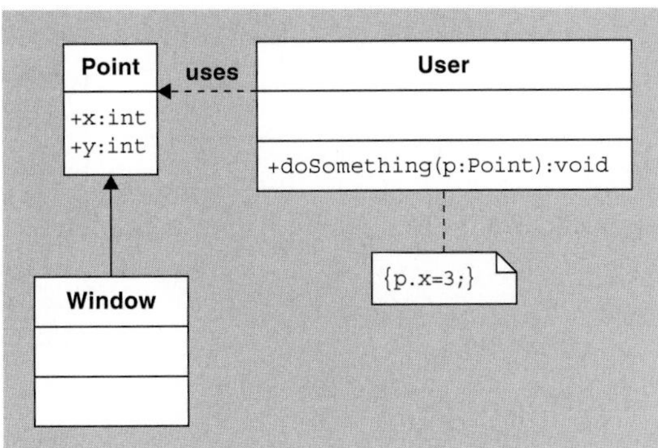

FIGURE 5.10 The Window may have no way of knowing the user changed the value of `p.x`.

Let us suppose you have a software system using a Point class with public integer instance variables `x` and `y`. Let us also suppose that in the next enhancement of the system, you need to display in a window the current values of `x` and `y` of a Point `p` and you need to keep the values in the display updated so that whenever `x` or `y` change, the value in the display changes accordingly. How can you ensure that the displayed value of `x` and `y` will always be updated when a change is made to `p`? Because of the public accessibility of `x` and `y`, any other object that is aware of `p` can arbitrarily change the value of `x` or `y` without notifying anyone. For example, in Figure 5.10 a User and a Window both have access to a Point `p`, but they are unaware of each other. When the User's `doSomething` method is executed, the value of `p.x` changes, but the Window may be unaware of that change.

One solution to this dilemma is to have the display window repeatedly poll `p` to see whether `x` or `y` have changed. Alternatively, we could restrict the knowledge of the existence of `p` to only a few other classes who know that they need to notify the window when they change the value of `p`'s `x` or `y` variables. However, both these solutions are suboptimal in terms of the inefficiencies they impose on the system and the brittleness of the code. This problem stems from the public accessibility of the Point's instance variables `x` and `y`.

In contrast, suppose that the Point class had instead been implemented with private instance variables `x` and `y` and public getter and setter methods for them. Although this class seems identical to the version of Point with public instance variables, it, in fact, allows a cleaner solution to the problem through the appropriate subclassing of Point. For example, we could define a new subclass of Point called NotifierPoint that overrides the `setX` and `setY` methods of Point. In this subclass, the overriding methods would, in addition to changing the value of `x` and `y`, notify the window (or anyone else that wishes to be notified) that a change has been made and give the window the new values. If `p` is of class NotifierPoint, then the window need not repeatedly poll to find the value of `p`'s `x` and `y` and, furthermore, we need not restrict access to `p` to objects that are aware of the need to notify the window of any change. If any object wishes to change `p`'s values, that object merely uses one of `p`'s setter methods and the window will automatically be notified of the change. Therefore, the version of point with getter and setter methods is more open for

FIGURE 5.11 The NotifierPoint notifies the Window of the change in x.

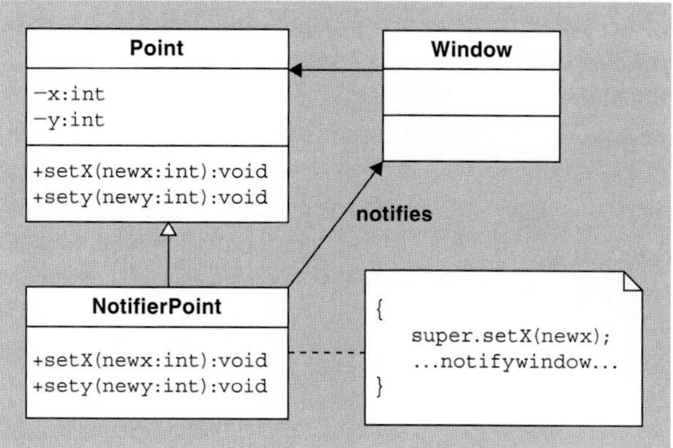

extension. See Figure 5.11. (By the way, this idea of notifying interested parties when something happens is called the *Observer* pattern and is discussed in Chapter 8.)

In summary, private instance variables and, if necessary, public getter and setter methods are almost always preferable to public instance variables.

What else can you do in terms of information hiding besides making instance variables private? You can also make auxiliary methods private (in other words, keep the public protocol of the class small and clean). In addition, widening the return type of the public methods as much as possible will help hide implementation details. For example, consider a class that stores data in a HashSet and suppose there is a getter method for the HashSet. The getter method could be declared as `public HashSet getHashSet()`. This is the narrow version. It gives away the fact that the data is stored in a HashSet (or subclass of HashSet). If the getter method is declared as `public Set getSet()`, then, even if the same HashSet is returned, the actual class of object being returned is hidden.

How much of a class' implementation do you encapsulate and hide? The general rule is to encapsulate and hide as much as possible. It is far easier to expose something later if it no longer needs to be hidden than it is to hide something that was previously exposed. Hiding an item that has been exposed may require global changes to the system.

In summary, one of the most important things you can do to make your code elegant is to design them to handle change. The Open-Closed Principle states more specifically what you should strive for. Coding to interfaces, minimizing coupling, and using encapsulation and information hiding are guidelines to help you reach this goal.

How well are our three word frequency counter classes from Figure 5.5 designed for change? One could argue that there are only three classes and that this is a very small program, so it is not worth worrying about it. But, for the sake of discussion, let us evaluate it anyway. If all methods except the ones shown in Figure 5.5 and all instance variables of the classes are kept private, then the three classes properly hide their implementation details. Is there a way we can further reduce the coupling to facilitate future changes in the design or code? If you review the design and code, you will notice that there are no interfaces used. We could make the WordFrequency-Analyzer more generally useful by changing `analyzeText` so that it takes a more general kind of input than a File. For example, it could take an Iterator<String> or a Readable object as its parameter. In addition, note that the analyzer returns a WordFrequencyCollection in the `getResults` method. But does the return type need to be WordFrequencyCollection? That is, does any user of the analyzer need to know that the particular class of the object returned is WordFrequencyCollection? If the only methods of that collection that the user invokes are its `iterator` and `getFrequency` methods, then the return type of `getResults` could be an interface whose protocol includes those methods.

SECTION 5.8 LAW OF DEMETER

There is one final topic we want to address in this chapter. It relates to the expert pattern and the coupling between classes. It can also influence greatly how well your software can handle change. This topic is the Law of Demeter.

To understand the Law of Demeter, consider a general in an army that is setting up a base of operations in the field. One of the many jobs that need to be performed is the digging of foxholes. Here is one way that task could be accomplished. The general could get one of his colonels and tell him to get a major. The general would then tell the major to get a captain. The general would then tell the captain to get a sergeant. The general would then tell the sergeant to get a private. The general would then tell the private to dig some foxholes.

This approach is quite ridiculous, isn't it? And yet we might easily see the equivalent of that approach in code:

```
general.getColonel(c).getMajor(m).getCaptain(c).getSergeant(s)
.getPrivate(p).digFoxhole();
```

Just as it is not appropriate for the general to go through all those steps for getting a foxhole dug, it is inappropriate for code to go down such a message chain to get a task done.

Consider a more realistic but similar chain that might appear in an ATM application, where the program reads from the ATM card the bank name `b`, the branch number `r`, the customer name `c`, the account number `a`, and then attempts, starting with some associated CentralControl object, to get the customer's balance in that account:

```
Balance balance = centralControl.getBank(b).getBranch(r)
                  .getCustomer(c).getAccount(a).getBalance();
```

where `b` is the bank name, `r` is the branch name, `c` is the customer name, and `a` is the account number. Do you see the problems with such code? One problem is that you have now strongly coupled the ATM application, CentralControl, Bank, Branch, Customer, Account, and Balance classes. Any changes to the structure of any of the latter classes could affect the code in all the former classes. Just as important, such `getter` methods give the user access to the Bank, Branch, Customer, Account, and Balance objects and so the user could manipulate them (that is, invoke methods on them) in ways that are not intended for anyone other than a privileged set of objects. This design has a bad smell called *inappropriate intimacy.*

What are better ways to handle these situations? Let us go back to the general in the army and consider what such a general would really do. Most likely he wouldn't even concern himself with details such as digging foxholes. But if he did, he would certainly call in one of his officers and tell him, "I don't care how it is done, but get someone to dig foxholes."

Similarly, one possible way to handle the request for an account balance would be to do something like the following:

```
Balance balance = centralControl.getBalance(b, r, c, a);
```

In this version, it is up to the CentralControl class to delegate or forward the responsibilities to other classes as necessary to get the desired balance. For example, the CentralControl could find the Bank with the name `b` and pass it the values of `r`, `c`, and `a` and ask it for the balance. The Bank could continue similarly. As a result, the classes are less strongly coupled in that the main application doesn't need to worry about the existence of Customer or Account objects and can leave those details to CentralControl or other classes with which the CentralControl communicates.

The distinction between the two ATM approaches can be seen in the UML sequence diagrams in Figures 5.12 and 5.13.

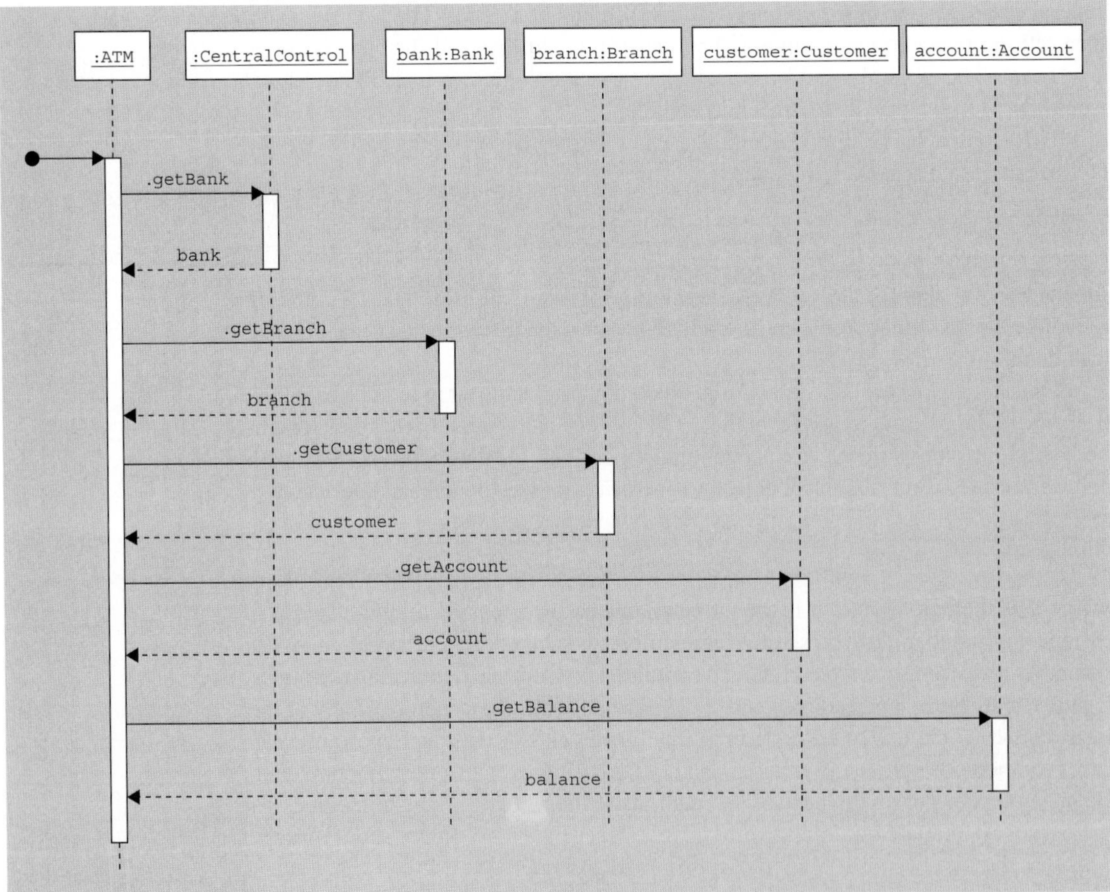

FIGURE 5.12 The UML sequence diagram for the first approach at getting the balance.

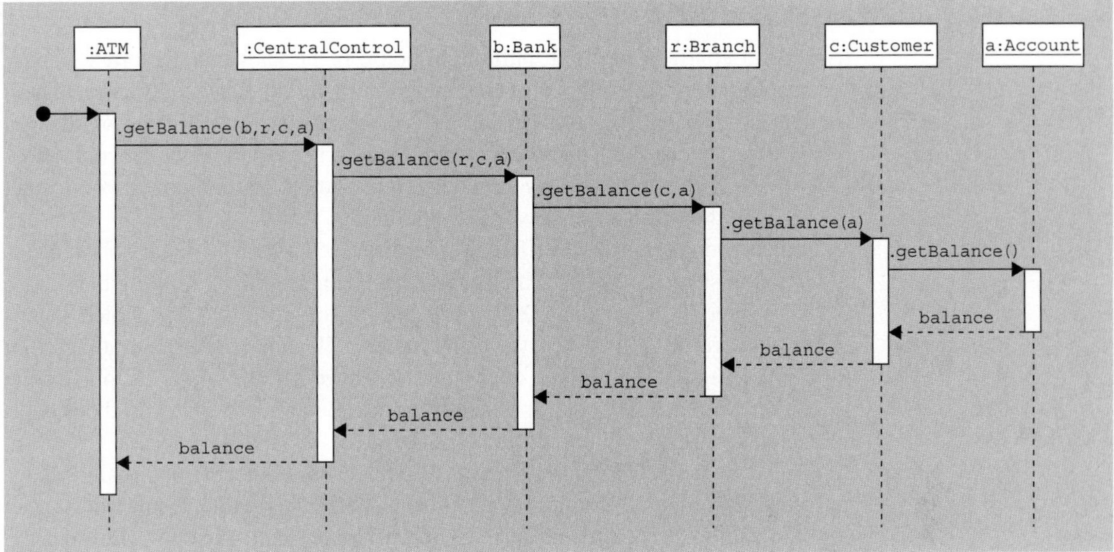

FIGURE 5.13 The UML sequence diagram for the second approach at getting the balance.

A UML *sequence diagram* is a diagram that shows message passing along a timeline so that you can see the order in which the messages are passed. Each rectangle at the top of the diagram corresponds to an object. Each object has a name and a class, separated by a colon. If the name or the class is not important, it can be omitted. The vertical axis corresponds to time, with time increasing as you go down. The thin white strip below each object indicates when the object is actively executing a method (i.e., when it has an activation record on the stack). The solid arrows between the timelines indicate the sending of a message and the dashed arrows indicate the return from the method call, with an optional label indicating the return value. The black dot with an arrow from it indicates a method call whose source is irrelevant. For more information about sequence diagrams, see Appendix A.

The method chaining seen in these examples are violations of the *Law of Demeter* [12], which states that, inside a method body, an object should send messages only to the following categories of objects:

1. This object itself
2. This object's instance variables
3. The method's parameters
4. Any object the method creates
5. Any object returned by a call to one of this object's methods
6. The objects in any collection that falls into these categories

Conspicuously absent are objects that are returned by messages sent to other objects. This law can also be stated as "Talk only to your immediate neighbors" or "Don't talk to strangers" [13].

Here are some more examples where this issue arises:

1. General contractors, when building a house or larger structure, often employ subcontractors. The subcontractors may in turn get other subcontractors to help them. The general contractor doesn't care about that second level of subcontractors. That is, the general contractor expects the first level of subcontractors to do the jobs for which they are contracted, and the general contractor doesn't care who they employ or how they get it done.
2. In the third example in Section 5.5, we discussed a canvas that displays a collection of shapes, some of which are selected (highlighted). Suppose the shapes know whether or not they are highlighted. If you need to know which shapes are highlighted, you can ask the panel for the collection and then iterate through it, gathering the highlighted ones yourself. However, this approach violates the Law of Demeter. A better approach is to ask the panel to give you the subcollection consisting of the highlighted shapes.
3. Similar to the ATM example above, suppose you are accessing a bank's database, and you need to find the customer with a given name. You could (a) ask the database for a collection of all the customers and then step through the collection looking for the one with the given name, (b) ask the database for a collection of all the customers and then ask the collection to find the desired customer for you, or (c) give the database the name and ask it to do the searching to find the customer for you. Clearly, version (c) is the preferable one from the perspective of the Law of Demeter.

What should you do if you encounter code that breaks Demeter's Law through long message chaining, and you want to refactor it to conform to the letter of the law? There are a variety of refactorings that might apply, including Hide Delegate, Extract Method, and Move Method[4]. The important thing is that you need to rethink your design to see why there is such a chain and how it might be avoided.

Guideline

Obey the Law of Demeter.

It is important also to mention here that the Law of Demeter should really have been called a "guideline" instead of a "law." It is not an absolute that must always be followed. Otherwise, it would place a tremendous burden on your neighbors in that all requests of their neighbors must be handled through them. Given that you don't always know what kinds of requests will be made (remember that "change happens"), it is hard to anticipate all future requests.

Do our word frequency counter classes obey the Law of Demeter? In fact, the implementation of the `main` method of the WordCounter class breaks the law. Can you spot where? The method gets the collection from the analyzer and then it invokes the collection's `iterator` and `getFrequency` methods (can you see where `iterator` was called?). Luckily for us, this is a misdemeanor rather than a felony. It would be possible to eliminate the crime, for example, by adding a `displayResults` method to the analyzer class that calls the collection's `iterator` and `getFrequency` methods and prints the results, but it is debatable whether the code would be made that much better by this change.

SECTION 5.9 SUMMARY AND FURTHER READING

Here is a list of the guidelines discussed in this chapter:

- When working in the early high-level design phase, keep the discussion at a high level. In particular, avoid wasting time on implementation details and low-level data representations at the initial stages.
- Every class should be responsible for doing one thing only and doing it well.
- Different kinds of responsibilities should be separated among different objects.
- (Expert pattern) The object that contains the necessary data to perform a task should be the object that performs the task.
- Only one class should be responsible for knowing and maintaining a set of data, even if that data is used by many other classes.
- Give classes a complete interface.
- Give classes a consistent interface.
- Design your classes and interfaces so that they can handle change.
- Follow the Open-Closed Principle when designing software. That is, design software to be open for extension but closed for modification.
- Code to interfaces, not classes. That is, wherever possible write your code so that objects are referred to by the interfaces they implement instead of by the concrete class to which they belong.
- Obey the Law of Demeter.

For more detailed discussions of these topics, consider the following references. Many of the topics in Section 5.1 can be found in [3]. The Bertrand Meyer text [10] is a classic that contains huge amounts of useful material on creating an elegant design. Another good explanation and example of the Law of Demeter can be found in [14]. The text [6] contains many good heuristics, similar to many of the guidelines in this text, to help you come up with an elegant design. The text [7] has similar guidelines but for lower-level implementations in Java rather than high-level design.

EXERCISES

1. Finish the design and implementation of the word frequency counting program in Section 5.1. It should gracefully handle all errors, including such errors as a missing command-line argument and nonexistent files.
2. In the design of the word frequency counting program in Section 5.1, the main method created a File, which it passed to the WordFrequencyAnalyzer. An alternative would be to pass the path name to the WordFrequencyAnalyzer constructor and have the analyzer create and deal internally with the File. What are any advantages or disadvantages to this alternate design?
3. In the design of the word frequency counting program in Section 5.1, the WordFrequencyAnalyzer has a void method that analyzes the files and a separate function that returns the results of the analysis. An alternative would be to combine these two behaviors into one method that would analyze the text file and return the resulting WordFrequencyCollection. What are any advantages or disadvantages to this alternate design?
4. In the design of the word frequency counting program in Section 5.1, the WordFrequencyAnalyzer is passed a File that it then analyzes by way of a Scanner that it creates. An alternative would be for the main

program in the WordCounter class to create the Scanner and then pass the Scanner to the WordFrequencyAnalyzer. What are any advantages or disadvantages of this alternate design?

5. In the design of the word frequency counting program in Section 5.1, a WordFrequencyCollection class was included. However, you may have noticed that a HashMap<String, Integer> that stores the words from the file as the keys and the numbers of occurrences as the corresponding values has all the functionality desired of the WordFrequencyCollection class. Therefore, one could eliminate the WordFrequency Collection class and just use this HashMap class in the design. What are any advantages or disadvantages of this alternate design?
6. In the design of the word frequency counting program in Section 5.1, the WordCounter program has one static `main` method in which everything happens. An alternative would be to move all the code from the current `main` method into a nonstatic `displayInfo` method (with the file name as a parameter) and have a new `main` method that just creates a WordCounter object and asks it to execute its `displayInfo` method. What are any advantages or disadvantages of this alternate design?
7. In Section 5.2, we mentioned that you should rethink your design if you have a class that maintains no data and just manipulates data passed to it from other classes. The Math class in the java.lang package is such a class. Have the Math class creators designed a poor class?
8. In Section 5.3, we gave the example of a drawing program and asked who should be responsible for keeping track of which shapes are currently selected. One possibility not mentioned there is the case where the shapes keep track of whether they are selected and, in addition, the view also keeps track of which shapes are selected. This design has the advantage that shapes know whether they are selected, which seems appropriate, but the view does as well, which simplifies manipulation (such as dragging or deletion) of all selected shapes. Give a disadvantage of this approach.
9. In Section 5.3, we used the example of a CarDealer object to get across the point that the object with the data should be the one to manipulate the data for you. In this example, we wanted the CarDealer object to filter the data for us. That is, a CarDealer object with only a `getAllCars()` method is less useful to customers than a CarDealer object with methods that filter the cars according to various criteria specified by the customer, such as `getAllCarsOfType(CarType)` or `getAllCarsOfColor(Color)`. However, there are many filtering criteria that might be applied besides type and color, such as the year, make, model, mileage. Also, the user might want to use the criteria in various combinations, such as "all those blue minivans manufactured by Ford or Chevrolet in the years 2001–2004 with at most 10,000 miles on them". How can a CarDealer object handle all possible combinations and types of filtering without have a separate method to deal with each one?
10. In Section 5.3, we said that a class that stores data for you should also manipulate it for you, as appropriate. One might conclude from this statement that a HashSet, for example, should not just store data, but should manipulate the data for you somehow. For example, consider a HashSet containing a collection of Person objects. The client of such a class might find it necessary to extract just the names of the people and put them in a new HashSet. Ideally, the HashSet class would have a method to do this extraction for you. However, there are an unlimited number of ways that the Person objects might be manipulated, and so you cannot fill the HashSet class with methods covering all possible cases.
    - **a.** Suppose you were asked to enhance the HashSet class. Suggest one new method for that class that could be used to manipulate the data in a variety of ways.
    - **b.** Why wasn't such a method ever added to the HashSet class?
11. Suppose you were told to implement a class whose objects need to store 10–20 pieces of data and the data is of several kinds. Some people might argue that you should store each piece of data in a separate instance variable in your object. Others might argue that it is ludicrous to have one instance variable for each piece of data, and so it would be better to store the data all in one instance variable, such as an array `data` of type Object[ ]. For example, a Person object could store the person's first name in location `data[0]`, the last name in `data[1]`, the address in `data[2]`, the age in `data[3]`, etc. Give your opinion on these two approaches. Discuss the approach you would use.
12. In Section 5.4, we mention that a vehicle management program should store information on the car dealers in a variable of type Dealer, rather than FordDealer, even if all cars are Fords. How should Dealer and FordDealer be related? For example, should Dealer be

an interface and FordDealer a class that implements the interface? Should Dealer be an abstract class and FordDealer a subclass? Is there a third alternative that might be better? Briefly explain.

13. A class designer is designing a Person class that he wants to be as popular and as reusable as the String class, and so he is attempting to maximize the reusability through the addition of as many methods as he can think of. Some of the methods he has added are listed below.
    - `Person(int age, String name, //String address) //constructor`
    - `String getName()`
    - `void setName(String name)`
    - `String toString() //returns the //name of the person`
    - `int getSSN() //returns the //person's Social Security Number`
    - `String getSSNAsString() //returns the SSN as a String`
    - `Person[] siblings() //returns //an array of the siblings of the //person`
    - `Race getRace()`
    - `Person getBoss() //returns the //person who is employing this //person`
    - `boolean isDogOwner()`
    - `boolean isUSCitizen()`
    - `String getAddress()`
    - `int numberOfCarsOwned()`
    - `int getAge()`
    - `int setAge()`

    a. For each method, indicate whether (a) it is a core (essential) method that should be included, (b) it is an inessential but convenient method and so should be included, or (c) it should not be included. Briefly explain your reasoning.

    b. Rewrite the signatures and return types of any of the methods if you think they can be improved. Explain each of your changes.

    c. Give the signature and return type of any missing methods that should be included in the Person class and explain why.

14. Suppose you are writing a method `getChildren()` in a Person class that returns an array of Persons. Then, among other things, you need to deal with the case where the person on whom the method is invoked has no children. What should your method return in that case? An obvious thing to return is null. Comment on this approach .

15. Suppose you have a class one of whose instance methods does not access (either read or write directly or indirectly) any of the class' instance variables. Comment on the design of this class.

16. We like to preach that all applications should have their `main` method in a class by itself, named for the kind of application it is. For example, if your application simulates rockets, you might call the class with the `main` method "RocketSimulationApp." Give a reason for putting the `main` method in its own class.

17. Suppose you have an IntegerList class that is an ordered mutable collection of (not-necessarily-unique) integers. Suppose it has only the following methods:

```
void cons(int x) //adds x to the front
    //of this list
int first() //returns the first integer
    //in this list
int second() //returns the second
    //integer in this list
int third() //returns the third integer
    //in this list
int nth(int n) //returns the n-th
    //integer in this list
IntegerList rest() //returns a new list
    //identical to this list
   //except that the first integer of
   //this list is omitted
int size() //returns the length of the
    //list (number of elements)
```

    Assume that `first`, `second`, `third`, and `nth`, respectively, throw an Exception if there is no first, second, third, or *n*-th integer, respectively, in the list.

    a. Show that `second`, `third`, `nth`, and `size` are convenience methods by implementing them using the other methods of the class.

    b. Is it appropriate to have the `second`, `third`, and `nth` methods? That is, do they really add enough convenience to be included in the IntegerList class? Briefly explain.

18. Suppose you have an IntegerSet class that represents an unordered mutable collection of integers without duplication (i.e., the same integer does not appear twice in the set). Suppose it has only the following methods:

```
void add(int x)    //adds x to this set
  //if it is not already there
void remove(int x)   //deletes x from
  //this set if it is in the set
```

```
int size() //returns the number of
  //integers in the set
boolean contains(int x)   //returns true
  //if x is in this set
```

Assume that add does nothing if x is already in the set. Similarly, assume remove does nothing if x is not in the set.

a. Show that contains is not necessary (although convenient) by showing that it can be implemented using the other methods in the class.

b. Using just these methods of IntegerSet, is it possible to write a loop that will print all the elements of this set? If so, do it. If not, say why not.

19. Suppose you are designing an IntegerSet class that represents an unordered collection of integers without duplication (i.e., the same integer does not appear twice in the set). Some methods you might wish to include are the following:

- `int[] toArray() //returns an array //containing the integers in this //set`
- `boolean contains(int x) //returns //true if x is in this set`
- `boolean containsAll(IntegerSet otherSet) //returns true if this //set contains all the integers in //the other set`
- `int size() //returns the number of //integers in this set`
- `boolean isEmpty() //returns true //if this set has no integers in it`
- `boolean equals(Object obj) // //returns true if obj is a Set //containing exactly the same //integers as this Set`

a. For each of these methods, determine whether it is essential. That is, determine whether it must be included in the IntegerSet class or whether it is a method that can be implemented by the user through the use of the other methods in the list above.

b. Find a minimal set of essential methods.

c. Should all six of these methods be included in the IntegerSet class even if they are not all essential methods? Why?

d. Suggest other methods that should be added to the IntegerSet class to make it a do-one-thing-only-and-do-it-well class. Explain.

20. As mentioned in Section 5.5, a well-designed class A will have a `toString()` method that provides a readable representation of objects of class A. It is nice when class A can also provide a kind of "inverse" constructor that takes such a String as a parameter and creates and returns an object of class A initialized with the data as it was displayed in the String. For example, the java.util.Date class' `toString()` method returns a string of the form "Fri Jul 01 12:00:00 EST 2002." It also provides a constructor (now deprecated) that takes such a string as a parameter and returns a new Date object initialized with the values given in that string. For this exercise, take the FixedPoint class given at the end of Section 5.6 and add a readable `toString()` method and a constructor that takes a string of the form returned by the `toString()` method and constructs a new FixedPoint object initialized with the values given in the string.

21. Let us suppose you are unhappy with the limitations of the java.awt.Rectangle class, and so you subclass it to get an EnhancedRectangle class. Suppose that one of the things that the new class has is a method `showCoordinates()` that creates and brings up a dialog box displaying the top, left, bottom, right coordinates of the rectangle. What do you think of this enhanced class? Is it a good design?

22. In Section 5.7, we mentioned that String objects are immutable. But what if you have a String s = "hello" and you execute the statement

```
s.replace('e', 'a');
```

Doesn't that change "hello" to "hallo" and so mutate the string? Explain this supposed contradiction.

23. In Section 5.6, we mentioned that subclasses of the Java.awt.Point class cannot hide the inherited public instance variables x and y. But are we really correct? Consider the following classes:

```
public class A { public int x = 3; }
public class B extends A {
private int x = 4; }
```

Also consider what happens when you try to access the public x inherited by B from A:

```
B b = new B();
System.out.println(b.x);
```

The Java compiler will give an error message when you try to compile those two lines, claiming that x is private in B. So in this case, it appears that the private instance variable x of B does in fact hide the public instance variable x that B inherits from A. Doesn't this example show that you *can* hide the inherited public instance variables of a superclass? Explain.

24. If a class is immutable, why is it important that no subclasses of it be allowed to override any of its methods?

25. The java.math.BigInteger class documentation says that it represents "Immutable arbitrary-precision integers." But the class is not final nor are its methods final, contradicting the discussion in Section 5.6 regarding how to make a class immutable. What's going on here?

26. The java.util.Date class represents low-level data corresponding to a specific instance in time.

a. By the discussion in Section 5.6, it ought to be immutable. However, the class was designed as a mutable class. Come up with some guesses as to why the Java designers made Date mutable. Was it a good design choice? Discuss.

b. Create an elegant FixedDate class that has similar behavior to the Date class except that it is immutable. Ignore the deprecated methods in the Date class.

27. As discussed in Section 5.6, the main disadvantage of immutable classes is that a whole new copy needs to be made whenever you want to create an object that is slightly different from the original, even if you don't need the original any more. This can lead to a significant amount of copying if you are incrementally constructing a large immutable object. For example, if you are constructing a large string in a loop by repeatedly appending another character using the statement "`s += c`" where `s` is the string and `c` is the character, you end up creating a large number of intermediate strings, all of which eventually need to be garbage collected. Suggest a better way of constructing such a large string.

28. Suppose you have Person objects and Location objects, and you need to keep track of the place of birth of each Person. There are at least three ways to organize this information:

a. Each Person object has an instance variable of type Location that stores the place of birth.

b. Each Location keeps a collection of references to Person objects corresponding to the people born at that location.

c. A third object keeps a table of Person objects and their place-of-birth Location objects.

Discuss the advantages and disadvantages of each of these three designs.

29. Suppose the Department of Motor Vehicles (DMV) hired a software firm to design and build a vehicle registration system, and suppose that the designers initially developed a MotorVehicle class and a VehicleOwner class. Among other methods in the design, the MotorVehicle objects have a method `getOwner()` that returns a VehicleOwner, and the VehicleOwner objects have a `getVehiclesOwned()` method that returns a collection of MotorVehicles. Furthermore, since both corporations and individuals can be vehicle owners and since the designers decided they want to distinguish between them, they created a Corporation subclass of VehicleOwner. Furthermore, they added a `getEmployer()` method to the VehicleOwner class that returns a Corporation object (the employer of the vehicle owner). See Figure 5.14 for a diagram of these relationships.

The designers felt this design was sufficient to handle all situations. For example,

- The employer of a corporation can be itself (i.e., in the design, a corporation that owns a car can be thought of as being an employee of itself).
- A self-employed person will be his or her own employer, like corporations, assuming that person has incorporated himself or herself.

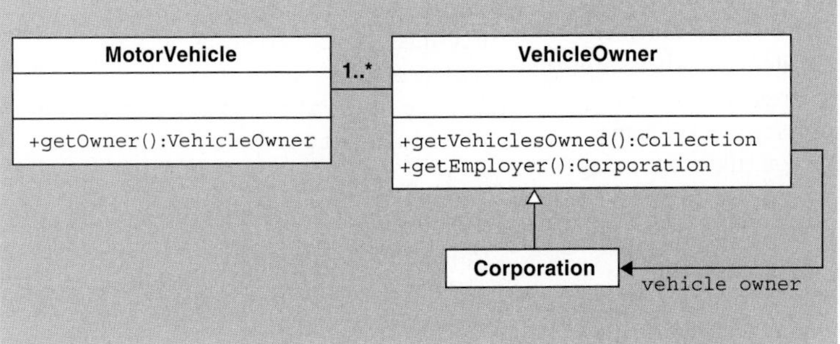

FIGURE 5.14 The relationship between vehicles and their owners.

- An unemployed owner could return null when asked for its employer.
- An unowned (e.g., abandoned) car could return null when asked for its owner.
- A person who doesn't own any cars could return an empty collection when asked for the vehicles he or she owns.
- You can easily distinguish between the two types of owners either by looking at their employers as follows:

```
if( owner.getEmployer() == owner )
   ...owner is a corporation...
else
   ...owner is a person...
```

or by testing the class of the owner as follows:

```
if( owner instanceof Corporation )
   ...owner is a corporation...
else
   ...owner is a person...
```

Analyze this design, listing all its faults, and then come up with an elegant alternate design.

30. To implement a Rectangle class which stores its position and size, you could use four integer instance variables `x`, `y`, `width`, `height` or you could use four Point instance variables that store the coordinates of the four corners of the rectangle.

a. Which of these two implementations is better and why?

b. Suppose the Rectangle has a method that allows it to be rotated by an arbitrary angle. In that case, the first implementation is insufficient, but what about the second implementation? Is it a reasonable implementation in this case?

c. Come up with a third better implementation in the case where the Rectangle can be rotated.

31. Consider the problem of designing grade book software for instructors to use to keep track of student grades on class assignments. Assume that the design includes four classes: a GradeBook class, a Student class, an Assignment class, and a Grade class. Tell how these classes should be related and what attributes and methods they should have.

32. Design a simple program for playing a poker game.

a. If you have never played poker, there are many Web sites devoted to poker that describe how to play the game and the many variations on basic poker.

b. Design your classes for one game of poker, but make it open to extension to other poker games and, more generally, other kinds of card games.

c. Include an explanation of why you designed your classes the way you did.

d. Include in your design your approach to comparing poker hands to see who is the winner.

e. You don't need to construct a GUI. In fact, you should design your code to make it easy for someone else to create various GUIs for your game, including console I/O and windows with buttons for clicking. In other words, you are to design the model for the poker game, not the view or controller. Your classes should do all the work relating to the game so that a view and controller would only need to call methods in your model.

f. Give sufficient details that one of your fellow students could easily implement the classes from your description.

g. Implement your poker game.

33. Often you have a Collection class and you want to remove or "filter" out some of the elements. For example, you might have a set of Integer objects, and you want to filter out all the odd integers, leaving only the even ones.

a. Design a way of filtering Collection classes. Your design should not require modification of the source code of existing Collection classes or interfaces. Your design should be as flexible and generally useful as possible. You should include an explanation of why you designed it the way you did.

b. Implement your design.

34. Suppose that you are using Java 1.4 or earlier and so there are no generics. In that case, if you want a list of strings, you might want to implement your own StringList class, as shown below. This class is elegant in that it allows you to work with lists of Strings, but it avoids all the downcasting that would be necessary if you were to use a general List class. What is inelegant about this implementation of the StringList class? There are several bad smells of varying importance.

```
public class StringList {
  private LinkedList v = new
    LinkedList();
  private Iterator iterator = new
    StringListIterator();

  //add a new string at the end
  public void add(String s) { v.add(s); }
  //get the i-th string
  public String get(int i){ return
    (String) v.get(i); }
  //remove and return the i-th string
```

```
public String remove(int i){ return
   (String)v.remove(i); }
//return the number of strings in
   //the list
public int size(){ return v.size(); }
//return an iterator over the list
public Iterator iterator() {
   return iterator; }
//inner class
class StringListIterator implements
   Iterator {
      int count = size();
      public boolean hasNext() { return
         count > 0; }
      public Object next() {
         if (count == 0)
            throw new
               NoSuchElementException
               ("StringList");
         return v.get(--count);
      }
      public void remove() {
         throw new
      UnsupportedOperationException();
      }
   }
}
```

35. Suppose you have created your own LinkedList class (not the java.util.LinkedList class) implemented with Nodes, each with data and next-node pointers. Furthermore, suppose you are stepping through such a list extracting the data from each node. As you step through the list, who should be responsible for keeping track of where you are in the list? There are several possibilities:

a. You (the user of the list) keep a reference to the current node, and you repeatedly follow the current node's next pointer to move on to the next node.

b The LinkedList object itself keeps a reference to the current node. You can ask the list for the data in the current node, and you can ask the list to move on to the next node, which causes the list to update its reference to point to the next node.

c. A third object keeps track of where you are in the list. You ask that third object to find and return to you the data in the current node. You can also ask the third object to move on to the next node.

Discuss these choices from the perspective of design elegance.

REFERENCES

1. Gamma, E., R. Hehn, R. Johnson, and J. Vlissides, *Design Patterns, Elements of Reusable Object-Oriented Software*. Professional Computing. 1995. Reading, MA: Addison-Wesley.
2. Larman, C., *Applying UML and Patterns: An Introduction to Object-Oriented Analysis and Design*. 1998. Upper Saddle River, NJ: Prentice Hall.
3. Wirfs-Brock, R. and A. McKean, *Object Design: Roles, Responsibilities, and Collaborations*. 2003. Reading, MA: Addison-Wesley.
4. Fowler, M., *Refactoring, Improving the Design of Existing Code*. Object Technology Series. 1999. Reading, MA: Addison-Wesley.
5. Astrachan, O., G. Berry, L. Cox, and G. Mitchener *Design Patterns: An Essential Component of CS Curricula*. in *SIGCSE Technical Symposium on Computer Science Education*. 1998. New York: ACM Press.
6. Riel, A.J., *Object-Oriented Design Heuristics*. 1996. Reading, MA: Addison-Wesley.
7. Bloch, J., *Effective Java Programming Language Guide*. The Java Series. 2001. Reading, MA: Addison-Wesley.
8. Shalloway, A. and J.R. Trott, *Design Patterns Explained*. Software Patterns Series. 2002. Reading, MA: Addison-Wesley.
9. Kernigan, B.W. and R. Pike, *The Practice of Programming*. Professional Computing Series. 1999. Reading, MA: Addison-Wesley.
10. Meyer, B., *Object-Oriented Software Construction*. 2nd ed. 1997. Upper Saddle River, NJ: Prentice-Hall.
11. Martin, R.C., *The Open Closed Principle*. C++ Report, 1996.

12. Lieberherr, K. and I. Holland, Assuring good style for object-oriented programs. *IEEE Software*, 1989. pp. 38–48.

13. Lieberherr, K. *Law of Demeter.* 1998. [Cited April 8, 2007; available from *http://www.ccs.neu.edu/home/lieber/LoD.html.*]

14. Bock, D. *The Paperboy, the Wallet, and the Law of Demeter.* Web page. [Cited April 8, 2007; available from *http://www.ccs.neu.edu/research/demeter/demeter-method/LawOfDemeter/paper-boy/demeter.pdf.*]

6

Simple Case Study of a Money Class

SECTION 6.0 INTRODUCTION

Software written for businesses will, of necessity, deal with money. A well-designed OO software package will represent money in some well-thought-out form appropriate to the application domain. In this chapter, we will attempt to design and implement a class representing the idea of money in a form that is as general and reusable as possible. This design process will provide us with a good opportunity in which to show the evolution of a design toward elegance. We will start with naive representations of money and will incrementally develop a series of new designs and implementations, each a little better in one or more respects than the preceding design and implementation. Along the way, we will use many of the design issues we've discussed in previous chapters.

Much of the material in this chapter is based on the discussions of money in [1–3], except that those sources use money as a context for introducing test-driven design techniques. We will instead focus on using the design principles in the preceding chapters in an attempt to come up with elegant designs.

When designing classes such as these, it is important to keep in mind the tradeoffs involved. As we stated, we will attempt here to design a general-purpose Money class. However, individual applications may need special representations of money. For example, to avoid the inefficiencies of using objects and because they may use money in such a simple way, some designers may prefer just to use integers to store quantities of money. Others may need variations on the classes we will design here and so cannot use them as they are. However, regardless of whether our design is useful in any particular application, the design guidelines and ideas discussed in this chapter are worth devoting time to understand.

SECTION 6.1 NAIVE REPRESENTATIONS OF MONEY

Instead of using the design guidelines as discussed in the last chapter to develop a good representation of money, let us first blindly try some of the simplest things that might come to mind, such as representing money using primitive values instead of objects, to see what can go wrong. Then we will back up and look at the issue properly. To keep things simple, we will start with U.S. money (dollars and cents) and generalize to other currencies later.

Representation 1: U.S. money is represented by two integers: dollars are represented by one integer and cents by another. The latter integer value is in the range 0 to 99.

If you have absorbed the material in the preceding chapters, then it should not take much thought to realize that this representation is very unappealing. Let us list some of its more obvious flaws:

1. U.S. money is a single concept, but the user must keep track of two separate variables to work with money.
2. Whenever arithmetic is done with money (e.g., adding two amounts together), the cents and dollar values will need to be adjusted to keep the cents within the range of 0 to 99.
3. When comparing two quantities of money, you need to compare two values instead of just one.
4. If you are to allow negative quantities of money (to represent debt or negative balances in accounts), then you can easily become confused as to how to deal with positive dollars and negative cents or vice versa.

Therefore, let us immediately move on to another representation that is still naive but that addresses many of these issues.

Representation 2: Dollars and cents are represented by one floating point number, such as a Java double. For example, the number 3.14 represents $3.14.

Floating point numbers have the advantage that you can represent far larger numbers and you can represent fractional parts of dollars conveniently. Furthermore, since the quantity of money is represented by a single number, the awkward calculations needed by Representation 1 to properly handle dollars and cents is avoided.

However, there are several issues regarding floating point values that can increase the complexity of the design. For example, do we really want to allow fractional cents, such as is represented by $3.141? More importantly, the round-off error caused by floating point approximations can raise significant problems (these problems are a central concern of the field of numerical analysis). For a simple example, note that a number of type double in Java has approximately 15 significant digits of accuracy, and so can quite accurately represent dollars and cents up to $10 trillion (the order of magnitude of the U.S. national debt). However, if you take two almost equal numbers of that magnitude and subtract them to get a number of much smaller magnitude, the number of significant digits of accuracy in the result is reduced. If that number is then used in other computations, you can easily introduce meaningless digits without realizing it.

For these reasons, let us try another representation that avoids floating point calculations.

Representation 3: Dollars and cents are represented by one long integer, whose value is in units of cents. For example, the long integer 314 represents 314 cents or $3.14.

This representation is advantageous in that (a) money is still represented by a single value and (b) it allows very large monetary values but avoids most of the problems of round-off error that occur with floating point numbers. Unfortunately, there are still several issues that can cause problems. For example, now that we are back to using integers, there are problems of integer division and the truncation of the result. If you divide $1 by 3, you will get 33 cents. When you multiply the result by 3, you get 99 cents. That is, a penny was lost from the original dollar when first divided by 3 and then multiplied by 3, a very undesirable outcome for those who need to keep track of every cent.

All of these primitive representations have one more problem: When we later introduce other currencies, how do we distinguish between U.S. dollars and those other currencies, such as British pounds, for example? We would also like to be able to consider mixed bags of money of arbitrary currencies, compare their values, and convert money from one currency to another. Implementing money using primitives leaves too much of this work on the client.

In summary, primitive values can be used to represent a quantity of money, but only in very limited situations.

SECTION 6.2 A USMONEY CLASS

Now that we have dealt with several possible primitive representations, let us start over and design a representation of money using the principles in the preceding chapter. In particular, let us design a USMoney class.

Let us think about what would be written on a CRC card for USMoney. In particular, what are the responsibilities of such a USMoney class? Without too much thought, you should be able to come up with several things. For example, the class should be able to tell us its worth and display its worth as a String in a standard format, such as "$3.14."

In addition to this "getter" behavior, should there be "setter" behavior? For example, should there be a `setValue` method that changes the amount of money represented by the object? To answer this question, think back to the discussion in Section 5.6 about mutability versus immutability. A class representing a value should ideally be immutable. Therefore, we will make USMoney immutable and avoid any mutator methods.

After very little more reflection on what is done with money, the following responsibilities should come to mind. USMoney objects should be able to:

- Represent positive or negative quantities of dollars and cents.
- Give you the number of dollars and cents that it represents.
- Draw itself as a string in a desired format, such as "$3.14" or "3.14USD."
- Determine whether it represents a quantity that is equal to, greater than, or less than the quantity represented by another USMoney object.
- Add or subtract itself to or from another USMoney object.
- Multiply or divide itself by a given positive or negative number.
- Negate the amount it represents.

Let's look at these behaviors in terms of specifying the public interface of the USMoney class. Here are method headers corresponding to the behaviors above:

```
public long getAmount()
public String toString()
public int compareTo(USMoney o)
public boolean equals(Object o)
public int hashCode()
public USMoney plus(USMoney)
public USMoney minus(USMoney)
public USMoney times(double factor)
public USMoney dividedBy(double denominator)
public USMoney negate()
```

Each of these method headers deserve some discussion.

The `getAmount` method returns the amount of money in cents. It can be positive or negative. Other getter methods are also possible. The `toString` method displays the money amount in a standard format, such as "$3.14" or "3.14USD." The `compareTo` method should look familiar. It is the method header from the Comparable<USMoney> interface. Therefore, we will have USMoney implement that interface.

Since USMoney objects are value objects, the USMoney class should override the inherited `equals` method to test whether two USMoney objects have the same amount of dollars and cents rather than testing whether they refer to the same object. This equality test makes sense in the same way that a $5 bill should be considered "equal to" five $1 bills or 500 pennies. Furthermore, since the inherited `equals` method is being overridden, the inherited `hashCode` method should also be overridden, as discussed in Section 5.5.

The arithmetic methods deserve special attention. Note that they are listed above as functions that return a value instead of void (that is, modifier) methods that modify this object. Since USMoney objects are immutable, the arithmetic operations do not change the current object, and instead they return a new USMoney object with the new amount of dollars and cents.

Note that the `times` and `dividedBy` methods use floating point calculations and, as a result, have round-off issues to deal with. Exercise 1(j) suggests one way of dealing with this problem.

Finally, we should consider what constructors should be included in our class. A constructor taking two integers, one for dollars and one for cents, makes sense, as does a constructor that takes one long integer containing the amount of money in cents. Other convenience constructors could be added as well, but we will include only these two for now.

We now have a complete public interface for our class, including all constructors and all methods unique to USMoney or that override inherited methods.

```
public class USMoney implements Comparable<USMoney>
{
  public USMoney(int dollars, int cents)
```

```
    public USMoney(long cents)
    public long getAmount()
    public String toString()
    public int compareTo(USMoney o)
    public boolean equals(Object o)
    public int hashCode()
    public USMoney plus(USMoney m)
    public USMoney minus(USMoney m)
    public USMoney times(double factor)
    public USMoney dividedBy(double divisor)
    public USMoney negate()
}
```

This class can easily be implemented using a long instance variable to store the amount of money. The details are left as an exercise.

Let us finish our discussion of the design of USMoney by reviewing some of the benefits of using this class instead of one or two primitive values to represent money. One benefit is encapsulation. Users of USMoney need not concern themselves about how positive and negative money are represented. Nor do they need to do any of the calculations when combining two quantities of money—instead the USMoney class does the calculations for you (the Expert pattern again). In addition, there is a benefit that we haven't yet mentioned. Namely, if you use objects to represent money, the Java compiler can detect logical errors in your program that might slip through if you use a primitive representation of money. For example, suppose the user accidentally adds a floating point value representing money to a floating point value representing current rainfall in inches. In that case, the result is quite meaningless but the logical error is not detected by the compiler. However, if the user tried to add a floating point value to a USMoney object, the compiler would detect the error. That is, only USMoney objects are allowed to be added to a USMoney object, which is what we desire.

SECTION 6.3 USING SUBCLASSES OF MONEY TO REPRESENT DIFFERENT CURRENCIES

Now let us extend our design so that it can handle different currencies. For example, we want to deal with Euros and Yen in addition to dollars.

One natural way to handle different currencies is to represent each of them with different classes.

What will those classes have in common and how will they interact with each other? That is, think again of what you would put on the CRC cards for these money classes. In particular, consider the responsibilities that we gave the USMoney class in Section 6.2. Shouldn't all money classes have the same responsibilities? In fact, let us consider the public interface of the USMoney class and see what needs to change now that we have more than one such class.

To allow mixed arithmetic using these money classes, it turns out that the only change we need to make to the USMoney interface is that all the methods will need to use a type other than USMoney for the parameters and return type. To allow any type of money to be passed as the parameter, we need a common superclass or interface Money for all our classes. In fact, we need only take the public interface given for USMoney in Section 6.2 and replace USMoney with Money everywhere to get the interface of the new Money superclass. Because we will want to move duplicated code up into the superclass, we will make Money an abstract class rather than a Java interface.

```
public abstract class Money implements Comparable<Money>
{
  public long getAmount()
  public String toString()
  public int compareTo(Money m)
  public boolean equals(Object o)
  public int hashCode()
  public Money plus(Money)
  public Money minus(Money)
  public Money times(double factor)
  public Money dividedBy(double divisor)
  public Money negate()
}
```

See Figure 6.1 for a class diagram of Money and some of its subclasses.

Let us now consider the implementations of these methods. How many of them can be implemented in the Money class and how many of them need to be abstract in the Money class with their implementation left to the subclasses? If the Money class, instead of its subclasses, holds an instance variable representing the amount of money, then the `getAmount`, `times`, `dividedBy`, and `negate` methods can be implemented in the Money class. Also, the `toString` method is going to be implemented almost identically in all the subclasses of Money except for the display of the currency.

Furthermore, consider the implementation of the `compareTo`, `plus`, and `minus` methods. We want these methods to work for all kinds of Money. We will

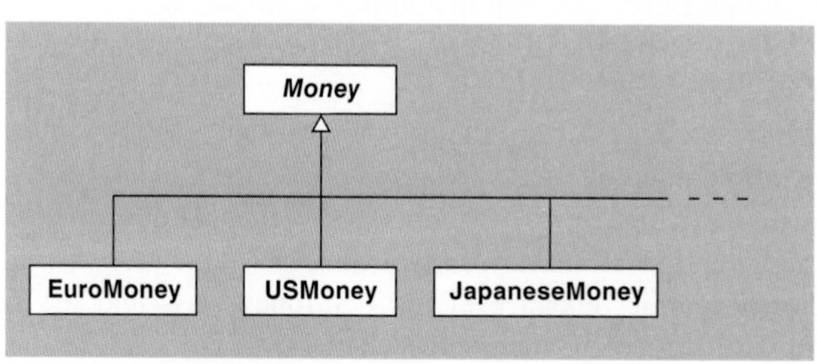

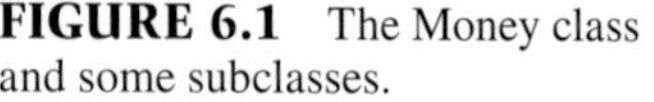
FIGURE 6.1 The Money class and some subclasses.

worry about the details of combining money of different currencies later, but you are probably getting the feeling that implementations of these methods in the subclasses would all be very similar and that most or all of the code could therefore be moved to the superclass Money.

In fact, by now you may be wondering whether there are enough differences among the classes to justify using separate classes for each currency. Their behaviors do not appear to vary from each other in any truly significant way.

Another reason to wonder whether using subclasses is the right way to go concerns the number of subclasses that must be dealt with if we wish to allow all of the world's currencies to be represented. There are over 170 different currencies currently in use. Do we really want a separate subclass of Money for each of them?

SECTION 6.4 USING ONE CLASS OF MONEY WITH A CURRENCY ATTRIBUTE

To deal with the problem of an explosion of subclasses, we turn to other techniques than inheritance. Since the subclasses all behave identically except with regard to their currency, it makes sense to get rid of the subclasses and instead add to the Money class another instance variable that represents the currency of the money. Money corresponding to different quantities of euros or yen or dollars will differ only in the values of the amount and currency instance variables.

How do we implement the currency instance variable? That is, what type should it be? One possibility is to make it a String. For consistency and uniformity, it would make sense to use the three-character ISO 4217 standard code for world currencies [4]. For example, U.S. dollars would be represented by the string "USD" and British pounds would be represented by "GBP."

Here is what Money might look like in this case. We have included the implementations of a constructor and the `toString` method.

```
public class Money
{
  private long amount;
  private String currency;

  public Money(long amount, String currency) {
    this.amount = amount;
    this.currency = currency;
  }
  public String toString() {
    return amount/100 + "." + amount%100 + currency;
  }
  //implementations not shown
  public long getAmount() { ... }
  public String getCurrency() { ... }
  public int compareTo(Money m) { ... }
  public boolean equals(Object o) { ... }
```

```
    public int hashCode() { ... }
    public Money plus(Money) { ... }
    public Money minus(Money) { ... }
    public Money times(double factor) { ... }
    public Money dividedBy(double divisor) { ... }
    public Money negate() { ... }
}
```

Before we attempt to go any further, you should see a problem with the implementation of the `toString` method, namely, that it assumes all currencies display a decimal point to the left of the rightmost two digits, indicating that the minor currency unit is 1/100 of the major currency unit. Unfortunately, that is not the case. For example, the currencies for Iraq and Jordan use three digits to the right of the decimal point and the Japanese use no decimal point when writing amounts of Yen. In other words, the `toString` method needs to have more information on the display format for each currency, including the number of fractional digits used.

It would be a terrible design to implement the `toString` method of the Money class with a large if-then-else statement for distinguishing between the layouts of 170 different currencies. To solve this problem more elegantly, we need to ask ourselves which object should be responsible for knowing such information as the number of fractional digits of each currency. The information is currency related, and therefore the information should be held by the currency. In other words, the solution is to use a Currency class, each instance of which represents a different currency that knows the necessary information for that currency, including the ISO code, the number of fraction digits, and another other currency-specific information. In the java.util package there is such a Currency class, with exactly the desired behavior, including a `getCurrencyCode` method that returns the three-character code for the currency it represents, a `getSymbol` method that the symbol for the currency (such as the "$" symbol for U.S. dollars) and a `getDefaultFractionalDigits` method that tells you where to place the decimal point.

See Figure 6.2 for a class diagram of our new design.

By using this Currency class, we can now easily display the money using the currency symbol or the currency's ISO 4217 code. For example, here is an implementation of a method that displays the money using the currency code and a decimal point:

```
public String toString()
{
    String sign = (amount < 0 ? "-" : "");
```

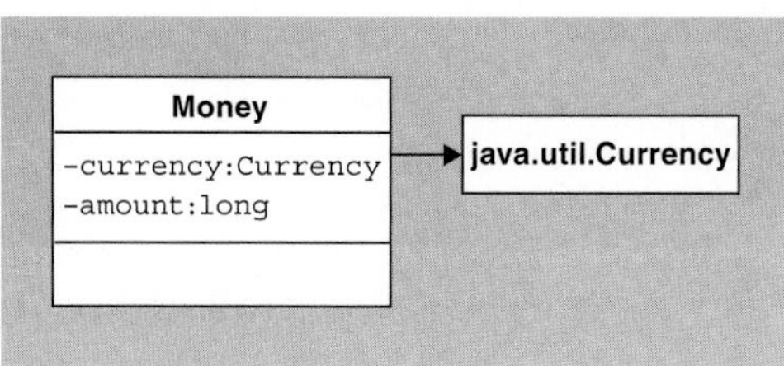

FIGURE 6.2 The Money class and Currency class.

```
    Long absAmount = (amount < 0 ? -amount : amount);
    String code = currency.getCurrencyCode();
    int fractDigits = currency.getDefaultFractionalDigits();
    int unit = tenToPower(fractDigits);
    if(fractDigits > 0)
      return sign + absAmount/unit + "."
                 + fill(fractDigits, absAmount % unit) + code;
    else
      return sign + absAmount + code;
}
```

where tenToPower and fill are auxiliary methods. Note that there is no conditional expression necessary for determining which currency symbol to display; instead, a Currency object gives the symbol to us.

Therefore, let us reimplement Money as follows:

```
public class Money
{
  private long amount;
  private Currency currency;
  public Money(long amount, Currency currency) {
    this.amount = amount;
    this.currency = currency;
  }
  public long getAmount() { return amount; }
  public Currency getCurrency() { return currency; }
  public String toString() { ...above... }
  public int CompareTo(Money o) { ... }
  public boolean equals(Object o) { ... }
  public int hashCode() { ... }
  public Money plus(Money) { ... }
  public Money minus(Money) { ... }
  public Money times(double factor) { ... }
  public Money dividedBy(double divisor) { ... }
  public Money negate() { ... }
}
```

The implementations of the rest of the methods are left as an exercise.

SECTION 6.5 MIXED CURRENCIES VS. SIMPLE CURRENCIES

The Money class in the last section is fine as long as your money is always in one currency. However, what if some of your money is in US dollars, some is in euros, and some is in Japanese yen? How should we design and implement classes to represent an amount of money in several currencies?

An obvious answer is to create a new MixedMoney class. An object of this class can be thought of as a "wallet" that contains bills and coins in any number of different currencies.

Let us look at this new class from the perspective of responsibilities. What should the MixedMoney class' behavior be? Clearly, it should be able to do most of the things that Money can do and, in addition, do some things unique to itself. For example, it should be able to

- Give you the amount of money of any given currency in the wallet.
- Give you a list of the Currencies with nonzero amounts in the wallet.
- Display the amounts of money of each currency in a string.
- Arithmetically combine itself with other Money or MixedMoney objects.
- Compare itself to other Money or MixedMoney objects.

Note that we will make MixedMoney immutable, just like Money.

Now, what is the relationship between Money and MixedMoney? If we use two different classes for simple money and mixed money, then we need to allow them to be combined easily. For example, we should be able to add a Money object to a MixedMoney object to get a new MixedMoney or Money object. We don't want to have lots of conditional statements testing whether a given object is of class Money or MixedMoney. Therefore, a natural design is to give the two classes a common superclass or interface. Because the two kinds of money are so different, let us use an interface this time instead of a superclass. Also, we will rename the old Money class to SimpleMoney and will use Money as the name of the new interface that both SimpleMoney and MixedMoney implement. See Figure 6.3 for the UML class diagram.

Here is such a Money interface:

```
public interface Money extends Comparable<Money>
{
  public int compareTo(Money o);
  public Money plus(Money money);
  public Money minus(Money money);
  public Money times(double factor);
  public Money dividedBy(double divisor);
  public Money negate();
}
```

FIGURE 6.3 The relationship between Money, MixedMoney, and SimpleMoney.

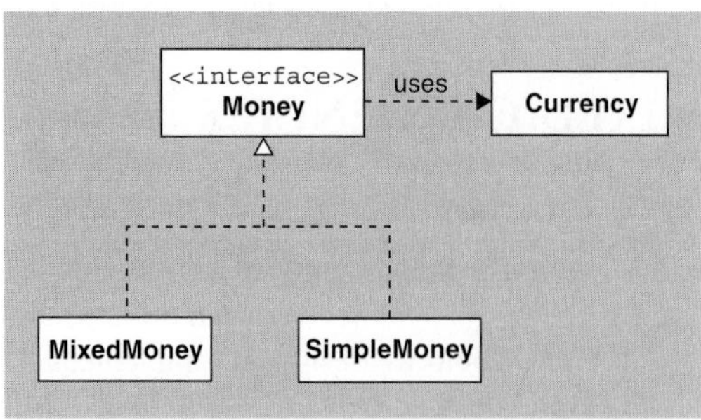

Note that our SimpleMoney class has methods unique to it (i.e., not mentioned in the Money interface), such as `getAmount` and `getCurrency`. Similarly, there are other things MixedMoney can uniquely do, as mentioned above, such as give you a list of the currencies of money it contains and give you the amount of money it contains of any specified currency.

Finally, the MixedMoney class needs one or more constructors. For now, let us just use a default constructor that creates a MixedMoney object corresponding to no money of any currency. To get mixtures of several currencies, we can use the `plus` method with SimpleMoney objects as the argument. Now our MixedMoney class can be specified as follows:

```
public class MixedMoney implements Money
{
  public MixedMoney() { ... }
  public String toString() { ... }
  public boolean equals(Object o) { ... }
  public int hashCode() { ... }
  public int compareTo(Money o) { ... }
  public Money plus(Money) { ... }
  public Money minus(Money) { ... }
  public Money times(double factor) { ... }
  public Money dividedBy(double divisor) { ... }
  public Money negate() { ... }
  public Collection getCurrencies() { ... }
  public long getAmount(Currency currency) { ... }
}
```

The implementation of these methods is left as an exercise.

SECTION 6.6 CONVERTING BETWEEN CURRENCIES

If you attempted to implement the MixedMoney class as suggested at the end of the last section, then you probably grappled with the semantics of the `equals` and `compareTo` methods. What does it mean for one MixedMoney object to be greater or less than another? The `compareTo` method in the Comparable interface is supposed to use a "natural ordering" of the objects being compared. What is that natural ordering? For example, what is the natural ordering between money consisting of U.S. $1 and money consisting of ¥100?

One could define two MixedMoney objects to be equal if and only if they have exactly the same amount of each of the same currencies. That is, a MixedMoney object consisting of U.S. $1 and SF 2 is not equal to any other MixedMoney objects except ones with exactly one dollar and two francs. Alternatively, one could consider two MixedMoney objects to be equal if they have the same total value in U.S.

dollars, for example, at the current exchange rate. A business would likely use the latter definition of equality and so we will use it also. Similarly, we will consider the natural ordering of MixedMoney objects to be the ordering of their total value after conversion to one common currency.

Note that we have now introduced a new concern, namely conversion between currencies. It is time to think in terms of CRC cards again. Who should have the responsibility for doing conversions? Who should be responsible for storing and maintaining the appropriate rates of conversion? Should the SimpleMoney class or MixedMoney class do it or neither? One complicating factor is the fact that exchange rates vary over time, and so a table of exchange rates composed of constants cannot be used.

After a moment of reflection, it should be clear that an elegant solution is to create a new class of object whose sole responsibility is to deal with conversions of currencies, including the maintenance of conversion rates. We will therefore add a new MoneyConverter class to our design. Here is the initial interface of this class:

```
public class MoneyConverter
{
  //returns the conversion rate between the two currencies
  public double getRate(Currency from, Currency to)
  //sets the conversion rate to the new rate for the two currencies
  public void setRate(Currency from, Currency to, double rate)
  //returns a Money object with value equal to the given money with
  //in the given currency
  public Money convertTo(Money money, Currency to)
}
```

For the purpose of this chapter, we will assume that there is also a constructor that creates a MoneyConverter object that is initialized with all the current rates of exchange at the time it was created (the details regarding how such an object is constructed so that it has the current rates of exchange are ignored here). Those rates can be changed with the `setRate` method.

Our new design can be seen in Figure 6.4.

FIGURE 6.4 The Money classes with Currency and MoneyConverter.

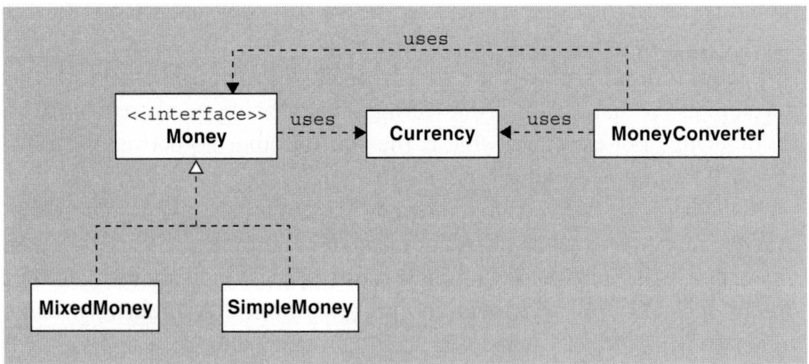

SECTION 6.7 MONEYCONVERTER ISSUES

Something about the design of the MoneyConverter class may have bothered you, since there is one unpleasant smell in the design of that class. To see more clearly what the problem is, consider how we would implement the MoneyConverter's `convertTo` method. Recall that this method takes a Money object and a Currency object as parameters. It returns a new Money object containing an amount of the given Currency that is equal in value to the Money object that was passed as the first parameter. If that parameter is a SimpleMoney object, then the amount of money of the new currency can easily be computed by multiplying the amount in the SimpleMoney object by the appropriate conversion rate. If the first parameter is a MixedMoney object, then the amount of the new currency can also be computed quite easily by extracting the currencies and amounts from the given Money object, multiply them by the appropriate rates of exchange, and create a new SimpleMoney object with the total amount of money of the desired currency. Here is such an implementation:

```
//in the MoneyConverter class
public Money convertTo(Money money, Currency to)
{
  if( money instanceof SimpleMoney ) {
    SimpleMoney simpleMoney = (SimpleMoney) money;
    long newAmount = simpleMoney.getAmount() *
                getRate(simpleMoney.getCurrency(), to);
    return new SimpleMoney(newAmount, to);
  }
  else {
    MixedMoney mixedMoney = (MixedMoney) money;
    long totalAmount = 0;
    for (Currency currency: mixedMoney.getCurrencies()) {
      long currentAmount = mixedMoney.getAmount(currency);
      totalAmount += (long) (getRate(currency,to) * currentAmount);
    }
    return new SimpleMoney(totalAmount, to);
  }
}
```

This implementation violates a couple of our principles in the preceding chapters because (a) it uses "instanceof" to create two cases for handling the two kinds of money, and (b) it requires the MoneyConverter to extract the data from a Money object and then manipulate it, violating the Expert pattern.

From the perspective of elegance of design, it makes more sense for a Money object to get rates from a MoneyConverter and use it to determine its total value in a given currency than for the MoneyConverter object to get the Currencies and amounts from a Money object and then convert and combine them. Therefore, it seems clear that Money objects should have a new public method

```
Money convertTo(Currency currency, MoneyConverter converter)
```

that returns a new Money object whose amount of the given currency is equal to the total value of this Money object (using the rates supplied by the given converter). Once this method has been added to the Money interface and subclasses, then the `convertTo` method in the MoneyConverter class can simply delegate the work to the Money object as follows:

```
//in the MoneyConverter class
public Money convertTo(Money money, Currency to)
{
  return money.convertTo(to, this);
}
```

Note that the Money subclasses can each implement their `convertTo` methods as they see fit, based on how they maintain their internal state. This one change eliminates both of the smells from the implementation of the MoneyConverter's `convertTo` method.

Once we have made this change, something else becomes a little clearer about our design. Namely, does the MoneyConverter class need a `convertTo` method? A Money object can convert itself, and so the MoneyConverter's `convertTo` method is now superfluous. If we eliminate that method, then the MoneyConverter's interface becomes more balanced (with just `getRate` and `setRate` methods). Furthermore, the MoneyConverter class is now only concerned with currency rates and doesn't refer to Money at all, and so we can change its name to something more appropriate, such as "CurrencyConverter." See Figure 6.5 for a diagram of the new design.

How has this change affected the coupling of the classes? With the original MoneyConverter class, the Money classes needed no knowledge of MoneyConverters since they just stored money and left the conversion to others. With the new CurrencyConverter class and with the addition of the `convertTo` method in the Money classes, the situation has been reversed. That is, the CurrencyConverter

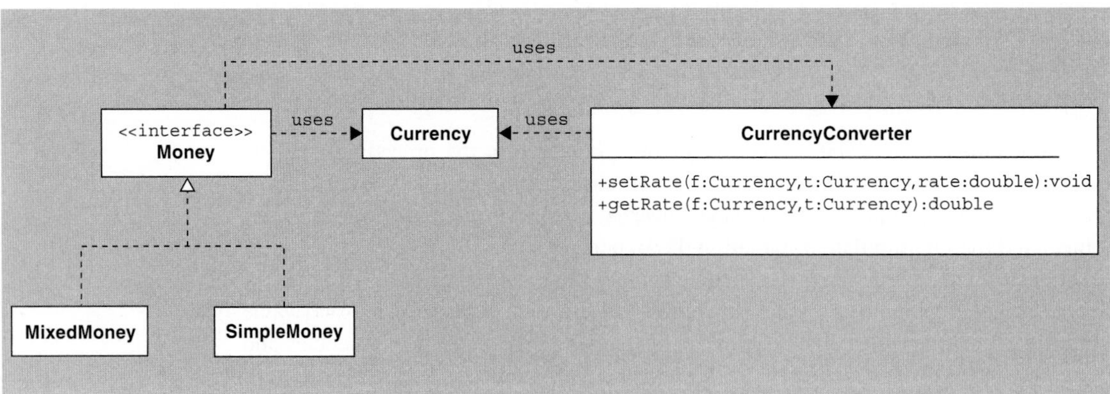

FIGURE 6.5 Money, Currency, and CurrencyConverter.

class needs no knowledge of Money classes, but the Money classes now need to know about CurrencyConverters. As with almost all design decisions, there are trade-offs like these that must be weighed and, depending on the application, different designs might be chosen.

SECTION 6.8. MIXEDMONEY AND SIMPLEMONEY ISSUES

Now let us consider the implementation of the MixedMoney and SimpleMoney classes. How are their internal states to be maintained? For example, how is the MixedMoney object to store all the data corresponding to the mixed currencies and the corresponding amounts?

One way to implement the MixedMoney class is to have it store a collection of SimpleMoney objects, each corresponding to a different currency. Alternatively, one could implement the MixedMoney class so that it stores the amounts and currencies in a HashMap that uses the currency as a key and either a SimpleMoney object or just a long integer as the value corresponding to that currency. For example, a MixedMoney object corresponding to U.S. $5 and £7 could have a HashMap with two key/value pairs: one pair being the Currency object for U.S. money and the long number 5 and and the other pair being the Currency object for British pounds and the long number 7.

If you attempt to implement MixedMoney in either of these ways, you will see that many of the methods in the SimpleMoney and MixedMoney classes are implemented identically. Therefore, it makes sense to change Money from a Java interface to an abstract class and move those duplicated implementations up into the Money superclass. So far, so good.

Unfortunately, as you attempt to implement the `plus` method using either approach, you will find yourself writing ugly conditionals on the type of Money objects with which you are dealing. In particular, when you are adding Money to a MixedMoney object, you need to have a conditional since the way a SimpleMoney object is added to a MixedMoney object is different than the way a MixedMoney object is added to a MixedMoney object. These conditionals are not so good.

There is another problem with our design from the user's perspective. Think of how a user would create an object representing U.S. $5 and SF 3 using these classes and interfaces. Here is one way:

```
Money dollars = new SimpleMoney(5, Currency.getInstance("USD"));
Money francs = new SimpleMoney(3, Currency.getInstance("CHF"));
Money total = dollars.plus(francs);
```

In an ideal world, the user should just be able to deal with objects implementing the Money interface without worrying about the actual class of the objects.

In other words, regardless of which of the two implementations of SimpleMoney and MixedMoney discussed here that you use, there will be ugly conditionals in the code. Also, the user is forced to treat SimpleMoney and MixedMoney objects differently instead of uniformly as Money objects. Can we come up with a design without these problems?

SECTION 6.9 MIXED MONEY ONLY

One way to avoid conditionals and to avoid forcing the user to be aware of all the classes implementing Money is to simplify things in terms of the number of classes involved.

In particular, one way is to use only mixed money objects! In that case, we could eliminate the Money interface and the SimpleMoney class, and we could have just one Money class that plays the role that MixedMoney played in our earlier versions. In this design, money of one currency, which used to be represented by a SimpleMoney object, can be represented by a Money object that refers to just one kind of currency.

This new Money class can be implemented in the same ways that we suggested implementing MixedMoney, such as using a HashMap whose key is a Currency and whose value is a long indicating the amount of money of that currency. You will be asked to implement the Money class in this way in the exercises. If you implement this class, you will notice that it will not have conditionals based on the type of money since there is now only one type.

We will still use the Currency class and the CurrencyConverter class, and so our diagram (see Figure 6.6) will consist of only three classes.

In summary, our Money classes have evolved significantly. We started with a single USMoney class and ended in this section with a Money class that acts more like the wallet of an international traveler that contains different amounts of different currencies. Along the way, we decided to use the java.util.Currency class and a CurrencyConverter class in our design.

Have we achieved our goal of an elegant design of a Money class? Has our design evolved to perfection? Of course not. There are always trade-offs. For example, by eliminating SimpleMoney, we removed undesirable conditionals from our code, but we also omitted some desirable properties of Money as well. Namely, when our design included the SimpleMoney class, the user could ask it for its currency and amount. Our new Money object does not necessarily represent just one currency, so to see whether the Money object is simple, you must get all the currencies included in the object and then determine whether at most one of the amounts associated with those currencies is nonzero.

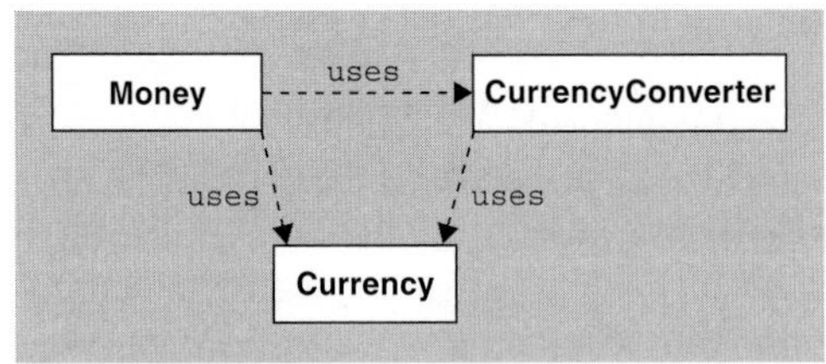

FIGURE 6.6 The (Mixed-)Money class and related classes.

SECTION 6.10 ALTERNATE IMPLEMENTATION WITH BINARY TREES

The design and implementation discussed in the preceding section is an improvement over the earlier versions, but there is still something inelegant about representing simple money such as 5 dollars by an object designed to represent mixed currencies of money that just happens to contain only money of one currency. Is it possible to bring back SimpleMoney and MixedMoney classes and the Money interface in a way that avoids ugly conditionals and complex code and avoids making the user aware of these classes?

In fact, there are ways of doing so. A clever way (see [1]) is to design each MixedMoney object to act as a sum of two other Money objects. In this design, the data is stored in a binary tree whose internal nodes are MixedMoney objects and whose leaves are SimpleMoney objects. The internal nodes hold no data except for the references to their two children. We will explore this design and its implementation in this section.

Therefore, let use go back to our design using a Money interface and the classes SimpleMoney and MixedMoney and consider the following implementation of the MixedMoney class:

```
public class MixedMoney extends Money
{
  private Money left;
  private Money right;

  public MixedMoney(Money left, Money right)
  {
    this.left = left;
    this.right = right;
  }

  public Collection getCurrencies()
  {
    Collection wholeSet = left.getCurrencies();
    wholeSet.addAll(right.getCurrencies());
    return wholeSet;
  }

  public long getAmount(Currency currency)
  {
    return left.getAmount(currency) + right.getAmount(currency);
  }

  public Money plus(Money other)
  {
    return new MixedMoney(this, other);
  }

  public Money times (double factor)
```

```
    {
        return new MixedMoney(left.times(factor), right.times(factor));
    }
    public Money convertTo(Currency to, MoneyConverter moneyConverter)
    {
        long amount = left.convertTo(to, moneyConverter).getAmount(to);
        amount += right.convertTo(to, moneyConverter).getAmount(to);
        return new SimpleMoney(amount, to);
    }
}
```

Note the elegance of this code, including how simple the implementations are when recursion is used to traverse the binary tree!

Our SimpleMoney class can be implemented as discussed earlier in this chapter:

```
public class SimpleMoney extends Money
{
    private long amount = 0;
    private Currency currency;
    public SimpleMoney( long amount, Currency currency)
    {
        this.amount = amount;
        this.currency = currency;
    }
    public Collection getCurrencies()
    {
        HashSet currencies = new HashSet();
        currencies.add(currency);
        return currencies;
    }
    public long getAmount(Currency currency)
    {
        if( this.currency.equals(currency))
            return amount;
        else
            return 0;
    }
    public Money plus(Money other)
    {
        return new MixedMoney(this, other);
    }
    public Money times(double factor) {
        return new SimpleMoney((long) (amount*factor), currency);
    }
```

```
    public Money convertTo(Currency to, MoneyConverter
                                moneyConverter)
    {
      double rate = moneyConverter.rate(currency, to);
      return new SimpleMoney((int)(amount*rate), to);
    }
  }
```

By the way, note that the `plus` method's implementation is identical in both classes, and so the Money interface can be changed to an abstract superclass and the `plus` method can be moved up to that class. In fact, several other public methods common to MixedMoney and SimpleMoney can also be implemented in the Money superclass.

We now have a nice elegant design and implementation of these classes. Furthermore, the users need never directly concern themselves with MixedMoney objects. For example, the user can create and manipulate some money as follows:

```
Money dollars = new SimpleMoney(5, Currency.getInstance("USD"));
Money francs = new SimpleMoney(3, Currency.getInstance("CHF"));
Money total = dollars.plus(francs);
```

The fact that we have been able to hide the existence of the MixedMoney class from the user raises the question as to whether we should similarly attempt to hide the SimpleMoney class as well. Coupling can be reduced if the user can avoid using the two subclasses of Money and instead use only Money. But if we do so, how can the user create some money to start with?

The answer is for the user to avoid the use of constructors for SimpleMoney and MixedMoney objects and instead use a "factory" method that generates Money objects for the user. That is, we can add a new method to the Money class:

```
  public static Money getMoney(long amount, String currency)
  {
    return new SimpleMoney(amount, currency.getInstance(currency));
  }
```

that allows the user to create money very simply. If this method is available, then the user code above can be replaced with the following code:

```
  Money dollars = Money.getMoney(5, "USD");
  Money francs = Money.getMoney(7, "CHF");
  Money total = dollars.plus(francs);
```

and all mention of subclasses of Money are eliminated.

Is the design in this section better than the design in the preceding section (using only MixedMoney objects storing the monetary amounts and currencies in a collection such as a HashMap)? It is not clear. From the user's perspective, they are identical except that in the first design the user would use a constructor to create a Money object and in the second design the user would use a factory (although a similar factory method could also be added to the first design). In terms of implementation, the second design might be slower if the tree gets large. Furthermore, it is possible for two leaves of a tree to have identical currencies, and so a complete traversal of the tree is necessary just to find out how many U.S. dollars there are in it. To make the binary tree version more efficient, there should probably be added a private method that simplifies the tree by combining nodes with like currencies. The decision as to the implementation to use will vary from situation to situation.

SECTION 6.11 SUMMARY

In this chapter, we considered the design and implementation of a Money class. Using the design principles and guidelines from earlier chapters, we considered the good and bad points of a design before moving on to a new, supposedly better, design.

We started with a discussion of the problems with using primitive values. We then designed a USMoney class. Next, we considered how to generalize the situation to allow money of other currencies, and we decided that the more elegant approach was to relegate any differences to a Currency object rather than creating many subclasses of Money. Then we had to address the issue of money of mixed currencies, which we did by creating SimpleMoney and MixedMoney classes. This discussion also led to the creation of a CurrencyConverter class to handle conversion rates. Finally, to simplify the design and implementation, we considered two alternatives. One way was to just use mixed money and eliminate the SimpleMoney class. The other way was to implement MixedMoney as the internal node to a binary tree with SimpleMoney as the leaves.

Which is the optimal one? There is no one design and implementation that is best for all applications, but the consideration of the design issues discussed in the previous chapters can result in a design and implementation that has a better chance of have a long useful life.

EXERCISES

1. These problems concern the USMoney class discussed in Section 6.2.

a. A default (no-argument) constructor was not included for the USMoney class. Should there be such a constructor? If so, how much money should it represent? Explain.

b. Because USMoney is immutable, the USMoney object representing $1 could theoretically be reused everywhere exactly $1 is needed. Describe a way that the USMoney class could be designed so that only one object is ever created that represents $1.

c. Should there be additional variations on the `getAmount` method that return the amount in some form other than the number of cents returned as a long value? Discuss the alternatives and their advantages and disadvantages.

d. Do we really need a `getAmount` method at all? What would it be used for?

e. Why do we add and subtract USMoney objects, but we multiply and divide by plain doubles? Why not multiply and divide by USMoney objects, like we did for addition and subtraction?

f. Add method headers that follow Javadoc conventions and completely describe the behavior of each of the methods in the USMoney interface.

g. Show that the `minus`, `dividedBy`, and `negate` methods are just convenience methods by implementing them very simply using the `plus` and `times` methods.

h. Implement the USMoney class using one long instance variable to store the amount of money in cents. Don't forget to override the inherited `equals` and `hashCode` methods.

i. Implement the USMoney class so that arbitrarily large amounts of money can be stored in a USMoney object. You are welcome to make minor changes to the method and constructor headers.

j. It was mentioned in earlier chapters that a class' interface should have symmetry. In particular, each method should have a complementary method to make the class elegant. Since the USMoney class is immutable, the `getAmount` method of course will not have a complementary `setAmount` method. The `plus` and `minus` methods nicely complement each other, as do the `times` and `dividedBy` methods. But what about other methods?

(a) Consider the `negate` and `compareTo` methods. Shouldn't they have complementary methods to make the class even more elegant? Explain.

(b) There is no complement to the `toString` method. For symmetry to this method, which converts a USMoney object into String object, it would be nice to have a method that converts a String into a USMoney object. One such method could be a `fromString` method that takes a String as its parameter. This method could be a static method in the USMoney class (why static?). Or, instead, we could create a new constructor that takes a String as its parameter and creates the corresponding USMoney object. Either way you do it, the string needs to be parsed to create an object with the appropriate value. For example, if the user wrote

```
USMoney money = USMoney
  .fromString("500");
```

then the variable `money` could refer to an object corresponding to $5. Note that this method will somehow need to handle Strings that have improper format. We could throw an IllegalMoneyFormatException, a new class of exceptions that we create. Implement the `fromString` method as part of the implementation of the USMoney class described in part (h) above and have it throw an IllegalMoneyFormatException if the input string is improperly formatted. You will need to create this new exception class yourself.

k. The `times` and `dividedBy` methods result in round-off errors, since they involve floating point calculations. To avoid this problem, we could require the factor and divisor to be integers, but even then the `dividedBy` method could have round-off errors. One way to avoid this problem is to return an array of USMoneys. That is, the return type of `dividedBy` would be USMoney[]. This approach is discussed in [1]. It corrects for the problem of lost cents when you divide an amount of money by an integer. If we use `dividedBy` to divide an amount of money by n, then the size of the array returned by `dividedBy` is n and each object in that array contains $1/n$th of the original amount of money, except that the first few objects in the array have one more cent so that the total sum of the objects in the array adds up to the original amount. For example, if you divide $1 by 3, the `dividedBy` method will return an array of three USMoney objects, the first one corresponding to 34 cents and the last two corresponding to 33 cents. For this exercise, implement these new `times` and `dividedBy` methods, assuming that the value of a USMoney object in cents is stored in a long instance variable:

(a) `USMoney times(int factor)`

(b) `USMoney[] dividedBy(int divisor)`

2. These problems concern the Money classes discussed at the end of Section 6.4.

a. Finish the implementation of the Money class given at the end of Section 6.4.

b. The `getCurrency` method of the Money class returns a reference to the same Currency object that is used by the Money object. Doesn't this method expose the innards of the Money object? Shouldn't the `getCurrency` method instead return a clone of the Currency object referred to by the Money's `currency` field?

c. The java.util.Currency class gives you the symbol and the number of fractional digits for each world currency. From that information you can display an amount of money in either of two forms. In one form, the amount is preceded by the currency symbol and includes a decimal point in the appropriate place, such as "$3.14" for U.S. currency. In the other form, the amount is followed by the three-letter currency code, such as "3.14 USD." However, what if a country likes to display its currency in some third form, such as using a comma instead of a period or putting the symbol at the end? In that case, our Money class would not display the money appropriately. Explain an elegant way to handle such currency-specific differences.

3. These problems concern the Money classes discussed in Section 6.5.

a. We did not include the `toString`, `equals`, and `hashCode` methods in the Money interface. Why not? We will want all of our subclasses to implement those methods, and so shouldn't they be included in the interface?

b. As we mentioned at the beginning of the section, a Money object representing a mixed bag of currencies can be thought of as a "wallet" for an international traveler. However, with a wallet, the amount of money of each currency in it will vary over time. When viewed this way, it seems that Money should be a mutable container object rather than an immutable value object. After all, every time you add or remove money from your wallet, you don't create a whole new wallet with the new amount of money. Discuss whether it is better to have Money be immutable or mutable.

4. These problems concern the Money and MoneyConverter classes discussed in Section 6.6.
   a. Although we said that the `convertTo` method in the MoneyConverter class should return a SimpleMoney object, we declared the return type to be Money instead of SimpleMoney. Why did we do that?
   b. We decided that two Money objects should be equal if they have the same value after being converted to one common currency, such as U.S. dollars. However, the conversion rate between currencies varies over time and so any two Money objects may be equal at one point in time but not equal at a later point in time. Discuss the ramifications of this fact with regard to the implementation of the `hashCode` method in the Money classes. Recall from Chapter 4 that if two objects are equal, then they must have the same hash code value.
5. In Section 6.7, we added a new method to the Money interface

```
Money convertTo(Currency to,
  CurrencyConverter converter)
```

Implement this method in the Money class using the interface given at the end of Section 6.4.

6. These problems concern implementations of the MixedMoney class discussed in Sections 6.5–6.8. Use the MixedMoney interface given at the end of Section 6.5 but also include the method with header `Money convertTo(Currency to, CurrencyConverter converter)` discussed in Section 6.7.
   a. Implement the MixedMoney class so that it stores the money in an ArrayList of SimpleMoney objects. Implement it so that there is only one SimpleMoney object in the list of any given currency. That is, combine SimpleMoney objects of the same currency in the list into a single SimpleMoney object.
   b. Implement the MixedMoney class as in the preceding problem except do not combine SimpleMoney objects of the same currency in the list into a single SimpleMoney object.
   c. Implement the MixedMoney class so that it stores the money in a HashMap whose key is a Currency and whose corresponding value is a SimpleMoney object of that currency. In implementing the arithmetic operations, delete any key/value pairs whose amount has been reduced to 0.
   d. Implement the MixedMoney class so that it stores the money in a HashMap whose key is a Currency and whose corresponding value is a long integer indicating the amount of money of that currency. In implementing the arithmetic operations, delete any key/value pairs whose amount has been reduced to 0.
   e. Compare the implementations of MixedMoney in the preceding four problems. Which is the most elegant? Why?
7. These exercises refer to the Money interface and subclasses in Section 6.8.
   a. Change the Money interface into an abstract class and then implement the following methods in the Money class without referring to either the SimpleMoney or MixedMoney subclasses: `equals`, `dividedBy`, `minus`, and `negate`.
   b. Even though the methods listed here can be implemented in the Money superclass because the same code will work for both classes, why might the developer choose instead to implement them separately in the SimpleMoney and MixedMoney subclasses?
8. Implement the Money class discussed in Section 6.9 by eliminating the Money interface and the SimpleMoney class and renaming MixedMoney as Money.
9. These problems concern the Money class discussed in Section 6.10.
   a. One of the potential drawbacks of the implementation of Money using binary trees is that the tree grows in size every time you perform a `plus` operation. This means that you may end up with a tree with 50 leaf nodes, all potentially referring to money of the same currency. Therefore, add and implement a new method in the Money class:

   ```
   private Money simplify()
   ```

   that returns a new Money object with the same amount of money of each currency as this Money object, but with all leaves of the same currency combined into one leaf.
   b. The `simplify` method in the preceding exercise was designated a private method. Why? When should this method be called?

REFERENCES

1. Beck, K., *Test-Driven Development by Example*. 2003. Reading, MA: Addison-Wesley.
2. Fowler, M. *Analysis Pattern: Quantity*. 2004. [Cited April 8, 2007; available from *http://www.martinfowler.com/ap2/quantity.html*.]
3. Unknown. *JUnit Test Infected: Programmers Love Writing Tests*. 2004 [Cited April 8, 2007; available from *http://junit.sourceforge.net/doc/testinfected/testing.htm*.]
4. ISO. *ISO 4217 Currency Names and Code Elements*. [Cited April 8, 2007; available from *http://www.iso.org/iso/en/prods-services/popstds/currencycodeslist.html*.]

7

Introduction to Design Patterns

SECTION 7.0 INTRODUCTION

In Chapter 5, we discussed the advantages and disadvantages of the various possible software designs, and we developed some guidelines and rules to follow that will help you develop good designs. Many of these guidelines and rules evolved over the years. Practitioners would notice that certain things would work well and others would work poorly. They saved, in the form of a set of rules, those practices that worked well. Sometimes these rules were discovered the hard way when designs that seemed good in the initial phase ended up being very ugly, brittle, or totally unworkable when attempts were later made to modify the designs.

In this chapter, we introduce more tools to help you create good software designs. These tools, which can be thought of as some of the software industry's best practices for developing elegant code, are called *design patterns*. As stated in [1], design patterns are "simple and elegant solutions to specific problems in object-oriented software design. Design patterns capture solutions that have developed and evolved over time." Kent Beck in [2] says that "patterns are a literary form for capturing and transmitting common practice. Each pattern records a recurring problem, how to construct a solution for the problem, and why the solution is appropriate."

The cataloging and organization of these patterns has been going on since the early 1990s. The most famous book on the subject is *Design Patterns* [1], which introduces 23 design patterns, including examples in Smalltalk and/or C++. Since then, many books have appeared on the subject, including some that discuss the same patterns but use examples in Java.

Why bother learning these design patterns? John Vlissides, one of the four authors of [1], lists four main benefits in his later book [3]:

1. They capture expertise and make it accessible to nonexperts.
2. Their names collectively form a vocabulary that helps developers communicate better.
3. They help people understand a system more quickly when it is documented with the patterns it uses.

4. They facilitate restructuring a system whether or not it was designed with patterns in mind.

We would like particularly to stress the second and third benefits. If designers on a team can say things like, "Let's use the Decorator pattern here to handle all the options," they can raise the discussion to a higher level of abstraction. As a result, they are able to deal with a larger piece of the whole design and can avoid getting bogged down in low-level details.

Design patterns are usually presented and discussed at the conceptual level (as defined in Section 4.0 of this text), but we will also include in this chapter some sample implementations to give examples of patterns in practice.

In this chapter, we will introduce a few of the simplest design patterns so that you can get a feeling for what design patterns are. More patterns will be introduced in the context of the case studies in the following two chapters. In all these chapters, we will introduce the design pattern by way of a motivational example. Then, inside a box, we will present the design pattern in more general terms, including a discussion of when to use a pattern and the trade-offs involved in doing so.

Keep in mind that our intent in this book is just to introduce design patterns. The *Design Patterns* book, other patterns books, and Web pages devoted to design patterns lay out the patterns more formally than we will, including detailed analysis of the applicability, structure, participants, collaborations, and consequences of using the patterns, as well as motivation, implementation issues, and sample code. We refer you to those other sources to understand the finer points of each of the patterns.

SECTION 7.1 THE ADAPTER PATTERN

One of the simplest, but very useful, patterns is the *Adapter* pattern [1]. Let us see how this pattern naturally appears when software engineers are designing with change in mind, as discussed in Section 5.7. Let us review the material in that section but use a different example.

Suppose you are working in a company on a team that built a front end (for example, a Web interface) for one of your company's main applications. The back end of the application contains all the data (maybe in a database) and tools for manipulating that data. Suppose that one of the data structures managed by the back end is a collection of Person objects containing customer information. Assume that your front end needs to access these Person objects regularly so your code includes lots of statements such as

```
Person customer = backend.getPerson(name);
Address customerAddress = customer.getAddress();
```

that gets a person with a given name and then gets the address of that person (in the form of an Address object) from the Person object.

Now suppose your company is purchased by Acme Corporation, and the new owners like your front end so much that they want to replace the current front end of their database with your front end. Unfortunately, the Acme back end almost surely has a different interface than the back end for which your front end was designed. For a simple example, suppose the Acme back end does not use the exact same Person class as your front end but instead it uses a Customer class that stores different information about the person and has different methods for extracting that information.

What are you to do to get your front end working with the existing Acme back end? The problem that you now have is due to incompatible interfaces. Your front end assumes, among other things, that the back end has a `getPerson` method that returns a Person object and that the Person object has a `getAddress` method that returns an Address object. However, the new back end has a `getCustomer` method that returns a Customer object that does not store information in the same form. Therefore, the two ends cannot communicate with each other.

Obviously, some code in the existing front end or new back end needs to be changed. One way to fix the problem is to modify the front end so that it uses the interface of the new back end. In particular, you could modify it so that it always uses Customers instead of Persons. Another way to fix the problem would be to take the Acme back end and modify its code to use the interface expected by the front end. A third way would be to assign some of the changes to the front end and some to the back end.

However, both the front end and back end are hopefully well-written and have been extensively debugged. Regardless of whether you are talking about the front or back end, you are asking for new bugs every time you change existing working code. How can you get your front end and new back end to communicate with minimum changes to the existing code?

An elegant way is to provide a new class to act as an "adapter" to adapt one interface to another interface. Objects of this class sit between the front end and back end. In our case, the front end will communicate with the adapter class instead of the Acme back end. The adapter will provide the interface that the front end expects, but it will actually get the data from the Acme back end and transform it into the data that the front end expects.

To show an example of how such an adapter class would work with our front end and Acme's back end, we need to be a little more precise regarding the classes and interfaces involved. Let's assume that the front end is connected to the back end through a reference `backend` to an object implementing a BackEnd interface. That interface includes methods such as `getPerson`. Also assume that the Acme back end is in the form of an AcmeBackEnd object that does not implement the BackEnd interface. Instead it has its own interface, including methods such as `getCustomer`. To connect the front end and new back end, we create a AcmeBackEndAdapter class that implements the BackEnd interface, so that the FrontEnd can communicate with it, but it forwards the actual work to an AcmeBackEnd.

```
public class AcmeBackEndAdapter implements BackEnd
{
  private AcmeBackEnd backend; //the backend doing the real work

  public AcmeBackEndAdapter(AcmeBackEnd acmeBackEnd)
```

```
    {
      this.backend = acmeBackEnd;
    }
    public Person getPerson(String name)
    {
      Customer customer = backEnd.getCustomer(name);
      Person person = ...transform a Customer to a Person...;
      return person;
    }
    //...other methods in BackEnd interface...
  }
```

To use this adapter class, there needs to be only *one* change made to the existing front end and *no* changes to the new back end. The one change to the front end is that, instead of assigning to the `backend` instance variable a reference to the original back end, it now assigns to that variable a reference to an AcmeBackEndAdapter.

The use of an adapter class, as in this example, to adapt an existing class to a different interface is what is called the *Adapter* pattern.

Figure 7.1 gives a UML diagram of our new design.

Another simple example of the Adapter pattern, this time in a nonsoftware context, concerns electrical outlets. In the United States, most appliances have two flat prongs and an optional third round prong that fit into standard American electrical outlets. However, in other countries, the outlets are designed for appliances with two or three round prongs or flat prongs oriented in different directions or in different

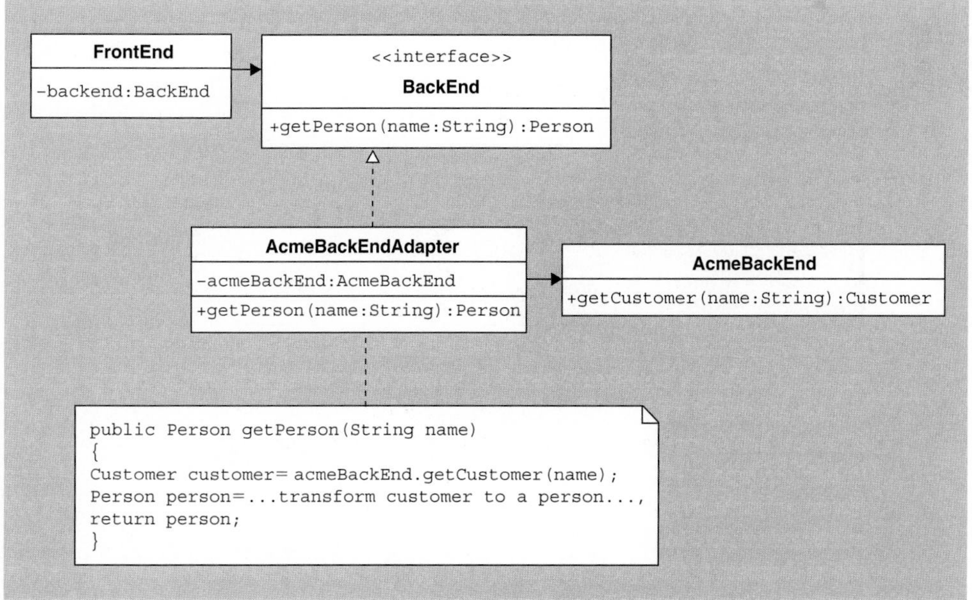

FIGURE 7.1 The FrontEnd and BackEnd adapter.

The Adapter Pattern

The Adapter pattern is useful when you have one client class that wants to use another class but that other class has the wrong interface. In that case, the solution provided by the Adapter pattern is to introduce an Adaptor class that connects the client class with the other class. The Adapter class is also called a *wrapper* class since it can be thought of as wrapping around the other class and so presenting a different interface to other classes.

The participants in the Adapter pattern are:

1. The Client, an existing class that uses a particular interface
2. The Target, the interface used by the Client
3. The Adaptee, a class that the Client would like to use except that it has a different interface than Target
4. The Adapter, the class that implements the Target interface using the Adaptee

See Figure 7.2 for a UML class diagram showing the relationships among the Adapter participants.

In our example, the front end plays the role of the Client, the BackEnd interface plays the role of the Target, the AcmeBackEnd is the Adaptee, and the AcmeBackEndAdapter is the Adapter class.

Another example of where the Adapter pattern might come in handy is an object-oriented business system that needs to use a legacy non–object-oriented database. A clean way to handle this situation is to isolate the non–object-oriented part behind a wrapper class. Only the wrapper class will communicate with the non–object-oriented database, and all other parts of the system

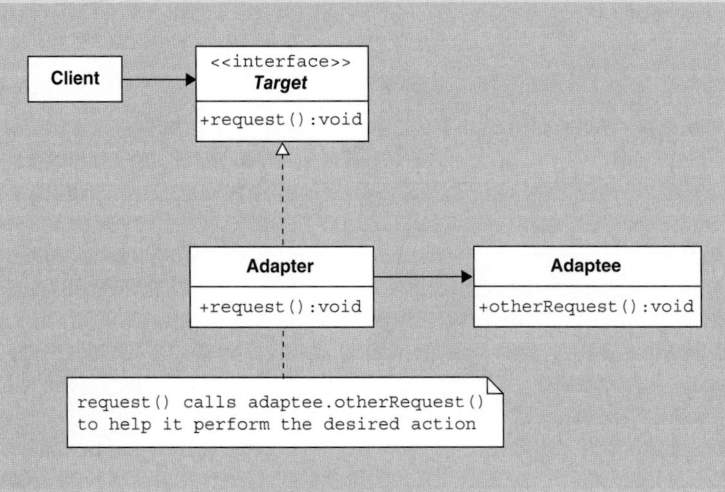

FIGURE 7.2 The Adapter pattern.

can blissfully assume the object-oriented wrapper class is actually an object-oriented database,

The main advantage of the Adapter pattern is that it allows the Client to use the Adaptee with minimal modifications to either class. The only new code that is needed appears in the Adapter class.

A disadvantage of using the Adapter pattern is that you have introduced yet another class into the design and therefore made it slightly more complex. Furthermore, there is now one more level of indirection in getting data to the front end from the back end; namely, the front end needs to ask the adapter class for the data, which then asks the actual back end for some data and converts that data into the form desired by the front end. But these disadvantages are usually far outweighed by the advantage of using an Adapter.

positions relative to each other. In those countries, the electrical interface does not match the interface for American appliances. So how can you use American appliances abroad? The solution is to purchase adapter plugs, with slots on one side into which American appliances fit and prongs on the other side that fit into the other country's outlets. Or to use the Acme clock example, in Section 5.7, the way to plug a general appliance into an outlet designed to accommodate only Acme electric clocks is to purchase or construct an adapter that plugs into the Acme clock outlet and that has slots into which general electrical appliances prongs fit.

SECTION 7.2 THE SINGLETON PATTERN

Consider a computer whose GUI is controlled by a WindowManager object. That object is responsible for displaying windows, dialogs, and icons when they are created or when they become exposed again after being covered by other GUI elements. Now consider what would happen if two such WindowManager objects were accidentally created. They would be stepping on each others toes, possibly displaying two copies of windows or icons or fighting to display a window. The screen would surely become unstable and unusable.

Similarly, consider a PrinterController object that controls all access to a set of resources such as printers. You do not want clients creating two or more PrinterControllers for the same set of printers, and so you need to restrict the number of PrinterController objects that can be created.

There is a similarity in both these examples in that we want to limit the number of objects of a class that are created to just one, but we want that one instance to be available to clients globally. How do you guarantee that there will be only one and make it accessible globally? The Singleton pattern [1] is a way of solving this problem elegantly.

To understand the Singleton pattern, let us start with a Singleton class of which we want to ensure that there will never be two or more instances created. To ensure such a thing, you clearly need somehow to hide the constructors for that class, such as making them private, so that clients cannot create new objects. As a consequence of this privatization, the class itself will need to create the instance. There are two or three standard ways that this creation can be implemented.

In the first approach, the object is created when the class is loaded, in which case the class could look something like this:

```
public class Singleton
{
    public static final Singleton instance = new Singleton();
    private Singleton() { }
    //...any other methods...
}
```

The key idea here is making the constructor private and creating one instance of the class, which is referenced by a public static variable, making it globally available. Any client could access the Singleton by the following code:

```
Singleton s = Singleton.instance;
...code that uses s...
```

An alternative approach would be to make the one instance a *private* static variable and provide a static method to get the instance. In that case, your class could look like this:

```
public class Singleton
{
    private static Singleton instance = new Singleton();
    private Singleton() { }
    public static Singleton instance() { return instance; }
    ...any other methods...
}
```

In this case, the user would access the instance by using the following code:

```
Singleton s = Singleton.instance();
...code that uses s...
```

You may wonder what advantage the second approach has over the first one. With these two particular implementations of Singleton, there is no advantage. However, the second approach is better in that it allows you to modify the implementation details of the Singleton class in a variety of ways without having to modify existing client code. For example, suppose the Singleton object takes a long time to create and you don't want a long delay during the start up of your application. Or suppose the object uses a lot of memory, and so you don't want to create it at all unless it is needed. In these cases, we could take a third approach called *lazy instantiation*. To implement this alternative, you only need make a minor change to the previous version:

```
public class Singleton
{
  private static Singleton instance = null;
  private Singleton() { }
  public static synchronized Singleton instance()
  {
    if (instance == null) {
      instance = new Singleton();
    }
    return instance;
  }
  ...any other methods...
}
```

As you can see, this approach avoids creating the one instance until the first time `instance` is called.

Although we have not discussed threads in this text, it should be noted that a "synchronized" modifier must be added to the `getInstance` declaration to prevent the Singleton's `getInstance` method from being executed by more than one thread at the same time. If two threads could execute the `getInstance` method simultaneously, there is the possibility that each thread would think that the instance is null and so create two instances.

An alternative way to accomplish the same result as the Singleton pattern is to make all the methods and attributes of the class static. In that way, there is re-

The Singleton Pattern

The Singleton pattern is a technique for ensuring that there is only one instance of a class and making that instance globally available.

This pattern is implemented by hiding the constructors for the class (i.e., making them nonpublic) and having the class itself provide you with the single instance through a static method. See Figure 7.3 for a UML diagram of this pattern.

The advantage of this approach over other approaches, such as making all methods and attributes static, is that it can easily be modified if you want a fixed number of instances greater than one or if you want to be able to create a subclass with a Singleton object.

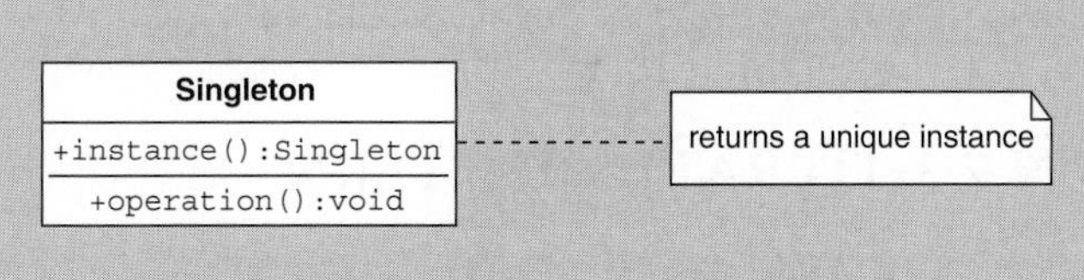

FIGURE 7.3 The Singleton pattern.

ally only one "object" to deal with, namely the class itself. Furthermore, since any instance of the class is irrelevant and possibly confusing to the user, the constructor could be made private.

The disadvantages of this alternative approach are twofold. First, it sometimes happens that you do not want just one instance of the class and instead want some other fixed number of instances. You cannot easily do so with the static method and static attribute approach. Second, it is much harder to subclass the Singleton class and use a single instance of that subclass instead of the Singleton class. These two issues are discussed further in the exercises.

Before leaving the subject of Singletons, it should be mentioned here that, in the case of Java, there are subtle issues that can cause the failure of the Singleton pattern. One such issue concerns Java's dynamic class unloading. When the Java runtime environment does garbage collection, it may check to see whether any classes (not just objects) that have been loaded into memory are currently reachable from objects in the program. If not, then the runtime environment unloads the class to save memory. In that case, if the class is later accessed, it is reloaded. Now, if the Singleton class is unloaded and reloaded in this way, the single instance before the unloading will not be identical to the single instance after the unloading and reloading. Depending on the role of the Singleton instance and the data it was maintaining, the creation and resulting initialization of a new Singleton instance can create subtle errors. More details can be found in [4].

Another subtle issue regarding Singletons in Java concerns object serialization in which a copy of an object or a collection of objects are stored ("serialized") in persistent memory (such as on disk) and later deserialized or reloaded. If the Singleton instance is serialized in this way and then deserialized, the deserialized Singleton may not be identical to the original Singleton, which can cause identity problems. For more details, see [5].

We need to mention here one final caution regarding the Singleton pattern. You might be tempted to decide to use the Singleton pattern for most of the objects in a software system so that those objects will be easily available everywhere in the system. After all, you don't need to worry about maintaining references to the Singleton object or pass it around as a parameter if you can always get a reference to it anywhere in your code by invoking `Singleton.instance()`. However, this temptation should be avoided since what you are really doing in that case is declaring those objects to be global, which is not good object-oriented design. As we discussed in earlier chapters, an object's scope should be as narrow as possible. The Singleton pattern's purpose is not to make objects globally available. The pattern should be used only in situations where the number of instances of a class must be limited. Furthermore, even in that case, the scope of those instances should be as narrow as possible, for example, by restricting access to the Singleton to the package in which it resides.

SECTION 7.3 ITERATOR PATTERN

There is a design pattern that you have surely seen in your data structures course and that has appeared in the preceding three chapters in this text, although it was never explicitly discussed as a pattern at that time, namely, the *Iterator* pattern [1].

In this section, we will review that pattern in the general context of iterating over any collection.

One of the most common activities involving a collection of objects is iteration, or stepping through the items in the collection. For example, you might iterate through the collection to search for a particular value, you might iterate to print the values of all the elements in the collection, or you might iterate to move the elements into a different collection, possibly filtering out some of the elements.

If you are using an array `A` as your collection, you might use a `for` loop for iteration:

```
for (int i = 0; i < A.length; i++) {
  Object data = A[i];
  ...do something with data...
}
```

If you are using a ordered collection with constant-time random access, such as an ArrayList v, you might use a similar loop:

```
for (int i = 0; i < v.size(); i++) {
  Object data = v.get(i);
  ...do something with data...
}
```

If you are using a home-grown linked list of nodes with `data` and `next` pointers, your code might look like this:

```
while( n != null ) {
  Object data = n.data;
  ...do something with data...
  n = n.next;
}
```

In every case, we might be doing the same thing with the data, but we are using slightly different control structures to iterate over the data because of the differences in the structures themselves.

But what if, after all your code is written, you decide to use a different collection, for example, you decide to swap out an ArrayList and replace it with a HashSet? It would be nice if you could avoid the hassle of modifying every iteration over the collection to use a new loop construct. A second problem, that is just as important, is that a client using the collection who only wants to traverse it shouldn't have to worry about the details of the implementation of the collection. That is, suppose you have a method that returns a Collection. The user of your method doesn't know what kind of Collection (i.e., what kind of class implementing the Collection interface) is returned. Without a common iteration technique that works across all Collection classes, the user would need to determine the actual class returned by your method in order to write a loop for iterating over the items in that collection.

To fix these problems, two standard, cross-collection approaches for iterating have been created. The first approach is to use the `for-each` loop construct in Java 1.5. This construct allows you to step through any array or Collection class in a uniform fashion. For example, let c be any Collection of objects or an array of objects. Then to step through the elements of c, you can write:

```
for(Object data : c) {
  ...do something with data...
}
```

You can read this loop as "for each Object data in c, do something with the data." If your client uses this construct when traversing the Collection, then the actual class of c doesn't matter.

The second cross-collection approach to iteration is useful in those cases where you want more direct control over the traversal process. In these situations, you can use an "iterator" over each Collection, as described by the Iterator pattern.

The Iterator pattern says that all collections should create Iterator objects associated with the collection to help you iterate over the elements in that collection. The Collection classes in the java.util package use an Iterator interface for just this purpose. The Iterator interface in the java.util package has three methods:

```
public boolean hasNext(); //returns true if the collection has more
                          //elements to be visited
public Object next();     //returns the next element in the collection
public void remove();     //optional method-removes from the collection
                          //the last element returned by the iterator
```

To traverse any collection, regardless of the actual class of the collection, you can use a control structure with the following form:

```
Iterator it = ...;
while (it.hasNext()) {
  Object data = it.next();
  ...do something with data...
}
```

Or if you prefer a for-loop format, you could write the traversal in the following form:

```
for( Iterator it = ...; it.hasNext(); ) {
  Object data = it.next();
  ...do something with data...
}
```

To repeat, the idea is that you can use such a control structure for iterating over *any* kind of collection, and so you don't need know or worry about the particular kind of collection you are dealing with.

Where does the Iterator for a collection come from? The Collection classes in the java.util package have an iterator method that returns a new Iterator object. So if you have a collection c, then your iteration control structure would look like:

```
Iterator it = c.iterator();
while (it.hasNext()) {
   Object data = it.next();
   ...do something with data...
}
```

Besides the advantage of the uniformity of this control structure among various data structures, there is another reason to use an Iterator to traverse a collection, as mentioned in the second example of Section 5.3. Namely, it separates into different objects the responsibility of iteration over a collection from the other responsibilities of a collection, such as storing and retrieving the data.

It should be pointed out that the `for-each` construct in Java is not independent of the `iterator` method in the Collection classes. The `for-each` construct is, in fact, just a convenient shorthand notation for the `for` loop using Iterators described above. In particular, if you create your own class that maintains a collection of objects but your class does not implement the Iterator interface, then you cannot use the `for-each` construct to traverse the objects in your class.

A variation on iterators is to use them to iterate over "virtual" collections. For example, suppose you want to step through arbitrarily many prime numbers. Because there are infinitely many primes, it is impossible to create a collection with all such numbers and then iterate over that collection. Instead, you can create a *virtual* collection of primes that represents all primes but only computes them when they are first needed, using lazy evaluation. Here is the interface to one such class:

```
public class SetOfPrimes
{
   //constructor
   public SetOfPrimes() { ... }
   //returns the i-th prime
   public BigInteger get(BigInteger i) { ... }
   //returns an iterator over the primes. The n-th call to
   //the iterator's next() method returns a BigInteger value
   //containing the n-th largest prime.
   public Iterator<BigInteger> iterator() { ... }
}
```

To avoid having to recalculate the primes every time an iteration is asked for, the class could store the already-calculated primes in an internal collection. In the exercises, you are asked to implement this class.

Another variation on the Iterator pattern to use internal iterators instead of external iterators, as described in the next section.

It should be noted that, although arrays can be traversed using the `for-each` loop, Java arrays do not have an `iterator` method. If you need such an iterator, you can create it indirectly by invoking the static `asList` method in the Arrays class to create a List from the array and then invoking the `iterator` method of that list. For

The Iterator Pattern

The Iterator pattern provides a uniform way to access sequentially the elements in a collection regardless of the structure of the collection. That is, it allows access to the collection's elements without exposing the representation of the collection. A client who is using a collection class need only know that the class implements the Collection interface.

The participants in this pattern (see Figure 7.4) are:

1. Client, which has access to a Collection it would like to traverse.
2. Collection, which is an interface that includes an `iterator` method.
3. ConcreteCollection, a class that implements the Collection interface.
4. ConcreteIterator, a class that implements the Iterator interface and is created and returned by the ConcreteCollection class' `iterator` method. This class keeps track of which elements in the ConcreteCollection that it has already traversed and determines the next element in the traversal.

The UML sequence diagram in Figure 7.5 shows the sequence of events that are used to traverse a collection using the Iterator pattern. The client first invokes the collection's `iterator` method, which creates an iterator object that implements the Iterator interface. The `iterator` method returns the iterator object to the client. The client then uses the iterator to traverse the collection's elements by repeatedly calling its `next` method as long as the iterator's `hasNext` method returns true.

The advantages of the Iterator pattern are several:

1. It allows the client to traverse a collection without needing to know the underlying structure of the collection.

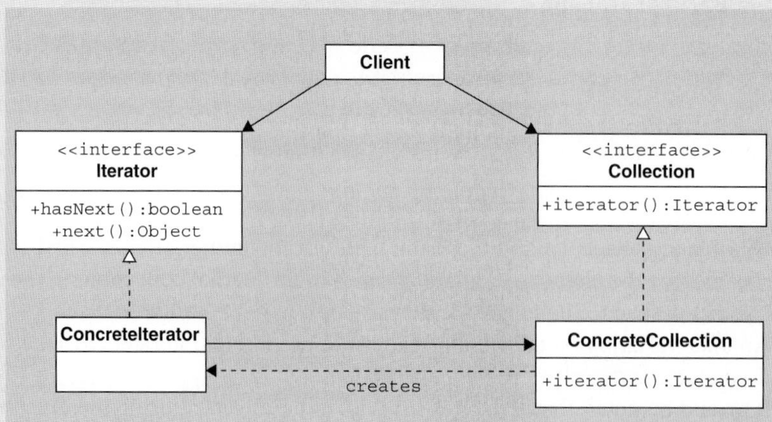

FIGURE 7.4 The Iterator pattern.

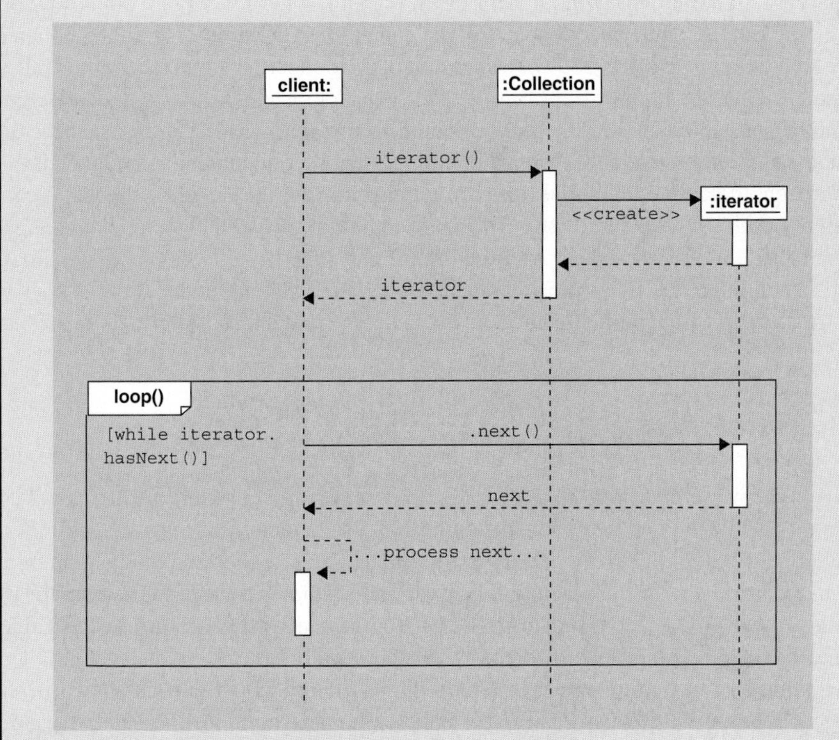

FIGURE 7.5 The sequence of operations in the Iterator pattern.

2. It separates the concerns of maintaining a collection from the concerns of traversing a collection.
3. It allows several traversals of the collection at the same time (as when two or more clients ask for iterators over the same collection).
4. It allows different forms of traversal of the same collection. For example, a binary tree collection could have both a preorder and a postorder iterator.

example, if `A` is an array of objects, then, to get an iterator over `A`, you can use the following code:

```
Iterator it = Arrays.asList(A).iterator();
```

By the way, in the java.util package, there is an older Enumeration interface that has the same functionality as the java.util.Iterator interface except for the `remove()` method, but it uses longer method names. You are encouraged to use the Iterator interface instead of the Enumeration interface because of its clarity and consistency.

One final note: The Iterator pattern seems simple, but, like the Singleton pattern, there are subtle issues that can cause problems. For example, what if the collection structure is modified during the iteration process, for example, by another thread that inserts or deletes an object in the collection? If the iterator is not carefully designed, the program could halt with an error or the iterator could merrily go on its way but miss or double-count some elements in the collection. One solution to this problem is for the iterator to create a copy or a snapshot of the collection when the iterator is first created. Then the iterator steps through the snapshot instead of the actual collection. Another possibility is that the iterator could throw an exception if any changes are made before it completes visiting all the objects in the collection. To implement this approach, the collection could have a version stamp that the iterator checks in each call to `next()` and the iterator throws an exception if the version stamp has changed since the iterator was created. A third possibility is that the collection could maintain a link to all iterators it has created and notify them if a client modifies the collection in any way, at which point the iterators could deal with it appropriately.

SECTION 7.4 THE COMMAND PATTERN

The iterators we discussed in the last section are certainly an improvement over using different kinds of loops for different kinds of collections. However, with these iterators, we are still getting the data from the collection and then doing something with that data, rather than having the collection do the operation on the data for us. This way of processing the data in the collection is directly contrary to the guidelines of the Expert pattern. We should be able to do better. For instance, a lot of code that use an iterator use it in a loop almost identical to the ones shown in the preceding section. Therefore, can't we factor out the common parts of the loop, leaving those common parts up to the collection and leaving only the unique parts to the client?

One way to do such refactoring is to use an *internal* iterator instead of an *external* iterator—the kind we discussed above. As previously discussed, iterators are called *external* since they produce an iterator object external to the collection that the user can use to loop through the data and manipulate it. In contrast, an internal iterator is one that the client never sees. It visits all the data in the collection in an internal (hidden) loop, and all the client needs to do is to tell it what action to perform on each piece of data when it visits that piece. In other words, when using an internal iterator, all the client has to do is to command the collection to "do something" to each of its elements. Note that the client is responsible only for specifying precisely what the command to "do something" means, and the collection is responsible for iterating (internally) over its elements and executing the command on each element.

Unfortunately, the java.util.Collection interface and implementing classes do not directly support internal iterators. Therefore, for the sake of an example, let us create our own ExtendedCollection interface that handles them. The new interface will add a `map` method to the Collection interface:

```
public interface ExtendedCollection extends java.util.Collection
{
  public void map(Command c);
}
```

The `map` method is the internal iterator method and is responsible for applying the given command to each of the elements in the collection. But what is a "Command"? What we really want to pass as a parameter to the `map` method is another method containing the code we want executed on each element of the collection. But how do you pass a method as a parameter? Only objects and primitive data can be so passed.

A natural solution is to put the method in an object and then pass that object as the parameter to `map`. This solution is one of the simplest forms of the *Command* pattern [1]. In this simple form, a client needs to pass some executable code as a parameter to a method so that the method can execute that code. Because code cannot be passed directly, the code is wrapped in an object and the object is passed as the parameter. The code the client wants executed is included in an `execute` method of the object.

In our case, the Command is an interface:

```
public interface Command
{
  public void execute(Object data);
}
```

Any object that implements this interface can be passed to the `map` method in our ExtendedCollection interface. Once such a Command object is passed to `map`, the `map` method is responsible for calling the object's `execute` method once for each element of the collection.

Let us now construct an example of a class that implements the ExtendedCollection interface so that we can see how internal iteration works in a complete program.

```
public class ExtendedArrayList extends ArrayList
  implements ExtendedCollection
{
  public void map(Command c)
  {
    for(Object data: this) {
      c.execute(data);
    }
  }
}
```

Notice that the Command's `execute` method is called on each element of the collection. Here is how a client might use an internal iterator to print all the values in an ExtendedArrayList:

```
//create a collection
ExtendedArrayList collection = new ExtendedArrayList();
//add elements to the collection
collection.add("Hello");
collection.add("Bye");
```

The Command Pattern

The Command pattern is useful when you want to encapsulate executable code as an object. This encapsulation is handled by wrapping the action in a Command object, which gets passed to the object that will invoke the action. To invoke the action, the object just needs to call the `execute` method of the Command.

See Figure 7.6 for a UML class diagram of this pattern.

The participants in the pattern are the following:

1. Command, which is an interface with an `execute` method
2. ConcreteCommand, a class that implements the Command interface and forms the encapsulation of an action
3. Invoker, a class that invokes the `execute` method of a Command
4. Client, who creates a ConcreteCommand object and passes it to an Invoker object

In this pattern, the Client creates the ConcreteCommand object and passes it to an Invoker object. The Invoker later (at an appropriate time) invokes the `execute` method of the ConcreteCommand.

One of the main advantages of the Command pattern is that it separates in a Command object the knowledge of what needs to be done (the action) from the object that invokes that code. The object invoking the `execute` method (the Invoker) need never know what action gets performed by that method. Similarly, the Command object need never know what object will be the Invoker. In this way, coupling is reduced.

Another advantage of the Command pattern is that the Invoker can be passed different Commands at different times and so in that way change dynamically the behavior of the invoker.

You can also collect and save actions for later execution. For example, you could add several Commands to a list of Commands. For a simple example of a situation where such a list would be useful, consider an application with an Undo menu item. Whenever an undoable action is performed, the opposite ac-

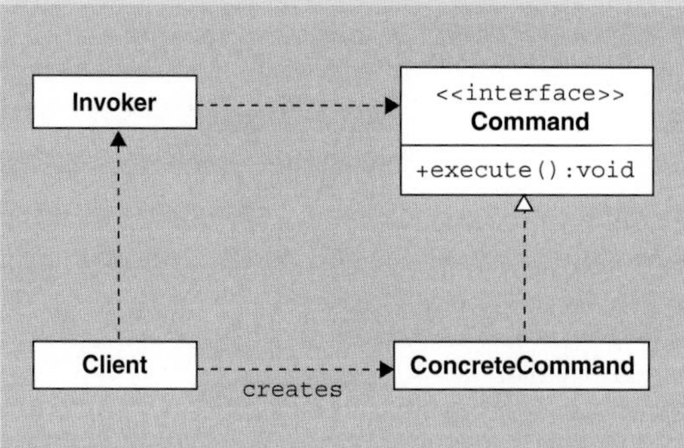

FIGURE 7.6 The Command pattern.

tion can be encapsulated in a Command object and pushed on a stack. Then, when the user selects the Undo menu item, the top Command on the stack is popped and its action is performed, thereby undoing the last action.

Another option with the Command pattern is to create a MacroCommand, which is a Command that maintains a list of other Commands. When the MacroCommand's `execute` method is invoked, it invokes the `execute` methods of all the contained Commands.

```
//print out the elements of the collection
collection.map(new Command() {
                  public void execute(Object data) {
                     System.out.println(data);
                  }
               });
```

Notice that the client does not have to deal with iterators. All the client has to do is tell the collection to map a particular Command to all of its elements.

Let us summarize the various approaches we've taken to visiting all the elements of a collection.

- Some collections, such as ordered lists or arrays, can have their elements visited using loops that get each element directly from the collection. This approach is useful if you want to visit the elements in an order different from the usual order supplied by an iterator.
- If the client doesn't care about the order in which the elements are visited or is satisfied with the default order used by iterators, then external iterators are preferable to other type-specific traversal methods since iterators reduce the coupling in the code.
- If a client only wants to execute some specific code on each of the elements of the collection, then an internal iterator, if available, is usually easier to use than an external iterator.

There is also a fourth way to visit all the elements of a collection that we haven't yet mentioned that is better, from the client's perspective, than all three of these approaches. If the collection's elements are often visited to perform a very specific task, then the collection's interface can be extended to include a method that performs that specific task for the user, in which case the client only needs to invoke that method. For example, a client often needs to know the size of a collection. If there were no more convenient way to get its size, the client might have to traverse the collection to compute it. But, anticipating this need, the Collection interface includes a `size` method, and so the client needs only to invoke that method to compute the size. Similarly, a collection often needs to be searched, and so, to avoid having to traverse the collection to find the desired item, the Collection interface includes a `contains` method that does the traversal for you.

SECTION 7.5 FACTORIES

The final topic in this chapter concerns creating objects and elegant ways of doing so.

Let us return to the case study of the polygon-drawing application we first mentioned in Section 3.9. In that section, we said that when the user clicks in the canvas, a polygon corresponding to the currently selected tool is drawn. Let us consider the code for the MouseListener that listens for mouse clicks in the canvas. We'll assume that this listener has access to a `currentTool` variable that stores the currently selected Tool. Because the polygon to be created depends on the value of `currentTool`, the MouseListener cannot just create one fixed type of polygon. A natural way to create the proper kind of polygon is to use a conditional in the `mouseClicked` method as follows:

```
public void mouseClicked(MouseEvent e)
{
  if( ...currentTool is a triangle tool... )
    ...add a triangle to the canvas where the click occurred...
  else if( ...currentTool is a rectangle tool... )
    ...add a rectangle to the canvas where the click occurred...
  else if ...
}
```

However, this code clearly has bad smells. A better way, that would avoid the conditional, would be to design the currently selected Tool to act as a factory that would create for you a new polygon of the shape corresponding to that tool. That is, we could add a method to the Tool class with the following header

```
public Polygon createPolygon(Point center)
```

that creates a new Polygon of the appropriate type with the given center point. Then the `mouseClicked` method can look like this:

```
public void mouseClicked(MouseEvent e)
{
  ...get centerPoint...
  Polygon p = currentTool.createPolygon(centerPoint);
  ...add p to the canvas...
}
```

and no conditionals are necessary. The `createPolygon` method is a factory method that creates objects for use by others, such as the MouseListener.

But how is the `createPolygon` method implemented in the Tool class? If there is a conditional in that method, then we have succeeded, in our redesign, only in moving the conditional to a new location and so have not removed the bad smell. An elegant way to solve this problem is to make the `createPolygon` method abstract in the Tool class since the Tool class doesn't know which kind of polygon to create. Instead, create subclasses of Tool (e.g., SquareTool, TriangleTool, RectangleTool) that

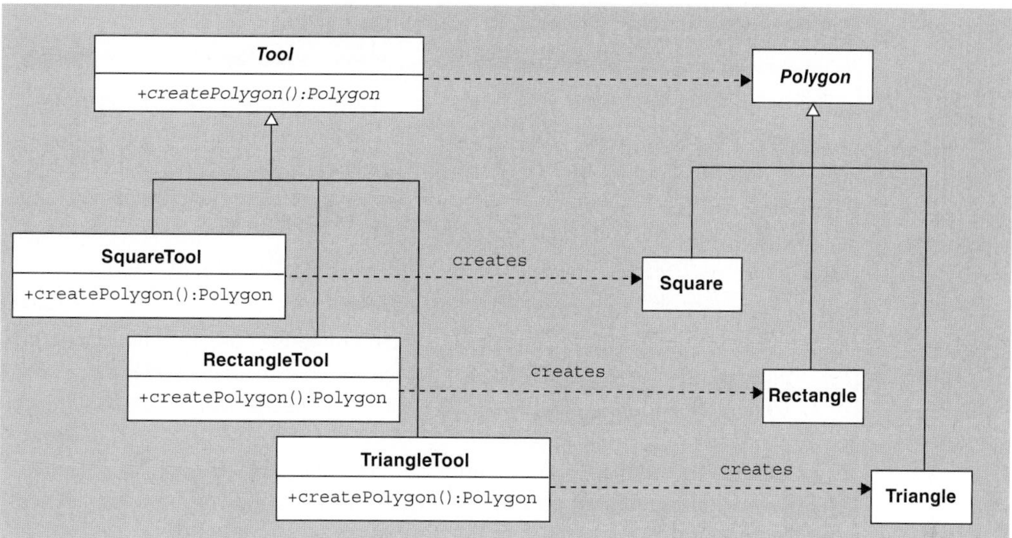

FIGURE 7.7 The Tool and Polygon hierarchies.

implement `createPolygon` differently so that the appropriate kind of object is created. See Figure 7.7 for a UML diagram of this situation.

This design is called the *Factory Method* pattern. In this pattern, a class (e.g., our Tool class) needs to create objects (e.g., Polygons) but it doesn't know which class of object to create. The solution is to add to the design of the class an abstract factory method for creating the objects, but leave the implementation of the factory method to subclasses, each of which creates a different type of object.

For another example of the Factory Method pattern, consider the java.util.Collection interface and java.util.AbstractCollection class. The AbstractCollection is a superclass of all classes in the java.util package that implement the Collection interface because it implements almost all methods in the Collection interface, thereby making it easier to implement the Collection classes. Now, in its implementation of those methods, the AbstractCollection class often creates Iterators to step through the elements of the collection. But the AbstractCollection class does not know exactly which subclass of Iterator to create because, for each subclass of AbstractCollection, a different Iterator is needed. The solution, according to the Factory Method pattern, is to create an `iterator` factory method in the AbstractCollection class and have the AbstractCollection's methods use that factory method whenever they need an Iterator, but have the implementation of the `iterator` method left up to the subclasses of AbstractCollection.

There are several variations on the Factory Method pattern. For example, the factory method could take parameters and, based on them, create several different kinds of products. That is, one concrete factory method need not just generate one kind of product. In a second variation, the factory method in the superclass is not abstract. Instead it provides a default implementation of the factory method, creating a default kind of product. In this situation, the subclasses need only override the

The Factory Method Pattern

The Factory Method pattern is useful in situations where a class (a "Factory") that needs to create other objects does not know which class of object to create and so leaves the actual creation up to its subclasses. The pattern is implemented by using a "factory" method for the creation of the objects rather than creating those objects by calling their constructors. The subclasses of the Factory can then override the factory method to create different types of objects.

The participants in this pattern are the following:

1. Factory, the abstract class that needs to create and use Products, but the particular type of Product needed varies with each subclass of Factory
2. ConcreteFactory, a subclass of Factory that needs to creates ConcreteProducts
3. Product, the interface for the products needed by the Factory
4. ConcreteProduct, which implements the Product interface and is created by the ConcreteFactory

See Figure 7.8 for a class diagram of these participants.

One of the advantages of using a factory method to create an object over direct object creation using a constructor is that it reduces coupling between the creator (the Factory) and the class being created (the Product). The abstract Factory class need know nothing about the specific subclasses of Product that are being created by the `create` method.

The Factory Method pattern is a technique in which an abstract class provides a "hook" for subclasses. That is, the abstract class provides a framework that uses some methods (such as the `create` method) to perform a task but leaves the implementation of those methods to subclasses. These methods are hooks upon which the subclasses can hang their specific behavior within the framework.

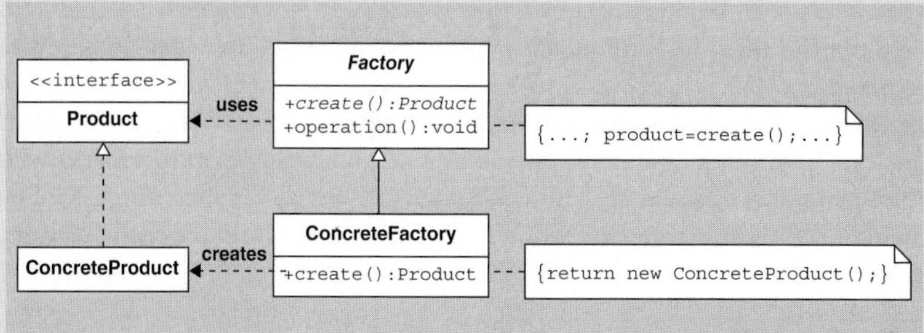

FIGURE 7.8 The Factory Method pattern.

factory method when they want a different kind of product. In a third variation, the factory method does not always call a constructor to create a new product. For example, the factory method might repeatedly return the same product, similar to the way the `instance` method in the Singleton pattern always returns the same object, or it might return one of the objects in a pool of objects that it maintains.

It should also be noted that there are many uses of factories in software design other than as described in the Factory Method pattern. For example, the javax.swing.BorderFactory class is aptly named because it is a class with a collection of public static factory methods, each of which creates and returns a different kind of Border. There is also another factory design pattern called the *Abstract Factory* pattern, which is addressed in the exercises.

SECTION 7.6 SUMMARY

In previous chapters, we introduced you to elegance in method implementation, elegance in class design, and finally elegance in interactions among classes. In this chapter, we introduced you to design patterns, which are designs that solve problems of class interaction in ways that have proven useful to practitioners in the software industry. Five of the simplest such patterns were presented. In those presentations, we motivated the pattern with an example, showed how the pattern helped the example's design, and then explained the pattern in more detail. These patterns are explained in even greater detail in the classic design pattern book [1].

EXERCISES

1. In the Java libraries, there are several classes with "Adapter" in their names, such as MouseAdapter and WindowAdapter. Are these classes playing the role of adapter classes in the Adapter pattern? Explain.
2. Prior to Java 1.5, if you needed a list of Strings, there were at least two approaches you could take. The first approach was to create an object, such as an ArrayList, that implemented the List interface and then populate it with Strings. However, whenever you fetched a String from the list, you needed to typecast the object returned by the list since the ArrayList's `get` method had a return type of Object. Furthermore, it was hard to ensure that no one accidentally added a non-String object to the list. Therefore, an alternative approach was to use the Adapter pattern and create a new StringList class that behaved just like a List except that its `add` methods took a String as its parameter and its `get` method had a return type of String. To store the Strings, the StringList class would reference an ArrayList or other List object. With the arrival of Java 1.5, a third, easier approach is possible. Explain that third approach.
3. Suppose you need a SimpleDate class that stores just a day, month, and year. Its `getDate` method returns a string with that date in the format (month day, year) or the format (day month year), depending on its parameter. Create an interface for SimpleDate and then create a class that implements it. Use the Adapter pattern with the Calendar class.
4. As mentioned in this chapter, a variation on the Singleton pattern is when an application needs a fixed number of instances of a class where the number of instances is greater than one.
   a. Come up with a situation where such a variation would be useful.
   b. Outline the design and implementation of this situation.
5. Investigate how one would go about subclassing a Singleton class so that a unique instance of the subclass is used instead of an instance of the Singleton class. There are several possible interfaces and implementations that can be used.
6. When we discussed the Singleton pattern, we mentioned that lazy evaluation is sometimes useful for

putting off the creation of an object until it is needed. The same lazy evaluation process is also useful during initialization of other kinds of objects. That is, instead of initializing all its instance variables of an object during construction, some of them can be initialized to null or some other invalid default value until they are first needed at which point they can be properly initialized.

a. What are the advantages of lazy initialization?

b. What are the disadvantages of lazy initialization?

c. Why would you not want to make publicly available instance variables that are initialized lazily?

7. An alternative design of the Iterator pattern is to require that, instead of an `iterator` method, all collections have a `get` method with the following interface:

```
public Object get(int i); //returns
  the i-th element
```

Then all collections `C` can be traversed with the same control structure:

```
for (int i = 0; i < C.size(); i++) {
  Object data = C.get(i);
  ...do something with data...
}
```

and so we have the advantage of iterators without having to create separate Iterator objects. What is wrong with this design?

8. Assume that the java.util.LinkedList class didn't have `iterator` or `elements` methods. Using the other methods of that class, create and implement a subclass called *IteratibleLinkedList* that has an `iterator` method. Try to make this method as efficient as possible.

9. Instead of a collection creating an Iterator object with which you communicate to do your iterating, the collection could create a "state" object that just stores the current state of the iteration. The user would hold onto the state object, but would never manipulate it (or even know its contents), passing it back to the collection whenever the user wants the next item or wants to advance to the next element, at which point the collection uses the state object to determine the next item and also update the state object to reflect the new state. Here's what the user's code would look like in this case, if the user was trying to iterate over a collection `c`. The user would first ask the collection for an initial state object. Then, whenever the user wants to move to the next element or determine whether there is a next element, she would pass the state object back to the collection to tell the collection where she is in the iteration process. The user code might look like this:

```
IterationState state = c.get
  InitialIterationState();
while( ! c.isDoneIterating(state) )
   {
   Object data = c.getCurrentItem
      (state);
   ...do something with data...
   c.advanceTheIteration(state);
   }
```

In this way, lots of users or threads could get their own state objects and use them to iterate through the collection concurrently. For this exercise, you are to create a new subclass of ArrayList called ArrayListWithIterationState that has `getInitialIterationState()`,`isDoneIterating(State)`, `getCurrentItem(State)`, and `advanceTheIteration(State)` methods so that the loop above will correctly step through the items in an object `c` of class ArrayListWithIterationState.

10. Implement the SetOfPrimes class defined in Section 7.3. The class should have a collection of BigIntegers in which the already-calculated primes are stored.

11. There is an alternative to creating a Command interface and then creating classes that implement that interface when you wish to use the Command pattern in Java. The alternative is to use the java.lang.reflect .Method class, each instance of which corresponds to a method in a class. If this approach is used, then the ExtendedCollection interface can be redefined to include the following declaration:

```
public void map(Method m)
```

a. Reimplement the ExtendedArrayList class from Section 7.4 so that it uses the new definition of ExtendedCollection using Method objects instead of Command objects.

b. What are disadvantages of using Methods instead of Commands in the ExtendedCollection interface?

12. Often Commands are compared to function *closures* (a feature available in some languages such as Lisp and Scheme).

a. Read about function closures, if you are not already familiar with them.

b. Describe the differences and similarities between Commands, as described in Section 7.4, and closures.

13. Any method that creates a new object and returns that object can be thought of as a "factory" method. However, the use of such a method does not necessarily mean that the Factory Method pattern is appropriate.

a. Give an example of a situation where such a factory method is useful outside of the Factory Method pattern.

b. Write a brief summary of other factory patterns, such as the Abstract Factory pattern [1], and explain how they differ from the Factory Method pattern.

14. Come up with a non–software-related example of the following design patterns:

a. Adapter
b. Singleton
c. Iterator
d. Command
e. Factory Method

REFERENCES

1. Gamma, E., R. Helm, R. Johnson, and J.Vlissides, *Design Patterns, Elements of Reusable Object-Oriented Software*. Professional Computing. 1995. Reading, MA: Addison-Wesley.
2. Beck, K., *Smalltalk Best Practice Patterns*. 1997. Upper Saddle River, NJ: Prentice Hall.
3. Vlissides, J., *Pattern Hatching, Design Patterns Applied*. Software Patterns Series. 1998. Reading, MA: Addison-Wesley.
4. Warren, N. and P. Bishop, *Java in Practice: Design Styles and Idioms for Effective Java*. 1999. Reading, MA: Addison-Wesley.
5. Bloch, J., *Effective Java Programming Language Guide*. The Java Series. 2001. Reading, MA: Addison-Wesley.

8

Figure-Drawing Application Case Study

SECTION 8.0 INTRODUCTION

In the previous chapters, we discussed design principles and patterns for making our code more elegant. In this chapter, we will use many of those principles and patterns and will introduce more patterns in the context of a drawing application. This application is based on HotDraw [1], a framework originally developed by Kent Beck and Ward Cunningham. The application discussed here is also based on the work of John Vlissides [2] and can be thought of as a much-simplified version of those works. Our approach is along the lines of the approach in [3] except that we will be implementing the application using the Java Swing package.

Aspects of this application already appeared previously in this text in Section 3.9 and briefly in Section 7.5. In this chapter, we will not assume that you have read those sections and will cover that material again from a slightly different angle here as it arises in the development of the application. We are doing so to keep this chapter somewhat independent of earlier chapters and also to reinforce the ideas and concepts covered in those earlier sections.

As you read the chapter, keep in mind that we will not just give you the "correct" answer to problems we encounter. Rather, we will usually consider several alternatives whenever we encounter a problem and will discuss some advantages and disadvantages of each before ultimately deciding on the path to take. Furthermore, sometimes we will head down a path that we later decide is not the best one. As a result, we will be doing some backtracking. To help you avoid getting confused or lost, we are providing guideposts along the way. In particular, at the end of most sections of this chapter, we provide working code for our application containing the latest version of the enhancements discussed in that and earlier sections. That working code should always be considered the starting point for the next section. Note that the code in the book has few, if any, comments or Javadoc headers. However, the code is also available electronically, and the electronic copy has proper documentation.

Before we begin, we should note that, in Chapter 5, we discussed the importance of using CRC cards, UML use case diagrams, and related tools when first designing a new application. However, we will not use them here. The reason is that we will be developing our application in incremental steps. In particular, the objects we will use will be added incrementally instead of all at once. Furthermore, our incremental software development process will consist of repeatedly finding something that works and then making it more elegant. At each step, we will not consider what the following step will be. One of the goals of this chapter is to see how well this development process succeeds.

SECTION 8.1 THE USER INTERFACE

As first introduced in Section 3.9, our application will consist of a window with two components: a toolbar and a drawing canvas. The toolbar, at the top of the window, will contain tools corresponding to various figures, in our case, rectangles, squares, and ellipses. The rest of the window will be a drawing canvas in which the figures can be drawn. See Figure 8.1 for a picture of the initial GUI.

At any given time, one of the tools will be selected. When the user clicks on the drawing canvas, a new figure of a fixed size will appear centered at the click. The shape of the figure will correspond to the selected tool. We will implement the tools in the toolbar with JButtons.

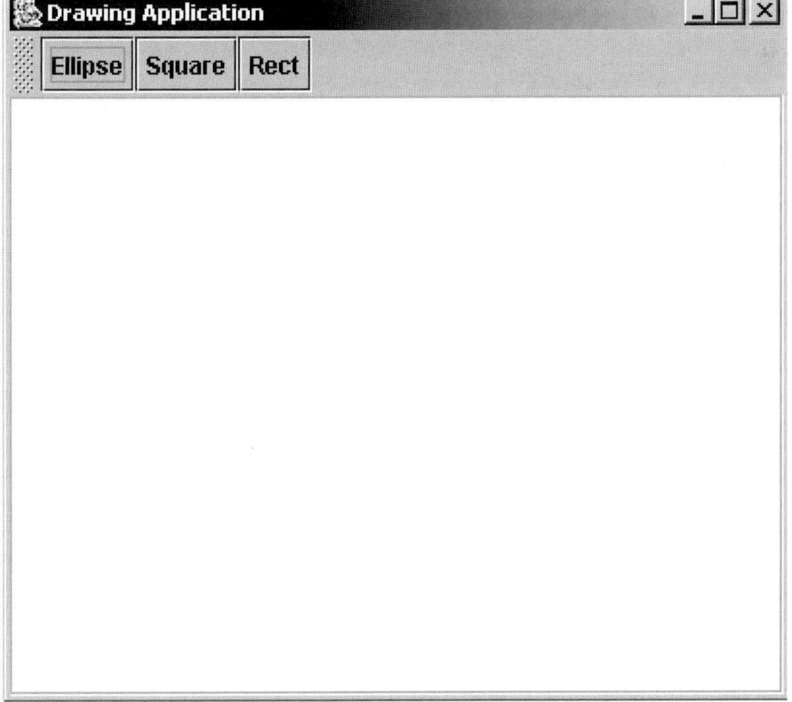

FIGURE 8.1
The initial drawing application GUI.

Here is Java source code for displaying the window shown in Figure 8.1 with a drawing canvas and a toolbar with three tools. A `main` method has been added to show you how to create and display the window. Note that this code is in a package called `drawer0`. Later versions of the application will appear in packages `drawer1`, `drawer2`, etc.

```
package drawer0;

import javax.swing.*;
import java.awt.*;

public class DrawingFrame extends JFrame
{
  public DrawingFrame() {
    super("Drawing Application");
    setDefaultCloseOperation(EXIT_ON_CLOSE);

    JComponent drawingCanvas = createDrawingCanvas();
    add(drawingCanvas, BorderLayout.CENTER);

    JToolBar toolbar = createToolbar();
    add(toolbar, BorderLayout.NORTH);
  }

  private JComponent createDrawingCanvas()
  {
    JComponent drawingCanvas = new JPanel();
    drawingCanvas.setPreferredSize(new Dimension(400, 300));
    drawingCanvas.setBackground(Color.white);
    drawingCanvas.setBorder(BorderFactory.createEtchedBorder());
    return drawingCanvas;
  }

  private JToolBar createToolbar() {
    JToolBar toolbar = new JToolBar();
    JButton ellipseButton = new JButton("Ellipse");
    toolbar.add(ellipseButton);
    JButton squareButton = new JButton("Square");
    toolbar.add(squareButton);
    JButton RectButton = new JButton("Rect");
    toolbar.add(RectButton);
    return toolbar;
  }

  public static void main(String[] args) {
    DrawingFrame drawFrame = new DrawingFrame();
    drawFrame.pack();
    drawFrame.setVisible(true);
  }
}
```

This code is available from the book's web site.

SECTION 8.2 THE OBSERVER PATTERN

If you try running the code given above, you will notice that most user input, such as clicking in a tool or on the canvas, is completely ignored. To handle such input, we need to enhance the code in several ways.

There are two fundamental user-generated events we need to handle: a click on a tool in the toolbar and a click in the drawing canvas. We need to decide which objects are going to deal with those events and how they are going to deal with them.

For clicking in the drawing canvas, we could have the canvas itself handle the events. In many ways, this approach makes sense since, after all, it is the canvas that is being clicked in. However, it is better to follow the principle of separation of responsibilities. That is, the canvas should be responsible just for displaying the figures, and some other object should be responsible for handling user input for the canvas. Let us call this second object the *CanvasEditor.* The CanvasEditor has one responsibility, namely, causing the appropriate shape to be drawn at the appropriate location in the canvas when the user clicks in the canvas. To design the CanvasEditor, we have to decide how the CanvasEditor knows where and when a click occurs in the canvas and how the CanvasEditor knows what shape is to be drawn in the canvas. Let us consider the second issue first.

In order to determine the appropriate figure to draw when the user clicks on the canvas, the CanvasEditor needs to know which tool button is currently selected, in other words, which tool button was last clicked. How can the CanvasEditor get that necessary information? It could have references to all three buttons, and, when a click occurs in the canvas, the CanvasEditor could poll them asking them when they were last clicked. See Figure 8.2 (a) for a class diagram. In this diagram, the three tool buttons are represented by a ToolButton class. Figure 8.2 (b) contains a sequence diagram of this design.

The design for our application displayed in these diagrams is not optimal. One problem is that the buttons need to keep track of their last click time. Furthermore, the CanvasEditor has to poll all of them each time it needs to know the selected one, which is more work than necessary.

Instead, consider a different approach in which all the buttons have references to each other and, whenever a button is clicked, it informs its fellow buttons that it is the most recently clicked. As a result, the CanvasEditor need only ask any one button which one was most recently clicked. However, this solution is actually worse in that all the buttons now need to keep track not only of each other but also the most recently clicked one. There is far too much message passing and information duplication going on here.

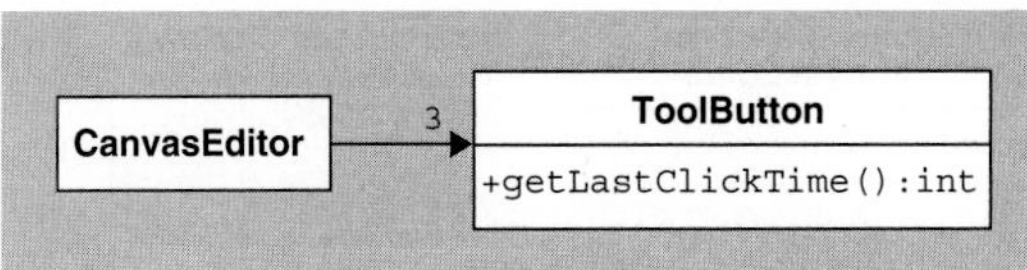

FIGURE 8.2 (a) Class diagram of CanvasEditor and ToolButtons.

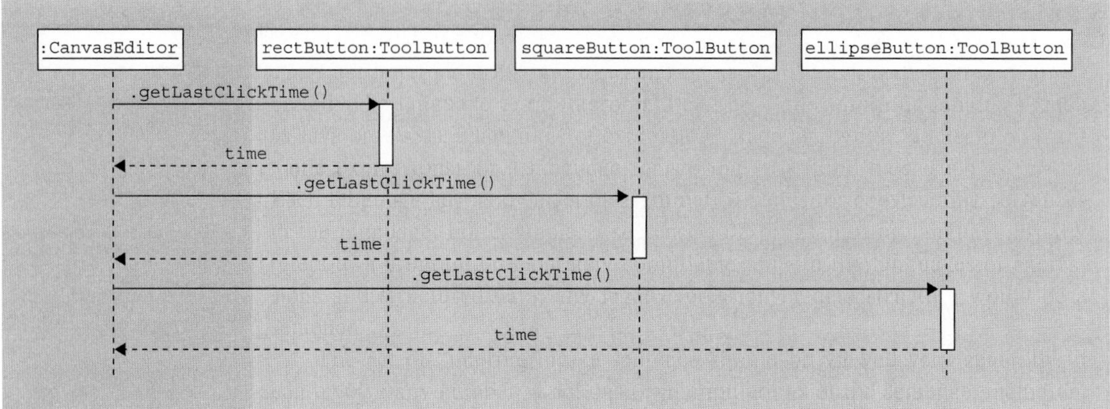

FIGURE 8.2 (b) Sequence diagram of CanvasEditor and ToolButtons.

Therefore, consider a third approach. Rather than the CanvasEditor polling the buttons when it needs to know which one was last clicked, it would be better for the buttons to have a reference to the CanvasEditor and directly notify it when they are clicked. The CanvasEditor then saves this information, and so always knows which button was most recently clicked. This makes much more sense in that the CanvasEditor is the one that needs the information, and so it should be the one responsible for maintaining the knowledge. See Figure 8.3 for a class diagram for this approach. When a button is clicked, it will call the `wasJustClicked` method of the CanvasEditor, passing itself as the parameter. The CanvasEditor then saves that button in the `lastClickedButton` attribute.

This third approach is better than the other two, but not quite as elegant as it could be. In the third version of our design, the buttons have references to the CanvasEditor, whereas in the other two approaches, the editor has references to the buttons. In every case, we have coupled the buttons and the editor together. Is there a way to reduce the coupling so that the CanvasEditor and/or the buttons are separately reusable in other contexts and yet still have the necessary communication between them?

Our solution is to use the *Observer* pattern [4]. In this design pattern, there are *observers* and there are *subjects* to be observed. The subjects are also called *publishers* or *broadcasters*, and the observers are also called *subscribers* or *listeners*. The publishers maintain a list of subscribers and, whenever there is something to publish, they notify all the subscribers. (Therefore, before an object can be a subscriber, it needs to ask the publisher to add it to the publisher's subscription list.) In this pattern, a publisher can have any number of subscribers.

FIGURE 8.3
The class diagram for the third approach.

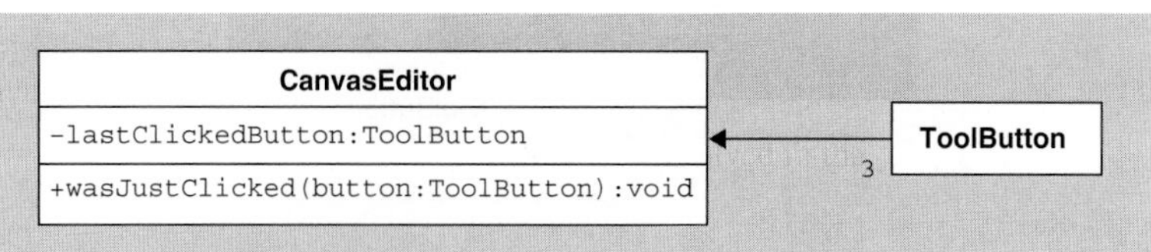

In our third approach, we were imitating the observer pattern in that the buttons play the role of publishers and the CanvasEditor plays the role of a subscriber. Whenever a button is clicked, the button notifies all subscribers—the CanvasEditor—of that event. But in that design, the CanvasEditor and the buttons are tightly coupled. To uncouple them, let us first look at how mouse clicks are handled in Java. In Java 1.1 or later, mouse-click event handling with Buttons is done through ActionListeners. Here is the definition of the ActionListener interface:

```
public interface ActionListener extends EventListener
{
  public void actionPerformed(ActionEvent e);
}
```

Note that the ActionListener interface has just one method (the EventListener superinterface has no methods). A listener that wants to subscribe to mouse-click events that occur in a button needs to implement this interface and must register with the button through the button's `addActionListener` method. Then, when the user clicks in the button, the button's default behavior is to generate an ActionEvent object that contains the details of the mouse click (such as a reference to the button itself, the timestamp of the click, and whether any modifier keys were down) and then call the `actionPerformed` method of all listeners, passing them the ActionEvent as the argument. Note that each of the listeners to the buttons, in the body of their `actionPerformed` methods, can do whatever they wish.

How does this ActionListener interface help reduce coupling? The key point is that the buttons, which are the publishers, no longer need to know exactly what kind of subscribers or listeners they have. All they care about is that all the listeners implement the ActionListener interface; that is, the buttons care only that the listeners have an `actionPerformed` method that the buttons can call when they are clicked in. We are therefore uncoupling the buttons from knowing the actual class of their listeners, and so we are allowing many kinds of objects (any kind that implement the ActionListener interface) to listen to the buttons.

In our fourth approach, we will use the Observer pattern as implemented in Java by the ActionListener interface. See Figure 8.4 for the class diagram of our new

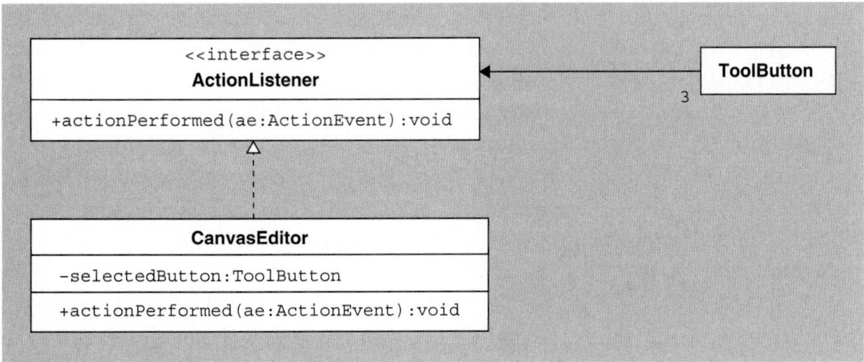

FIGURE 8.4 Using the Observer pattern through ActionListeners.

design as it relates to our CanvasEditor and ToolButtons. In this case, the CanvasEditor implements the ActionListener interface and the tool buttons, when clicked, call the `actionPerformed` method of the CanvasEditor. Furthermore, in its `selectedButton` attribute, the CanvasEditor can save a reference to the button that sent the `actionPerformed` message.

We end up with the following code for the CanvasEditor:

```
import javax.swing.*;
import java.awt.event.*;

public class CanvasEditor implements ActionListener
{
  private JButton selectedButton;

  public CanvasEditor(JButton initialSelectedButton)
  {
    this.selectedButton = initialSelectedButton;
  }

  public void actionPerformed(ActionEvent e)
  {
    selectedButton = (JButton) e.getSource();
  }
}
```

Note that, because we were able to uncouple the CanvasEditor from the ToolButtons, we are able to use the standard Swing JButton class for our toolbar buttons, and so we don't need to create a special ToolButton class.

To finish our implementation of the Observer pattern in the case of the CanvasEditor and the buttons, we only need to modify the `createToolbar` method of the DrawingFrame so that it registers the CanvasEditor subscriber with the three button publishers. The modification involves adding the following code to that method:

```
CanvasEditor CanvasEditor = new CanvasEditor(ellipseButton);
ellipseButton.addActionListener(CanvasEditor);
squareButton.addActionListener(CanvasEditor);
rectButton.addActionListener(CanvasEditor);
```

If you were to execute the code with these enhancements, you wouldn't see any visibly different behavior, but, behind the scenes, the CanvasEditor would change the value of its `selectedButton` instance variable whenever a different button is clicked.

At this point, we have dealt with handling clicks in tools in the toolbar. The other fundamental events we said at the beginning of this section that we need to handle are clicks in the drawing canvas. Therefore, let us continue with our design plans and let the CanvasEditor deal with these mouse clicks. Interestingly enough, we will see the Observer pattern appear a second time.

When the user clicks in the canvas, the CanvasEditor needs to draw the current figure (based on the button currently selected) centered at the click. Just as in the case of a click in one of the buttons, the CanvasEditor needs to be notified by the canvas when a click occurs in the canvas. Therefore, it makes sense that the communication between the canvas and the CanvasEditor should again be done using the Observer pattern. In this case, the CanvasEditor needs to be a listener to the canvas so that it is notified when a mouse click occurs in the canvas.

In Java, we can make the CanvasEditor a listener to clicks in the canvas by making the CanvasEditor implement the MouseListener interface and by registering it with the canvas through the canvas' `addMouseListener` method. (Clicking a JButton generates an ActionEvent whereas clicking a canvas—actually a JPanel—generates a MouseEvent.) The MouseListener interface is defined as follows:

```
public interface MouseListener extends EventListener
{
  public void mouseClicked(MouseEvent e);
  public void mousePressed(MouseEvent e);
  public void mouseReleased(MouseEvent e);
  public void mouseEntered(MouseEvent e);
  public void mouseExited(MouseEvent e);
}
```

We don't care about any events except mouse clicks so our CanvasEditor will implement the last four methods by just giving them empty bodies. We will, however, add code to the `mouseClicked` method in the CanvasEditor class to draw the desired figure in the canvas. Once we make these changes, our code for the CanvasEditor looks like the following:

```
public class CanvasEditor implements ActionListener, MouseListener
{
  private JButton currentButton;
  public CanvasEditor(JButton initialButton)
  {
    this.currentButton = initialButton;
  }
  public void actionPerformed(ActionEvent e)
  { //handle clicks in the buttons
    currentButton = (JButton) e.getSource();
  }
  public void mouseClicked(MouseEvent e)
  { //handle clicks in the canvas
    //get the location of the click and get the canvas
    int x = e.getX();
    int y = e.getY();
    JPanel canvas = (JPanel) e.getSource();
    //draw the correct figure
    if (currentButton.getText().equals("Ellipse"))
      canvas.getGraphics().drawOval(x - 30, y - 20, 60, 40);
    else if (currentButton.getText().equals("Rect"))
      canvas.getGraphics().drawRect(x - 30, y - 20, 60, 40);
```

The Observer Pattern

The Observer pattern is a technique for allowing an object, when it changes state, to notify other dependent objects so that they can appropriately update their state.

The object doing the notifying is often called a *subject* or *publisher* and the dependent objects are called *observers* or *subscribers*. When the publisher changes state, it broadcasts that information to its subscribers.

The participants in the pattern (see Figure 8.5) are the following:

1. Subject, which is the publisher that notifies the subscribers when its state changes
2. Observer, which is the interface of all subscribers
3. ConcreteObserver, which is a subscriber that implements the Observer interface and is notified when the Subject changes state

When the Subject's state has changed, it invokes its `notify` method, which in turn calls the `update` method of all the registered Observers. The `update` methods use the information passed in as a parameter to help them determine what needs updating in the Observers.

Two of the benefits of using the Observer pattern are (a) a publisher can have an arbitrary number of subscribers that can change at any time and (b) the publisher and subscribers are not tightly coupled. The second benefit is a consequence of the fact that the Subject knows only that its subscribers are Observers, and so doesn't need to know the actual class of the subscribers.

There are several variations in this pattern. For example, instead of the Subject calling its `notify` method after its state changed, the client that caused the change in the Subject might be responsible for invoking the Subject's `notify`

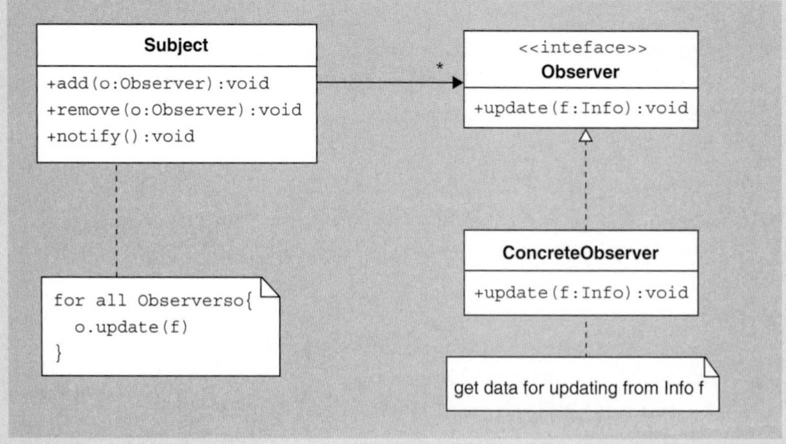

FIGURE 8.5 The Observer pattern.

method. The advantage of the first approach is that the clients do not have to remember to call `notify`. The advantage of the second approach can be seen when the client causes many consecutive state changes in the Subject. It is inefficient to have each of those changes cause the `notify` method to be invoked, which is what would happen if the Subject called `notify` after any state change. In contrast, the client can wait until all changes have been made and then invoke the Subject's `notify` method, thereby avoiding the inefficiency.

The amount of information passed as a parameter in a call to `update` can vary significantly in this pattern. At one extreme, the Observer already has a reference to the Subject, and that Subject is the only object being observed by the Observer. In that case, no information need be passed in the update method, and instead the Observer can poll the Subject for the information. This is the *pull* model. At the other extreme is the *push* model, in which all possibly useful information is passed as a parameter to `update`, whether the Observer needs that information or not.

It should be noted that this pattern is used extensively in the Java libraries in the form of various kinds of Listeners. There is also an Observer class and Observable interface in the java.util package to aid you in implementing the Observer pattern in other contexts.

```
        else //if( currentButton.getText().equals("Square") )
            canvas.getGraphics().drawRect(x - 25, y - 25, 50, 50);
    }
    //ignore mouse press, release, enter, and exit events
    public void mousePressed(MouseEvent e) {}
    public void mouseReleased(MouseEvent e) {}
    public void mouseEntered(MouseEvent e) {}
    public void mouseExited(MouseEvent e) {}
}
```

Notice that we again reap the benefits of low coupling through the use of the Observer pattern. The canvas does not need to know about CanvasEditors and only needs to know about MouseListeners. As a result, we do not need to subclass JPanel to create our canvas and instead can use a JPanel object for our canvas directly.

All the code up to this point can be found in the drawer1 package. If you compile and run the code in that package, you will see a working drawing application that draws the appropriate shape in the appropriate place.

See Figure 8.6 for a class diagram showing the relationships between the drawing canvas, the CanvasEditor, and the buttons.

Note that, in the drawer1 package, the `main` method of the DrawingFrame class has been moved to a separate Main class. The movement of the `main` method to its own class has the following benefits:

1. It makes it easier for the readers of the source code to find the starting point of the application.

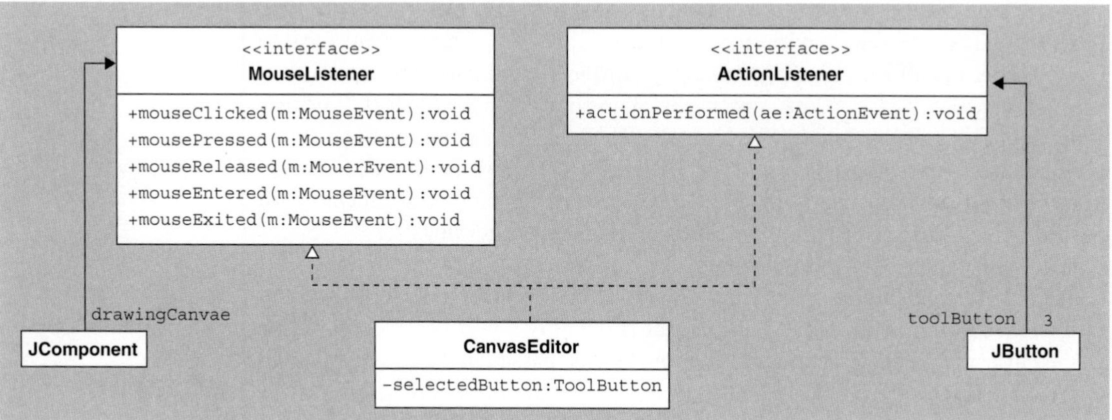

FIGURE 8.6 The CanvasEditor listens to both the buttons and canvas. Note that the tool buttons are implemented as JButtons and the drawingCanvas is implemented as a JComponent.

2. It separates the responsibilities of creating the initial objects and starting them communicating from the responsibilities of the individual objects during the execution of the program.
3. It frees up the other classes to have main methods for unit tests, for example.

SECTION 8.3 THE FIGURE HIERARCHY

Hopefully, you noticed at least one ugly feature of the code in the preceding section. (If you haven't, look again for ugliness in the code in package drawer1 before continuing.) One such feature is the conditional statement in the `mouseClicked` method in the CanvasEditor class. If you have learned all the material covered in previous chapters of this text, you should find yourself asking whether we should use polymorphism here instead of a conditional. In addition, you might have noticed that there are some less-than-optimal aspects of the behavior of the package from the user's perspective. For example, the drawing in the canvas is neither preserved nor manipulatable. That is, if the user drags another window across our drawing window, our drawing will be erased for good. Also, the user is unable to move or resize a figure after it has been drawn on the canvas. Let us tackle the conditional first, which will eventually aid in solving the other problems.

When you have a conditional statement based on the currently selected button, how do you replace it with polymorphism? One natural solution is to create EllipseButton, RectButton, and SquareButton subclasses of JButton, each with their own implementation of a `drawFigure` method, so that the `if` statement in the `mouseClicked` method of the CanvasEditor can be replaced with the simple statement:

```
currentButton.drawFigure(canvas, x, y);
```

In this approach, each button knows how to draw its associated figure. In order for this approach to work, we would need some kind of FigureButton abstract superclass (or interface) of our three Button classes that contains an abstract drawFigure method, and we would need the CanvasEditor's currentButton instance variable to be of type FigureButton. We will not implement this approach because it is moving in the wrong direction for a variety of reasons, one of which is that the buttons shouldn't be responsible for drawing. We will see additional reasons shortly.

A better way to design the program is to have an abstract Figure class with Rect, Ellipse, and Square subclasses that know how to center and draw themselves (using a given Graphics object) and have the CanvasEditor keep a reference to the currently selected *figure* object rather than the currently selected *button*. Then the body of the CanvasEditor's mouseClicked method can be implemented with just three lines:

```
public void mouseClicked(MouseEvent e)
{
   JPanel canvas = (JPanel) e.getSource();
   currentFigure.setCenter(e.getX(), e.getY());
   currentFigure.draw(canvas.getGraphics());
}
```

Here are what the Figure class and its subclasses would look like with such a design:

```
package drawer2.figure;
import java.awt.*;
public abstract class Figure
{
   private int centerX, centerY; //the center coordinates
   private int width;
   private int height;
   public Figure(int centerX, int centerY, int w, int h)
   {
      this.centerX = centerX; this.centerY = centerY;
      this.width = w; this.height = h;
   }
   public int getWidth() { return width; }
   public int getHeight() { return height; }
   public void setCenter(int centerX, int centerY)
   {
      this.centerX = centerX; this.centerY = centerY;
   }
   public int getCenterX() { return centerX; }
   public int getCenterY() { return centerY; }
   public abstract void draw(Graphics g);
}
```

```
public class Ellipse extends Figure
{
  public Ellipse(int centerX, int centerY, int w, int h)
  {
    super(centerX, centerY, w, h);
  }
  public void draw(Graphics g)
  {
    int width = getWidth();
    int height = getHeight();
    g.drawOval(getCenterX() - width/2, getCenterY() - height/2, width, height);
  }
}
public class Rect extends Figure
{
  public Rect(int centerX, int centerY, int w, int h)
  {
    super(centerX, centerY, w, h);
  }
  public void draw(Graphics g)
  {
    int width = getWidth();
    int height = getHeight();
    g.drawRect(getCenterX() - width/2, getCenterY() - height/2, width, height);
  }
}
public class Square extends Rect
{
  public Square(int centerX, int centerY, int w)
  {
    super(centerX, centerY, w, w);
  }
}
```

We'll be adding more methods to these classes later. Also, in the exercises you will be asked to add more Figure subclasses.

Notice that all figures inherit a width and a height. You should think of these values as the width and height of the smallest rectangle that encloses the figure. Notice also that we've made the Square a subclass of Rect. Why is that design decision an appropriate one at this point?

There is, however, one slight problem with using Figures in our design—namely, the CanvasEditor's `actionPerformed` method now gets more complicated. How is the CanvasEditor going to determine the currently selected figure from the button that was clicked in the toolbar? One way would be to use a conditional:

```
public void actionPerformed(ActionEvent e)
{
  JButton currentButton = (JButton) e.getSource();
    if (currentButton.getText().equals("Ellipse"))
      currentFigure = new Ellipse(0, 0, 60, 40);
    else if (currentButton.getText().equals("Rect"))
      currentFigure = new Rect(0, 0, 60, 40);
    else //if( currentButton.getText().equals("Square") )
      currentFigure = new Square(0, 0, 50);
  }
```

Unfortunately, this approach just moves the conditional from the `mouseClicked` method to the `actionPerformed` method. A slightly cleaner and faster way to get the figure associated with the clicked button is to use a hash table with keys consisting of the names of the buttons and values consisting of the associated figure. Or one could use reflection to create a new figure whose class is constructed using the name of the button. This latter option is further pursued in the exercises.

However, we will follow a different approach that also clears up another questionable aspect of our code. You may have noticed and questioned the earlier decision to let the CanvasEditor listen both to the canvas and to all the buttons, thereby requiring it to do two things instead of just one thing well. It would be better for the CanvasEditor to deal just with clicks in the canvas, let some other object or objects listen to the buttons, and then notify the CanvasEditor of any changes. In particular, why not have a separate listener for each button? In the `createToolbar` method of the DrawingFrame, we can replace

```
ellipseButton.addActionListener(canvasEditor);
```

with the only slightly more complicated code

```
ellipseButton.addActionListener(new ActionListener() {
  public void actionPerformed(ActionEvent e) {
    canvasEditor.setCurrentFigure(new Ellipse(0, 0, 60, 40));
  }
});
```

Similarly, the action listeners for the other buttons will tell the canvas editor to set the current figure appropriately. To implement this change, we also need to add a `setCurrentFigure` method to the CanvasEditor class.

The resulting relationship between the buttons, listeners, and editor can be seen in Figure 8.7. In summary, each tool button (JButton) has an associated anonymous (unnamed) ActionListener. When a tool button is clicked, it notifies the associated ActionListener, which in turn tells the CanvasEditor to set its current figure to the appropriate figure.

All of the code for this new version is in the package drawer2.

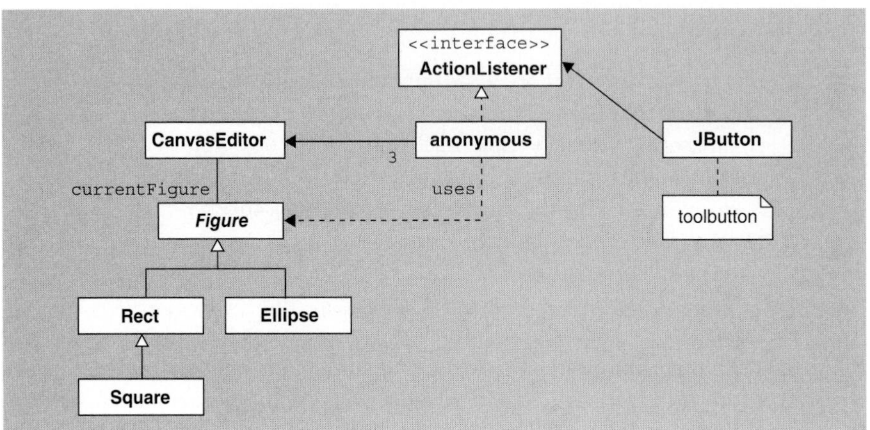

FIGURE 8.7 Part of the drawer2 package.

SECTION 8.4 THE MODEL-VIEW-CONTROLLER ARCHITECTURE

Now let's tackle the problem mentioned in the preceding section concerning the preservation and manipulability of the figures in the drawing. In order to be able to redraw the figures when necessary, their properties need to be stored for retrieval on demand. One approach would be to save the image on the canvas as an Image object and just redraw the image when necessary. However, this approach doesn't let you select and manipulate (e.g., drag or delete) the figures in the canvas. Clearly, a more appropriate action is to preserve the actual figures themselves or at least the data necessary to reconstruct the figures.

To implement this approach, we need to give some object the responsibility of storing the data regarding the figures that have been drawn on the canvas. Who should store it? Cleary, the canvas is responsible for drawing the figures so it makes sense to give the canvas a list of figures to draw. Although this decision is a logical one, we can actually do better in terms of separation of responsibilities.

To see how to improve our design, it is worth stepping back briefly to discuss the design of our application at a higher level. Three of the main components in our application up to this point are (a) the drawing itself, consisting of the collection of figures currently displayed in the canvas, (b) the canvas, on which the figures are drawn, and (c) the canvas editor, which deals with user input. These three objects can be called the *model*, the *view*, and the *controller*, respectively, in the *Model-View-Controller* architecture or *MVC*. A key benefit of using this software architecture is the separation of responsibilities. The model contains the data and is not concerned with how it is displayed or with interactions with the user. It can informally be viewed as a database in which data can be added, deleted, modified, or retrieved. Separate from the model is the view, which displays some or all of the model data. Finally, we have the controller, which handles interactions with the user.

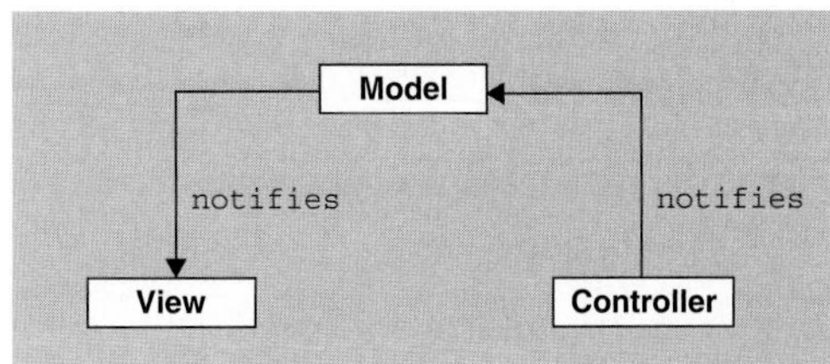

FIGURE 8.8 A very generic MVC architecture.

One advantage of such a separation of responsibilities is that, by using the MVC, we can easily implement several views displaying the same data in different forms (e.g., a pie chart and table could be two views of the same spreadsheet information), and we can easily add several controllers for handling different kinds of interactions with the user. In the simplest form of the MVC architecture, the model, view, and controller interact with each other via the Observer pattern. That is, the view registers with the model so that whenever the model changes, it notifies the view so the view can update the display to reflect the changed model. Similarly, the model registers with the controller so that when user action occurs, the model can update its data appropriately. See Figure 8.8 for a very generic MVC UML diagram.

For our application, we will consider a variation on the generic MVC architecture that similarly separates the responsibilities among three classes—the model (drawing), view (canvas), and controller (editor)—but that varies slightly the interconnections between the classes:

1. Since the view needs to display the data, the view will maintain a reference to the model. Therefore, our view will consist of a new DrawingCanvas subclass of JPanel that has an instance variable corresponding to the drawing and that has a `paintComponent` method for drawing the figures stored in that model.
2. Since the controller needs to interpret user actions on the view, the controller will be a MouseListener for the canvas, and so the canvas will maintain a link to the controller through the canvas' list of listeners.
3. The controller needs to tell the model to change its data based on user actions. For ease of implementation, we will not add a direct reference from the controller to the drawing. Instead, the controller will access the model in a two-step process by first getting the canvas from the MouseEvent object and then by telling the canvas to modify the drawing.

Note that in our approach, the view holds the only reference to the model, which holds the drawing to be displayed. The controller communicates only with the view and tells it to update its drawing based on user actions. That is, when a mouse click occurs in the canvas, the canvas notifies the editor of that event (since the editor is a MouseListener registered with the canvas), and the editor turns around and tells the canvas to add another figure to the drawing. See Figure 8.9 for the UML class diagram of our new design. Notice that we have added a Drawing class that stores the figures. We added this class because we want to have an object that

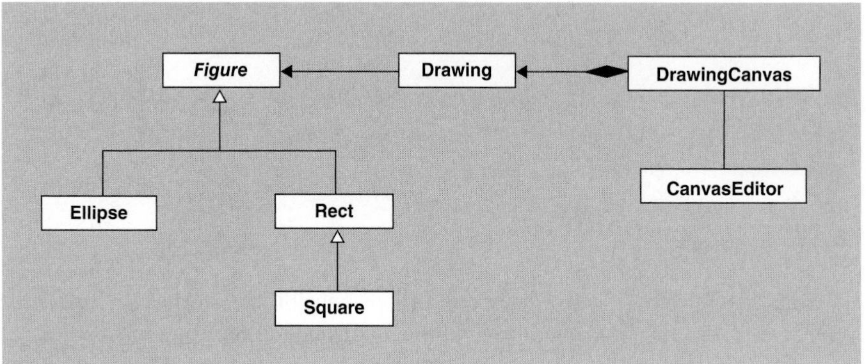

FIGURE 8.9 The MVC architecture in the drawer3 package.

directly corresponds to the model and that hides the details of how it stores the figures.

Here is the new code for the CanvasEditor class:

```
public class CanvasEditor implements MouseListener
{
  private Figure currentFigure;
  public CanvasEditor(Figure initialFigure)
  {
    this.currentFigure = initialFigure;
  }
  public void setCurrentFigure(Figure newFigure)
  {
    currentFigure = newFigure;
  }
  public void mouseClicked(MouseEvent e)
  {
    Figure newFigure =
             ...a new figure based on the currentFigure and
               centered at the mouse click...;
    ((DrawingCanvas) e.getSource()).addFigure(newFigure);
  }
  public void mousePressed(MouseEvent e) {}
  public void mouseReleased(MouseEvent e) {}
  public void mouseEntered(MouseEvent e) {}
  public void mouseExited(MouseEvent e) {}
}
```

Here is one way of implementing the new DrawingCanvas class to handle the design changes:

```
public class DrawingCanvas extends JPanel
{
    private Drawing drawing;
    public DrawingCanvas()
    {
        this.drawing = new Drawing();
        setBackground(Color.white);
        setPreferredSize(new Dimension(400, 300));
        setBorder(BorderFactory.createEtchedBorder());
    }
    public void paintComponent(Graphics g)
    {
        super.paintComponent(g);
        for (Figure figure : drawing) {
            figure.draw(g);
        }
    }
    public void addFigure(Figure newFigure)
    {
        drawing.addFigure(newFigure);
        repaint();
    }
}
```

Notice the use of polymorphism in asking all the figures to draw themselves in the `paintComponent` method. The use of an internal iterator in the Drawing class to draw the figures instead of this external iteration is explored in the exercises.

Let us look at the implementation of the Drawing class now. From what we have seen above, we know that it needs to have at least the following responsibilities:

1. Allow the creation of a new empty Drawing.
2. Store the collection of the currently drawn figures.
3. Allow the user to iterate through the collection of figures.
4. Allow the user to add a new figure to the collection.

Later on we will add more methods to this class. Here is one implementation of the Drawing class:

```
public class Drawing implements Iterable<Figure>
{
    private List<Figure> figures; //collection of Figures
    public Drawing()
    {
        figures = new ArrayList<Figure>();
    }
    //precondition: newFigure is non-null and is not already in
    //this Drawing
```

```
    public void addFigure(Figure newFigure)
    {
        figures.add(newFigure);
    }
    public Iterator<Figure> iterator()
    {
        return figures.iterator();
    }
}
```

Notice the precondition to the `addFigure` method. Alternative approaches would be to allow duplicate figures in the Drawing or to check whether the new figure is already in the Drawing and, if so, do nothing. These alternatives are pursued in an exercise.

SECTION 8.5 THE PROTOTYPE PATTERN

To finish up the drawer3 package, we need to make one more important change. That change is in the implementation of the `mouseClicked` method of the CanvasEditor. As shown above, that method has the following form:

```
public void mouseClicked(MouseEvent e)
{
    Figure newFigure = ...new figure based on the currentFigure
                          and centered at the mouse click...;
    ((DrawingCanvas) e.getSource()).addFigure(newFigure);
}
```

How do we construct the `newFigure` object? We can't use the `currentFigure` itself. (Why not?) It is hard to use a constructor to create the `newFigure` object since the actual object referred to by `currentFigure` can be from a variety of subclasses of Figure. We could have a conditional statement of the form:

```
if( currentFigure instanceof Ellipse )
    newFigure = new Ellipse(...);
else if( currentFigure instanceof Rect )
    newFigure = new Rect(...);
else
    newFigure = new Square(...);
```

but we all know by now that such statements do not make elegant code. We could use a factory to create the `newFigure` object, as discussed in the previous chapter. But then the factory would have to figure out the class of the object to create, and so we would just be moving the problem to a different class rather than eliminating it. We could also use reflection to create a new object of the same class as `currentFigure`.

There is a better way: use the *Prototype* design pattern [4]. One of the problems the Prototype pattern addresses concerns the need to create an instance of a class, but the particular class is not known until runtime. The pattern's solution is to use a prototypical instance and create the new object by cloning that prototype.

This pattern fits our situation perfectly. In our application, the Figure referred to by `currentFigure` can act as the prototype, and we can create new copies of it by cloning it. Furthermore, because our figures are so simple, we don't need to worry about most of the subtle problems with cloning mentioned in Section 4.8. We can clone the figures by just calling the inherited Object class' `clone()` method, and so we need only declare our Figure class as implementing the Cloneable interface and then add the following method to it:

```
public Object clone()
{
   try {
      return super.clone();
   } catch (CloneNotSupportedException e) {
      assert false; //this code block should never execute
      return null;
   }
}
```

Once this change has been made to the Figure class, the `mouseClicked` method of the CanvasEditor can be implemented as follows:

```
public void mouseClicked(MouseEvent e)
{
   Figure newFigure = (Figure) currentFigure.clone();
   newFigure.setCenter(e.getX(), e.getY());
   ((DrawingCanvas) e.getSource()).addFigure(newFigure);
}
```

The complete source code for the drawing application up to this point can be found in the package drawer3. If you compile the code in that package and run it, you should notice that the drawing gets redisplayed when the window is covered and then uncovered, as desired.

SECTION 8.6 THE STATE PATTERN

Now let us enhance the package further to allow manipulation of the figures drawn on the canvas. In particular, let us allow selection of one or more figures and dragging of the selected figures. As part of this process, we will need somehow to highlight the currently selected figures in the canvas.

To accommodate the new behavior, we will add a new tool to the toolbar—a selection tool. When the selection tool is chosen and

1. The user clicks the mouse button inside an unselected figure, then that figure becomes the only selected figure.

The Prototype Pattern

The Prototype pattern is useful in situations where your system needs to create a new object, but it does not know until runtime the class of the object it needs to create. In the Prototype pattern, a prototypical instance of the class is maintained, and, when a new object of that class is needed, the prototypical instance is cloned.

The participants in the pattern are the following (see Figure 8.10):

1. Client, which calls the `clone` method of the prototype to create a new instance
2. Prototype, which is an interface or abstract superclass for the classes for which instances will be cloned
3. ConcretePrototype, which is a class that implements the Prototype interface

In our drawing application, the Client is the CanvasEditor, the Prototype is the Figure abstract class, and the ConcretePrototypes are the Rect, Square, and Ellipse classes.

The benefits of using the Prototype pattern include the fact that you don't need to create a set of factory classes in order to create objects of different classes, as is done in the Factory Method pattern.

You also do not need to know ahead of time all the kinds of objects that will be created. As long as a prototypical instance can be accessed, new copies of that object can be created, even if the class of that prototype is unknown at compile time. For example, the prototype might be a composite object built from several other objects at runtime.

The main disadvantage of the Prototype pattern concerns the fact that the prototypical instance must be clonable. If the instance belongs to a class that does not implement Cloneable, then this pattern is hard to use. Implementing a `clone` method can also be difficult, as noted in Section 4.8.

Another minor disadvantage is that the newly created object will have the same state as the prototype, which is not always the desired state. Therefore, after cloning, you may need to initialize the new object to a different state.

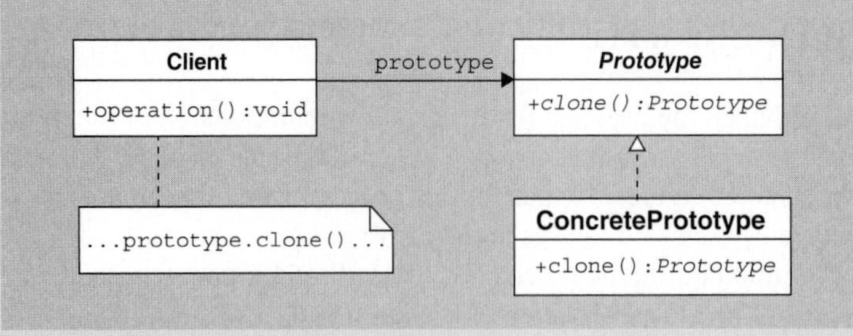

FIGURE 8.10 The Prototype pattern.

> One variation on the Prototype pattern is to keep all prototypical instances in a registry maintained by a prototype manager. In this case, the client might ask the manager for the appropriate prototypical instance before cloning it. The client might even be able to browse through the set of prototypes.

2. The user clicks the mouse button inside a selected figure, nothing changes.
3. The user clicks the mouse button outside of all the figures, all figures become unselected.
4. The user presses the mouse inside an unselected figure and drags, then that figure becomes the only selected figure and is dragged along with the mouse.
5. The user presses the mouse inside a selected figure and drags, then that figure and all other currently selected figures are dragged with the mouse.
6. The user presses the mouse outside all figures and drags the mouse, a selection area is outlined and all the figures intersecting the selection area become the selected figures.

See Figure 8.11 for a UML state diagram of the states of the canvas when the selection tool is chosen. Note that a mouse click corresponds to a mouse press followed immediately by a mouse release.

A UML *state* diagram displays the set of states of an object and the transitions between them. The rounded rectangles denote states, and the arrows between the states indicate how the object changes states. The arrows are usually labeled with the event that provokes the state change. Optionally, the event can be followed by a slash "/" and an action that is performed when the object changes state. The black circle points to the initial or starting state. In our diagram in Figure 8.11, the canvas starts in the state labeled *mouse button not pressed*. When the mouse button is pressed, the canvas transitions to another state and, in the process, selects, unselects, and/or drags some figures. For example, if, from the start state, the mouse button is pressed in an unselected figure, then all figures are unselected except for the figure in which the mouse press occurred, which is selected. At this point, the canvas is in the state labeled *pressed in a figure*. If the mouse button is now released without dragging, the canvas transitions back to the start state.

The set of behaviors listed above when the selection tool is chosen is the conventional one for drawing applications, which is why we have included it here. However, it should be pointed out that it would be more elegant to separate the responsibilities of selecting from the responsibilities of dragging, which would mean separate selection and dragging tools. Unfortunately, if we are to avoid confusing the user who is used to other drawing applications, we need to follow this convention.

To accommodate these enhancements, our old design will need to change considerably (again). Until now, the CanvasEditor has created new figures with mouse clicks and ignored mouse presses, mouse drags, and mouse releases. (In particular, the CanvasEditor does not implement the MouseMotionListener interface and so cannot deal with mouse drags at all.) However, if the new selection tool is chosen,

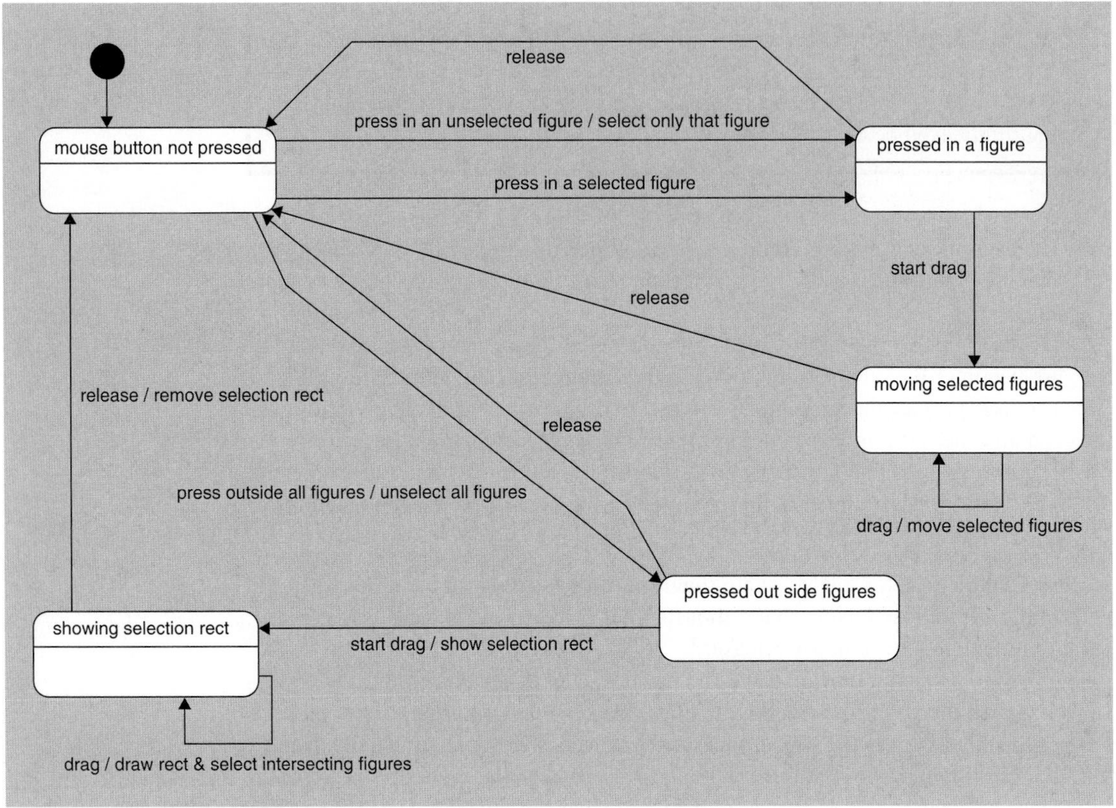

FIGURE 8.11 The UML state diagram when the selection tool is chosen.

the editor will need to have a whole new set of behaviors for dealing with these mouse events.

How can the editor exhibit such different behaviors depending on the choice of tool and still be simple and elegant? One solution would be to have the Canvas-Editor implement the MouseMotionListener interface and then add conditionals in the `mouseClicked`, `mousePressed`, `mouseDragged`, and `mouseReleased` methods that test for the currently selected tool and then have different actions based on which tool is selected. However, that solution is not optimal. (Why?)

Alternatively, the fact that we want the editor to exhibit different behavior at different times suggests that different classes (which have different behaviors) be used for the editor. That is, when one tool is selected, we would like the editor to belong to one class (e.g., the current CanvasEditor class) and so have one set of behaviors, and, when a different tool is selected, we would like the editor to belong to a different class and so have a different set of behaviors. Unfortunately, we can't change the class of the editor (nor any other existing object) dynamically in Java, and nor is it necessarily the best design decision even if we could do so.

There is a second related problem we need to address here. In the drawer3 package, the CanvasEditor held a `currentFigure` reference as an aid in adding new figures to the canvas. In our new version of the application, the idea of a "current figure" makes no sense when the selection tool is chosen. What should we do with the `currentFigure` instance variable in the case of the selection tool being chosen? Should we just ignore it? Alternatively, could we use the current figure to distinguish between all the tools? For example, we could set the value of `currentFigure` to null or set it to a new subclass of Figure to represent the fact that the selection tool was chosen so that the editor can check the `currentFigure` and determine from it which kind of tool is currently selected. Hopefully, you feel very uncomfortable with such a design. The problem we are having here stems from the fact that our old design assumes that we are always selecting a *creation* tool, and so the editor only needs to know which figure to create. But now we have another kind of tool, a *selection* tool, and so a `currentFigure` instance variable is no longer appropriate.

We can solve both these problems at the same time in a rather elegant way. The first step is to have the editor store a reference to the currently selected *tool* rather than the currently selected *figure*. Does this mean we go back to our drawer1 package where the editor kept track of the currently selected button? No, the buttons are just part of the GUI and so shouldn't have tool-like behavior. Instead, associated with each button should be a Tool object. In this design, there will be the SelectionTool and a CreationTool, both of them subclasses of an abstract Tool class. We will also create three CreationTool objects, each with a reference to the particular figure (Rect, Ellipse, or Square) it is to create. That is, the CanvasEditor will have a `currentTool` reference to a Tool, which will be either a SelectionTool object or one of the three CreationTool objects. The behavior of the CanvasEditor will depend on which of those tools the `currentTool` currently refers to.

The second step is to use the *State* pattern [4]. This pattern is a way of dealing elegantly with an object that needs different behavior depending on its state. In the State pattern, the object needing different behavior will maintain a reference to another object representing its current state. All behavior of the first object that might vary is delegated to the state object.

We can understand the State pattern better by studying how it can aid in our particular problem. In our case, the CanvasEditor needs different behavior depending on the state of its `currentTool` instance variable. Therefore, the State pattern tells us that the editor should delegate all varying behavior to the state object, namely the Tool referenced by `currentTool`. This means that the `mouseClicked` method and the other mouse event-handling methods of the CanvasEditor should just call a method in the current Tool to perform the actual work. The refactoring of the `mouseClicked` method can be done most simply by making the Tools into mouse listeners and having the `mouseClicked` method of the editor call the `mouseClicked` method of the current tool, as follows:

```
public void mouseClicked(MouseEvent e) { //in the CanvasEditor
  currentTool.mouseClicked(e);
}
```

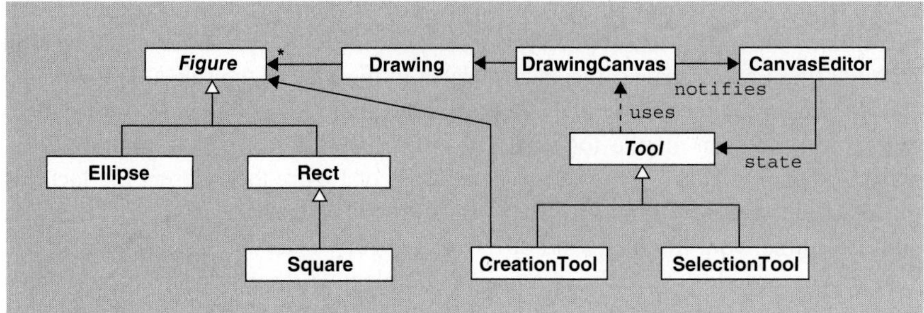

FIGURE 8.12 The drawer4 package.

As part of this refactoring, the body of the old version of the editor's `mouseClicked` method is moved to the body of the `mouseClicked` method of the Tool. Similar delegation is done for the other mouse event methods.

After doing this refactoring, when a mouse event occurs in the canvas, the canvas broadcasts that event to its subscribers (the CanvasEditor). The CanvasEditor then delegates the job of dealing with the event to the current Tool. As a result, the CanvasEditor's behavior (i.e., how it responds to mouse events) varies, depending on its state (the current value of its `currentTool` instance variable), exactly as we desired.

This new design is included in the package drawer4. The details of how the selection tool selects and drags the selected figures are quite straightforward and are included in the drawer4 package, but are not discussed here. In this package, the figures are responsible for knowing whether they are selected and for drawing themselves with a highlighted bounding rectangle when they are selected. Also, to simplify the code further, the figures no longer maintain their size and position in four separate integer instance variables and instead store that information in a `boundingRect` instance variable of type Rectangle.

A UML class diagram of this package is shown in Figure 8.12. Note that the CanvasEditor has an associated state consisting of a Tool. The Tool class has CreationTool and SelectionTool subclasses, each with different behaviors when mouse events occur. The CreationTool maintains a reference to a Figure, and, when the user clicks in the canvas, it creates an instance of that Figure and asks the canvas to add it to the drawing. The SelectionTool accesses the DrawingCanvas to find out which figures were clicked in and so which figures are to be selected and/or dragged.

SECTION 8.7 THE COMPOSITE PATTERN

The next enhancement we will make to our drawing application is to allow the user to group figures together to make a composite figure. For example, the user should be able to build a snowman from three ellipses and then group the three ellipses together to form a composite figure. This group, from the user's perspective, should

The State Pattern

The State pattern is useful when you have an object that needs to behave differently depending on its internal state. In this pattern, the object has a reference to a State object and delegates its varying behavior to that object.

The participants in the pattern are the following (see Figure 8.13):

1. Context, which is the object of interest to clients. Its state is determined by the particular State object to which it refers.
2. State, which is an abstract class or interface that defines the interface for the objects that represent the state of the Context.
3. ConcreteState subclasses, which implement the State interface and provide different behaviors.

When a client invokes the `request` method of a Context object, the request is passed to the state through a call to its `handleRequest` method. Different subclasses of State will handle the request differently. As a result, it will appear to the client as if the Context object changed class.

Any of the clients, the Context, or the State subclasses can be responsible for changing the state of the Context and determining under what circumstances the state will change.

One of the benefits of using the State pattern is the fact that the Context object will not need to have a conditional in its `request` method that tests the current state of the Context to see which behavior to exhibit. Instead the differing behaviors are delegated to different subclasses of State.

Another benefit is that it separates the responsibilities of the objects into cohesive groups. A ConcreteState subclass will have all the behavior appropriate for one state of the Context.

In addition, a Context object's behavior can be extended, through the creation of new subclasses of State, to include forms of behavior not anticipated in the original design.

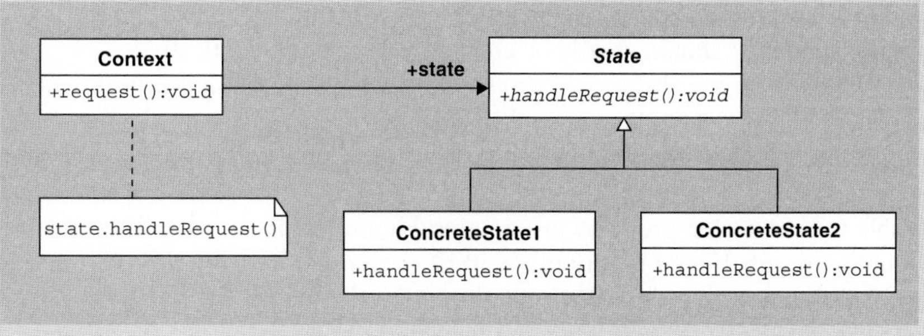

FIGURE 8.13 The State pattern.

behave exactly the same as a "primitive" figure (i.e., a square, ellipse, or rectangle) in that it should be selectable and draggable.

To create a composite figure, the user will need to select one or more figures in the canvas and then choose the "Group" menu item in the "Edit" menu in the menu bar. At this point, the selected figures are removed from the canvas and replaced with one group figure which, when drawn, looks like the drawing of the selected figures but is otherwise identical to a primitive figure. In particular, when selected, the group will have one bounding rectangle displayed for the whole group rather than having individual rectangles displayed for each component figure of the group. Furthermore, group figures can be selected and grouped into even larger group figures. Finally, we will enhance the application with an "Ungroup" menu item that reverses the process for all selected group figures.

How can we implement these group figures in an elegant way? Recall that the Drawing object stores all its figures in a ArrayList<Figure> named `figures`. Each group could similarly be represented by an ArrayList of all the figures making up the group, and that ArrayList could be stored as one of the elements of `figures`. That is, to implement the "Group" menu item action, we can just remove all the selected figures from `figures`, put those selected figures into a new ArrayList, and add that ArrayList to `figures`. We would need to change figures to be of type ArrayList<Object> instead of ArrayList<Figure>, but that change is easy to make.

This implementation seems simple and clean until one looks at the resulting code in the Drawing class. In the package4 version of our application, the class' methods assume that only Figure objects, and not other ArrayLists, are in the `figures` ArrayList. Therefore, all Drawing methods would now have to be rewritten to contain a conditional statement of the form:

```
if( figures.get(i) instanceof ArrayList)
  //...do the desired processing on the group...
else
  //...do the desired processing on the figure...
```

Such code is very inelegant. Furthermore, since we want to allow a group figure to contain other group figures, the code would need to be even messier. The Drawing shouldn't have to concern itself with differences between grouped figures and ungrouped figures. It should ideally be able to treat them all identically.

To get the desired behavior, we use the *Composite* pattern [4]. In this pattern, individual objects and collections of objects are treated uniformly. In our drawing application, Ellipses, Rects, and Square can be treated uniformly by referring to them as Figures. Therefore, to treat groups of Figures the same way, we need to be able to treat such a group as just another Figure. To do so, we will create a new GroupFigure subclass of Figure that will be composed of a collection of other Figures. See Figure 8.14 for the UML diagram.

Once these classes have been implemented, the Drawing can treat groups the same way as primitive figures by treating them all as just Figures. It need not worry about whether any particular figure is primitive or a group. Furthermore, since a GroupFigure is just a collection of Figures, those Figures can include other GroupFigures, and so we can form tree-like structures of GroupFigures within Group-

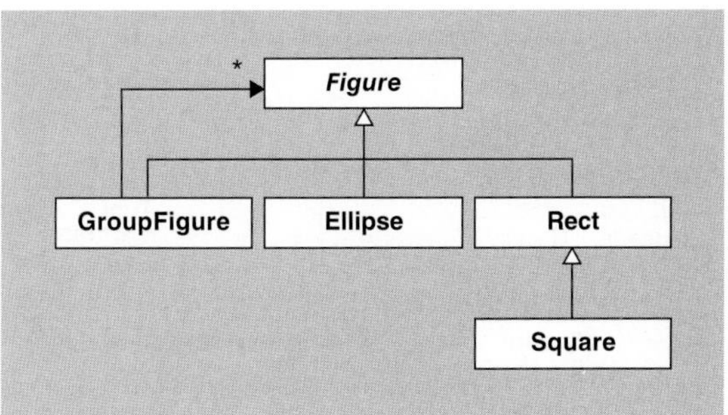

FIGURE 8.14 The subclasses of Figure in the drawer5 package.

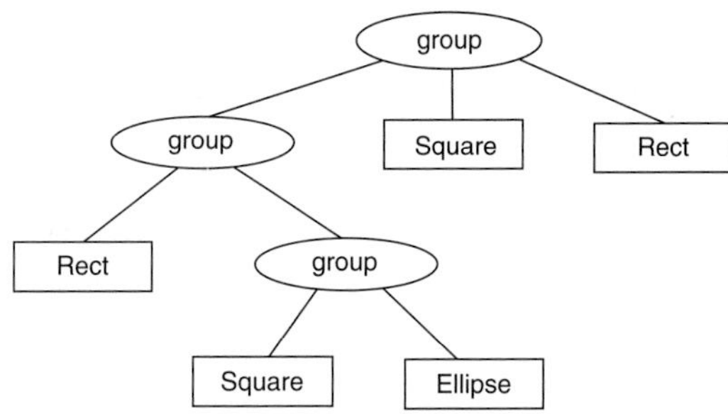

FIGURE 8.15 A tree of primitive Figures and GroupFigures.

Figures, with the primitive Figures forming the leaves of the tree. See Figure 8.15 for an example.

Let us now consider how we might implement such a GroupFigure class. By making the GroupFigure a subclass of Figure, it inherits all of the Figure class' behavior. If you study that behavior, you will see that the GroupFigure class can inherit almost all of it without modification. In fact, it only needs a constructor and overriding implementations of five methods:

1. drawShape
2. setSize
3. move
4. moveTo
5. getComposedFigures

The constructor takes a collection of figures (its "children") as its parameter. The GroupFigure's `drawShape` method just calls `drawShape` on all of its children. The `setSize` method adjusts the width and height of all children figures as well as the group figure. Similarly, the `move` and `MoveTo` methods call `move` and `moveTo` on all of the children. The `getComposedFigures` method is a new method in the GroupFigure subclass that is used to ungroup the figures. To avoid having to test whether a figure is a GroupFigure, we will add a `getComposedFigures` method to the Figure class as well, so that all Figure subclasses have such a method. In the case of a primitive (non-group) figure, the `getComposedFigures` method returns a list containing only the figure itself.

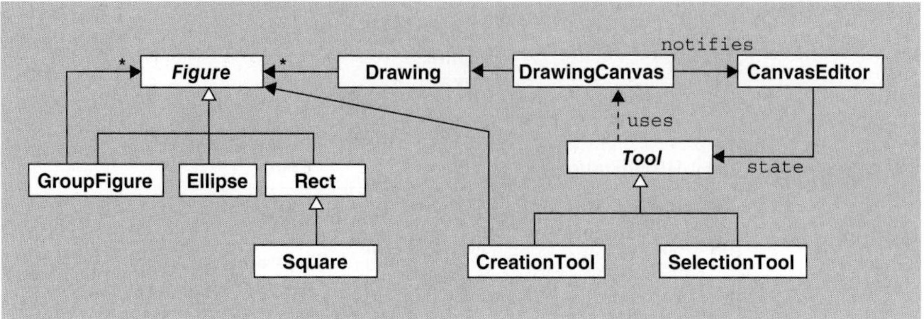

FIGURE 8.16 The drawer5 package.

The "Group" menu item's behavior is implemented by an ActionListener that calls a new `groupSelectedFigures` method in the DrawingCanvas. This new method simply removes all selected figures from the drawing and adds to the drawing a new GroupFigure object composed of the figures that were removed. The "Ungroup" button has the reverse behavior and calls a new `ungroupSelectedFigures` method in the DrawingCanvas class.

The almost-complete code for the drawing application up to this point can be found in the drawer5 package. The only code not included is the code for the `setSize` and `moveTo` methods in the GroupFigure class, which have been left to the reader as an exercise (see Exercise 22 below). A UML class diagram for the package can be found in Figure 8.16.

Note that the only difference between the drawer5 diagram in Figure 8.16 and the drawer4 diagram in Figure 8.12 is the addition of a new GroupFigure subclass of Figure.

SECTION 8.8 THE MEMENTO PATTERN

A standard feature of a drawing application that our application is still missing is the ability to undo and redo the last action. A well-constructed application will have "Undo" and "Redo" menu items that, when selected, execute arbitrarily many Undo and Redo commands. To implement undoability, we somehow need to be able to restore the canvas to a previous state. The most straightforward way to implement restorability is to store all previous states of the canvas in an "undo" stack. We will take this approach to adding undoability and redoability.

Our application will have the invariant that the state at the top of the undo stack always corresponds to the current state of the canvas. Each time an action is performed that changes the state of the canvas, a copy of the new state is pushed on the undo stack. Each time the undo command is executed, the stack is popped and the canvas is restored to the state stored in the stack's top item. What do we do with the state popped off the stack? We push it onto a "redo" stack. Then when the redo command is executed, the redo stack is popped, the popped state is pushed on the undo stack, and the canvas is restored to that state.

The Composite Pattern

The Composite pattern is useful when you want to treat individual objects and collections of objects uniformly. It helps you compose objects into a tree-like structure.

In this pattern, there are one or more "Leaf" classes, representing individual objects, and there is a "Composite" class, representing collections of objects. The Composite class and the Leaf classes are subclasses of the same abstract "Component" class or interface. If a client refers to these two kinds of components only as elements of type Component, then that client need never know whether the components are actually composites or leaves, and so the client can treat them all identically. Similarly, a Composite object may contain Leaf objects or other Composite objects. To treat them all uniformly, it refers to them only as Component objects. See Figure 8.17 for the UML class diagram of the Composite pattern.

The participants in the pattern are the following:

1. Client, who is able to treat composite objects and single objects uniformly through the Component interface
2. Component, which is an abstract class or interface that defines the interface for the individual objects and composite objects
3. Leaf, which is a single or noncomposite subclass of Component
4. Composite, which is a subclass of Component storing a collection of Components

One of the issues that needs to be addressed when the Composite pattern is used is what methods should be included in the Component interface. In particular, should it include the operation `getChildren` to allow other Components or the Client to traverse the tree of Components?

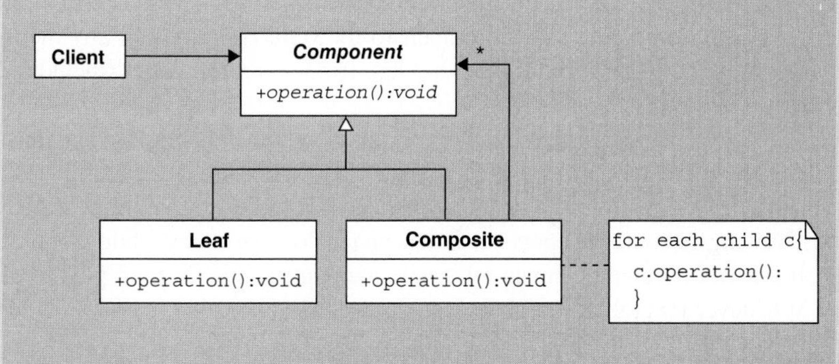

FIGURE 8.17 The Composite pattern.

Continued

> It makes sense for the Composite class to have a `getChildren` method, but, if this method does not also appear in the Component interface, then the Client cannot call that method on a Component without first checking whether the Component is actually a Composite and then typecasting the Component into a Composite. In contrast, if the `getChildren` method does appear in the Component interface, then it needs to have some appropriate behavior in the Leaf subclass, which has no children. Regardless of the implementation of this method in the Leaf class, just the existence of it is misleading. Therefore, neither option is completely satisfactory from the perspective of elegance.
>
> There are also the issues of whether to include a `getParent` or `getParents` (if components are shared) method in the Component interface and whether Component should be an abstract class with default implementations of some or all of the methods. These issues must be addressed on a case by case basis.

Who is going to manage the undo and redo stacks and the storing and restoring of the state? A natural choice is to have the DrawingCanvas do all of it since it is the object whose state needs to be stored and restored (what pattern are we using here?). But making the DrawingCanvas handle all the details of storing, unstoring, and restoring states is giving it too many responsibilities. It should be concerned only with displaying the Display object to which it refers. However, to have any other object take care of storing backup states would seemingly require exposure of the internal implementation of the DrawingCanvas. After all, how can another object store and restore the state of the DrawingCanvas without knowing how the DrawingCanvas is implemented?

The *Memento* pattern [4] solves this problem. This pattern says that we should create "memento" objects that encapsulate a snapshot of the internal state of the DrawingCanvas, and we should create a "caretaker" who is responsible for the safekeeping of the mementos. The DrawingCanvas should create the mementos and should be able to restore itself to the state contained in any memento. The mementos' contents should be hidden from everyone else (including the caretaker).

In our case, we will create a new inner class called DrawingCanvas.State that will act as the memento, and we will create a UndoRedoManager class that will act as the caretaker. We will implement the UndoRedoHandler so that it has a reference to the DrawingCanvas. Whenever it is instructed to save a new state on the undo stack, it asks the DrawingCanvas for a new memento, which it then pushes on the stack. Whenever it is told to undo the last change, it

1. Pops the top memento off the undo stack and pushes it onto the redo stack.
2. Gives a reference to the memento now on top of the undo stack to the DrawingCanvas, and tells the canvas to restore itself to that memento.

Here is the code for the UndoRedoHandler:

```
public class UndoRedoHandler
{
    private Stack<DrawingCanvas.State> undoStack, redoStack;
    private DrawingCanvas canvas;

    public UndoRedoHandler(DrawingCanvas canvas) {
        undoStack = new Stack<DrawingCanvas.State>();
        redoStack = new Stack<DrawingCanvas.State>();
        this.canvas = canvas;
        //store the initial state of the canvas on the undo stack
        undoStack.push(canvas.createMemento());
    }

    //save the current state of the DrawingCanvas
    public void saveState()
    {
        DrawingCanvas.State canvasState = canvas.createMemento();
        undoStack.push(canvasState);
        redoStack.clear();
    }

    public void undo()
    {
        if( undoStack.size() == 1)
            return; //only the current state is on the stack

        DrawingCanvas.State canvasState = undoStack.pop();
        redoStack.push(canvasState);
        canvas.restoreState(undoStack.peek());
    }

    public void redo()
    {
        if( redoStack.isEmpty()) return;

        DrawingCanvas.State canvasState = redoStack.pop();
        undoStack.push(canvasState);
        canvas.restoreState(canvasState);
    }
}
```

The Undo and Redo menu items in our application have listeners that tell the UndoRedoHandler to invoke `undo` or `redo`. Various objects tell the handler that the canvas is in a new state that needs to be saved. These objects include the tools in the toolbar and the Group and Ungroup menu items.

Note that we need to add only two new methods in the DrawingCanvas class. These methods are `restoreState(DrawingCanvas.State)` that takes a state as parameter and `createMemento` that creates and returns a new state object. Therefore, we have maintained low coupling and high cohesion in this design. That is, the DrawingCanvas need not be concerned with what is done with the mementos after it creates one and is only concerned with restoring its state to that in such a

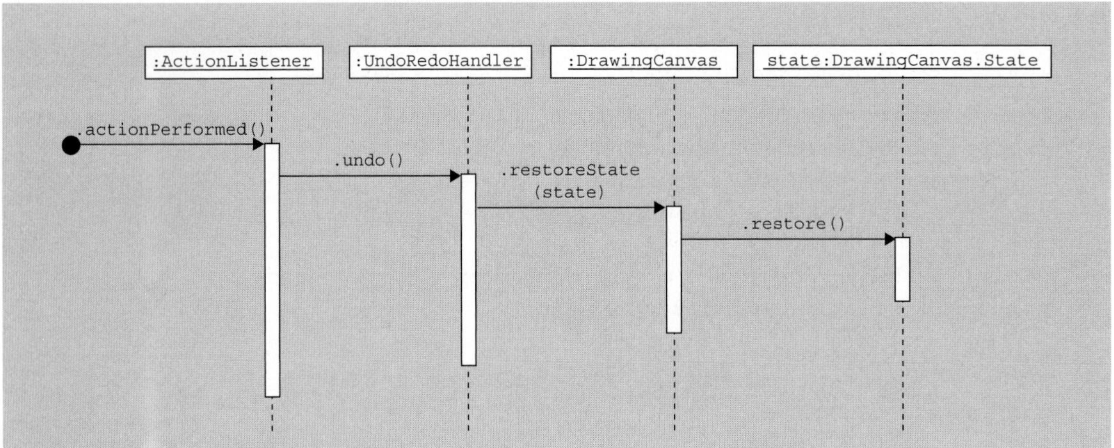

FIGURE 8.18 The sequence diagram showing how the undo operation is performed.

memento when asked to do so. Other objects are involved in storing and manipulating the mementos, but they have no knowledge of the internals of the mementos and how the canvas uses them to restore its state.

The last details to consider are how the states are implemented and how the canvas uses a state object to restore itself. Since the DrawingCanvas state is intimately involved with the implementation of DrawingCanvas, a natural design is to have the state be an internal class to the DrawingCanvas, thereby allowing it access to all the private instance variables of the canvas. The DrawingCanvas' `createMemento` method calls the constructor of DrawingCanvas.State, which copies the canvas' Drawing (by cloning it) and stores that copy in an instance variable of the State. When the canvas is asked to restore its state to that in a State object, it turns around and asks the State object to restore the drawing to the one the state saved. The State object does so by copying the Drawing it saved to the drawing attribute of the DrawingCanvas. The UML sequence diagram in Figure 8.18 shows the process of restoring a state.

In Figure 8.18, the ActionListener for the Undo menu item signals the UndoRedoHandler to undo. The UndoRedoHandler then extracts the State to be restored from its undo stack and signals the DrawingCanvas to restore its state to that State. Since the internals of the State object are private, the DrawingCanvas cannot access them, but it can ask the State object to restore the canvas' state for it.

Here is the new code for the DrawingCanvas class.

```
public class DrawingCanvas extends JPanel
{
  private Drawing drawing;
  public State createMemento()
  {
    return new State();
  }
```

The Memento Pattern

The Memento pattern is useful when you need to save a snapshot of an object's internal state for later restoration and you want to avoid exposing the object's internal state.

In this pattern, there is an Originator whose internal state is to be stored, a Memento, which encapsulates a snapshot of the internal state of the Originator, and a Caretaker, who is responsible for the safekeeping of the Mementos. The Originator is responsible for creating the Mementos and restoring its state to that contained in a Memento. The Memento hides its contents so that no object other than the Originator can inspect it. The Caretaker never cares about the contents of the Memento. In many ways, the Caretaker is like a bank with safe deposit boxes, in that the bank is responsible for the safekeeping of the boxes, but is never concerned with the contents of those boxes.

The participants in the pattern (see Figure 8.19) are the following:

1. Originator, whose internal state needs to be saved in snapshots. It is responsible for creating the Mementos and restoring its state to that of a Memento.
2. Memento, which stores a snapshot of the Originator's state. It hides the state's implementation details.
3. CareTaker, which is responsible for safekeeping the Mementos.

One of the nice features of the Memento pattern is the way it separates responsibilities among the classes. One class stores the snapshot, another class safekeeps the mementos, and the third class creates mementos and restores itself to the state in a memento.

One possible disadvantage of this pattern is that the Mementos might be expensive to create and keep since the system might need a lot of resources to create the Mementos and the Caretaker might need a lot of memory to store them. Therefore, one option is to store in a Memento only part of Originator's state or just the change in its state.

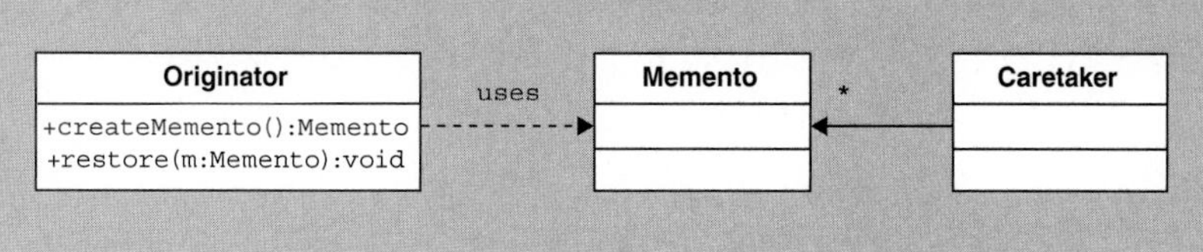

FIGURE 8.19
The Memento pattern.

```
public void restoreState(State canvasState)
{
  canvasState.restore();
  repaint();
}
public class State
{
  private Drawing drawing;
  public State()
  {
    drawing = (Drawing) DrawingCanvas.this.drawing.clone();
  }
```

```
        public void restore()
        {
            DrawingCanvas.this.drawing = (Drawing) drawing.clone();
        }
    }
        ...other instance variables and methods...
}
```

Notice the cloning of the drawing that the State's constructor performs. It is apparent that a deep clone is needed here. That is, we must clone all the figures inside the drawing since each object stores its current position, which can be different in different states. Therefore, the Drawing class' `clone` method invokes the (deep) `clone` method of the List of figures that it references. The List's `clone` method in turn invokes the `clone` method of each of the Figures in the list. The GroupFigure's `clone` method similarly deep clones the List of its children.

The complete code for the application with this new feature can be found in the package drawer6.

SECTION 8.9 SUMMARY

In this chapter, we have incrementally developed a drawing application. In each evolution of the application, a new feature was added. Various alternative designs and implementations for each new feature were compared for elegance. Along the way, new design patterns were discussed and used. Through the use of the design patterns and, more generally, good design principles, it was quite easy to add the new features to the application without having to do major refactoring or redesign.

There are many more features that could be added to this package, and there are other designs for the existing features that are viable alternatives. Some of these features and alternatives are explored in the exercises.

EXERCISES

1. When you are trying to reach an executive in a company, you have at least three choices:
   a. Call and be put on hold until the executive is free.
   b. Keep calling back every few minutes until the executive is free.
   c. Leave a message asking the executive to call you back when she is free.

   Which one of these choices corresponds most closely to the Observer pattern?

2. The Observer pattern is used in the design of the JButton class, which has a method `addActionListener` to let listeners register with the button so that they can be notified when the button is clicked. When such a click occurs, the JButton notifies all listeners by calling their `actionPerformed` methods. How are these two actions implemented? That is, what is in the body of the `addActionListener` method, and how does the JButton go about notifying the listeners? To get a feeling for how this is done, create your own Publisher class with an `addSubscriber` method and a `broadcast` method and create a Subscriber class with a `somethingHappened` method. The Publisher's `broadcast` method should call all the `somethingHappened` methods of the Subscribers.

3. Does the ActionListener interface use the push model or the pull model of communication? (See Section 8.2 for a discussion of the two models.) Briefly explain.

4. As mentioned in Section 8.2, Java provides an Observable class and an Observer interface to aid in using the Observer pattern. To use these classes, you would typically subclass Observable to get a class with the specific observable behavior you want and all observers would implement the Observer interface. Study the features of the Observable class. Is it good design to subclass Observable when you need to use the Observer pattern? Why or why not? Give an alternate design using Observer and Observable to get the same behavior. Hint: See the java.beans.PropertyChangeSupport class.

5. Refactor the code in the CanvasEditor class of package drawer1 so that it uses the java.awt.event.MouseAdapter class to eliminate the methods with empty bodies. Then briefly discuss whether the new version is better than the old version.
6. In Section 8.3, it is mentioned that you can use reflection to get a new object of one of the subclasses of Figure from the name of that subclass (given as a String). However, in package drawer2, we didn't use reflection. Instead, in the DrawingFrame's constructor, we created three almost-identical ActionListeners, one to listen to each button. If the button is clicked, its listener tells the CanvasEditor to set the current figure to the figure corresponding to that button. In this exercise, you are to use reflection to avoid the duplication in these three ActionListeners. That is, replace the three listeners with one listener that listens to all three buttons. When a button is clicked, the listener gets the name of the button and uses reflection to create a figure of the class with that name. It then tells the CanvasEditor to set its current figure to that newly created figure.
7. As stated in Section 8.4, in the MVC pattern, the model, view, and controller usually interact via the Observer pattern. That is, the view registers with the model so that whenever the model changes, it notifies the view so that the view can update the display to reflect the changed model. Similarly, the model registers with the controller so that when user action occurs, the model can update its data appropriately. In the drawer3 package, we didn't use the Observer pattern at all when connecting the model and the controller and when connecting the model and the view. Reimplement the drawer3 package so that the Observer pattern is used between the model and the view. Is the new design more elegant?
8. In the drawer3 package, the DrawingCanvas' `paintComponent` method uses an iterator to loop through the figures to draw each of them. An alternative to using such an external iterator is to use an internal iterator. Implement such an internal iterator by adding to the Drawing class a `draw(Graphics)` method, in which the drawing itself loops through the figures, calling each of their `draw` methods. Then modify the DrawingCanvas class so that the `paintComponent` method in the DrawingCanvas class calls `super.paint(g)` and then calls `drawing.draw(g)`.
9. In drawer3, we include the following line of code in the `mouseClicked` method of the CanvasEditor class:

```
((DrawingCanvas) e.getSource())
  .addFigure(newFigure);
```

Doesn't this code break the Law of Demeter in that we ask the MouseEvent `e` for an object and then ask that object to do something? Briefly explain your answer and what, if anything, should be done about it.

10. At the end of Section 8.4, we mentioned two alternatives to the precondition to the `addFigure` method of the Display class.
    a. Implement the two alternatives.
    b. Discuss the advantages and disadvantages of the three approaches.
11. In the drawing3 and later packages, we defined a Drawing class. However, that class does nothing that an ArrayList<Figure> can't already do. Why did we introduce the class? What design pattern are we using here?
12. One problem with our drawing3 package is that the currently selected button is not clearly indicated in the GUI. Enhance the application to put a red border around the currently selected button. Try to do this by adding new code rather than changing existing code.
13. In the drawer4 package, we used the State pattern to change the behavior of the CanvasEditor based on its state instead of creating subclasses of CanvasEditor with different behaviors. We can look at the Figure heirarchy similarly. In the design of the drawer4 package, each of the subclasses of Figure are identical except for their behavior when asked to draw themselves. Use the State pattern to eliminate the need for subclasses of Figure, and instead change the behavior of each Figure based on its state. Then critique your design compared to the design of package drawer4.
14. In the Figure's `getBoundingRect` method in the drawer4 package, we return a new Rectangle object instead of the value of the `boundingRect` instance variable. Why not just return `boundingRect`?
15. In the drawer4 package, there is a Tool abstract class with no methods or fields that extends MouseInputAdapter. Why include such a class in our design?

16. In the discussion in Section 8.6, we refactored the design of the drawing application using the State pattern to avoid conditionals in the `mouseClicked` method in the CanvasEditor. In Section 7.5, we used the Factory Method pattern to get a slightly different solution to an almost identical problem. Compare the two solutions, describing any advantages and disadvantages of each.
17. In the code in the drawer5 package, the figures are stored in an ArrayList<Figure>, which is an ordered collection. Why maintain an order to the figures?
18. Add a new "Filled Rect" button to the drawer5 package that, when clicked, allows filled rectangles to be drawn on the canvas. Keep track of exactly how many (a) new files need to be created, (b) existing files need to be modified, and (c) places existing files need to be modified.
19. Add a new "Delete" menu item to Edit menu in the drawer5 package that, when clicked, removes the selected figures from the drawing. Keep track of exactly how many (a) new files need to be created, (b) existing files need to be modified, and (c) places existing files need to be modified.
20. Add a new "Rotate right" menu item to the Edit menu in the drawer5 package. This menu item causes all selected figures to be rotated clockwise 90 degrees around their center point. The center point of a group figure is the center of the figure's bounding rect. If you rotate a figure right four times, it should be restored to its original position and orientation. Keep track of exactly how many (a) new files need to be created, (b) existing files need to be modified, and (c) places existing files need to be modified.
21. The DrawingFrame has many almost-identical calls to `addActionListener` to the tool buttons. Refactor this class so that the duplication is eliminated by creating one ActionListener that has a hash table that associates each button with its tool and by having this listener listen to all buttons in the toolbar.
22. As described in Section 8.7, the drawer5 package is incomplete in that the GroupFigure class needs to override the `setSize` and `moveTo` methods of the Figure class so that all children figures are similarly moved or stretched along with the GroupFigure. Implement these two overriding methods.
23. In the drawer5 package, the GroupFigure class is implemented so that when the GroupFigure is moved, all figures in the group are moved, and so they maintain their position relative to the drawing canvas. Reimplement the GroupFigure class so that each figure in the group maintains its position relative to the position of the GroupFigure. That is, the *x* and *y* position of a figure in a group is not its absolute position in the drawing canvas and instead indicate offsets from the position of the bounding rectangle of the group figure.
24. In the drawer5 package, we added a new `getComposedFigures` method to the Figure class. In the case of a nongroup Figure, the method just returns a list containing the Figure itself. Can you find anything inelegant about this design?
25. In Section 7.4, the Command pattern is discussed. Describe where the Composite pattern appears (without the name) in that section.
26. Reimplement the UndoRedoHandler in drawer6 so that it uses one doubly linked list of States instead of two stacks of States. The handler maintains a reference to the current State in the list, which matches the state of the canvas. An undo action moves the reference to the previous state in the list and a redo action moves the reference to the next state. A save-state action causes every state after the current state to be deleted and replaced with a new state, which becomes the current state.
27. Refactor drawer6 so that the UndoRedoHandler can be reused in settings other than with DrawingCanvases. That is, generalize the UndoRedoHandler so that it doesn't refer to DrawingCanvas and the DrawingCanvas.State classes.
28. Reimplement the UndoRedoHandler in drawer6 so that it stores only incremental changes in state instead of a complete snapshot of the state in each memento. Note that in this case the memento will not store a state, but rather a *change* in state. Therefore, it might be appropriate to make each memento contain a command or an action that can be executed to cause the desired change.
29. One shortcoming of the drawer6 package is that a new state may be saved on the undo stack that is identical to the state immediately below it (e.g., if the user selects the same figures that are already selected or if the user drags a figure in a circle back to its starting place). Rewrite the package so that no new state is saved if the new state is equal to the previous state. To implement this feature, you will need to test the equality of two states, which, in turn, will require testing the equality of the drawings, and so the figures within the drawings. Therefore, `equals` methods will need to be added to many classes.
30. Enhance the drawer6 package in the following ways:
    a. Add "Delete," "Cut," "Copy," and "Paste" menu items to the Edit menu in the drawer6 package.

The Delete menu item removes the selected figures from the canvas. The Copy menu item creates copies of the currently selected figures and puts them in a clipboard for later pasting. Cut is just like Copy except it deletes the currently selected figures after copying them. The Paste menu item should take the figures in the clipboard and paste them down and to the right a few pixels from where the original figures were at the time they were copied. Ideally you will use the system clipboard so that copied figures can also be pasted into other applications if they support such pasting. To get the system clipboard using Java, have your DrawingCanvas class call

```
getToolkit().getSystemClipboard()
```

b. Implement resizing. To do so, add a new "Resize" tool. When the user selects the resize tool and drags one of the corner (light green) boxes on a selected figure, that figure is stretched with the dragging. The corner of the selected figure opposite to the dragged corner remains fixed.

c. Add context menus. That is, when the user right-clicks on a figure using the selection tool, that figure is selected and a popup menu appears with appropriate options for the type of figure selected. For this exercise, the popup menu should just have a "Delete" menu item unless the selected figure is a GroupFigure, in which case there should also be an "Ungroup" menu item.

31. Other objects can traverse an ArrayList<Figure> by invoking the list's `iterator` method, which returns an Iterator. Such an Iterator is used quite a few times in the Drawing class and in the GroupFigure class in the drawer6 package. Clean up this code by providing an *internal* iterator. That is, do the following:

a. Create a FigureCommand interface with one method: `public void execute(Figure f)`.

b. Create a FigureList class with a `map(Figure Command c)` method that calls `c.execute(f)` for all figures `f` in the list. This `map` method is an internal iterator.

c. Change the type of the `children` field of the GroupFigure class to FigureList, and similarly change the type of the `figures` field of the Drawing class to FigureList.

d. Then replace as many of the external iterator loops in all drawer6 classes as you can with a call to the internal iterator of the FigureList class.

32. Look at the API for the java.awt.Component and java.awt.Container classes, and decide which, if any, design patterns were used in developing them.

REFERENCES

1. Beck, K. and R. Johnson. *Patterns generate architectures.* In *European Conference on Object-Oriented Programming (ECOOP'94).* 1994. Bologna, Italy: Springer-Verlag.
2. Vlissides, J., Tooled composite. *C++ Report,* 1999. 11(8): 43–47.
3. Johnson, R., *Documenting Frameworks Using Patterns.* Proceedings OOPSLA '92, 1992. NewYork: ACM Press, pp. 63–76.
4. Gamma, E., R.Helm, R.Johnson, and J.Vlissides, *Design Patterns, Elements of Reusable Object-Oriented Software.* Professional Computing. 1995. Reading, MA: Addison-Wesley.

9

Language Parser Case Study

SECTION 9.0 INTRODUCTION

If you have written Java programs using a modern IDE (integrated development environment) such as Eclipse or NetBeans, you probably appreciate all the tools it provides to make life easier for you as you write and debug your code. One of the helpful tools such environments provide is autoformatting, which does things like automatically indenting lines of code properly or reformatting poorly formatted code. Another tool modern IDEs provide is refactoring support. For example, they allow you to rename methods, and the IDE automatically updates all calls to the renamed methods. Yet another tool provided by such environments is automatic checking of your code for errors such as missing semicolons or misspelled words. If such errors are found, they are immediately highlighted.

Such tools can be written completely independently of each other, each taking the user's source code and doing something different with it. However, although there might be some advantages to such independence, this approach is sure to lead to a large amount of code duplication because there are so many similar things these tools all need to do to the code before they can perform their jobs. How can we avoid such duplication?

In this chapter, we will answer this question by creating some tools for manipulating programs written in a very simple subset of Java and showing you how code duplication can be avoided. In the process, we will encounter more design principles and patterns.

SECTION 9.1 VSSJ: A VERY SIMPLE SUBSET OF JAVA

To allow us to focus on design principles without having to spend a lot of time on the intricacies of a fully modern programming language such as Java, we will use a very small subset of Java as the programming language to study in this chapter. We won't execute programs in this language, but instead will look at issues such as formatting programs or searching for particular structures in the programs.

Our language VSSJ (Very Simple Subset of Java) consists of three kinds of declarations, four kinds of statements, and integer literals. These features are combined according to certain rules to form a legal program.

The three VSSJ declarations are:

1. A variable declaration, consisting of two symbols followed by a semicolon—the first symbol represents the variable's type and the second symbol represents the variable's name. A *symbol* consists of a letter a–z or A–Z followed by zero or more letters or digits.
2. A method declaration, which starts with two symbols—the first indicating the return type and the second being the method name—followed by an empty set of parentheses (no parameters are allowed in VSSJ), and ends with a body consisting of a *block* of statements, which is a set of braces "{" and "}" surrounding zero or more statements.
3. A class declaration, which starts with the word "class" followed by a symbol indicating the name of the class. Last, there is a class body consisting of a set of braces "{" and "}" surrounding zero or more method, variable, or class declarations. Note that a class body can include other class declarations (called *inner* classes in Java).

The four VSSJ statements are:

1. An empty statement, consisting of just a semicolon ";"
2. An assignment statement, consisting of a symbol followed by an equal sign (=), then an integer literal, and finally a semicolon
3. A while statement, consisting of the word "while" followed by a set of parentheses surrounding a symbol, and then a block of statements
4. A method call statement, consisting of a symbol, an empty pair of parentheses, and a semicolon

A legal VSSJ program consists of a class declaration. Inside a VSSJ program, you can have *white space* (any combination of space, tab, new line, and return characters) anywhere, except within a symbol, since such white space indicates the beginning or ending of a symbol. An example of a VSSJ program, that includes all kinds of declarations and statements, is given in Figure 9.1.

As we said above, we will not be executing these programs, and so you shouldn't worry about what the program will do when executed. Furthermore, we won't, at the moment, concern ourselves with other Java necessities, such as declaring variables before using them or whether their types match their usage.

SECTION 9.2 PRETTY PRINTING

As stated in the introductory section of this chapter, our goal is to learn more about design and design patterns through the study of tools for a programming development environment. Let us start with a fairly simple but useful tool: Given a program in VSSJ with an arbitrary layout, the tool reformats the program with proper indenting following the usual Java conventions.

FIGURE 9.1 A sample VSSJ program.

```
class A {                     —a class declaration
   int x;                     —a variable declaration
   void foo() {               —a method declaration
      ;                       —an empty statement
      x = 3;                  —an assignment statement
      while(x) {              —a while statement
         foo();               —a method call
      }
   }
   class B {                  —an inner class
      int y;
      void bar() {}
   }
}
```

To develop this tool, we will create a PrettyPrinter class with a public method with the following header:

```
public String prettyPrint(String program)
```

This method will return a program identical to the program that was given to it as its argument except that white space will be added or removed in order to properly format the program as in Figure 9.1. In particular, if the input to the `prettyPrint` method were the string

```
"class A{int x;void foo(){;x=3;while(x){foo();}}class B{int y;void bar(){}}}"
```

then the output would be exactly the program in Figure 9.1.

Before continuing reading, spend a little time thinking about how you would implement the `prettyPrint` method.

The first thing you may have realized is that the program (the input parameter to the `prettyPrint` method) is just a String, and so it needs to be stepped through one character at a time. Your `prettyPrint` method will need to look for the special words “class” and “while,” symbols such as “foo” and “void,” and special characters such as parentheses, braces, and semicolons. It will add these words, symbols, and characters to the output string, and, as it does so, it will add or remove white space. In the process of doing so, it will need to keep track of indentation levels. A method that accomplishes all this work sounds pretty complicated. The problem here, of course, is that one method is trying to do too much. The solution to all this complexity is to spread the responsibilities among different methods and objects.

SECTION 9.3 SCANNING

Notice that some of the basic meaningful units of the VSSJ program, called *tokens*, consist of single characters such as semicolons, parentheses, and braces, but other tokens are multiple-character ones, such as “class,” “while,” and words indicating variable and method names and types. During pretty printing, these tokens need to be extracted from the program. Should the PrettyPrinter’s `prettyPrint` method do this extraction? The design principle that says that "objects and methods should do one thing only and do it well" would suggest that a separate object should take the program string and convert it into a list of tokens. Such an object is typically called a *scanner* or *lexer* (for "lexical analyzer"). A Scanner object would be given the program string to scan. It would repeatedly determine which characters form the next token. More precisely, a Scanner class typically has a public method with the following header:

```
public Token getNextToken()
```

A PrettyPrinter would use a Scanner by repeatedly calling this method to ask it for the next token. A Scanner is a form of factory in that the PrettyPrinter asks it to create new "Token" objects for the PrettyPrinter instead of expecting the PrettyPrinter to create the objects itself.

Note that the return type of the `getNextToken()` method is Token. The `getNextToken()` method could just return a String consisting of the characters that make up the token, but it is useful to have a Token object that contains the string of characters that made up the token. A Token typically also stores information indicating the "type" or "kind" of token it is—for example, whether the token refers to a symbol, a key word such as "class" or "while," or an integer literal. Finally, it is useful—for error messages, for example—to have a Token contain the index or location of its string of characters in the program. Here is such a Token class:

```
public class Token
{
  //constants - the kinds of tokens
  public static final int EOF = 0;
  public static final int ERROR = 1;
  public static final int INTLITERAL = 2;
  public static final int SYMBOL = 3;
  public static final int CLASS = 4;
  public static final int LEFTBRACE = 5;
  public static final int RIGHTBRACE = 6;
  public static final int LEFTPAREN = 7;
  public static final int RIGHTPAREN = 8;
  public static final int SEMICOLON = 9;
  public static final int WHILE = 10;
  public static final int EQUALS = 11;

  //instance variables
  private int kind;           //the kind of token
  private int position;       //starting position of token in the input
  private String spelling;  //the characters in this token

  public Token(int k, String s, int p) //constructor
  {
    kind = k;
    spelling = s;
    position = p;
  }
```

```
    public String getSpelling()
    {
      return spelling;
    }
    public int getKind()
    {
      return kind;
    }
    public int getPosition()
    {
      return position;
    }
    public String toString()
    {
      return spelling + " " + kind + " " + position;
    }
}
```

How does the Scanner determine which token to build next? It repeatedly gets the next available character from the input string and adds it to the spelling of the token being built until it reaches the end of that token. We will not go into the details of how the Scanner works at this time. You can find the source code in the ast1 package. In this package, we have also included a Main class to demonstrate how the user might use these classes.

One important thing to note is that the Scanner always returns a nonnull Token when the `getNextToken` method is invoked. Eventually, it will return a Token of kind Token.ERROR or Token.EOF (indicating the end of the program), at which point the PrettyPrinter should finish up the formatting process.

SECTION 9.4 A SIMPLE PRETTY PRINTER

Now let us implement the `prettyPrint` method. It is quite easy to implement a loop that repeatedly asks the Scanner for the next token and then adds that token and appropriate white space to the formatted output string. It is easy to tell where space characters are needed and, by looking at Figure 9.1, you can see that new lines need to be added only after semicolons, right braces, and left braces, unless the next token is a right brace. The only stickler concerns proper indentation of lines of code. This issue, however, can be addressed by the use of a variable that keeps track of the indentation level at each point in the pretty printing process and by the use of both the current token and next token to determine the white space to be used between those tokens in the formatted version. See Figure 9.2 for a complete implementation of such a method.

How elegant is this implementation of `prettyPrint`? It nicely uses a Scanner to separate the responsibility of creating tokens from using tokens. It also seems to handle all the special cases very nicely with the conditionals.

```
/**
 * constructs a string of tab characters of the given number
 * @param numTabs the number of tabs to be included
 * @return the string of tabs that was constructed
 */
private String indent(int numTabs)
{
  String indentString = "";
  for (int i = 0; i < numTabs; i++)
    indentString += "\t";
    return indentString;
}
/**
 * constructs a new copy of the program with proper formatting
 * according to Java conventions.
 * It keeps track of the "indent level" and uses the current token
 * and next token to determine the formatting to be used between
 * those tokens.
 * @param program the program string to be reformatted
 * @return the string containing the properly formatted version
 *         of the program
 */
public String prettyPrint(String program)
{
  Scanner scanner = new Scanner(program);
  String result = "";
  int indentLevel = 0;
  //get the first 2 tokens
  Token currentToken = scanner.getNextToken();
  int currentTokenKind = currentToken.getKind();
  Token nextToken = scanner.getNextToken();
  Int nextTokenKind = nextToken.getKind();
  //repeatedly add the current token and the
  //appropriate white space to precede the next token
  while (currentTokenKind != Token,EOF &&
        currentTokenKind != Token.ERROR) {
    //add current token
    result += currentToken.getSpelling();
    //add spaces, indent, & newlines before the next token
    if (currentTokenkind == Token.CLASS ||
        CurrentTokenKind == Token.EQUALS ) {
          result += " ";
    }
    else if (currentTokenKind == Token.SYMBOL) {
      if (nextTokenKind    != Token.LEFTPAREN &&
        nextTokenKind      != Token.RIGHTPAREN &&
        nextTokenKind      != Token.SEMICOLON)
          result += " ";
```

FIGURE 9.2 A prettyPrint implementation. *Continued*

```
    }
    else if (currentTokenKind == Token.RIGHTPAREN) {
      if (nextTokenKind != Token.SEMICOLON)
        result += " ";
    }
    else if (currentTokenKind == Token.SEMICOLON ||
         currentTokenKind == Token.RIGHTBRACE) {
      result += "\n";
      if (nextTokenKind == Token.RIGHTBRACE)
          indentLevel--;
        result += indent(indentLevel);
      }
    else if (currentTokenKind == Token.LEFTBRACE) {
      if (nextTokenKind == Token.RIGHTBRACE)
        result += " ";
      else {
        indentLevel++;
        result += "\n" + indent(indentLevel);
      }
    }
    //update the currentToken and nextToken
    //for the next time through the loop
    currentToken = nextToken;
    currentTokenKind = nextTokenKind;
    nextToken = scanner.getNextToken();
    nextTokenKind = nextToken.getKind() ;
  }
  return result;
}
```

FIGURE 9.2 *Continued*

However, what if you now want/need to modify this code so that there are blank lines between declarations? That is, suppose that Figure 9.1 should be replaced with Figure 9.3 as the new model of correct formatting.

Before reading further, take the `prettyPrint` code in Figure 9.2 and try to modify it so that it inserts the blank lines between declarations.

You should quickly see a problem, namely, knowing the indentation level and knowing the current token and next token are not sufficient to determine whether a blank line should be included between the tokens. In particular, consider the following program:

```
class A {
  void foo() {
    while(x) {}
    bar();
  }
  int x;
}
```

According to our formatting conventions, we do not want a blank line between lines 3 and 4 (between the `while` loop and the call to `bar`), but we do want a blank line between lines 5 and 6 (between the declaration of `foo` and the declaration of `x`). However, in both cases, the `prettyPrint` method, as implemented in Figure 9.2, sees only a right brace followed by a symbol, and so there is no way to determine, based on just those two tokens, whether to insert a blank line between them. To solve the problem, we need more contextual information than just the current token and next token.

At the cost of making the `prettyPrint` method a little more complex, we could fix it so that it uses contextual information to correctly insert blank lines where appropriate (See Exercise 3 at the end of the Chapter). Furthermore, this increased complexity could be ignored if nothing else were ever to be done with the PrettyPrinter. However, as we said earlier, one of the central tenets of software today is "change happens." Someone always wants more features or wants the current features to be made more sophisticated. For example, someone might want your PrettyPrinter to print an error message if the program does not have legal syntax, such as a missing semicolon or misspelled key words. Another user might want your PrettyPrinter to highlight key words.

Your code must be able to adapt to changes and must be robust and flexible so that it will not break when such changes are attempted. One way to get the desired robustness and flexibility is to use another design pattern, called the *Interpreter* pattern.

SECTION 9.5 INTERPRETER PATTERN

VSSJ is a language with grammar rules and so one of the best ways to construct manipulators of "sentences" (programs) in that language is by way of the *Interpreter* pattern [1]. In the Interpreter pattern, a VSSJ program is converted, through the use of the grammar of the VSSJ language, into a data structure representing the

```
class A {
  int x;


  void foo() {
    ;
    x = 3;
    while(x) {
      foo();
    }
  }

  class B {
    int y;

    void bar() {}
  }
}
```

FIGURE 9.3 A sample VSSJ program with blank lines between declarations.

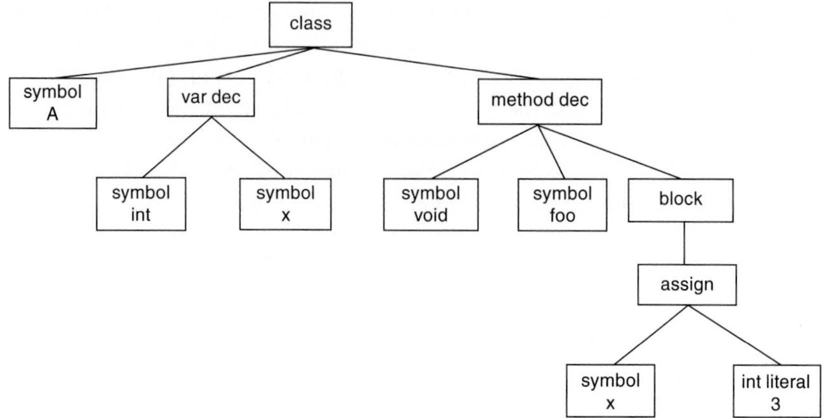

FIGURE 9.4
A sample AST.

program. The user can then take appropriate actions on that structure (e.g., pretty printing). The data structure we will use here is an *abstract syntax tree* (AST), a structure typically generated by compilers when they are processing source code. Each leaf node of this tree corresponds to a value (e.g., a constant or a symbol), and the internal nodes correspond to more complicated structures, such as declarations or statements, with subtrees of internal nodes corresponding to substructures within those structures. For example, an AST is given in Figure 9.4, corresponding to the following VSSJ program:

```
class A {
   int x;
   void foo() {
      x = 3;
   }
}
```

With the help of the Interpreter pattern, we will break down our process of pretty printing into the following phases:

1. Convert the program string into a list of Tokens as before (done by a Scanner object).
2. Build the AST from the list of Tokens (done by a Parser object).
3. Manipulate the AST to produce a new string (done by a PrettyPrinter object).

See Figure 9.5 for a diagram of how these phases are related.

Besides the nice separation of responsibilities demonstrated by this design, another advantage of following this route is that we can reuse the AST for other actions that the user may also want to perform on the program. For example, suppose the user wants only to search a VSSJ program for methods named `foo`. The AST is a very

FIGURE 9.5 The phases of manipulating a program. The rounded items are the data and the rectangular items are the manipulators.

helpful data structure for conducting such a search. We'll look at this search process in more detail in a later section. We can easily imagine other uses of the AST as well.

Because the AST is so central to source code manipulation processes, we need to design it carefully—in particular, we need to design carefully the classes that make up the nodes of the tree. After we have designed the AST, we will consider the manipulations of this tree. Finally, we will design and implement a Parser that will construct such an AST from a list of tokens.

SECTION 9.6 DESIGN OF THE AST

When designing an AST, it is helpful to consider how it will be manipulated, for example, by a PrettyPrinter. Based on Figure 9.5, we would expect the new PrettyPrinter to have a method with the following header:

```
public String prettyPrint(Node root)
```

that takes the root node of the tree (instead of a String) as its parameter and returns a String containing the reformatted program represented by the tree. Or, to add a little more generality, the following header could be used:

```
public String prettyPrint(Node root, String indent)
```

The indent would be a string of white space, and this method would pretty print the program, adding the given indentation string at the front of every line.

During the printing process, the method needs somehow to traverse the tree and visit each node. When visiting each node, it prints the source code corresponding to the subtree rooted at that node. Therefore, during the visit to a node, the PrettyPrinter might need to print something and then recursively visit the children to print the source to which they correspond, possibly doing more printing between the visits to the children, and finally return a String. For example, for a node representing a class declaration, the PrettyPrinter could print the word `class`, the name of the class, a left brace, and then recursively visit all the node's children declarations to pretty print them before finally printing the closing right brace.

First attempt

Let us first attempt to implement our AST with a general tree and see how elegant our AST and PrettyPrinter turn out to be. Consider a tree where each internal node corresponds to a program structure and each leaf node corresponds to a value or symbol. Since different structures within the program have different numbers and types of substructures (for example, a `while` statement has more tokens than an assignment statement), we will assume that all internal nodes can have arbitrarily many children nodes.

Every node will need to store some information indicating the structure it represents and references to any children nodes. For example, a node corresponding to a class declaration could store the string "class," a child containing the name of the class, and zero or more children corresponding to the declarations in the class. A node corresponding to an assignment statement could store the string "assignment," a child indicating the variable and another child indicating the value. The tree in Figure 9.4 is an example of such a tree.

In our implementation of this design, let us make the nodes immutable and so provide getter methods but not setter methods. Here is some of the code for one such implementation scheme:

```
public class Node
{
  private String kind;
  private List<Node> children;

  public Node(String k, List<Node>) {...} //constructor
  public String getKind() {...}
  public Node getChild(int index) {...}
  public int getNumberOfChildren () {...}
}
public class Leaf extends Node
{
  private String value;

  public Leaf(String k, String v) {...} //constructor
  public String getValue() { return value; }
}
public class PrettyPrinter
{
  public String prettyPrint(Node root, String indent)
  {
    if(root instanceof Leaf)
      return indent + ((Leaf) root).getValue();
    else if(root.getKind().equals("assign") ) {
      return indent + ((Leaf) root.getChild(0)).getValue() +
            " = " + ((Leaf) root.getChild(1)).getValue() + ";";
    }
    else if(root.getKind().equals("var dec") ) {
      return ident + ((Leaf) root.getChild(0)).getValue() +
              ((Leaf) root.getChild(1)).getValue() + ";";
    }
    else if( root.getKind().equals("class") ) {
      String result = indent + "class ";
      result += ((Leaf) root.getChild(0)).getValue() + " { ";
      for( int i = 1; i < root.getNumberOfChildren(); i++ ) {
        result += prettyPrint(root.getChild(i), indent + "\t");
      }
      return result;
    }
    else ...
  }
}
```

```
public class Main { //test code
  public static void main(String[] args) {
    Node root;
    ...construct the tree using a Scanner and Parser...
    PrettyPrinter printer = new PrettyPrinter();
    System.out.println(printer.prettyPrint(root));
  }
}
```

This code is clearly ugly. The children of each node are used for different purposes, depending on the kind of node. As a result, the code is not very readable without comments describing the role of each child. Also the code has too many conditionals based on the kind of node.

One could modify the Node class so there is more than one field in a Node besides a string and the list of children, but for some uses of the Node class, any extra fields are unneeded, and so this modification is no more elegant.

Second attempt

A better design declares a new class of node for each type of construct. For example, a ClassDeclaration node would represent a class declaration, an AssignStatement node would represent assignment statements, and an IntLiteral node would represent integer literals. The ClassDeclaration node would have two fields: a name field and a field corresponding to the list of declarations within the class declaration. The AssignStatement node would have two fields: a string naming the variable being assigned to and an IntLiteral node containing the value being assigned. An IntLiteralNode would have one field: a string containing the integer value represented by the node. All node classes would be subclasses of an abstract Node class or a Node interface. If we make this change but no others, then our PrettyPrinter's `prettyPrint` method would look like this:

```
public String prettyPrint(Node root, String indent)
  {
    if( root instanceof IntLiteral )
      return indent + ((IntLiteral) root).getValue();
    else if(root instanceof AssignStatement) {
      return indent + ((AssignStatement) root.getVariable() +
           " = " +
          ((AssignStatement) root.getValue()).getValue() +
           ";";
    }
    else if( root instanceof ClassDeclaration ) {
      String result = indent + "class " +
                     ((ClassDeclaration) root).getName() + " { ";
      List<Node> children =
                ((ClassDeclaration) root).getDeclarations();
      for( int i = 0; i < children.size(); i++ ) {
        result += prettyPrint(root.getChild(i), indent + "\t");
      }
```

```
            return result;
        }
        else ...
    }
```

Clearly this version is not much cleaner than the previous version. In particular, there is still a huge, ugly set of conditionals.

Third attempt

Hopefully by now, you see a more elegant design for this code. Let us recall two of the design rules mentioned in earlier chapters:

1. Ask not what you can do to an object; ask what an object can do for you.
2. Use polymorphism instead of conditionals.

Therefore, instead of the PrettyPrinter having to pretty print each node, nodes should know how to pretty print themselves. In other words, each node should have a method

```
public String prettyPrint(String indent)
```

that returns the pretty printed version of the code represented by the subtree rooted at that node, with every line indented by the given amount. Because each method is specific to the type of node, the conditional tests can be eliminated.

With these changes, the PrettyPrinter's `prettyPrint` method merely calls the prettyPrint method on the root of the AST and returns the result:

```
public String prettyPrint(Node root, String indent)
{
    return root.prettyPrint(indent);
}
```

In fact, one could go a step further. In this design, the PrettyPrinter object has only one method and that method does nothing but invoke the root's `prettyPrint` method. Therefore, one could argue that there is no real need for a PrettyPrinter object anymore. Our main method need only contain the following code:

```
ClassDeclaration root = ...generate the tree from the program...;
String result = root.prettyPrint("");
System.out.println(result);
```

However, we will continue to include the PrettyPrinter object for the sake of consistency with later versions of our design.

Note that we do not have any common behavior (or data) that can be implemented in the Node superclass, and so we are using a Node interface instead of abstract class. Here is a complete set of node classes and interfaces:

```
public interface Node {
    public String prettyPrint(String indent);
}
```

```
class AssignStatement implements Node { ... }
class Block implements Node { ... }
class ClassDeclaration implements Node { ... }
class EmptyStatement implements Node { ... }
class IntLiteral implements Node { ... }
class MethodCall implements Node { ... }
class MethodDeclaration implements Node { ... }
class VarDeclaration implements Node { ... }
class WhileStatement implements Node { ... }
```

See Figure 9.6 for the UML class diagram relating these classes and interfaces. The complete code for these classes can be found in the ast2 package.

Let us look at the implementations of the `prettyPrint` methods in some of the node classes to show you how straightforward they are.

AssignStatement:

```
public String prettyPrint(String indent)
{
  return indent + getVariable() + " = " +
    getValue().prettyPrint("") + ";";
}
```

IntLiteral:

```
public String prettyPrint(String indent)
{
  return indent + getValue();
}
```

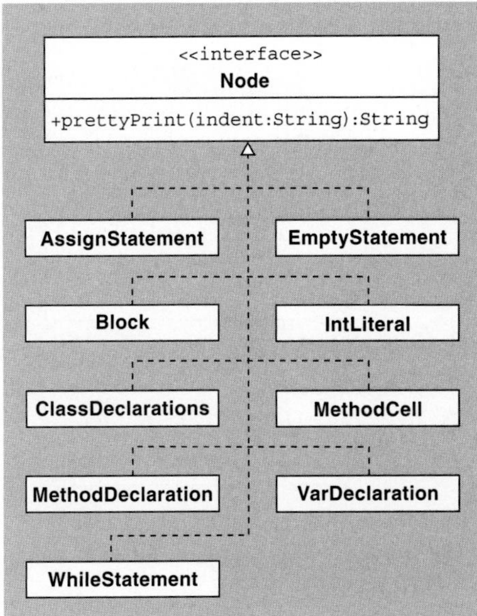

FIGURE 9.6 The class diagram for the nodes of our AST.

The Interpreter Pattern

The Interpreter pattern is useful when sentences in a language need to be interpreted. The language to be interpreted can be a programming language (such as Java or VSSJ), a language of expressions (such as regular, boolean, or arithmetic expressions), or a language for storing structured data (such as XML). Each language has its own set of grammatical rules for constructing sentences in the language. For example, a sentence in a programming language usually refers to a program or separately compilable unit. In the languages of expressions and structured data, any legal expression or data structure would be a sentence.

The act of "interpreting" a sentence should be viewed very generally. It can involve any number of actions or manipulations of the sentence, including, for example, executing the sentence (in the case of a programming language), evaluating the sentence (in the case of a language of expressions), or translating the sentence by converting it into another form. Also, an expression might be interpreted in a way that produces an equivalent but simplified expression. A sentence in a programming language might be interpreted in a way that creates an equivalent sentence in another language, such as machine language (the traditional role of a compiler).

In the Interpreter pattern, the grammatical rules of the language are used to construct an AST for a sentence in the language and then the AST is interpreted. More precisely, the grammatical rules are used to construct classes of nodes for the AST. The leaves of the tree correspond to tokens in the sentence, and the internal nodes correspond to grammatical structures in the language such as declarations, expressions, loops, or conditional statements. There is typically one class for each different grammatical structure. All the classes are subclasses of an abstract Node class or interface with an abstract `interpret` method. Each

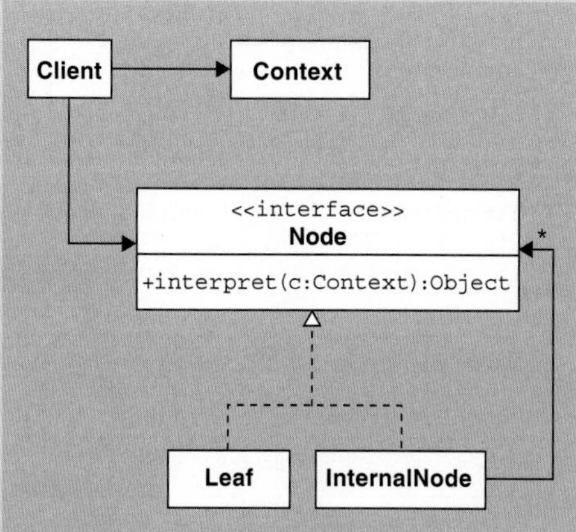

FIGURE 9.7 The classes involved in the Interpreter pattern.

subclass implements `interpret` differently, depending on the grammatical structure the class represents. Each `interpret` method recursively calls the `interpret` methods of its children nodes, as necessary, to fulfill its task.

The participants in the Interpreter pattern are the client, the context, and the AST node classes. See Figure 9.7. The context is global information provided by the client. The client passes the context to the nodes when the client calls the Node class' `interpret` method. The `interpret` method can modify the context or return a value.

In our pretty printer design, the `prettyPrint` method plays the role of the `interpret` method and the indentation level plays the role of the context. In this case, the act of interpretation involves creating a new program identical to the original program except for the formatting.

By the way, the bottom part of Figure 9.7 (the Node class and subclasses) should appear familiar. If you read the preceding chapter of this text, then you should recognize the Composite pattern here. The Interpreter pattern uses the Composite pattern for structuring the AST.

ClassDeclaration:

```
public String prettyPrint(String indent)
  {
    String result = indent + "class " + getName() + " {\n";
    for (Iterator it = getDeclarations().iterator();
                                          it.hasNext();) {
      Node node = (Node) it.next();
      result += node.prettyPrint(indent + "     ") + "\n";
      if (it.hasNext() )
        result += "\n"; //add blank line between declarations
    }
    result += indent + "}";
    return result;
  }
```

MethodDeclaration:

```
public String prettyPrint(String indent)
  {
    String result = indent + getType() + " " + getName() +
               "() ";
    result += getBody().prettyPrint(indent);
    return result;
  }
```

Isn't this design much more elegant than the previous design attempts? Each node is smarter, does more work, and has more responsibility, resulting in methods that are shorter, clearer, and do one thing only and do it well.

SECTION 9.7 METHOD FINDER

Now that we have handled pretty printing, let us see how we can reuse the AST for other purposes. Consider the very simple-looking problem: Given a program in VSSJ, does there exist a particular class in the program containing a particular method? More precisely, given a class name, a method name, and a program, does there exist a method of the given name in the class of the given name in the program?

To solve this problem, we will attempt to create a MethodFinder class with a public method with the following header:

```
/**
 * determines whether the given code contains a method by the
 * given name in a class with the given name.
 * If the class is an inner class, then its full name including the
 * outer class names separated by periods is used.
 * For example, if class A contains class B which contains class C,
 * then the innermost class is referred to by "A.B.C".
 * @param methodName the name of the method we are searching for
 * @param className the full name of the class containing the
 *                  desired method
 * @param program the VSSJ program we are searching for the given
 *                  method
 * @return true if a method with the desired name is found in the
 *                  desired class.
 */
public boolean findMethod(String methodName, String className,
                          String program)
```

Note, as the header says, that for inner classes, we prepend the inner class' name with the name of the enclosing class using a period as a separator. This notation applies to classes nested arbitrarily deep.

For example, using the program in Figure 9.1, there is a method in class A named `foo`, and so `findMethod("foo", "A", ...program...)` would return true. Similarly, there is a method named `bar` in a class B that is an inner class of a class A, and so `findMethod("bar", "A.B", ...program...)` would return true. Any other calls to `findMethod` using the program in Figure 9.1 would return false.

Before continuing reading, spend a little time thinking about how you would implement the method `findMethod` both without creating the AST and with creating the AST.

You hopefully see how messy it would be to implement `findMethod` by inspecting just the tokens of the program instead of using the AST, as we did in our original version of the PrettyPrinter. However, using the AST, we can implement our method finder similarly to our pretty printer. That is, we can use a Parser and Scanner to create an AST from the program and then let the MethodFinder traverse the tree looking for the desired method. Moreover, as with the PrettyPrinter, it is appropriate to let each node class be responsible for finding whether its subtree contains the desired method, and so we will give each node a method of the form:

```
public boolean findMethod(String methodName,
                          String desiredClassName,
                          String currentClassName)
```

that returns true if the subtree contains the method with the desired name in the class with the desired name. Note that we added an extra parameter `currentClassName` to keep track of the outer class names, as the tree is traversed downward.

As a result of these changes, the MethodFinder's `findMethod` method can now be modified to take the AST as a parameter instead of the original program:

```
public boolean findMethod(String methodName, String className,
                          Node root)
{
    return root.findMethod(methodName, className, "");
}
```

Notice, as in the case of the PrettyPrinter, the MethodFinder class now has only one method and that method has just one line of code, rendering the MethodFinder class itself somewhat superfluous. However, the class will be useful in later versions of our package.

The interesting thing about these `findMethod` methods in the node classes is that all but two of them just return false. The two remaining methods are in the ClassDeclaration and MethodDeclaration nodes, as you may have suspected. The implementations of these two methods are very simple:

```
//in class ClassDeclaration
public boolean findMethod(String methodName,
                          String desiredClassName,
                          String currentClassName)
{
    String newCurrentClassName = (currentClassName.equals("") ?
                          getName() : currentClassName+"."+getName());
    for (Node node : getDeclarations()) {
        if (node.findMethod(methodName, desiredClassName,
                                        newCurrentClassName))
            return true;
    }
    return false;
}
//in class MethodDeclaration
public boolean findMethod(String methodName,
                          String desiredClassName,
                          String currentClassName)
```

```
{
    return desiredClassName.equals(currentClassName) &&
           getName().equals(methodName);
}
```

The complete code for the `findMethod` methods in all node classes is given in the package ast3.

SECTION 9.8 SOME PROBLEMS WITH THESE ELEGANT IMPLEMENTATIONS

Everything looks nice and elegant, doesn't it? In package ast3, we have node objects sharing the responsibilities of pretty printing and method finding as appropriate so that each object's methods are nice and clean. Furthermore, as you hopefully see by now, the AST can be used to answer many more questions about the original program than just pretty printing and method finding, many of which can be implemented by adding new, simple methods in each node class.

Unfortunately, there still are a couple of problems with this design and implementation. The first problem is that the pretty printing and method finding code is spread all over among all the node classes. That is, in our code in the ast3 package, the PrettyPrinter object is not responsible for all pretty printing and the MethodFinder object is not responsible for all the searching for the desired method. Instead, the code for each of these jobs is spread all over the place, and each node has the responsibility of handling these jobs for itself and its children. It would be more elegant if all the code for each of the jobs were conveniently organized together.

There is another related problem. What if we later want to add code to solve another problem that involves traversing the tree? For example, we might want to display the tree graphically using rectangles for nodes and lines for connecting nodes to children. This job, if implemented in a manner similar to pretty printing and method finding, would require us to modify each class of nodes by adding new `display` methods to them. But what if we were only given the compiled node classes in a library so that we couldn't modify them? In that situation, we would have to take some less elegant approach such as subclassing all of the node classes. If we later wanted to add another job that requires AST traversal, we would need to subclass our nodes yet again.

There's a pattern here. We want to be able to visit each node of the AST to do something specific based on the type of node. To implement these visits, we have added a new method to each of the node classes so that we can use polymorphism to handle dispatching the correct method on each node. See Table 9.1 for a listing of the method implementations for the three jobs we have discussed so far on the AST nodes.

The way the code is organized now is that the methods in each row are implemented together in one class (in one file). But from a coder's perspective, it would be nice to have the code organized so that all methods in one *column* are together in the same class, for example, in a PrettyPrinter, MethodFinder, or Displayer class. Furthermore, we want to be able later to add new visitors that visit each node and do something specific based on the class of each node. Adding such a visitor cor-

TABLE 9.1 The organization of methods for our three jobs.

	PrettyPrinter	MethodFinder	Displayer
AssignStatement	prettyPrint	findMethod	display
Block	prettyPrint	findMethod	display
ClassDeclaration	prettyPrint	findMethod	display
EmptyStatement	prettyPrint	findMethod	display
IntLiteral	prettyPrint	findMethod	display
MethodCall	prettyPrint	findMethod	display
MethodDeclaration	prettyPrint	findMethod	display
VarDeclaration	prettyPrint	findMethod	display
WhileStatement	prettyPrint	findMethod	display

responds to adding another column to this table. It would be nice to be able to add this visitor without having to modify every node. But we also want to be able to use polymorphism to avoid ugly tests that use the `instanceof` operator, so we can't remove all intelligence from the nodes. Each of them will still need to know what is to be done when it is visited.

Let us consider how we might redesign our classes to move all the `prettyPrint` methods into the same class. First consider the AssignStatement node. We will leave the `prettyPrint` method in that node for the sake of polymorphism, but we will move the *body* of that method into a new method called `prettyPrintAssignStatement` in the PrettyPrinter class. Then the AssignStatement's class' `prettyPrint` method need only call that method in the PrettyPrinter class, and so the AssignStatement method looks something like this:

```
//in AssignStatement class
public String prettyPrint(String indent)
{
  return printer.prettyPrintAssignStatement(this, indent);
}
```

The modified code has been highlighted with bold text. Note that we have to pass the node itself as the first parameter to the PrettyPrinter's `prettyPrintAssignStatement` method since the PrettyPrinter needs some way to access the AssignStatement's attributes.

The PrettyPrinter class now has a new method containing the body of the old AssignStatement's `prettyPrint` method:

```
public int prettyPrintAssignStatement(AssignStatement node,
                                      String indent)
{
  return indent + node.getVariable() + " = " +
                 node.getValue().prettyPrint("") + ";";
}
```

We can do the same refactoring to all the other nodes. Once this refactoring is completed, the important code for evaluating the AST has been grouped together in one PrettyPrinter class, and all the `prettyPrint` methods in the node classes are used just to call polymorphically the correct method in the PrettyPrinter class.

There is one remaining detail before the new code will compile: There is a reference in the new version of the AssignStatement's `prettyPrint` method to a `printer`, but this variable is undeclared. How do we fix this problem? The AssignStatement needs to have a reference to the PrettyPrinter object so that it can invoke the PrettyPrinter's `prettyPrintAssignStatement` method. The easiest way to handle this situation is to pass the PrettyPrinter as another parameter to the `prettyPrint` method in the AssignStatement class.

```
//in AssignStatement class
public String prettyPrint(PrettyPrinter printer, String indent)
{
   return printer.prettyPrintAssignStatement(this, indent);
}
```

This requires us to make a small change to the PrettyPrinter's method as well:

```
public String prettyPrintAssignStatement(AssignStatement node,
                                         String indent)
{
    return indent + node.getVariable() + " = " +
         node.getValue().prettyPrint(this, "") + ";";
}
```

In summary, in the `prettyPrintAssignStatement` method, the PrettyPrinter is asking the child of the node to pretty print itself, using this object (the PrettyPrinter) and the empty string as parameters. In passing itself as the first argument, it is telling the child node where to go to find the code that is used to form the body of its `prettyPrint` method.

In the `main` method that gets things started, our code would appear as follows:

```
PrettyPrinter printer = ...create an PrettyPrinter...;
ClassDeclaration root = ...create an AST using a Parser...;
String result = root.prettyPrint(printer, " ");
```

We can also do exactly the same refactoring for method searching using the MethodFinder class and for displaying the tree using the Displayer class. After these changes, each node will still have `findMethod` and `display` methods, but those methods will just call the appropriate methods in the MethodFinder and Displayer classes, respectively. So each node *XXX* will have the following `findMethod` method:

```
public boolean findMethod(MethodFinder finder, String methodName,
              String desiredClassName, String currentClassName)
{
   return finder.findMethodXXX(this, methodName,
                         desiredClassName, currentClassName)
}
```

and a similar `display` method. Once again, the important code is now all nicely organized into the MethodFinder and Displayer classes, just as it was done in the PrettyPrinter class.

We are not going to give you the full code for this design because, although it is getting closer to elegance, there are still three problems:

1. We now have three short `prettyPrint`, `findMethod`, and `display` methods in all the node classes. They are so similar, one would think that there must be a better way of handling this situation.
2. If we want to compute something new, for example, check the validity of the program in terms of variable declarations before use, we need to create a Validator class where all the real computation is done, but we also need to add short `validate` methods to each of the node classes to call the Validator's methods. So now we are adding twice as many methods as before!
3. We haven't solved the problem of what to do if the node classes come precompiled so you can't just add new methods without subclassing all the node classes.

SECTION 9.9 THE VISITOR PATTERN

To solve these problems, we will use the *Visitor* pattern [1]. Think of the PrettyPrinter, MethodFinder, and Displayer as "visitors" to the nodes. We can nicely simplify all their visits by replacing the `prettyPrint`, `findMethod`, and `display` methods in the node classes with just one `accept` method. That `accept` method will be reused by each of the three (and all future) visitors. In each node class *XXX*, the `accept` method will look like this:

```
public Object accept(Visitor v, Object obj)
{
   return v.visitXXX (this, obj);
}
```

Note that we changed the return type to Object to generalize things and we included a second parameter `obj` of type Object for any extra information that needs to be passed along (such as the indentation level in the case of the PrettyPrinter).

Next, in all the visitor classes (PrettyPrinter, MethodFinder, and Displayer), we will name all the methods `visit`*XXX* instead of `prettyPrint`*XXX*, `find-Method`*XXX* or `display`*XXX*.

After these changes are made, we end up with the following code. In each node class, we have one generic `accept` method, mentioned above, that all visitors will call. In each visitor class, we have a full set of `visitXXX` methods, one for each node class *XXX*. For example, in the PrettyPrinter class, we would have the following method (and eight more methods like it):

```
public Object visitAssignStatement(AssignStatement node,
                                  Object obj)
{
  //obj is a string of whitespace giving the indentation
  return obj + node.getVariable() + " = " +
         node.getValue().accept(this, "") + ";";
}
```

To help start things off elegantly when the user wants to pretty print a program, the PrettyPrinter class would have the following public method:

```
public String prettyPrint(ClassDeclaration root)
{
  return (String) root.accept(this, "");
}
```

and so the user's main method could look like this:

```
PrettyPrinter printer = ...;
ClassDeclaration root = ...;
String result = printer.prettyPrint(root);
```

To do validating using a Validator visitor, we don't need to add anything new to the node classes. Instead, in the Validator class we would just have a collection of `visitXXX` methods.

As the primary interface with the user, the Validator class could have the following public method:

```
public boolean validate(ClassDeclaration root)
{
  return (Boolean) root.accept(this, null);
}
```

and the user's main method could look like this:

```
Validator validator = ...;
ClassDeclaration root = ...;
boolean result = validator.validate(root);
```

Notice how the Visitor pattern takes care of all three problems:

1. The node classes are no longer full of short methods, one for each activity. There is just one `accept` method in each node class that is used by all visitors.
2. Any new visitor we want to add later just needs to implement the appropriate `visitXXX` methods to do the real work, and we don't need to change any existing node files. All the new code is stored in one place, namely the new visitor class.

3. Since we are not modifying the node classes when adding new visitors, it doesn't matter whether we are working with compiled versions of the node classes, as long as the compiled versions have the appropriate `accept` methods in them.

There is one last detail to consider, namely the `accept` method's `visitor` parameter that is declared of type Visitor. We haven't yet explained what the Visitor type is, but the definition of Visitor should hopefully be clear by now. The Visitor is an interface, and all Visitor classes, such as PrettyPrinter, MethodFinder, etc., implement this interface. Here's the complete code for the Visitor interface:

```
public interface Visitor
{
  Object visitAssignStatement(AssignStatement node, Object obj);
  Object visitBlock(Block node, Object obj);
  Object visitClassDeclaration(ClassDeclaration node, Object obj);
  Object visitEmptyStatement(EmptyStatement node, Object obj);
  Object visitIntLiteral(IntLiteral node, Object obj);
  Object visitMethodCall(MethodCall node, Object obj);
  Object visitVarDeclaration(VarDeclaration node, Object obj);
  Object visitWhileStatement(WhileStatement node, Object obj);
  Object visitMethodDeclaration(MethodDeclaration node,
                                                    Object obj);
}
```

The complete code for our ast3 package after being refactored using Visitors can be found in package ast4.

Let us now update Table 9.1 to handle the node classes and the new Visitor classes (see Table 9.2). Each cell in the table corresponds to a `visit`*XXX* method on each node by each visitor.

Note that, with the introduction of the Visitor pattern, we now have the methods in each column grouped into one class, as we had desired, but we still get the benefit of polymorphism through the invocation of the `accept` methods in each node

TABLE 9.2 The organization of methods using Visitors.

	PrettyPrinter	MethodFinder	Displayer
AssignStatement	visitAssignStatement	visitAssignStatement	visitAssignStatement
Block	visitBlock	visitBlock	visitBlock
ClassDeclaration	visitClassDeclaration	visitClassDeclaration	visitClassDeclaration
EmptyStatement	visitEmptyStatement	visitEmptyStatement	visitEmptyStatement
IntLiteral	visitIntLiteral	visitIntLiteral	visitIntLiteral
MethodCall	visitMethodCall	visitMethodCall	visitMethodCall
MethodDeclaration	visitMethodDeclaration	visitMethodDeclaration	visitMethodDeclaration
VarDeclaration	visitVarDeclaration	visitVarDeclaration	visitVarDeclaration
WhileStatement	visitWhileStatement	visitWhileStatement	visitWhileStatement

The Visitor Pattern

The Visitor pattern is useful for situations in which you have a data structure and you want to define new operations on the elements of the data structure, but you don't want to (or may not be allowed to) modify the classes of the elements. More precisely, it is useful in situations where (a) you have elements of many different classes in your structure and the operation to be added will vary in its actions depending on the classes, (b) you want to or need to avoid "polluting" the classes with new methods corresponding to the new operation, and (c) the classes defining the structure rarely change but the desired operations on the elements of the structure change.

For our pretty printing example, the AST corresponds to the data structure in the Visitor pattern. The operations we want to perform on the AST nodes are pretty printing, method finding, displaying, and others. We want to avoid adding new methods, such as `prettyPrint`, `findMethod`, and `display` to each of the Node subclasses every time we want to perform a new operation on the AST structure.

The Visitor pattern solves this problem using Visitor classes, each of which encapsulates an operation on all the elements of the data structure. That is, suppose the elements of the data structure belong to classes A and B, both of which implement an interface I. Then define a new Visitor interface as follows:

```
public interface Visitor
{
  Object visitA(A a, Object o);
  Object visitB(B b, Object o);
}
```

In these methods, the second parameter provides optional extra information needed to perform the desired action on A or B. The return type of the `visitA` and `visitB` methods is Object so that, optionally, a value can be returned by the `visitA` and `visitB` methods.

Now add one new method to interface I and the classes A and B:

In interface I, add the abstract method with header

```
Object accept(Visitor v, Object o);
```

In class A, add the method

```
public Object accept(Visitor v, Object o)
{ return v.visitA(this, o); }
```

In class B, add the method

```
public Object accept(Visitor v, Object o)
{ return v.visitB(this, o); }
```

The addition of these methods will be the only change that needs to be made to these classes, regardless of the number of actions you later want to perform on the data structure.

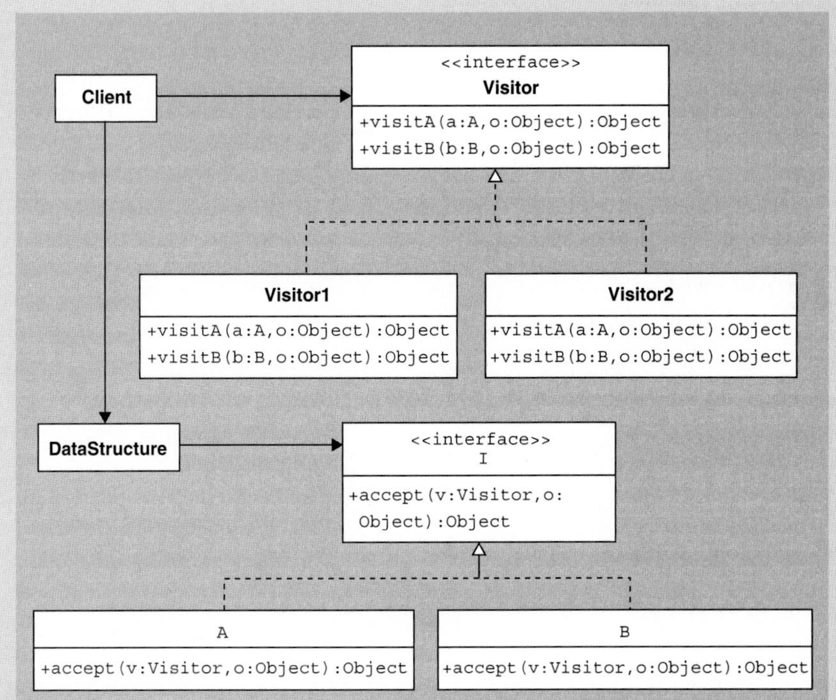

FIGURE 9.8 The Visitor pattern.

Every time you want to perform a new action on the elements of the data structure, you need to create a new class that implements the Visitor interface. The `visitA` and `visitB` methods, in your new class should perform the desired action on elements of type A and B, respectively.

Figure 9.8 shows a UML diagram of the Visitor pattern. In this diagram, we show two visitors, Visitorl and Visitor2.

The participants are all shown in Figure 9.8. The client obtains a visitor (e.g., Visitorl or Visitor2) for performing an operation on the data structure. Then the data structure is traversed, and the `accept` method is invoked on each of its elements, with the Visitor passed in as an argument. There are at least three ways the data structure can be traversed:

1. The data structure can use an Iterator to access all its elements and call their `accept` methods.
2. Each element's accept methods could recursively call the `accept` methods of their neighbors.
3. The visitor could do the traversing, in that each of its `visit` methods could call the `accept` methods of other elements.

Our pretty printer example used the third method. The visitor, when visiting a node, called the `accept` methods of the children of that node.

Continued

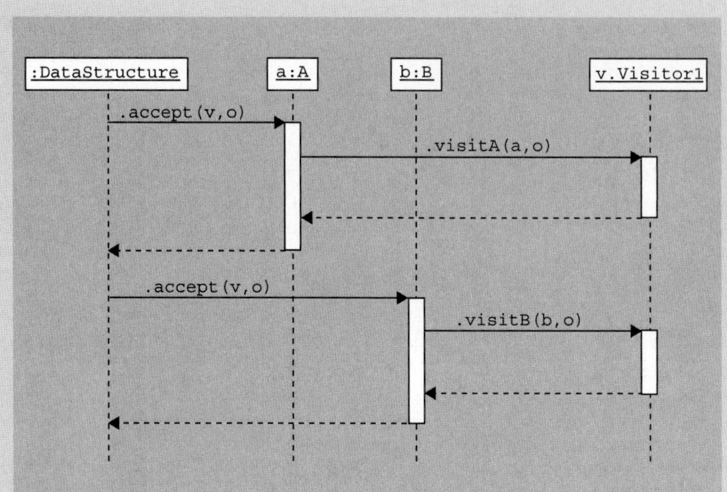

FIGURE 9.9 The Visitor pattern sequence diagram.

Note that the Visitor pattern is useful in other cases than traversing trees to visit their nodes. For example, a collection such as an ArrayList might contain elements from a variety of classes. Many different visitors could be created to traverse the list and visit each element. Such visitors could include ones that search for particular elements in the list or ones that modify different elements in the list in particular ways.

It is helpful to view the Visitor pattern through a sequence diagram (see Figure 9.9). It shows how the `accept` method of an element (`a` or `b`) is invoked and that method in turn calls the `visitA` or `visitB` method of the Visitor (`v`).

class. Also, if we now add new visitors (corresponding to adding new columns to Table 9.2), we do not need to modify the node classes.

You should be aware that there are some downsides to using the Visitor pattern. As we mentioned earlier, the `visit`*XXX* methods are no longer in the node classes, and so the methods cannot access the private attributes or methods of the node classes. As a result, we had to add public getter methods for all node attributes. In essence, the Visitor is getting the data from a node and then manipulating that data, a violation of the Expert pattern.

Also there is a downside to grouping the `visit`*XXX* methods by columns as in Table 9.2. If later we decide to add more rows to the table, for example, if we add a new node class for a new grammatical structure in our VSSJ language, we have to add new visit methods to the Visitor interface and to all the classes implementing the interface. Therefore, the Visitor pattern is best if you have a fixed set of node classes that you wish to visit and a variable number of visitors. If, conversely, you have a fixed number of visitors and a variable number of nodes, it is probably better not to use the Visitor pattern.

SECTION 9.10 VISITORS AND DOUBLE-DISPATCHING

To better understand what is really going on with the Visitor pattern, it is worth spending some time understanding "single dispatch" and "multiple dispatch" languages. For the purposes of this section, let us pretend that there are no second parameters of type Object in the `visit`*XXX* methods in Table 9.2 and that the names of all the methods are just `visit`. Then every entry in Table 9.2 is invoked by a call to `v.visit(n)` where `v` is a visitor and `n` is a node.

In an ideal world, an invocation `v.visit(n)` would act polymorphically based on the actual type (as compared to the declared type) of both the visitor `v` and the node `n`. That is, when we call `v.visit(n)`, the `visit` implementation we would like to be executed is the one in Table 9.2 that is in the row corresponding to the actual type of `n` and in the column corresponding to the actual type of `v`.

Unfortunately, Java is a single dispatch language. That is, a call in Java of the form `v.visit(n)` will behave polymorphically based on the actual class of the visitor `v` but not on the node `n`. This behavior, as we discussed in Chapter 3, is due to the fact that the compiler chooses which of the overloaded versions of `visit` to execute based on the declared type of the parameter, not the actual value of the parameter.

Some other languages have the desired kind of behavior. That is, they have *multiple dispatch* or *multimethods*, which means that the method implementation to be executed is chosen at runtime based on the object being sent the message and the actual values of the parameters, not just the declared types of the parameters, as in Java. Common Lisp, for example, has an object-oriented extension called CLOS with multimethods. If we were using CLOS to implement our pretty printer, then each of the `visit` methods in Table 9.2 could be declared as follows, using Lisp syntax:

```
(defmethod visit((v PrettyPrinter) (n AssignStatement)) ...)
(defmethod visit((v PrettyPrinter) (n EmptyStatement)) ...)
(defmethod visit((v PrettyPrinter) (n MethodCall)) ...)
...
```

or

```
(defmethod visit((v MethodFinder) (n AssignStatement)) ...)
(defmethod visit((v MethodFinder) (n EmptyStatement)) ...)
(defmethod visit((v MethodFinder) (n MethodCall)) ...)
...
```

When a call of the form `(visit a b)` is made, the Lisp environment dynamically looks at the actual type of `a` and `b` and chooses the appropriate implementation of `visit` to execute.

Note that in CLOS, a call of `visit` is written `(visit v n)`, and so the visitor `v` is not accorded a special syntactical position in the method call (e.g., in front of the method name, as is done in Java). That is, `v` is just treated as another parameter instead of being treated as the owner of the method. The reason for this treatment is that both parameters play symmetrically identical roles in determining which implementation of `visit` is executed. In other words, the `visit` method that takes a PrettyPrinter and AssignStatement as its parameters can be thought of as jointly owned by both the PrettyPrinter and AssignStatement classes.

Since, as we stated above, Java is a single dispatch language, we have to do something slightly more complicated to get the desired behavior of double dispatch. In order to get Java to act polymorphically on both `v` and `n`, we have to make both `n` and `v` receivers of messages. That is, we first make a call `n.accept(v)`, which in turn makes a call `v.visit(n)`.

It should be noted that there is a way to use Java's reflection capabilities to implement the `visit` methods to act polymorphically on all the parameters as well as on the object being sent the message and so get Java to act more like a multimethod language. In such an implementation, the visitor has a generic `visit` method that uses reflection to find the actual class of the parameters and then uses that information to find the specific implementation of `visit` to execute. For more details, see [2]. In the exercises, you are asked to explore this idea further.

SECTION 9.11 FACADE PATTERN

Let us now stop for a moment and reflect on what we have accomplished and think about whether and how we can further improve on everything we've done so far in this chapter. In particular, let us look for more patterns in the work we've done that we might use again in the future.

Our current setup consists of a nice collection of classes for processing and manipulating a VSSJ program. We can parse the program to get an AST, and we can construct any kind of visitor we want to manipulate the AST. Furthermore, we have implemented two such visitors, the PrettyPrinter and the MethodFinder. These are powerful tools.

However, look at the `main` method in the Main class in packages ast2 through ast4. To use all our powerful tools, a client must create a Parser, understand about ASTs and all the node classes, create Visitors, and combine them in appropriate ways. What if our clients don't care about and don't want to learn about all the details regarding visitors and parsers? Suppose they don't intend to create new Visitor classes and instead just want a fixed set of operations that they can perform on a VSSJ program, including, for example, pretty printing and searching for methods with a given name? In such a case, it is inappropriate to require the user to manipulate all of our classes and understand all of the tools.

In a situation such as this one, it is better to provide a new class, say a ProgramTool class, that handles all the details of working with the parser, AST, visitors, etc., and provides a cleaner interface for what the clients want. All the other powerful classes that we have created can still be made publicly available to the clients if they wish to use them, but, if we provide a ProgramTool class that hides the details in the most commonly used situations, then our clients might only need to deal with one ProgramTool object and ask it to do the various jobs. Such a class could easily be implemented as follows:

```
public class ProgramTool
{
  public String prettyPrint(String program)
  {
    Node root = new Parser().parse(program);
    return new PrettyPrinter().prettyPrint(root,"");
  }
  public boolean findMethod(String methodName,
                            String className,
                            String program)
  {
    Node root = new Parser().parse(program);
    return new MethodFinder().findMethod(methodName, className,
                            root);
  }
  ...other similar visitor actions...
}
```

These methods handle all the details regarding visitors and ASTs for the client. All the client needs to write is the following code:

```
//client code in the main method
ProgramTool tool = new ProgramTool();
String code = "class A { void main() { print(); } }";
String reformattedCode = tool.prettyPrint(code);
boolean found = tool.findMethod("foo", "A", code);
```

This idea of creating a class or a small set of classes to hide the details of the most common uses of a set of powerful tools is called the *Facade* pattern [1].

The ProgramTool appears in the ast5 package, along with the modifications we will make in the next section.

SECTION 9.12 PARSERS AND BUILDERS

Up to this point, we have ignored the construction of the AST from the original program. Now it is time to back up and study this tree-generation process.

In our packages ast2, ast3, and ast4, we have used a Parser object to build the tree from the program (a string). That is, the Parser's public `parse(String)` method creates and returns the AST corresponding to the program passed in as the argument.

This `parse(String)` method uses "recursive-descent" to build the tree. In this approach, a tree is constructed by the Parser using a collection of methods that each build a subtree of the tree. That is, each such method creates one kind of node and calls other methods in the collection using recursion to build each subtree of that node.

A recursive-descent parser relies on the fact that there is a structure or "grammar" that defines legal programs. In our case, the grammar for legal VSSJ programs

Facade Pattern

The Facade pattern is intended to shield clients from the complexities of a system while still allowing them access to the full functionality of the system.

Suppose you have a system composed of many classes with many interfaces. The system may be very powerful and so provide a lot of services to the client. These features make the system very appealing. However, if clients have simple needs but have to learn how to combine all the classes in complex ways just to handle those needs, then the system isn't as elegant as it should be. Furthermore, as systems evolve, they generally add more classes and interfaces. This evolution can add power and flexibility to the system but can make the situation even worse for the client.

The solution is to create a simple public interface to the system to handle the more common tasks and shield the clients from the details. This public interface is called the *Facade*. The system's many classes and interfaces can still be made publicly available for those clients who need to customize their tasks.

There are other benefits to this approach besides making handling the common tasks easier. It also weakens the coupling between the system and the clients, in that many clients will use only the Facade, allowing the system design to change without forcing the client's code to change. Furthermore, the Facade pattern can be used within such a system. That is, it can be used between layers of the system, further decoupling the classes in the system by having the classes in the higher layers of the system access the classes in the lower layers through their Facade.

See Figure 9.10 for a UML class diagram showing the participants in the Facade pattern and their associations.

When clients want to access the system to perform common actions, they can ask the Facade to perform the actions and the Facade will, in turn, handle all the details of asking the elements of the system to perform the task. If the sys-

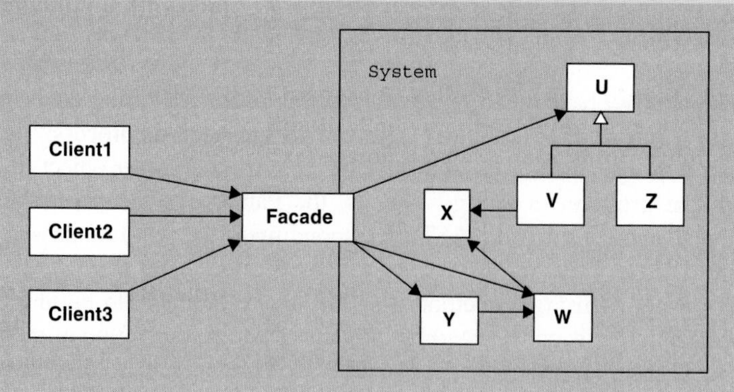

FIGURE 9.10 The Facade pattern.

tem's classes are made publicly accessible, then clients can also directly access the classes in the system in the cases when they have more specialized needs.

An example of the Facade in the Java Swing package is the JTable class. It is part of a system that also includes JTableHeader, TableModel, TableCellRenderer, TableCellEditor, TableColumnModel, TableColumn, TableModelListener, and ListSelectionListener classes. Those clients who want to create specialized JTables need to access most of these classes. However, those clients who want a simple table need not work with any of those classes except for the JTable class itself. They can, for example, call the JTable constructor passing in a two-dimensional array of data and an array of column header names, and the constructor will handle all the details regarding the rest of the system classes.

was already defined somewhat precisely when it was introduced in Section 9.1. Here are the grammar rules again:

1. A program consists of a class declaration.
2. A class declaration consists of the word "class" followed by a symbol giving the name of the class, followed by the class body, which consists of zero or more method, variable, or class declarations surrounded by left and right braces.
3. A variable declaration consists of a symbol followed by another symbol, and then by a semicolon.
4. A method declaration consists of two symbols followed by left and right parentheses and then a block of statements.
5. A block of statements consists of zero or more statements surrounded by left and right braces.
6. A statement consists of one of the following:
   a. An empty statement consisting of just a semicolon
   b. An assignment statement, consisting of a symbol followed by an equal sign, then an integer literal, and finally a semicolon
   c. A while statement, consisting of the word "while" followed by parentheses containing a symbol, and then a block of statements
   d. A method call statement, consisting of a symbol, an empty pair of parentheses, and a semicolon
7. An integer literal consists of one or more digits 0–9 optionally preceded by a "+" or "−" sign.
8. A symbol consists of a letter a–z or A–Z followed by zero or more letters or digits 0–9. No white space (space, tab, and newline characters) is allowed within a symbol.
9. There may be white space between the parts of each rule to avoid confusion (e.g., to separate two consecutive symbols) or to make the program more readable.

By following these grammatical rules, you can create a new program or determine the structure of an existing program. For example, the program

```
class A { int x; void foo(){;}}
```

can be broken down into a class declaration whose body contains one variable declaration and one method declaration. The method declaration's body consists of one empty statement.

Our parser uses this grammar to structure its recursive calls. Each part of a VSSJ program has a Parser method associated with it that generates an AST representing that part of the program. For example, the `parseDeclaration` method creates and returns an AST representing a class, method, or variable declaration, the `parseStatement` method creates and returns an AST representing a statement, the `parseBlock` method creates and returns an AST representing a block of statements, and so on. These methods call each other recursively as necessary to construct the tree. For example, the `parseBlock` method calls the `parseStatement` method to create the node's children. Similarly, if the `parseStatement` method is parsing a while statement, it calls `parseBlock` to create the subtree corresponding to the body of the while statement.

Such a recursive-descent parser is not necessarily the fastest way to build an AST, but it is one of the clearest ways to understand what is going on in each step and so, in that sense, it is quite elegant. Before continuing, you are strongly encouraged to study the Parser class in the ast4 package to understand how it works.

If you have looked at the Parser class implementation, you should have noticed two aspects of it that go against the design principles for elegant code:

1. The Parser is actually doing two things instead of one. It is both determining (i.e., parsing) the structure of the program and it is building the AST.
2. There are a significant number of conditional statements. We normally like to replace such conditionals, especially if they involve testing based on the type of an object, with polymorphism.

What can we do about these two problems?

Considering the first problem, suppose that the user wants merely to determine whether the program's structure is legal. In that case, the tree returned by the Parser in the ast4 package is not needed, and so it would be nice if we could avoid the construction process.

The solution, of course, is to separate out the parsing of the program from the construction of the AST. There should be a separate Builder class that does the construction. Whenever the parser reaches a point where, in the old version (in the ast4 package), it constructed a new node, it should instead ask the Builder to construct and return the new node for the parser. Then, we can substitute different builders to be used with our parser depending on our needs. If we want the AST to be constructed, we use a builder that actually constructs the nodes in the same way the old parser did. But if we just want to test the legality of the program, then nothing needs to be built, and so we can use an "empty" builder that returns null when asked to build a node. Furthermore, if we just want to count the number of nodes that would be created if we were to build the AST, we could use a builder that is identical to the empty builder except it keeps a count of the number of nodes it was asked to build. This idea of separating the actual construction of a complex object from the directing of that construction is called the *Builder* pattern [1].

The Builder Pattern

The Builder pattern is a creational pattern in which the algorithm responsible for creating a complex object is separated from the actual creation of the object. That is, there is a separation of responsibilities in that one participant, a Director, decides the steps involved in the creation of the complex object but another participant, the Builder, actually does the construction.

The Director need not be aware of how or what the Builder is actually constructing. The Director knows only that the Builder has a specific interface. Such a separation allows the same Director to use several Builders and so construct several different representations of the complex object.

The participants in the Builder pattern are the Director, the Builder interface, a concrete Builder class that implements the interface, and the Product, which is the complex object being constructed. The client first constructs a Director and concrete Builder. The client then instructs the Director to construct the Product using the provided Builder. The Director repeatedly decides what part of the Product is to be built next and directs the Builder to construct that part and add it to the Product. When the construction is finished, the client asks the Builder for the completed Product.

In the case of our PrettyPrinter, the Parser plays the role of Director. It parses the original VSSJ program and determines which part of the AST, the Product, is to be constructed next. But the Parser does not do the actual construction. Instead it asks the ASTBuilder to construct the nodes and add them to the AST.

See Figure 9.11 for a class diagram of the Builder pattern. In the diagram, there are two concrete Builders, each of which produces a different representation of the final product.

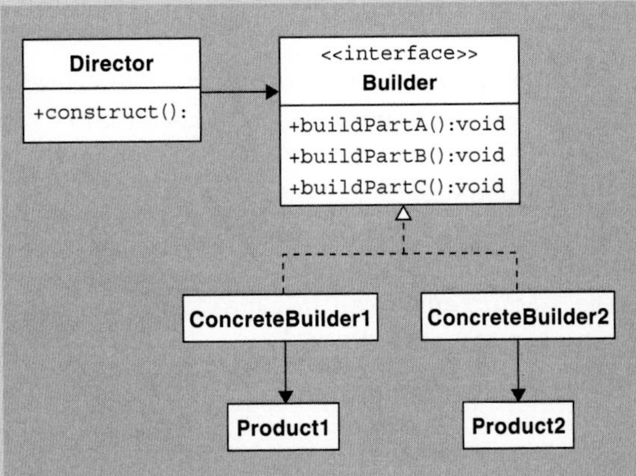

FIGURE 9.11 The Builder pattern.

A natural way to design Builder classes is to create an "default" Builder class whose methods all return null. This class can then be subclassed whenever the user wants to actually construct part or all of the AST. In this way, the user needs to override only those methods of interest.

The complete code for the DefaultBuilder class and an ASTBuilder subclass, as well as the modified Parser class that uses a Builder and a ProgramTool class as discussed in the preceding section, are available in package ast5.

SECTION 9.13 TOKENS, VISITORS, AND POLYMORPHISM (OPTIONAL SECTION)

What about the second aspect of the parser, as mentioned in the preceding section, that smelled a little badly? Namely, what about all the conditionals in the Parser's methods? Is there anything we can do about that? In particular, can we replace these conditionals with polymorphism? The answer to the last question is "yes," and it can be done in a very interesting way using visitors, based on the ideas of Dung "Zung" Nguyen at Rice University.

To convert the Parser's methods from using conditionals to using polymorphism, we need to determine what classes will be used to drive the polymorphism. If you study the Parser's methods, you will note that the conditionals are based on the kind of tokens referred to by the `currentToken` instance variable. Therefore, the first step of the conversion is to make the Token class abstract, remove the "kind" instance variable, and instead create subclasses of the Token class, one for each kind. Then the parsing methods that test the kind of the token can be refactored to test the class of the token. For example, if we create appropriate Token subclasses (see the ast6.token package), then the `parseDeclaration` method in the Parser class can be refactored from the following old version:

```
private Node parseDeclaration()
{
  if (currentToken.getKind()  != Token.SYMBOL &&
       currentToken.getKind() != Token.CLASS) {
    error(...);
  }
  String type = currentToken.getSpelling();
  advance();
  String name = currentToken.getSpelling();
  matchAndAdvance(Token.SYMBOL);
  if( currentToken.getKind() == Token.SEMICOLON) {
    advance();
    return builder.buildVarDeclaration(type, name);
  }
  else if( currentToken.getKind() == Token.LEFTPAREN) {
    advance();
    matchAndAdvance(Token.RIGHTPAREN);
```

```
    Block body = parseBlock();
    return builder.buildMethodDeclaration(type, name, body);
  }
  else if( currentToken.getKind() == Token.LEFTBRACE) {
    advance();
    List<Node> children = new ArrayList<Node>();
    while( currentToken.getKind() != Token.RIGHTBRACE) {
      children.add(parseDeclaration());
    }
    advance();
    return builder.buildClassDeclaration(name, children);
  }
  else {
     error(...);
  }
}
```

to the following new version (the changes are highlighted in bold):

```
private Node parseDeclaration()
{
  if (! (currentToken instanceof SymbolToken) &&
       ! (currentToken instanceof ClassToken) {
    error(...);
  }
  String type = currentToken.getSpelling();
  advance();
  String name = currentToken.getSpelling();
  matchAndAdvance(SymbolToken.class);
  if( currentToken instanceof SemicolonToken) {
    advance();
    return builder.buildVarDeclaration(type, name);
  }
  else if( currentToken instanceof LeftParenToken) {
    advance();
    matchAndAdvance(RightParenToken.class);
    Block body = parseBlock();
    return builder.buildMethodDeclaration(type, name, body);
  }
  else if( currentToken instanceof LeftBraceToken) {
    advance();
    List<Node> children = new ArrayList<Node>();
    while( currentToken instanceof RightBraceToken) {
      children.add(parseDeclaration());
    }
    advance();
    return builder.buildClassDeclaration(name, children);
  }
```

```
    else {
      error(...);
    }
  }
```

Note that we have had to modify the `matchAndAdvance` method to use the subclasses of Token.

As the next step, we would like to move the bodies of each case in the conditional statement above into an `execute` method in the appropriate Token subclass. In other words, we would like to define the following methods:

In the abstract Token class:

```
public Object execute()
{
  return error(...some message...); //default behavior
}
```

In the SemicolonToken class:

```
public Object execute()
{
  advance();
  return builder.buildVarDeclaration(type, name);
}
```

In LeftParenToken class:

```
public Object execute()
{
  advance();
  matchAndAdvance(RightParenToken.class);
  Block body = parseBlock();
  return builder.buildMethodDeclaration(type, name, body);
}
```

In LeftBraceToken class:

```
public Object execute()
{
  advance();
  List<Node> children = new ArrayList<Node>();
  while( currentToken instanceof RightBraceToken) {
    children.add(parseDeclaration());
  }
  advance();
  return builder.buildClassDeclaration(name, children);
}
```

If we were able to create such methods, we could then rewrite `parseDeclaration()` much more elegantly with only one conditional, which is used for error checking:

```
public Node parseDeclaration()
{
  if (! (currentToken instanceof SymbolToken) &&
      ! (currentToken instanceof ClassToken) {
    error(...);
  }
  String type = currentToken.getSpelling();
  advance();
  String name = currentToken.getSpelling();
  matchAndAdvance(SymbolToken.class);
  return currentToken.execute();
}
```

Unfortunately, this refactoring won't work for two reasons. First, many of the method calls, such as `advance();` are calls to private methods in the Parser class, and such calls cannot occur in methods in the Token subclasses. We could pass the Parser as a parameter and change the accessibility (from private to public) of some of the Parser's methods in order for them to be called in the Token subclasses' `execute` methods, but we have a better way, as you shall see.

The second problem we need to solve can be seen when we attempt to refactor similarly the `parseStatement` method in the Parser class to get rid of the conditionals. The problem is that the `parseStatement` method requires different `execute` methods for the Token subclasses than the `parseDeclaration` method requires. For example, in order to refactor the `parseDeclaration` method as we did above, we needed to add an `execute` method to the SemicolonToken class with the following body:

```
{
  advance();
  return builder.buildVarDeclaration(type, name);
}
```

But to refactor similarly the `parseStatement` method, we would need to add an `execute` method to the SemicolonToken class with the following body:

```
{
  advance();
  return builder.buildEmptyStatement();
}
```

Unfortunately, you cannot have an `execute` method in one class with two separate bodies.

One way to handle this problem is to create several different `execute` methods in each Token subclass, such as `executeDeclaration` and `executeStatement`. But we can do even better than this approach.

Let us create a table (see Table 9.3), where each row corresponds to a Token subclass and each column to a `parse`*XXX* method and whose entries are the new

TABLE 9.3 The new methods needed for each Token subclass.

	parseDeclaration	parseStatement	...
LeftParenToken	executeDeclaration	executeStatement	...
LeftBraceToken	executeDeclaration	executeStatement	...
SemicolonToken	executeDeclaration	executeStatement	...
...	...	...	...

`execute`*XXX* methods that need to be added to the Token subclass corresponding to the row.

Doesn't this table look familiar? It has the same structure as Table 9.1 and so we can apply the same analysis here that we did when analyzing that table. Namely, if we think of each column (i.e., each `parse`*XXX* method) as a visitor, then we can use the Visitor pattern! That is, we can refactor our code by grouping all the `executeDeclaration` methods in the second column of Table 9.3 into a ParseDeclarationVisitor class. We can similarly group all the `executeStatement` methods in the third column into a ParseStatementVisitor class, etc. Instead of all the `execute`*XXX* methods, each Token subclass will need only an `accept(TokenVisitor, Object)` method, where TokenVisitor is the interface implemented by the ParseDeclarationVisitor and ParseStatementVisitor. For example, the LeftParenToken will need only one constructor and one `accept` method, and so here is the complete class implementation:

```
public class LeftParenToken extends Token
{
  public LeftParenToken(String s, int p) { super(s, p); }
  public Object accept(TokenVisitor v, Object obj)
  {
    return v.visitLeftParenToken(this, obj);
  }
}
```

Once these visitor classes have been created, then the `parseDeclaration` method can be rewritten as follows:

```
private Node parseDeclaration()
{
  ParseDeclarationVisitor v = ...; //initialize v
  if (! (currentToken instanceof SymbolToken) &&
    ! (currentToken instanceof ClassToken) {
    error(...);
  }
  String type = currentToken.getSpelling();
  advance();
  String name = currentToken.getSpelling();
```

```
    matchAndAdvance(SymbolToken.class);
    return currentToken.accept(v, null);
}
```

where v is a ParseDeclarationVisitor, whose `visit`*XXX* methods correspond to the `executeDeclaration` methods in the second column of Table 9.3. Here is an outline of the code for the ParseDeclarationVisitor class:

```
public class ParseDeclarationVisitor
  implements TokenVisitor
{
  public Object visitSemicolonToken(SemicolonToken token,
                                    Object obj)
  {
    advance();
    return builder.buildVarDeclaration(type, name);
  }
  public Object visitLeftParenToken(LeftParenToken token,
                                    Object obj)
  {
    advance();
    matchAndAdvance(RightParenToken.class);
    Block body = parseBlock();
    return builder.buildMethodDeclaration(type, name, body);
  }
  public Object visitLeftBraceToken(LeftBraceToken token,
                                    Object obj)
  {
    advance();
    List<Node> children = new ArrayList<Node>();
    while( currentToken instanceof RightBraceToken) {
      children.add(parseDeclaration());
    }
    advance();
    return builder.buildClassDeclaration(name, children);
  }
  //all remaining visit methods are of the following form:
  public Object visitXXXToken(XXXToken token, Object obj)
  {
    return visitToken(token, obj);
  }
  public Object visitToken(Token token, Object obj)
  {
    error(...error message...);
    return null;
  }
}
```

We are almost finished with our refactoring, but not quite. In particular, the code above for the ParseDeclarationVisitor will not compile because of the calls to private methods in the Parser class (we also need to finish implementing the error message in the `visitToken` method).

An easy way to make the code compilable is to use anonymous inner classes that extend a DefaultTokenVisitor class whose `visit`*XXX* methods just call the `visitToken` default method, which returns null. The anonymous inner classes need only override the `visit`*XXX* methods of importance and override the default `visitToken` method if necessary. Furthermore, because we are using inner classes, we don't need to worry about the accessibility of the Parser's private methods, since they are accessible to inner classes.

Here's what the Parser's `parseDeclaration` method looks like with such an anonymous inner visitor (the visitor code is highlighted in bold):

```
private Node parseDeclaration()
{
  DefaultTokenVisitor visitor = new DefaultTokenVisitor()
  {
    public Object visitToken(Token t, Object o)
    {
      error("The wrong kind of token (" + currentToken + ") " +
        "was found at position" + currentToken.getPosition());
      return null;
    }
    public Object visitSemicolonToken(SemicolonToken t, Object o)
    {
      String[] args = (String[]) o;
      advance();
      return builder.buildVarDeclaration(args[0], args[1]);
    }
    public Object visitLeftParenToken(LeftParenToken t, Object o)
    {
      String[] args = (String[]) o;
      advance();
      matchAndAdvance(RightParenToken.class);
      Block body = parseBlock();
      return builder.buildMethodDeclaration(
                                     args[0], args[1], body);
    }
    public Object visitLeftBraceToken(LeftBraceToken t, Object o)
    {
      String[] args = (String[]) o;
      advance();
      List<Node> children = new ArrayList<Node>();
      while (!(currentToken instanceof RightBraceToken)) {
        children.add(parseDeclaration());
      }
```

```
            advance();
            return builder.buildClassDeclaration(args[1], children);
        }
    };
    if (! (currentToken instanceof SymbolToken)
          && ! (currentToken instanceof ClassToken)) {
        error("The wrong kind of token (" + currentToken +
          ") was found at position " + currentToken.getPosition());
    }
    String type = currentToken.getSpelling();
    advance();
    String name = currentToken.getSpelling();
    matchAndAdvance(SymbolToken.class);
    return (Node) currentToken.accept(visitor,
                                      new String[]{type, name});
}
```

In this method, the anonymous subclass of DefaultTokenVisitor overrides the `visitToken`, `visitLeftParenToken`, `visitLeftBraceToken`, and `visitSemicolonToken` methods in the DefaultTokenVisitor superclass. All other `visit`*XXX* methods in the anonymous subclass are inherited from the DefaultTokenVisitor, and so those other methods just call the default method `visitToken`, which calls an `error` routine. Note that, because this visitor is an inner class, its methods can call the Parser's private methods like `error`.

Whether practical or not, this design is a good example of how the Visitor pattern can be used to replace conditionals with polymorphism.

The complete code for these classes can be found in the package ast6.

SECTION 9.14 SUMMARY

We have now completed the design and implementation of classes for manipulating VSSJ programs. The classes we used enabled us to minimize coupling and isolate the parts that change, and they made it easy for us to add enhancements to the code. In the exercises, you will have the opportunity to add further enhancements to the package to see for yourself whether we were successful in our endeavors.

EXERCISES

1. Suppose an abstract class A has subclasses B and C and consider the following method in another class D:

```
public int classify(A a1, A a2) {
  if( a1 instanceof B && a2
    instanceof B)
    return 1;
  else if( a1 instanceof B &&
    a2 instanceof C)
    return 5;
  else if( a1 instanceof C &&
    a2 instanceof B)
    return 13;
  else if( a1 instanceof C &&
    a2 instanceof C)
    return 29;
}
```

Refactor this design using dynamic method invocation to eliminate as many conditionals as possible and as many uses of `instanceof` as possible. You are welcome to add new methods to any class if you wish. Try to do it without introducing any Collection classes.

2. Note that the Token class in packages ast1 through ast5 have getter methods but no setter methods. Is this the best design for the class? Explain.
3. Modify the `prettyPrinter` method in Figure 9.2 so that it properly adds blank lines between declarations. Do it in a way that doesn't require the use of a Parser or an AST.
4. One feature missing from our VSSJ language is comments.
   a. Extend the language to allow comments. Come up with your own syntax. You should be able to insert comments anywhere in the code between tokens. Then fix the Scanner to ignore the comments.
   b. Modify the classes in the ast2 package so that the PrettyPrinter pretty prints the comments as well as the code.
5. Implement another Visitor class for VSSJ programs. Here are some possibilities:
   a. A VariableValidator visitor that checks to see whether all variables used in the program have been declared somewhere in the program.
   b. A MethodValidator visitor that checks to see whether all methods called in the program have been declared somewhere in the program.
   c. A VariableFinder visitor that searches the program for a variable of the given name.
   d. A MethodTypeChecker visitor that checks to see whether the return types of all methods are void, int, or boolean.
   e. A Renamer visitor that searches for a variable or method with a given name and replaces it with a new name. It should also replace all applied occurrences of the variable or calls of the method.
   f. A VariableCounter visitor that determines the total number of variable declarations in the program.
6. The name `findMethod` is somewhat inappropriate for the MethodFinder's public method, because functions that return values should have names indicating the value returned. Since `findMethod` returns a boolean value, a better name would be `containsMethod`. If a method is named `findMethod`, then it should return a method (that is, a MethodDeclaration node) or null.
   a. What changes would need to be made to MethodFinder in the ast3 package so that `findMethod` returns a MethodDeclarationNode instead of a boolean value, and how can you use this new `findMethod` to implement a boolean `containsMethod` in the MethodFinder class?
   b. Implement these changes.
7. The design used in Section 9.12 in which a default builder is subclassed to create new builders imitates the design of some of the classes in the Java Swing or AWT package. Find some of the classes in those packages that the default builder imitates, and explain how they are similar to the default builder.
8. If we subclass DefaultBuilder to get various builders, then variables that need to refer to any of these builders must be declared to have type DefaultBuilder, which is an awkward name. Come up with a better naming scheme. For example, should DefaultBuilder just be renamed "Builder"? Why or why not?
9. The ProgramTool class is somewhat limited in what it can do.
   a. One useful method that should be in the ProgramTool class is a method that just builds and returns the AST for the user without applying any visitors to it. Implement such a method. (Hint: It should only need a couple of lines of code.)
   b. Name some methods besides `prettyPrint`, `findMethod`, and the method in part (a) that should be included in a useful ProgramTool class, and explain why they should be included.
   c. If possible, implement one of the methods you named in part (b) by creating a new visitor if necessary.
10. Rewrite the Token class in package ast5 so that, instead of using integer constants to represent the types of tokens, it uses an enumerated type.
11. Rewrite the Scanner class in package ast5 so that it has an instance variable of type java.io.StreamTokenizer. The Scanner should use the StreamTokenizer to break down the expression into token substrings, which it then uses to form the Tokens to be returned by the `getNextToken()` method. Simplify the Scanner class as much as possible (i.e., try to utilize StreamTokenizer to do as much of the work as possible).
12. In both the Facade and the Adapter patterns, there are behind-the-scene classes that are doing most of the work. How is the Facade pattern, as described in Section 9.11, different from the Adapter pattern?
13. Create a subclass of DefaultBuilder that always returns null except when it is asked to build a ClassDeclaration node, in which case, it still returns null, but it also keeps track of the number of times it was asked to create such a node. It should also have a method with the following header:

```
public int numberOfClassDeclarations()
```

that returns the number of class declarations the builder counted during the parsing of a program and a method with header

```
public void reset()
```

that resets to 0 the number of class declarations the builder found.

14. Construct a TreePrinter class for the ast3 package that lays out the structure of the tree using text in the console window. Each node should have a method of the form

```
public void treePrint(String indent)
```

that print the subtree rooted at this node indented by the given amount. The `treePrint` method should print the String returned by the node's `toString()` method (that you'll need to write), which should include the name of the class of the node (e.g., IntLiteral) and any other instance information that distinguishes it (e.g., the integer value stored in the IntLiteral node). Then it should recursively call `treePrint` on each of its children, using a larger indentation, for example, four more spaces than its indentation.

15. Construct a TreePrinter for the ast4 package, similar to the preceding exercise, but using a Visitor.

16. Consider what would happen if we refactored the code in package ast4 by renaming all the methods in the Visitor interface (and in all classes that implement this interface) so that they all were just "visit" instead of "visitClassDeclaration," "visitWhileStatement," etc. Would the ast4 package still compile and run correctly? Answer this question either (a) by reasoning about method overloading or (b) by rewriting the Visitor interface and the classes that implement the interface, trying to run the resulting code and explaining what happened and why.

17. Using the ideas in [2], rewrite the ast4 package so that the Visitors use reflection to choose which visit method to call. Here are some hints:
   a. Delete the Visitor interface, get rid of the phrase "implements Visitor" in the PrettyPrinter and MethodFinder classes, and get rid of the `accept(Visitor, Object)` method in all the node classes. We don't need them anymore.
   b. In the PrettyPrinter class, add the following new methods

```
public Object visit(Object node,
  Object obj) {
  // Class.getName() returns package
      // information as well,
   // so strip off the package
   String methodName =
     node.getClass().getName();
   methodName = "visit" + methodName.
     substring(methodName.
     lastIndexOf('.') + 1);
   try {
     // Get the method visitXXX
     Method m = getClass().
       getMethod(methodName,
       new Class[]{node.getClass(),
         Object.class});
     // Try to invoke visitXXX
     return m.invoke(this,
       new Object[]{node, obj});
   } catch (NoSuchMethodException e) {
       return defaultVisit(node, obj);
   } catch (IllegalAccessException e) {
       return defaultVisit(node, obj);
   } catch (InvocationTargetException
     e) {
       return defaultVisit(node, obj);
   }
}
public Object defaultVisit(Object
  node, Object obj) {
      return "";
}
```

   c. In each of the PrettyPrinter's `visit`*XXX* methods, replace occurrences of `node.accept(this, obj)` with `visit(node, obj)`.
   d. Make similar changes to the MethodFinder class.

18. The ast6 package differs from the ast5 package in that TokenVisitors were added in order to replace conditionals with polymorphism in the `parse`*XXX* methods. However, the Parser in the ast6 package still has some conditional statements, in particular, in the `visitSymbolToken` method in the TokenVisitor inner class in the `parseStatement` method.
   a. Outline how we could use polymorphism to replace that conditional statement.
   b. Implement this change.

19. In this project, you are asked to develop an expression evaluator that imitates the ast5 package in its design. The project is broken down into several steps. Ultimately, your goal is to create an Evaluator class with an `evaluate` method with the following method header

```
public int evaluate(String expression,
  Environment environment)
```

that returns the value of the integer infix expression in the parameter, using the environment to get the value of any variables in the expression. For example, the method call

```
evaluate("x+4*5", env);
```

will return the integer 23 if the environment `env` indicates that `x` has the value of 3. The Environment object can be thought of as a table of variables and their values. You can design the Environment class however you want, but it should include `int get(String var)` and `void set(String var, int value)` methods.

The grammar for expressions consists of the following rules:

- An expression is an additive expression.
- An additive expression is one or more multiplicative expressions separated by "+" or "−".
- A multiplicative expression is one or more primary expressions separated by "*" or "/".
- A primary expression is either (i) an integer literal, (ii) a variable, or (c) an expression surrounded by parentheses.
- An integer literal is one or more digits optionally preceded by a "+" or "−".
- A variable consists of one or more letters a–z or A–Z.

Here are the steps necessary to construct the desired Evaluator class using a design similar to the design of the ast5 package.

a. Implement the Environment class.

b. Implement a Scanner similar to the ast5.Scanner class that converts an expression string into consecutive tokens.

c. Create the node classes for an AST that represents legal expressions.

d. Create a Visitor interface and add `accept` methods to all the node classes.

e. Write a Parser similar to the ast5.Parser class that parses an expression string and constructs an AST. It should detect all illegal input and print an error message if such input is found.

f. Write the Evaluator visitor.

20. Enhance the preceding problem in any of the following ways:

a. Implement a VariableChecker visitor that has a method with header

```
public boolean check(AST root,
  Environment environment)
```

that returns true if all variables in the AST rooted at the given node have valid values in the given environment.

b. Implement a ConstantFolder visitor that has a method with header

```
public AST fold(AST root)
```

that returns an new AST that is equal to the given AST except that all subtrees representing constant expressions have been replaced with the value of that expression. For example, if the original AST represents the expression `x + y*(3+4) - 16/(2+2)`, then the `fold` method will return an AST representing the expression `x + y*7 - 4`.

c. Implement a PrettyPrinter visitor that has a method with header

```
public String prettyPrint(AST root)
```

that prints out the expression represented by the AST in infix notation with no unnecessary parentheses.

d. Implement a PrefixPrinter visitor that has a method with header

```
public String prefixPrint(AST root)
```

that prints out the expression represented by the AST in prefix notation. Each prefix expression should be surrounded by parentheses. For example, `2 + x` should appear as `(+ 2 x)`. Print a space between the operators and operands.

REFERENCES

1. Gamma, E., R. Helm, R. Johnson, and J. Vlissides, *Design Patterns, Elements of Reusable Object-Oriented Software*. Professional Computing. 1995. Reading, MA: Addison-Wesley.

2. Blosser, J. *Java Tip 98: Reflect on the Visitor design pattern*. Implement visitors in Java, using reflection. [Web page.] 2000. [Cited April 8, 2007; available from http://www.javaworld.com/javatips/jw-javatip98.html.]

Appendix A

An Introduction to UML

SECTION A.0 INTRODUCTION

The Unified Modeling Language (UML) is "a standard language for writing software blueprints. The UML may be used to visualize, specify, construct, and document the artifacts of a software-intensive system" [1]. In other words, just as architects create blueprints to be used by the construction company to build a building, software architects create UML diagrams to help software developers build the software. If software developers understand the vocabulary of UML (the diagrams' pictorial elements and their meanings), then they can much more easily understand a system and explain the design of that system to others through the use of UML diagrams in addition to textual descriptions.

UML was developed by Grady Booch, Jim Rumbaugh, and Ivar Jacobson, with much feedback from the software development community, in the mid-1990s as a way of merging the many competing modeling notations that were in use by the software industry at the time. In 1997, UML 1.0 was submitted to the Object Management Group, a nonprofit consortium involved in maintaining specifications for use by the computer industry. UML 1.0 was revised to UML 1.1 and adopted later that year. The current standard is UML 2.0, and is now an ISO standard. Because this standard is so new, many older references, such as [2], do not use UML notation and instead use one of the earlier notations.

UML 2.0 provides thirteen different diagrams for use in software modeling. In this appendix, we will discuss only four of those diagrams: class, state, sequence, and use case diagrams. These are the diagrams we have found most useful when teaching object-oriented design and are the only ones that appear in this text.

It should be noted that UML is a programming language-independent notation, and so UML does not map exactly to the way objects and classes are defined and implemented in Java. However, many of the differences are just terminology differences, and so students with a background in Java should have few problems with understanding the UML concepts and applying them to Java programming.

It should also be noted that, in UML diagrams, many of the features are optional. The UML language was designed not only to give the creators of UML diagrams a large number of options so that they are able to express all the important aspects of the system the diagram is modeling, but also to give them the flexibility to suppress those parts of the diagram that are not relevant to the aspect being modeled in order to avoid cluttering the diagram with irrelevant details. Therefore, the omission of a particular feature does not mean that the feature is absent; it may mean that the feature was suppressed. We will not exhaustively cover all the features of the four UML diagrams presented here. Instead, we will focus on the standard options, especially those options we have used in this text.

SECTION A.1 CLASS DIAGRAMS

To model classes, including their attributes, operations, and their relationships and associations with other classes, UML provides a *class* diagram. A class diagram is a static view of the system in that it does not show the dynamic nature of the communications between the objects of the classes in the diagram.

The main elements of a class diagram are boxes, which are the icons used to represent classes and interfaces. Each such box is divided into horizontal parts. The top part contains the name of the class.

The middle section contains the attributes of the class. An *attribute* refers to something that an object of that class knows or can provide all the time. Attributes are usually implemented as fields of the class, but they need not be. They could be values that the class can compute from its instance variables or values that the class can get from other objects of which it is composed. For example, an object might always know the current time and be able to return it to you whenever you ask, in which case, it would be appropriate to list the current time as an attribute of that class of objects. However, the object would most likely not have that time stored in one of its instance variables because it would need to continually update that field, which is quite wasteful of computer resources if its value is needed only occasionally. Instead, the object would likely compute the current time, for example, through consultation with objects of other classes, at the moment when you ask for it.

The third section contains the operations or behaviors of the class. An *operation* refers to something objects of the class can do. It is usually implemented as a method of the class.

See Figure A.1 for an example of a Thoroughbred class that models thoroughbred horses. It has three attributes displayed: mother, father, and birth year. The diagram also shows three operations: `getCurrentAge`, `getFather`, and `getMother`. There may be other suppressed attributes and operations not shown in the diagram.

FIGURE A.1 A class diagram for a Thoroughbred class.

Thoroughbred
-father:Thoroughbred -mother:Thoroughbred -birthyear:int
+getFather():Thoroughbred +getMother():Thoroughbred +getCurrentAge(currentYear:Date):int

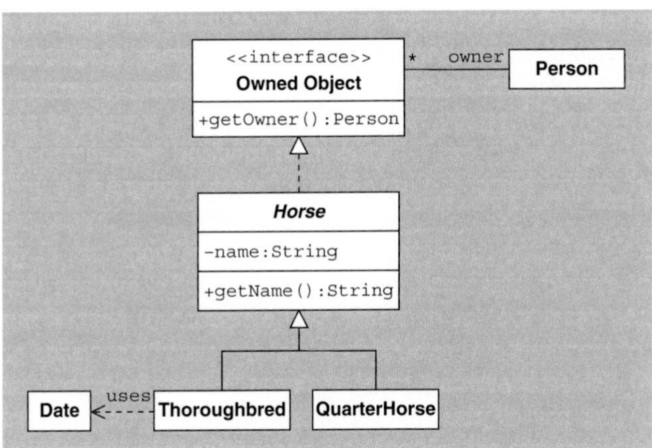

FIGURE A.2 A class diagram regarding horses.

Each attribute can have a name, a type, and a level of visibility. The type and visibility are optional. The type follows the name and is separated from the name by a colon. The visibility is indicated by a preceding "–", "#", "~", or "+", indicating, respectively, private, protected, package, or public visibility. In Figure A.1, all the attributes have private visibility, as indicated by the leading minus sign "–". You can also specify that an attribute is a static or class attribute by underlining it.

Each operation can similarly be optionally displayed with a level of visibility, parameters with names and types, and a return type.

An abstract class or abstract method is indicated by using italics for the name. See the Horse class in Figure A.2 for an example. An interface is indicated by adding the phrase «interface» (called a *stereotype*) above the name. See the OwnedObject interface in Figure A.2. An interface can also be represented graphically by a hollow circle.

It is worth mentioning that the icon representing a class can have other optional parts, such as a fourth section at the bottom containing a list of the responsibilities of the class. This section is particularly useful when transitioning from CRC cards to class diagrams in that the responsibilities listed on the CRC cards can be added to this fourth section in the class box in the UML diagram before creating the attributes and operations that carry out these responsibilities. This fourth section is not shown in any of the figures in this appendix.

Class diagrams can also show relationships between classes. A class that is a subclass of another class is connected to it by an arrow with a solid line for its shaft and with a triangular hollow arrowhead. The arrow points from the subclass to the superclass. In UML, such a relationship is called a *generalization*. For example, in Figure A.2. the Thoroughbred and QuarterHorse classes are shown to be subclasses of the Horse abstract class. A similar arrow except using a dashed line for the arrow shaft indicates implementation of an interface. In UML, such a relationship is called a *realization*. For example, in Figure A.2, the Horse class implements or realizes the OwnedObject interface.

An *association* between two classes means that there is a structural relationship between them. Associations are represented by solid lines. An association has many optional parts. It can be labeled, as can each of its ends, to indicate the role of each class in the association. For example, in Figure A.2, there is an association between OwnedObject and Person in which the Person plays the role of owner. Arrows on either or both ends of an association line indicate navigability. Also, each end of the association line can have a multiplicity value displayed. Navigability and multiplicity are explained in more detail below. An association might also connect a class with itself, using a loop. Such an association indicates the connection of an object of the class with other objects of the same class.

An association with an arrow at one end indicates one-way navigability. The arrow means that from one class you can easily access the second associated class to which the association points, but from the second class, you cannot necessarily easily access the first class. Another way to think about it is that the first class is aware of the second class, but the second class object is not necessarily directly aware of the first class. An association with no arrows usually indicates a two-way association, which is what is intended in Figure A.2, but it could also just mean that the navigability is not important and so was left off.

It should be noted that an attribute of a class is very much the same thing as an association of the class with the class type of the attribute. That is, to indicate that a class has a property called *name* of type String, one could display that property as an attribute, as in the Horse class in Figure A.2. Alternatively, one could create a one-way association from the Horse class to the String class with the role of the String class being "name." The attribute approach is better for primitive data types whereas the association approach is often better if the property's class plays a major role in the design, in which case it is valuable to have a class box for that type.

Another connection besides associations between classes that can be displayed in class diagrams is the *dependency* relationship, indicated by a dashed line (with optional arrows at the ends and with optional labels). One class depends on another if changes to the second class might require changes to the first class. An association from one class to another automatically indicates a dependency, and so no dashed line is needed between classes if there is already an association between them. However, for a transient relationship, that is, for a class that does not maintain any long-term connection to another class but does use that class occasionally, we should draw a dashed line from the first class to the second. For example, in Figure A.2, the Thoroughbred class uses the Date class whenever its `getCurrentAge` method is invoked, and so the dependency is labeled *uses*.

The *multiplicity* of one end of an association means the number of objects of that class associated with the other class. A multiplicity is specified by a nonnegative integer or by a range of integers. A multiplicity specified by "0..1" means that there is 0 or 1 objects on that end of the association. For example, each person in the world has either a social security number or no such number (especially if they are not U.S. citizens) and so a multiplicity of 0..1 could be used in an association between a Person class and a SocialSecurityNumber class in a class diagram. A multiplicity specified by "1..*" means one or more, and a multiplicity specified by "0..*" or just "*" means zero or more. A "*" is used as the multiplicity on the OwnedObject end of the association with class Person in Figure A.2 to indicate that a Person could own zero or more objects.

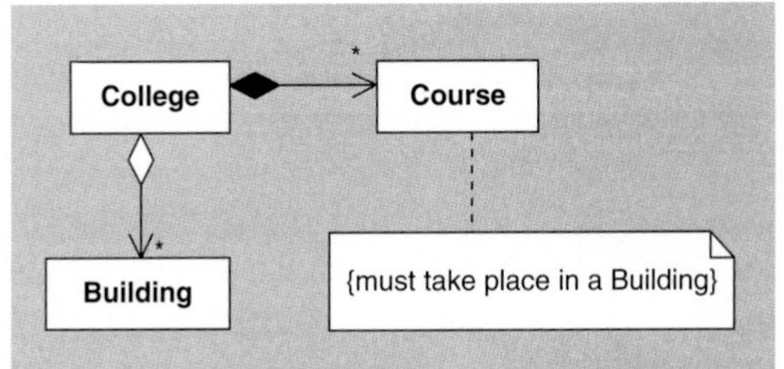

FIGURE A.3 The relationship between Colleges, Courses, and Buildings.

If one end of an association has multiplicity greater than 1, then the objects of the class referred to at that end of the association are probably stored in a collection, such as a set or ordered list. One could also include that collection class itself in the UML diagram, but such a class is usually left out and is implicitly assumed to be there due to the multiplicity of the association.

An *aggregation* is a special kind of association indicated by a hollow diamond on one end of the icon. It indicates a "whole/part" relationship, in that the class to which the arrow points is considered a "part" of the class at the diamond end of the association. A *composition* is an aggregation indicating strong ownership of the parts. In a composition, the parts live and die with the owner because they have no role in the software system independent of the owner. See Figure A.3 for examples of aggregation and composition. A College has an aggregation of Building objects, which represent the buildings making up the campus. The College also has a collection of Courses. If the college were to fold, the buildings would still exist (assuming the college wasn't physically destroyed) and could be used for other things, but a Course object has no use outside of the College at which it is being offered. If the college were to cease to exist as a business entity, the course object would no longer be useful and so it would also cease to exist.

Another common element of a class diagram is a *note*, which is represented by a box with a dog-eared corner and that is connected to other icons by a dashed line. It can have arbitrary content (text and graphics) and is similar to comments in programming languages. It might contain comments about the role of a class or constraints that all objects of that class must satisfy. If the contents are a constraint, the contents are surrounded by braces. In Figure A.3, we see a constraint attached to the Course class.

SECTION A.2. SEQUENCE DIAGRAMS

In contrast to class diagrams, which show the static structure of a software component, a *sequence diagram* is used to show the dynamic communications between objects during execution of a task. It shows the temporal order in which messages are sent between the objects to accomplish that task.

In Figure A.4, you see a sequence diagram for a drawing program. The diagram shows the steps involved in highlighting a figure in the drawing when it is clicked.

In a sequence diagram, there is a row of boxes across the top. Each box usually corresponds to an object, although it is possible to have the boxes model other

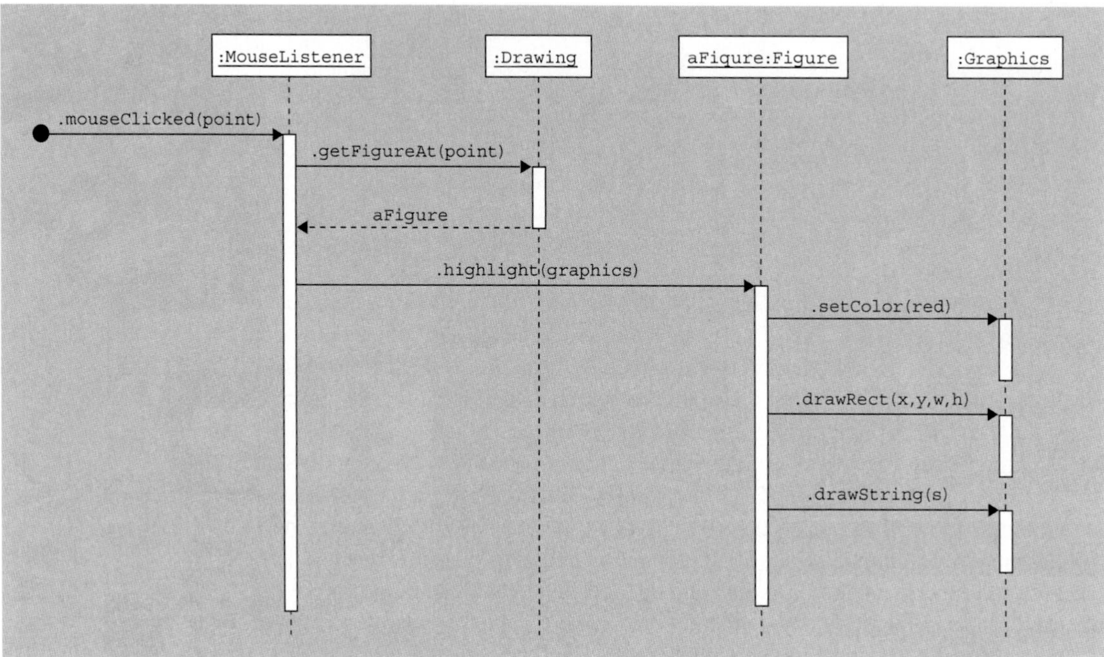

FIGURE A.4 A sample sequence diagram.

things, such as classes. If the box represents an object (as is the case in all our examples), then inside the box you can optionally state the type of the object preceded by the colon. You can also precede the colon and type by a name for the object, as was done in the third box in Figure A.4. Below each box there is a dashed line called the *lifeline* of the object. You should think of the vertical axis in the diagram as corresponding to time, with time increasing as you move down.

A sequence diagram shows method calls using horizontal arrows from the caller to the callee, labeled with the method name and optionally including its parameters, their types, and the return type. For example, in Figure A.4, the MouseListener calls the Drawing's `getFigureAt` method. When an object is executing a method (i.e., when it has an activation frame on the stack), you can optionally display a white bar, called an *activation bar*, down the object's lifeline. In Figure A.4, activation bars are drawn for all method calls. The diagram can also optionally show the return from a method call with a dashed arrow and an optional label. In Figure A.4, the `getFigureAt` method call's return is shown labeled with the name of the object that was returned. A common practice, as we have done in Figure A.4, is to leave off the return arrow when a void method has been called since it clutters up the diagram while providing little information of importance. A black circle with an arrow coming from it indicates a *found message* whose source is unknown or irrelevant.

You should now be able to understand the task that Figure A.4 is displaying. An unknown source calls the `mouseClicked` method of a MouseListener, passing in the point where the click occurred as the argument. The MouseListener in turn calls the `getFigureAt` method of a Drawing, which returns a Figure. The Mouse-

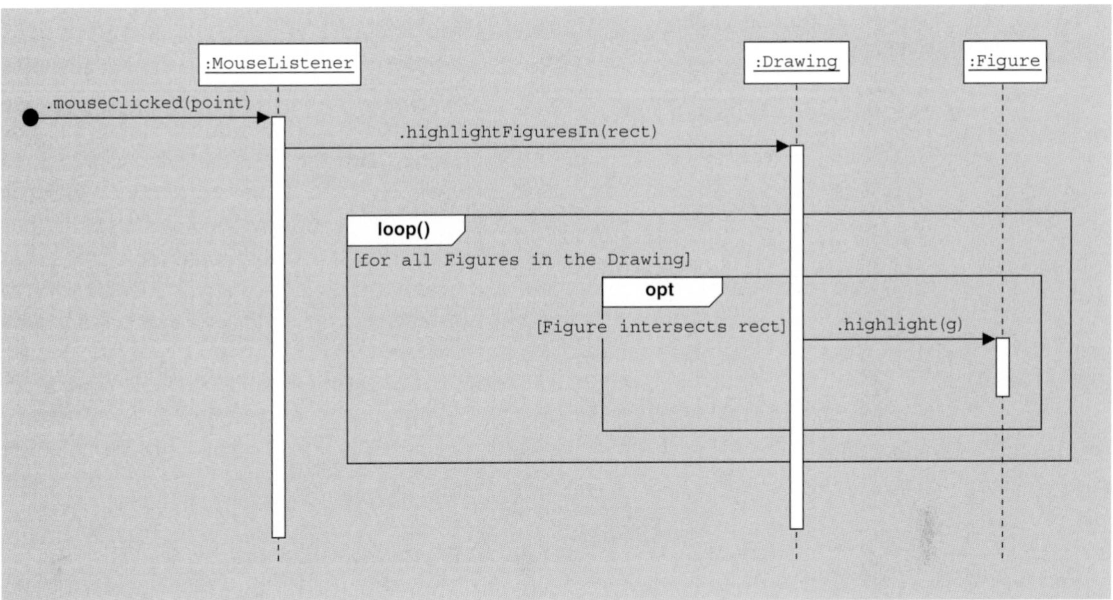

FIGURE A.5 A sequence diagram with two interaction frames.

Listener then calls the `highlight` method of the Figure, passing in a Graphics object as argument. In response, the Figure calls three methods of the Graphics object to draw the Figure in red.

This diagram is very straightforward, with no conditionals or loops. How do you draw sequence diagrams with these control structures? Probably the best way is to draw a separate sequence diagram for each case. That is, if the message flow can take two different paths depending on a condition, then draw two separate sequence diagrams, one for each possibility.

If you insist on including loops, conditionals, and other control structures in a sequence diagram, then you can use *interaction frames*, which are rectangles that surround parts of the diagram and that are labeled with the type of control structures they represent. In Figure A.5, you see two such frames. This diagram shows the process involved in highlighting all the figures inside a given rectangle. The MouseListener is sent the `rectDragged` message. The MouseListener then tells the drawing to highlight all figures in the rectangle by calling the Drawing's `highlightFiguresIn` method, passing the rectangle as the argument. That method loops through all Figures in the Drawing, and, if the Figure intersects the rectangle, the Figure is asked to highlight itself. The phrases in square brackets are called *guards*, which are boolean conditions that must be true if the action inside the interaction frame is to continue.

There are many other special features that can be included in a sequence diagram. For example,

1. You can distinguish between synchronous and asynchronous messages. Synchronous messages are shown with solid arrow heads while asynchronous messages are shown with stick arrow heads.

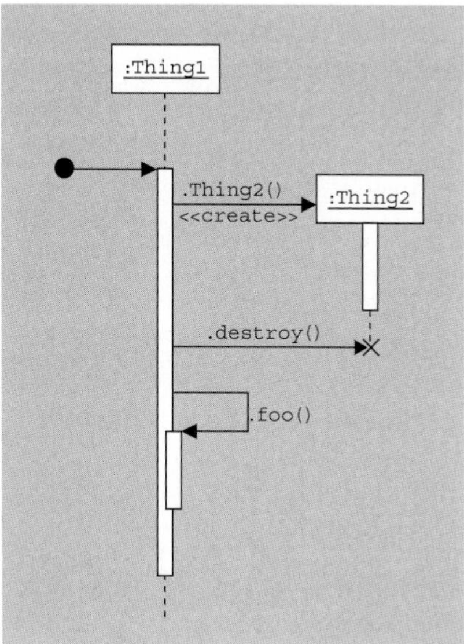

FIGURE A.6 Creation, destruction, and loops in sequence diagrams.

2. You can show an object sending itself a message with an arrow going out from the object, turning downward, and then pointing back to the same object.
3. You can show object creation by drawing an arrow appropriately labeled (for example, with a «create» label) to an object's box. In this case, the box will appear lower in the diagram than the boxes corresponding to objects already in existence when the action begins.
4. You can show object destruction by a big X at the end of the object's lifeline. Other objects can destroy an object, in which case an arrow points from the other object to the X. An X is also useful for indicating that an object is no longer usable and so is ready for garbage collection.

The last three features are all shown in the sequence diagram in Figure A.6.

SECTION A.3 STATE MACHINE DIAGRAMS

The behavior of an object at a particular point in time very often depends on the state of the object, that is, the values of its variables, at that time. For a trivial example, consider an object with a boolean instance variable. When asked to perform an operation, the object might do one thing if that variable is true and do something else if it is false. If an object has many different states and performs many different actions depending on those states, then, to ensure the object is behaving properly, it is critical to have a complete picture of all states, the actions in each state, and the transitions between the states of the object. UML *state* diagrams provide such a picture.

For an example of a UML state diagram, we will consider a Java compiler. The input to the compiler is a text file, which can be thought of as a long string of characters. The compiler reads those characters one at a time and, from them, determines the structure of the program. One small part of this process of reading in the characters involves ignoring "white space" characters (which, for this discussion, we will assume are the space, tab, and end-of-line characters) and characters inside a comment.

Let us focus just on this process of white space and comment elimination. Suppose that the compiler delegates to a WhiteSpaceAndCommentEliminator the job of advancing over white space characters and characters in comments. That is, this object's job is to read input characters until all white space and comment characters have been read, at which point it returns control to the compiler to read and process non–white space and noncomment characters. Think about how the WhiteSpaceAndCommentEliminator, as it reads in characters, determines whether the next character is white space or part of a comment. The WhiteSpaceAndCommentEliminator can check for white space by just testing the next character against `' '`, `'\t'`, `'\n'`, and `'\r'`. But how does it determine whether the next character is part of a comment? For example, when it sees a `'/'` for the first time, it doesn't yet know whether that character represents a division operator, part of the /= operator, or the beginning of a line or block comment. To make this determination, the WhiteSpaceAndComment Eliminator needs to make a note of the fact that it saw a `'/'` and then move on to the next character. If the character following the `'/'` is another `'/'` or a `'*'`, then the WhiteSpaceAndCommentEliminator knows that it is now reading a comment and can advance to the end of the comment without processing or saving any characters. If the character following the first `'/'` is anything other than `'/'` or `'*'`, then the WhiteSpaceAndCommentEliminator knows that the `'/'` represents the division operator or part of the /= operator and so it stops advancing over characters.

In summary, as the WhiteSpaceAndCommentEliminator reads in characters, it needs to keep track of several things, including whether the current character is white space, whether the previous character it read was a `'/'`, whether it is currently reading characters in a comment, whether it has reached the end of comment, etc. These all correspond to different states of the WhiteSpaceAndCommentEliminator. In each of these states, the WhiteSpaceAndCommentEliminator behaves differently with regard to the next character read in.

To help us visualize all the states of this object and how it changes state, we will use a UML state diagram. See Figure A.7. A state diagram displays states using rounded rectangles, each of which has a name in its upper half. There is also a black circle called the *initial pseudostate*, which isn't really a state and instead just points to the initial state. In Figure A.7, the Start state is the initial state. Arrows pointing from one state to another state indicate transitions or changes in the state of the object. Each transition is labeled with a trigger event, a slash ("/"), and an activity. All parts of the transition labels are optional in state diagrams. If the object is in one state and the trigger event for one of its transitions occurs, then that transition's activity is performed and the object changes into the new state indicated by the transition. For example, in Figure A.7, if the WhiteSpaceAndCommentEliminator is in the `Start` state and the next character is `'/'`, then the WhiteSpaceAndCommentEliminator advances past that character and changes to the `saw'/'` state. If the character after the `'/'` is another `'/'`, then the object advances to the `line comment` state and stays there until it reads an end-of-line(eoln)character. If instead the next character after the `'/'` is a `'*'`, then the object advances to the `blockcomment` state and stays there until it sees another `'*'` followed by a `'/'`, which indicates the end of the block comment. Study the diagram to make sure you understand it. Note

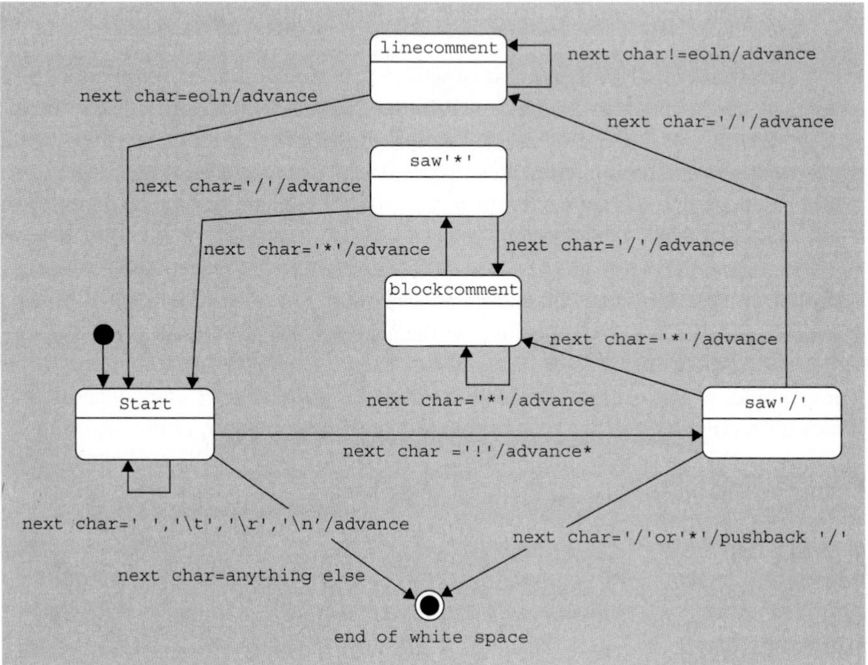

FIGURE A.7 A state diagram for advancing past white space and comments in Java.

that, after advancing past white space or a comment, the WhiteSpaceAndComment-Eliminator goes back to the Start state and starts over. That behavior is necessary since there might be several successive comments or white space characters before any other characters in the Java source code.

An object may transition to a final state, indicated by a black circle with a white circle around it, which indicates there are no more transitions. In Figure A.7, the WhiteSpaceAndCommentEliminator is finished when the next character is not white space nor part of a comment.

Note in our diagram that all transitions except the two transitions leading to the final state have activities consisting of advancing to the next character. The two transitions to the final state do not advance over the next character because the next character is part of a word or symbol of interest to the compiler. Note that if the object is in the `saw '/'` state but the next character is not `'/'` or `'*'`, then the `'/'` was the division operator or part of the /= operator and so we don't want to advance. In fact, we want to back up one character to make the `'/'` into the next character, so that the `'/'` can be used by the compiler. In Figure A.7, this activity of backing up is labeled as `pushback '/'`.

One advantage of using state diagrams is that it helps you to avoid missed or unexpected situations. That is, with a state diagram, it is relatively easy to ensure that all possible trigger events for all possible states have been accounted for. For example, in Figure A.7, you can easily check that, in every state, we have included transitions for all possible characters.

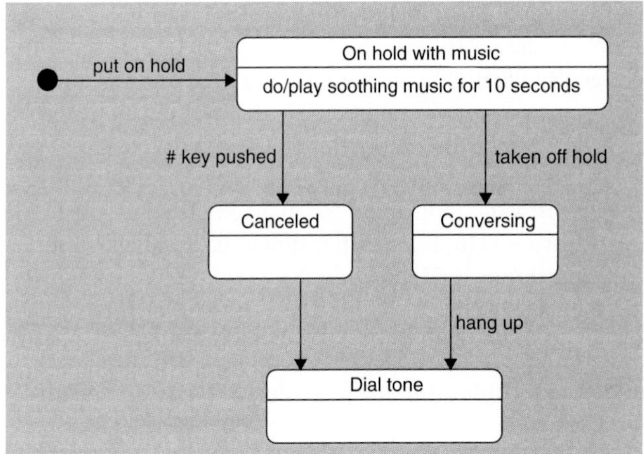

FIGURE A.8 A state diagram with an activity state and a triggerless transition.

UML state diagrams can contain many other features not included in Figure A.7. For example, when an object is in a state, it usually does nothing but sit and wait for a trigger event to occur. However, there is a special kind of state, called an *activity state*, in which the object performs some activity, called a *do-activity*, while it is in that state. To indicate that a state is an activity state in the state diagram, you include in the bottom half of the state's rounded rectangle the phrase "do/" followed by the activity that is to be done while in that state. The do-activity may finish before any state transitions occur, after which the activity state behaves like a normal waiting state. If a transition out of the activity state occurs before the do-activity is finished, then the do-activity is interrupted.

Also, as was mentioned earlier, a transition's trigger event is optional, and so it is possible that there is no trigger event listed as part of a transition's label. For normal waiting states, the object will immediately transition from that state to the new state. For activity states, such a transition is taken as soon as the do-activity finishes.

For a simple example of activity states and transitions without triggers, see Figure A.8, which shows some of the states that a telephone may be in. When a caller is placed on hold, the call goes into the "On hold with music" state, at which time soothing music is played for 10 seconds. After those 10 seconds, the do-activity of the state is completed, after which the state behaves like a normal nonactivity state. If the caller pushes the # key when the call is in the "On hold with music" state, the call transitions to the "Canceled" state and then transitions immediately to the "Dial tone" state. If the # key is pushed before the 10 seconds of soothing music has completed, the do-activity is interrupted and the music stops immediately.

SECTION A.4 USE CASE DIAGRAMS

During the requirements gathering phase of software development, before any software has been written, one of the things the developers need to decide is the functionality of the system from the user's perspective. The developers need to ask themselves questions like the following: Who are the users? What should the system be able to do for its users? How is the system going to interact with a user to accomplish these goals? Ideally, a complete list of all the uses to which the system will be put should be created in the requirements phase of development. Use cases and UML use case diagrams are helpful in this stage of software development.

To give you a feeling for how use cases and use case diagrams work, we will create some for a software application for managing digital music files, similar to Apple's iTunes software. Think about the functionality such an application should have. Here are some things it might do:

- Download an mp3 music file, and store it in the application's library.
- Capture streaming music, and store it in the application's library.
- Manage the application's library (e.g., delete songs or organize them in play lists).
- Burn a list of the songs in the library onto a CD.
- Load a list of the songs in the library onto an iPod or mp3 player.
- Convert a song from mp3 format to AAC format and vice versa.

This is not an exhaustive list, but it is sufficient to understand the role of use cases and use case diagrams.

A *use case* explains the functionality of a software system through a series of steps the user takes as he or she interacts with the system to accomplish a goal. For example, consider how the music application would accomplish the goal of burning a list of songs onto a CD. We can describe it as a series of steps, such as the following:

1. User creates a new empty list.
2. User browses the library and adds songs to the list.
3. User tells the application to burn the list to a CD.

These steps form a use case. They could be further subdivided to give a more detailed picture of the use case, but it is often best to leave out low-level details, including user interface details, until they are needed.

There can be variations in each use case. For example, what if the user, after telling the music application to burn the CD, wants to cancel the burn before it is done? Or what if all the songs in the list don't fit on one CD? What if, after telling the application to burn the list to a CD, the user realizes she doesn't have a blank CD to be burned? These variations, as well as the main sequence of steps, forms *scenarios,* which can be defined as sequences of steps in a use case describing one branch of the possible variations. For example, here's one scenario for the use case we've been discussing:

1. The user creates a new empty list.
2. The user adds some songs to the list.
3. The user tells the system to burn the list to a CD.
4. The system responds that the songs won't fit on a CD and asks how to proceed
5. The user cancels the burn request.

One could say that a use case is just a collection of scenarios with a common user goal [3].

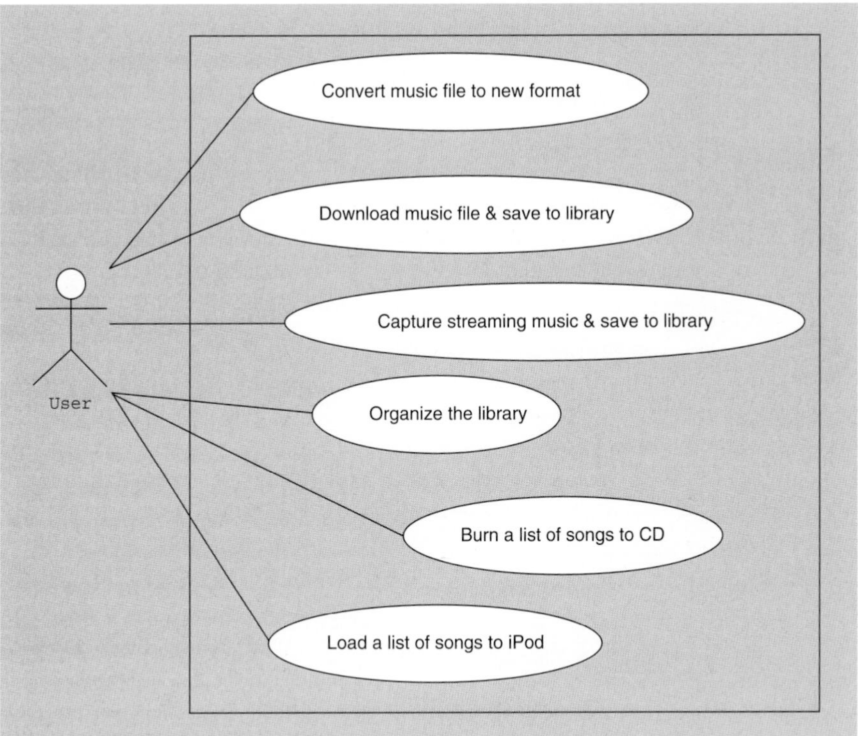

FIGURE A.9 A use case diagram for the music application.

Once all the use cases and variations have been described, then the developers have a good idea of the functionality of the system. It is at this point that UML use case diagrams come in handy. Such a diagram is an overview of all the use cases and how they are related, and so gives the big picture of the functionality of the system. In Figure A.9, there is a use case diagram for the digital music application discussed above.

In this diagram, there is a stick figure representing an actor. *Actors* are the different roles that users play when they interact with the system. An actor usually represents a person but can represent other things, such as another software system. Use case diagrams for more complex systems typically have more than one actor. For example, a vending machine application might have three actors representing customers, repair personnel, and vendors who refill the machine.

In the use case diagram, the use cases are displayed as ovals. The actors are connected by lines to the use cases that they carry out. Note that none of the details of the use cases are included in the diagram and instead need to be stored separately. Note also that the use cases are placed in a rectangle but the actors are not. This rectangle is a visual reminder of the system boundaries and that the actors are outside the system.

Some use cases in a system might be related to each other. For example, there are similar steps in burning a list of songs to a CD and in loading a list of songs to an iPod. In both cases, the user first creates an empty list and then adds songs from

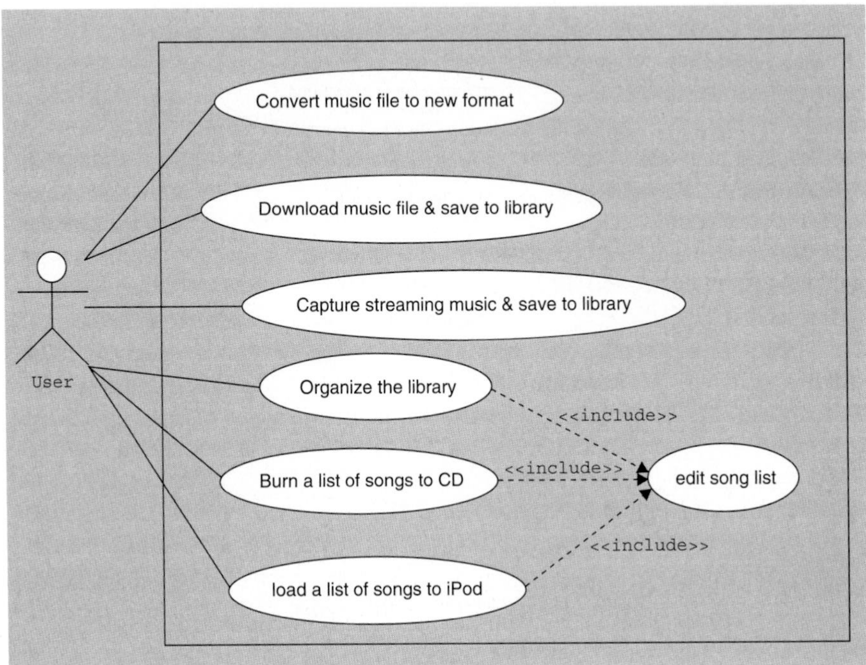

FIGURE A.10. A use case diagram with included use cases.

the library to the list. To avoid duplication in use cases, it is usually better to create a new use case representing the duplicated activity and then let the other use cases include this new use case as one of their steps. Such inclusion is indicated in use case diagrams, as in Figure A.10, by means of a dashed arrow labeled «include» connecting a use case with an included use case.

A use case diagram, because it displays all use cases, is a helpful aid for ensuring that you have covered all the functionality of the system. In our digital music organizer, we would surely want more use cases, such as a use case for playing a song in the library.

But keep in mind, that the most valuable contribution of use cases to the software development process is the textual description of each use case, not the overall use case diagram [3]. It is through the descriptions that you are able to form a clear understanding of the goals of the system you are developing.

SECTION A.5 SUMMARY

We have provided an overview of the four UML diagrams used in this text: class, sequence, state, and use case diagrams. For more details regarding those diagrams and to learn about other UML diagrams, you are referred to Martin Fowler's book [3], which is a convenient reference manual for UML 2.0, giving short and concise descriptions of each of the diagrams. If you are interested in all the gritty details of UML 2.0, then you should read either the UML reference manual [4] or the user guide [1]. You can also find much information online at Web sites such as www.uml.org and www.uml-forum.com.

EXERCISES

1. Why is it often important to include a dependency relationship in a UML diagram? That is, who cares about such relationships?
2. In Figure A.2, the Thoroughbred class could have been drawn with an association from that class back to itself. Why?
3. In Section A.3, we said that the space, tab, and end-of-line characters are white space characters. What other characters are also white space characters for Java?
4. Implement the WhiteSpaceAndCommentEliminator discussed in Section A.3. It should have one public method

```
public void advanceOverWhiteSpace-
  AndComments(PushbackInputStream
                           input)
```

that reads the input, one character at a time, until all consecutive white space characters and characters in comments have been read—that is, until a non–white space or noncomment character is the next character in the input stream.

REFERENCES

1. Booch, G., J. Rumbaugh, and I. Jacobsen, *The Unified Modeling Language User Guide*, 2nd ed. Object Technology. 2005. Reading MA: Addison-Wesley.
2. Gamma, E., *Design Patterns, Elements of Reusable Object-Oriented Software*. Professional Computing. 1995. Reading, MA: Addison-Wesley.
3. Fowler, M., *UML Distilled*, 3rd ed. Object Technology (ed). 2004. Reading, MA: Addison-Wesley.
4. Rumbaugh, J., I. Jacobsen, and G. Booch, *The Unified Modeling Language Reference Manual*, 2nd ed. Object Technology (ed). 2004. Reading, MA: Addison-Wesley.

B Appendix

Coding Conventions and Javadoc Comments

SECTION B.0 INTRODUCTION

Software developers are, of course, free to layout their source code files any way they wish, including the order of the methods, fields, and constructors, as well as the layout of the comments in the source code. However, it is beneficial, as mentioned in Chapter 4, for everyone on a project to follow some convention to make reading the source files easier for everyone on the team.

Sun Microsystems has developed some standard conventions for Java source code layout and, unless you have specific reasons to do otherwise, it is recommended that you follow these conventions. One advantage of doing so is that it enables you to use the Javadoc tool.

In this appendix, we will present a sampling of the many style guidelines that appear in Sun Microsystem's coding conventions [1] and in the many Java trade books.

You have likely learned most or all of these guidelines in your programming classes. Furthermore, many modern development environments will reformat your source files for you, making it easier for you to properly lay out the files. However, the material is included here as a refresher and as a reminder of the importance of some of these guidelines in terms of making your code readable.

We will also cover Javadoc notation in somewhat more detail so that you can properly write source code using that notation.

It should be noted that this text follows most, but not all, of the Java conventions. The author, like most people, has his own idiosyncrasies and his own preferences, which he has used here.

SECTION B.1 INDENTATION AND SPACING

For a simple example of how following conventions can improve readability, consider the conventions regarding spacing and indenting. As simple an action as lining up data can greatly improve readability. For example, a two-dimensional array A can be initialized with a fixed set of Strings as follows:

```
String[][] A = {{"Maurice","Wilkes"}, {"Richard","Hamming"}, {"Marvin", "Minsky"},
  {"John","McCarthy"}, {"Ole-Johan","Dahl"}, {"Kristen","Nygaard"}};
```

However, the following spacing and indentation scheme makes the code more readable.

```
String[][] A = {{ "Maurice"  , "Wilkes"   },
                { "Richard"  , "Hamming"  },
                { "Marvin"   , "Minsky"   },
                { "John"     , "McCarthy" },
                { "Ole-Johan", "Dahl"     },
                { "Kristen"  , "Nygaard"  }};
```

Improper spacing within a line can also *reduce* the readability of the code. For example [2, Chap. 18], consider the arithmetic expression

```
2+3  *  4+5
```

Although it looks like you are performing two additions to get 5 and 9 followed by the multiplication of 5 * 9 to get 45, in fact you are computing 2 + 12 + 5.

Indentation can similarly provide significant help in making code readable and cause significant problems when done improperly. In particular, if the writer of code does not indent the body of a method or a loop or doesn't line up sequential statements, the code becomes horribly unreadable. Also, anyone who has ever written a statement like the following and then wondered why only the first statement gets executed in the body of the loop is a victim of misleading indentation:

```
while (foo())
  statementOne();
  statementTwo();
  statementThree();
```

Guideline

Use proper indentation and spacing to improve readability.

SECTION B.2 PUNCTUATION AND LAYOUT

In the preceding section, you saw how the expression `2+3  *  4+5` is misleading because of the spacing. One way that this problem could have been avoided is by including parentheses, such as `2+(3 * 4)+5` to indicate the order of operations. Such parentheses are necessary if you want the operations performed in an order other than their standard precedence order, but it is valuable to use parentheses even in cases where it is unnecessary, as in the expression above, because of the clarity it adds to the expression.

For another example, no parentheses or spaces are needed in the expression `x*4-5/2.67/788` but parentheses and spacing, such as `(x*4) - (5/2.67)/788`, can improve its readability.

In the preceding section, we saw how misleading the following expression is:

```
while (foo())
  statementOne();
  statementTwo();
  statementThree();
```

One way to avoid this problem is to include braces around the body of every block, regardless of whether they are required. If such braces were included above, as in

```
while (foo()) {
  statementOne();
}
  statementTwo();
  statementThree();
```

then there would be little confusion as to which statements are in the loop.

Problems with readability come in other forms as well. For example, when a line of code needs to be wrapped because the line is too long, there are readable and unreadable ways of wrapping it. In particular, if your lines are required to be at most 80 characters long (one of the Java conventions), don't automatically break the line at the 80th character. Instead, break it where it makes the most sense for readability. For example, the line

```
throw new NumberFormatException("The number " + inputLong +
  " won't" + " fit in the first " + numBits + " bits.");
```

For another example, consider a method declaration with too many parameters to fit on one line. It is best to break between parameters and indent the continuation line to line up with the parameters on the first line, if possible. For example, a good layout would be

```
public void doSomethingToFourStrings(String first, String second,
                                     String third, String fourth)
```

A loop that has a conditional that won't fit on one line should break at a place in the conditional that is at as high a level as possible (that is, avoid breaking inside deeply nested parentheses) and should be indented in a way that distinguishes it from the body of the loop. For example, a good break and indentation would be the following:

```
while( longBooleanExpression1 && longBooleanExpression2 &&
       longBooleanExpression3 ) {
  foo(x);
}
```

Notice how the continuation of the conditional lines up with the conditionals above it instead of with the statement in the body of the loop, which helps the reader distinguish between the parts.

In addition to lines that are longer than 80 characters and so need to be broken, there are also lines that are shorter than 80 characters but still should be broken. For example, it is perfectly legal to have two or more statements on the same line, and so you might see a line of code like the following:

```
x++; System.out.println(x+y); y++;
```

This may save lines on the screen, allowing you to view more code at once, but it is not good style. Each statement should be on its own line.

Furthermore, each declaration should also be on its own line. It is perfectly legal to have

```
JFrame oldFrame, newFrame;
```

but it is better to write it as

```
JFrame oldFrame;
JFrame newFrame;
```

Not only is it more readable, but you also now have room at the end of the line for comments explaining the role of each of the variables.

Blank lines should also be used frequently to make the code more readable. In particular, there should be blank lines separating class, interface, and method declarations. There should also be blank lines within method bodies separating blocks of code that perform different functions, such as blank lines between the declarations at the beginning of a block and the statements in the rest of the block.

Guideline

Use punctuation such as parentheses, braces, and lines to your advantage to make your code more readable, even in situations where they are not needed.

SECTION B.3 FORMATTING A LOOP

Java language constructs such as loops can be written in many formats, but not all of them are equally readable.

Consider a loop that steps through an array A and prints all the values. Such a loop can have many forms, including the following six forms. Study them to determine whether they all do the same thing. (Hint: The answer is no.)

- ```
  for( int a: A ) {
    System.out.println(a);
  }
  ```
  ```

- ```
  for( int i = 0; i < A.length; i++ ) {
    System.out.println(A[i]);
  }
  ```
- ```
  for( int i = 5; i - 5 < A.length; i++ ) {
    System.out.println(A[i-5]);
  }
  ```
- ```
  for( int i = 0; i <= A.length - 1; i++ ) {
    System.out.println(A[i]);
  }
  ```
- ```
  int i = 0;
  while(i < A.length) {
    System.out.println(A[i]);
    i++;
  }
  ```
- ```
  int i;
  for( i = 0; i < A.length; i++ ) {
    System.out.println(A[i]);
  }
  ```

In fact, there is a subtle difference between the first four forms and the last two. The difference is that, in the last two forms, the variable `i` has been declared outside the loop and so its scope (that is, where it can be used) extends beyond the loop body to the end of the enclosing body of code (for example, the end of an outer loop or the end of the method that contains this code). The programmer may or may not have intended to use `i` after exiting the loop. If not, then one of the first four forms is preferable because, in those cases, the compiler will catch any accidental use of `i` after exiting the loop.

The main point we are trying to make here is that it takes the reader valuable time to convince himself or herself that these loops are or are not equivalent. This time can be better spent on other things.

So which of the forms should you use? It is somewhat a matter of preference. The first one is the standard form since Javal.5 and is, in our opinion, the most readable of them. That is, it takes the least amount of mental effort to convince ourselves that the statement actually accomplishes its objective. The fifth example is nonstandard because `while` loops are generally used when you do not know ahead of time how many times the loop body will be executed. A `for` loop is preferable in cases where you know the number of times the loop body will be executed, as is the case when stepping completely through an array.

Guideline

If a variable is supposed to be used only in the body of a loop, declare it in the body. More generally, give a variable the narrowest scope you can.
  ```

SECTION B.4 INCREMENTING INTEGER VARIABLES

Consider again the second of the loops in the preceding section. There are many ways to increment `i` inside that loop. Here are some examples. Do they all do the same thing? (Hint: The answer is no.)

- ```
  for( int i = 0; i < A.length; i++ ) {
    System.out.println(A[i]);
  }
  ```
- ```
  for( int i = 0; i < A.length; ) {
    System.out.println(A[i]);
    i++;
  }
  ```
- ```
  for( int i = 0; i < A.length; ++i ) {
    System.out.println(A[i]);
  }
  ```
- ```
  for( int i = 0; i < A.length; i = i + 1) {
    System.out.println(A[i]);
  }
  ```
- ```
  for( int i = 0; i < A.length; i += 1) {
    System.out.println(A[i]);
  }
  ```
- ```
  for( int i = 0; i < A.length; ) {
    System.out.println(A[i++]);
  }
  ```
- ```
  for( int i = 0; i < A.length; ) {
    System.out.println(A[++i]);
  }
  ```

The first six of these examples are equivalent, although some are easier to read than others. The last example is not equivalent in that it crashes with an ArrayIndex-OutOfBoundsException (can you see why?). The first version is the form we prefer. Once again, the whole point of following standard coding conventions is to make your code easier to read. If `i++` is a standard convention for updating the index when stepping through an array A and if you write `i=i+1`, then the reader will have to waste a small amount of mental effort convincing herself or himself that this loop really does step through the whole array.

In the examples above, it is important to realize that the phrase `i++` (as well as `++i`) is both an assignment statement and an arithmetic expression. That is, it

Guideline

Use the "++" operator as an assignment operator only. More generally, avoid embedding any assignment statements in expressions.
  ```

increments the value of `i` and also can be used in expressions to represent the value of `i`, as was done in the last two examples above. Such double use, if done indiscriminately, can result in legal but horribly unreadable code. Consider the following legal code:

```
int x = 1;
x += x++;
System.out.println(x);
```

Can you tell us what value is printed without actually running the code? (The answer is "2." Can you see why?)

For the same reason, you should also avoid multiple assignments in the same statement, such as

```
x = y = 3;
```

It is harder to read than

```
x = 3;
y = 3;
```

SECTION B.5 WORKING WITH BOOLEAN VARIABLES

Let's now take a look at boolean expressions and consider ways of making them more readable. A simple example is the following statement where `b` is a boolean variable:

```
if (b == true)
  return true;
else
  return false;
```

This statement is far too verbose. An equivalent and much more readable statement is:

```
return b;
```

This statement can be made even more readable by using an intention-revealing name for the variable.

It is also valuable to make complex boolean expressions as simple as possible using DeMorgan's laws and other Boolean algebra laws. For example, assume that `foo()` and `bar()` are methods that return a boolean value and that `a, b, c,` and `d` are boolean variables and consider the following expressions:

- `true || foo()`
- `false && bar()`
- `a && !b || !d && c`
- `!(b || !(c && d))`

The first expression can be simplified to `true` and the second to `false` due to Java's short-circuit evaluation of boolean expressions. The third expression above is crying out for parentheses, such as `(a && !b) || (!d && c)` to make it easier to read. The fourth expression could be simplified by an application of DeMorgan's laws as follows:

```
!(b || !(c && d)) ⇔ !b && (c && d)
```

Such simplifications usually make the code much more readable.

Another situation in which boolean variables are used in a confusing way involves conditional expressions in multiway branch statements. For example, consider the following code used to test for all possible values of two boolean variables `a` and `b`:

```
if(a && b)
   return 1;
else if(a && !b)
   return 2;
else if(!a && b)
   return 3;
else if(!a && !b)
   return 4;
else
   return 5;
```

After briefly studying this code, you should realize that the last `else` clause will never get executed because the preceding four cases cover all possibilities. Therefore, the last `else` clause should be removed. But an additional change should be made as well. If the first three conditionals all fail, then the fourth conditional must succeed and so there is no need to test for it. However, it is good to include a comment reminding you of the conditions under which the fourth case happens. Therefore, a good way to write the `if` statement above is:

```
if(a && b)
   return 1;
else if(a && !b)
   return 2;
else if(!a && b)
   return 3;
else //if(!a && !b)
   return 4;
```

Guideline

Simplify boolean expressions to make the conditions clearer.

SECTION B.6 LINE AND BLOCK COMMENTS

There are a few guidelines you should follow in the way you use line comments (starting with "//") and block comments (surrounded by "/*" and "*/").

Block comments should be used instead of line comments if you have several consecutive lines of comments. Also, block comments should have asterisks lined up on every line on the left side as a visual clue to the reader that every line is part of the comment.

In particular, when commenting out a section of code, you should not just add a "/*" before the section and "*/" after the section. For commenting out a section of code, it is recommended that you add "//" in front of every line. This use of line comments is a good clue that the code has been temporarily removed.

Luckily modern development environments help out by adding special styles to commented code, such as a different color or italics. Such environments also make it easy to add and remove "//" in front of every line of a section of code.

SECTION B.7 FILE LAYOUT

Sun's layout conventions for Java source files suggest that you include the following components in the order given:

1. A block comment including the name of the file, the date, and any copyright information.
2. An optional `package` declaration and `include` statements.
3. The public class or interface declaration.
4. Any nonpublic class or interface declarations.

Within each class declaration, the class components (comments, fields, constructors, and methods) should be laid out in the following order:

1. A comment block containing class implementation details. These comments include any information that is not appropriate for doc comments, such as class invariants that are implementation specific.
2. Static fields, ordered in decreasing accessibility (public fields first, then protected, package, and private).
3. Instance fields, ordered similarly.
4. Constructors.
5. Methods, ordered by functionality.

Figure B.1 gives an example of a source file laid out according to these guidelines. It is complete except for doc comments, which will be added later. It assumes there is a Horse class with `getFather`, `getMother`, `getName`, and `isMale` methods.

SECTION B.8 JAVADOC SYNTAX

In this section, we will discuss Sun's coding conventions regarding Javadoc.

Javadoc is a tool for generating documentation that uses specially formatted documentation comments or "doc comments" in the source code. When the Java-

```
/*
 * RapFamily.java
 * Jan. 1, 2000
 */
package horses;
import java.util.*;
public class RapFamily
{
/*
   * This class leaves it to the users to ensure the
following
   * class invariants hold:
   * (a) sire is a stallion,
   * (b) sire's male lineage goes back to Rap
   * (c) null is never added to the list of children
   * (d) all Horses in the list of children actually have
sire as their father.
   */
   public static final String ANCESTOR_NAME = "Rap";
   private final Horse sire;
   private ArrayList<Horse> children;
   public RapFamily(Horse sire) {
      this.sire = sire;
      this.children = new ArrayList<Horse>();
   }
   public void addChild(Horse foal) {
      children.add(foal);
   }
   public List<Horse> getChildren() {
      return new ArrayList<Horse>(children); }
}
```

FIGURE B.1 A Java source file following Sun's conventions except it is missing doc comments.

doc tool is run, it finds the doc comments in the source files and constructs HTML pages containing the documentation in the doc comments. The HTML pages form an API (application programming interface) for the classes. For an example of the kind of HTML pages generated, see the API for the Java 1.5 libraries at `http://java.sun.com/j2se/1.5.0/docs/api/`.

Doc comment general format

There should be a doc comment immediately preceding each class or interface declaration, field declaration, constructor, and method declaration in a Java source file.

We will first explain the general format of doc comments, and then we will give more specific information concerning doc comments associated with each of these types of declarations.

All doc comments begin with the delimiter "/**" and end with the delimiter "*/" and so look similar to Java block comments except for the double asterisk in the beginning delimiter.

The first sentence or phrase of each doc comment is included in the summary table in the HTML pages generated and so should always be a concise but complete summary of the role of the class, interface, field, constructor, or method or what it models.

All the information in a doc comment is included in the HTML files generated by Javadoc. To help Javadoc lay out the HTML files, you are allowed to add some HTML tags in your doc comment. For example, you can add underline `<u>` or italic `<i>` tags to format sequences of characters. You can add paragraph `<p>` tags between paragraphs in a doc comment. You are encouraged to use code `<code>` tags for Java keywords and for names of packages, classes, interfaces, fields, methods, and arguments. You should also use the `<code>` tag for sample code inside doc comments. Links to other pages and pictures can also be included.

Doc comments also can include special Javadoc tags, all of which begin with "@" such as `@param` and `@return`. These tags are provided to help Javadoc properly lay out the information in the HTML file. The use of the most common doc tags is explained below.

Doc comments for classes and interfaces

The doc comment that immediately precedes a class or interface declaration should have the following elements:

1. A concise and complete phrase or statement describing what the class or interface models.
2. More details and any other information that the user of the class should know about it in order to use it correctly.
3. Author information preceded by the `@author` tag.
4. Version information preceded by the `@version` tag.

Doc comments for fields

The doc comment preceding each field should have the following elements:

1. A concise and complete phrase or statement describing the role of the field and what it models.
2. The value of the field if it is a public constant of a primitive type or String. Otherwise, include the range of possible valid values of the field if it is not otherwise clear.
3. For nonprimitive fields, a statement saying whether null is a valid value and, if so, what that value represents.

Doc comments for constructors and methods

The doc comment preceding each method or constructor should have the following elements:

1. A concise and complete verb phrase or statement describing the intended behavior of the method or constructor.
2. The behavior of the method or constructor in special circumstances, for example, when it will throw exceptions.
3. The range of valid values for the arguments and the range of valid values returned by methods with a nonvoid return type.
4. For each parameter, a line starting with the `@param` tag followed by the name of the parameter and then by a description of the parameter. The description should start with the type of the parameter (except words such as "a," "an," "the" are allowed in front of the type).
5. For each method with a nonvoid return type, a line starting the `@return` tag followed by a description of the value being returned.
6. For each checked exception and for each likely unchecked exception (other than NullPointerException), a line starting with the `@throws` tag followed by the type of exception thrown and an explanation of what causes the exception to be thrown.

The set of lines with the `@param` tags should be preceded by a blank line. The descriptions should be listed in the order of the parameters in the method or constructor signature. These descriptions should be included even if the name of the parameter gives all the information you need, making the description redundant. Similarly, the line with the `@return` tag should be included even if the description is redundant.

Figure B.2 shows the same source file as in Figure B.1 above except with doc comments added.

```
/*
 * RapFamily.java
 * Jan. 1, 2000
*/

package horses;

import java.util.*;

/**
 * Represents one male stallion in the lineage of Rap and all
 * that stallion's offspring.
 * If you follow the chain of male ancestors from the sire,
 * you will eventually reach the famous stallion Rap.
 */
public class RapFamily
{
   /*
    * This class leaves it to the users to ensure the following
    * class invariants hold:
```

FIGURE B.2 A Java source file following Sun's conventions including doc comments. *Continued*

```
     * (a) sire is a stallion,
     * (b) sire's male lineage goes back to Rap
     * (c) null is never added to the list of children
     * (d) all Horses in the list of children actually have sire as their father.
     */

    /** the family name "Rap" */
    public static final String ANCESTOR_NAME = "Rap";

    /**
     * the father for this family.
     * The sire must be a Horse who is male and whose
     * lineage goes back to Rap.
     */
    public final Horse sire;

    /**
     * the collection of offspring of the sire
     * It should never be null, although it could be empty.
     */
    private ArrayList<Horse> children;

    /**
     * constructs a new RapFamily for the given stallion.
     * The user is responsible for ensuring that sire != null
     * and that sire is actually a stallion that is a descendent of
Rap.
    **
     * @param sire the Horse whose offspring will be stored in this RapFamily
     */
    public RapFamily(Horse sire) {
      this.sire = sire;
      this.children = new ArrayList<Horse>();
    }

    /**
     * adds a new foal to the collection of children of this sire.
     * The user is responsible for ensuring that foal != null and
     *   foal.getFather() == sire.
     *
     * @param foal the Horse being added to the set of children of
sire.
    **/
    public void addChild(Horse foal) { children.add(foal); }

    /**
     * creates and returns a new ArrayList<Horse> containing the
     *   children of sire.
     * If there are no children, it returns an empty list.
     *
     * @return a new List<Horse> with all the children of sire.
     */
    public List<Horse> getChildren() {
      return new ArrayList<Horse>(children);
    }
}
```

FIGURE B.2 *Continued*

SECTION B.9 SUMMARY

In this chapter, we reviewed some of the coding conventions from Sun microsystem, including how to write Javadoc comments.

To learn more about Sun's coding conventions, see the online documentation at *http://java.sun.com/docs/codeconv/html/CodeConvTOC.doc.html*. To learn more about Javadoc, see *http://java.sun.com/j2se/javadoc/* and especially *http://java.sun.com/j2se/javadoc/writingdoccomments/*.

EXERCISES

1. When talking about indenting and tabbing code, we used an example of a two-dimensional array containing the first names and last names of six people: Maurice Wilkes, Richard Hamming, Marvin Minsky, John McCarthy, Ole-Johan Dahl, and Kristen Nygaard. Find out what these computer scientists have in common.

2. Consider the following legal Java statements. In each case, first guess and then compute the value of x that is printed. Then justify the correct answer by referring to the Java Language Specs. If you guessed incorrectly, explain where your reasoning went wrong. Do (a)–(e) all yield the same answer? Should they?

a. `int x = 3; x += x++ + x++ + ++x; System.out.println(x);`

b. `int x = 3; x += 2 * x++ + ++x; System.out.println(x);`

c. `int x = 3; x = (x=x+1)+(x=x+1)+(x=x+1) + x; System.out.println(x);`

d. `int x = 3; x = x + (x=x+1)+(x=x+1)+(x=x+1); System.out.println(x);`

e. `int x = 3; int y = 5; x = y+++x; System.out.println(x);`

3. The following code is perfectly legal but inelegant. Why is it inelegant?

```
if (x < 3)
   System.out.println("yes");
else if (x > 3)
   System.out.println("no");
else if (x == 3)
   System.out.println("equal");
else
   System.out.println("other");
```

4. Suppose that `f()` is a boolean function and `g()` is a void method in a class A, and suppose that the body of `g` includes the following code:

```
if (f() && false)
   System.out.println("yes");
else
   System.out.println("no");
```

Can this statement be simplified? If so, to what? Explain.

5. If you know that an array A of integers has a length of 10, then is there any advantage to either of the following forms for looping through A and printing the values? Explain.

```
for (int i = 0; i < A.length; i++)
  System.out.println(A[i]);
for (int i = 0; i < 10; i++) System.out.
  println(A[i]);
```

6. Consider a program that needs to store 32 zeros and ones in a variable x and occasionally needs to flip all 32 bits (that is, replacing the zeros with ones and vice versa).

a. If x is an integer array of 32 zeros and ones, what is a better way of flipping the bits than using the statement `if(x[i] == 0) then x[i] = 1 else x[i] = 0`?

b. If x is a (32-bit) integer variable using twos complement notation and if the 32 zeros and ones are stored as the 32 bits in x, what is an easy way to flip all 32 bits?

7. What is inelegant about the following two lines of code? Assume that v is a Vector that was declared and initialized earlier.

```
Object[] A = new Object[10];
A = v.toArray();
```

8. Simplify the following boolean expressions. Assume a, b, and c are boolean variables and `f()` and `g()` are boolean-valued functions with no side effects.

a. `!(a || !b || c)`

b. `!(false || f())`
c. `(f() && g()) || c || !c`
Do any of your answers change if `f()` and `g()` have side effects? Explain.

9. Which of the following phrases might be legal statements, which might be legal expressions, and which are illegal? If phrase might be legal, what types must each of the variables be for it to be legal?
a. `(x = y) = z`
b. `(x = y) == z`
c. `(x == y) = z`
d. `(x == y) == z`
e. `x = (y = z)`
f. `x = (y == z)`
g. `x == (y = z)`
h. `x == (y == z)`

10. Come up with three coding style guidelines not mentioned in this appendix that you feel are very important for readable code.

11. Sometimes when you are reading code, you come across a method whose body consists of exactly one method call, for example,

```
public void foo(...) { bar(...); }
```

Why isn't the call to `bar` inlined? That is, why not replace the call to `bar` in `foo` with the code in the body of `bar`? It would seem to be more efficient to inline `bar`, in that you avoid another method call. What is there to gain by `foo` calling `bar`?

12. The RapFamily class example used in this appendix when explaining layout and Javadoc conventions is less useful than it could be because it is applicable only to descendents of the great horse Rap. Rewrite the class so that it is more generally useful for other horse family trees.

REFERENCES

1. Sun Microsystems, Inc., *Code Conventions for the Java Programming Language.* Web page, 1999. [Cited April 23, 2007; available from *http://java.sun.com/docs/codeconv/*]
2. McConnell, S., *Code Complete, A Practical Handbook of Software Construction.* 1993. Redmond, WA: Microsoft Press.

Index

Page references followed by f denote figures.

D

I

J

K

L

T

U